THE
STRATEGIC PARTNERING
HANDBOOK

THE PRACTITIONERS' GUIDE TO PARTNERSHIPS AND ALLIANCES

EDITION
4

THE
STRATEGIC
PARTNERING
HANDBOOK

THE PRACTITIONERS' GUIDE TO PARTNERSHIPS AND ALLIANCES

EDITION 4

TONY LENDRUM

The **McGraw·Hill** Companies

Sydney New York San Francisco Auckland
Bangkok Bogotá Caracas Hong Kong
Kuala Lumpur Lisbon London Madrid
Mexico City Milan New Delhi San Juan
Seoul Singapore Taipei Toronto

First edition, 1995
Reprinted, 1997
Second edition, 1998
Third edition, 2000

Text © 2003 Tony Lendrum
Design © 2003 McGraw-Hill Australia Pty Ltd
Cartoon on page 46 by Jock Macneish
Additional owners of copyright are acknowledged on the Acknowledgments page.

National Library of Australia Cataloguing-in-Publication data:

Lendrum, Tony.
The strategic partnering handbook: the practitioners'
guide to partnerships and alliances.

4th ed.
Includes index.
ISBN 0 074 71326 4.

1. Strategic alliances (Business). 2. Strategic alliances (Business) – Australia – Case studies. 3. Partnership. 4. Organizational change. I. Title.

658.042

Published in Australia by
McGraw-Hill Australia Pty Ltd
Level 2, 82 Waterloo Road, North Ryde NSW 2113
Acquisitions Editor: Javier Dopico
Production Editors: Sybil Kesteven, Rosemary McDonald
Editor: Christine Eslick
Proofreader: Tim Learner
Indexer: Diane Harriman
Cover design: Jan Schmoeger/Designpoint
Illustrator: Alan Laver, Diane Booth
Typeset in 11/14 pt Berkeley Book by Post Pre-press Group
Printed on 80 gsm matt art by Pantech Limited, Hong Kong.

The McGraw-Hill Companies

About the author

Tony Lendrum is CEO and Head Coach at Strategic Partnering Pty Ltd, a management consulting firm he formed in September 1994 to focus on the development of strategic partnering and alliance relationships. Tony has established himself as a recognised authority in this new and exciting field. Since 1995 Tony has worked extensively with Australian and international organisations in both the public and the private sectors.

Tony's experience in partnering, alliancing and relationship management generally spans over 20 years, 14 of which were spent with ICI, the global chemical company. An honours degree physical chemist by education, Tony has worked in many and various technical, sales, marketing, management, business development and manufacturing roles. This included two years in South Korea with responsibility for acquisitions and joint ventures. He was also Operations Manager for one of ICI Australia's petrochemical plants. Tony has extensive experience as a successful Partnering and Alliance Manager pioneering the ICI/Tetra Pak partnership which became a role model for both organisations.

The Strategic Partnering Handbook is widely used by small, medium and large organisations as a model and guide for implementing effective partnering and alliance strategies and is a recognised benchmark for relationship management generally.

This book is dedicated to Julie,
my wife and partner in life
for over twenty-five years,
my two sons, Simon and Mark,
and my parents Betty and Ross
for their love and support.

Contents

Preface

Never before has the world seemed so small, the marketplace so competitive, change more rapid and the pressure to perform so intense. Confrontation is turning into cooperation, competition into collaboration, separate and often conflicting strategies into shared visions with common goals. No longer can a single organisation, public or private sector, be all things to all people. Going it alone is clearly not the smartest option and the business landscape is littered with poorly performing firms that have refused to share. However, attaining genuine and sustainable competitive advantage has never been more challenging to understand or more difficult to achieve.

Partnering is really a logical response to the globalisation of markets, increasingly intense competition, the need for faster innovation and the growing complexity of technology. It makes good common sense that connected people, departments, companies, customers and suppliers, who don't have to compete with each other, should actually work with each other for some agreed common purpose. This same common sense applies to traditional competitors who now see the opposition not as existing individual firms but competing markets and supply chains. Past adversaries are quickly becoming collaborative colleagues.

Since the publication of the first edition in August 1995, the second edition in 1998 and the third edition in 2000, *The Strategic Partnering Handbook* has been used successfully by organisations worldwide as a model and practitioners' guide for building partnering relationships and alliances with selected customers and suppliers both internal and external to the organisation. The level of interest in strategic partnerships and alliances has never been greater, with estimated numbers growing at 25 per cent each year.

However, the results to date have not matched initial expectations. With surveys in the United States suggesting that less than 50 per cent of partnerships and alliances are successful, for many there needs to be both a redefining of the definition and a rethink of the approach. As occurred with total quality, many organisations find the language, principles and concepts of partnering and alliancing compelling, but have great difficulty 'walking the talk' into effective practice. Many so-called partnerships and alliances are nothing more than glorified, conventional contractual relationships with a twist of cooperative rhetoric. Signing off on a partnering charter is next to useless if not actively supported by the executive teams and the details delivered by an informed, competent, committed and empowered workforce.

Although common sense in principle, the reality is that genuine partnering is far from easy. Many organisations still tend to be combative and tribal, particularly in these times of cost-downs, restructuring, re-engineering, downsizing, right-sizing, outsourcing, de-layering and divesting. This departmental command and control approach often restricts communication, destroys initiative and creativity and leaves the organisation diminished in its capacity to relate effectively with the outside world. For most, partnering is a new paradigm. Old ways of doing things, old attitudes and mind sets will count for little in this brave new world. The concepts of interdependence, no-contract, no-term relationships, and payment on performance, not unit price, are just some of the mind-set shifts to be embraced practically.

There is no question that the future success of your business will depend critically on the quality of relationships developed with customers and suppliers, both internal and external. Strategic partnerships and alliances with selected customers and suppliers will continue to play a fundamental part of the business strategy of world-class organisations in the future. How we determine and manage these relationships to ensure continuous improvement in competitive advantage and customer satisfaction will be the key to that success.

The principles and concepts detailed in the *Partnering Handbook* have proven of great value for many organisations, and therefore remain unaltered in this fourth edition. Nevertheless, the partnering and alliance world is quite different from five years ago. In reviewing *The Strategic Partnering Handbook* for the fourth edition I have attempted to add my own experience and knowledge gained over the last three years as well as current best practices from organisations I have worked with or heard about. And there are many. These are the real life stories from the shop floor, the coalface, the operating levels, through to the boardrooms of what went right, what have been the lessons learnt, opportunities for improvement and where to go from here. The passion, knowledge, competence and courage being displayed by the leading-edge partnering and alliance practitioners is truly inspiring. The account of the outstanding global alliance between Alcoa and Honeywell has been updated, as has the Transfield Services and Worley case study and their highly successful integrated partnering and alliance strategies. A new case study that looks at Sydney Water Corporation and its strategic 'triple bottom line' approach to relationship management has been added. The steps on 'Selecting a partner' and 'Reviewing process with partner and sharing information' have been expanded and further detail has been added to Chapter 7 which looks at the link between performance, measurement, risk/benefit and options for risk/reward, performance-based remuneration. This, together with new anecdotes, real-life experiences of others, additional concepts and research data, will give the partnering and alliance practitioner fresh tools and skills to build successful and sustainable customer/supplier relationships well into the new millennium.

The book is divided into four parts. Part A (Chapters 1–4) looks at the general environment within the organisation and the corporate culture required if customer/supplier partnerships are to be developed and sustained. The concept of 0 to 10 relationship management is expanded upon from previous editions. Comparisons are made between the various types of customer/supplier relationships together with the characteristics and qualities of the organisations that inspire them. The critical link between strategic partnering and the rest of the business strategy in achieving sustainable competitive advantage is also discussed, along with the supporting organisational structures.

Part B (Chapters 5–7) deals specifically with the partnering process: the who, how, when, where and why of developing and maintaining long-term strategic relationships, key success factors, performance measures and methods of remuneration. This section has been extensively updated for the fourth edition.

Part C (Chapters 8 and 9) profiles the individual who will develop and manage the partnership—the partnering/alliance manager. Understanding the qualities and competencies required of them is critical to the success of the process. The management of change and complexity in partnerships is also explored.

Part D comprises three Australian-based case studies.

The Strategic Partnering Handbook provides the experienced professional as well as the initiate with the concepts and tools to take strategic partnering and alliance relationships to the next levels and beyond.

To understand the relevance of strategic partnering to your business, carry out the exercise on the next page.

Following the 80:20 rule, whereby 80 per cent of the business is with 20 per cent of the customers, calculate the potential turnover, profit and/or return on investment of the top 20 per cent of your customers, over the next five years. (Five years is the minimum time for the development of long-term, strategic customer/supplier partnerships and alliances.)

Also, what percentage of your revenue do you pay to suppliers? For most organisations the answer is most likely somewhere between 50 and 80 per cent. Therefore, supplier relationships are just as important as internal and external customer relationships.

Now answer these questions:

1. Are the numbers you calculated large enough and important enough, in your context, to be worthy of a clear, long-term strategy?
2. Do you have the long-term strategies and the people in place to manage them?
3. Do you understand which of the top 20 per cent of customers (current and potential) over the next five years are more important than others, and why?
4. Do you know which customers and suppliers you want to partner with, and why?
5. Do you know which customers and suppliers want to partner with you, and why?
6. Do you understand what customer/supplier partnerships and alliances mean, how they are managed and what benefits they can bring?

Should the answer to any of these questions be 'No', then read on: there is much to learn. Should the answer to any of the questions be 'Yes', then the following chapters will provide valuable cross-references and opportunities for improvement.

Acknowledgments

I am indebted to many people who generously gave their time and insight to the fourth edition, especially those people who contributed to the three major case studies (Alcoa/Honeywell, Transfield Services/Worley and Sydney Water). Frankly the list is endless, but in particular I would like to thank Clive Nielsen (Alcoa), John Taylor (Honeywell), Joseph Sadatmehr (Transfield Services), Peter Meurs (Worley), Ron Quill (Sydney Water), Rory Brennan (Sydney Water) and the entire Sydney Water Team who helped me in putting the Sydney Water case study together.

Thanks to all those stubbornly passionate innovators and champions I have been fortunate enough to work with and meet over the last twenty years, and to those people and organisations with an uncompromising belief in the value of partnerships and alliances. You have been an inspiration for this fourth edition.

Openness, humility, and the desire to share information and to learn are inherent qualities in partnering and alliance practitioners. The contributions of the many people and organisations to this fourth edition reinforce this view. My sincere thanks to you, champions one and all.

PART A

THE ENVIRONMENT

The Vision
Making our world a better place

The Definition
Strategic partnering and alliance relationships:

The cooperative development of successful, long-term, strategic relationships, based on mutual trust, world class/best practice, sustainable competitive advantage and benefits for all the partners; relationships which have a further separate and positive impact outside the partnership/alliance.

The Way
- Keep the faith.
- Stay focused.
- Enjoy the journey.

CHAPTER 1

An introduction to strategic partnerships

> *As each commercial organisation marches to its objective of customer satisfaction, it is self-evident that the quality of our offerings will be the sum total of the excellence of each player in our supply stream . . . Virtual perfection cannot be accomplished without cooperation. Cooperation is a synonym for partnership.*
>
> Robert W. Galvin[1]
> Chairman, Motorola Inc.

WHAT ARE CUSTOMER/SUPPLIER PARTNERSHIPS?

Customer/supplier partnerships are all about trust, commitment and leadership at every level, shared vision, common goals, respect, the long-term view, resolving conflicts, flexibility, clear and effective strategies, sustained competitive advantage, ownership, empowerment, attitude, innovation, removing hidden agendas, teamwork, people, suppliers, customers, customers' customers, suppliers' suppliers, communication, hard work, making/taking the time (a lot of it), cooperation, respect, win/win, compromise, risk taking, interdependence, sharing everything (information strategy, vision, people, ideas, risks and benefits), imagination, creativity, initiative, lateral thinking, friendship, centres of excellence, role models, over-delivering, unravelling/managing complexity, getting the basics right the first time every time as appropriate, exceeding requirements and expectations, achieving world class/best practice—and a whole lot more.

Simple enough, isn't it? In fact, like total quality management (TQM), strategic partnering is fundamentally about applied common sense. However, common sense is not always common practice.

A common misconception is that partnerships and alliances are mainly about sales and marketing, or supply and distribution, or are the latest flavour-of-the-month project from the corporate TQM unit. In fact, a true partnering/alliance relationship has little to do with sales and marketing or supply management in the traditional sense and is certainly not the exclusive domain of the TQM department or any other business unit or function. Strategic partnering requires the involvement, from all parts of the business, of highly skilled, committed and empowered people developing multilevel, cross-functional relationships focused on continuous and breakthrough improvement for mutual benefit and based on competence and trust. The 'whole' customer/supplier relationship then becomes greater than the sum of its parts.

WHY ARE CUSTOMER/SUPPLIER RELATIONSHIPS IMPORTANT?

Many world-class companies now understand the importance of developing successful customer/supplier relationships. Tetra Pak, world leader in processing, packaging and distribution systems for liquid food, is just one.

> ### Our Contribution to the Coming Decade
> *Tetra Pak is no longer purely a packaging company. We have expanded our technology base to include the processing, packaging and distribution of liquid foods. In fact, we are the first company in the world with the ability to design and construct entire plants with integrated production and distribution systems under the same roof. Our strategy is based on Innovation, Integration and Partnership.*[2]

With the global economy now a reality, the objectives of becoming internationally competitive and world class are imperatives for all successful businesses entering the 21st century. Critical to this success, and to the development of sustainable competitive advantage, will be the quality of the relationships developed between customers and suppliers, both internal and external to the organisation. Strategic partnerships and alliances are now regarded as a legitimate, fourth, growth option for business alongside organic growth, acquisitions/mergers and divestments. They are the way in which business will be done between world-class and best practice organisations in the future and will form a fundamental part of business strategy. A true partnering/alliance relationship positively influences and permeates the whole organisation, giving employees a greater sense of purpose, providing an improved return on investment, and acting as the benchmark for customer satisfaction and competitive advantage generally. Innovation is a key factor in the evolution and revolution of partnering/alliance relationships, and the driving force behind the process.

The stability and complexity of customer/supplier partnerships might at first appear to conflict with Tom Peters' view of a fashion-based, fickle and ephemeral future.[3] The disorganisation of the 'nanosecond nineties' seems not to lend itself to five-year-plus time frames within which trust and long-term sustainable innovation might be built. Partnerships, however, will provide the links and the stability around which all this instability, chaos and 'zaniness' can occur. They provide a melting pot in which people, skills and ideas can develop at extraordinary speed, and a mechanism by which organisations will not only survive but lead.

A senior manager once told me: 'Get them (the customers) to the position where you have them so linked into the organisation that they become so dependent on you they have nowhere else to go. They get hooked, just like with heroin. That's when you have a strong customer relationship.' The point is, smart customers don't become dependent on anyone or anything unless there is mutual benefit, mutual risk and a whole lot of trust in between. Smart customers, and certainly future partners, don't get hooked. Partnerships are about two-way synergy, not one-way dependence.

Partnerships are not about equity participation either. Equity, or even full ownership, may exist, but these are not the driving forces behind success or failure, nor are they the tools for developing a mutually beneficial environment. The traditional 'them (49 per cent) versus us (51 per cent)' approach has never worked as regards power and control, because it hinders the creation of mutual trust and respect. I have seen it happen many times. When the going gets tough, the majority shareholder turns into a ruthless, mean SOB. Sharing and caring are thrown out the door, and slash, burn and destroy become the order of the day. The difference between 51 per cent and 50 per cent equity is, quite simply, control! Partnering and alliance relationships based on compliance and control don't work.

Strategic partnering is a complex mix of human behaviour and organisational, market and technological diversity. It involves people—all differing in their idiosyncrasies, personalities, conflicts (personal or otherwise), ambitions, motivations, skills, capabilities and needs—at all levels of the customer/supplier organisations. This is what makes customer/supplier partnerships so difficult to develop and so much hard work to sustain, but so rewarding and enjoyable when they succeed. People and communication are the key.

How often have you seen the 'deal' done and the relationship cemented, only to have it fall apart for some reason? Everyone has their own view as to why a customer/supplier relationship has deteriorated or failed. This failure is then personalised. Get it right the first time, as post-mortems on failed business relationships are often severe and unforgiving. The steps normally involve a search for the guilty, punishment of the innocent and eventual praise for the non-participants: a far-from-perfect environment for engendering initiative, creativity and risk taking! The real casualties from this macabre and ruthless exercise are often the employees, who become demoralised and bewildered; access to future markets; greater share of existing markets; and product and service development times, which become longer.

A DETAILED DEFINITION OF STRATEGIC PARTNERING

The terms or labels 'strategic partnering', 'partnerships' and 'alliances' are in themselves quite unimportant. What is important are the underlying principles, concepts, practices, attitudes, mindsets and behaviours that go into making them work. To that end, it doesn't matter what words are used to describe these types of relationships—for example, strategic partnerships, strategic alliances, alliancing, partnering, partnering relationships, relationship marketing, alliance contracting, relationship contracting, performance contracting, 'co-opetition', co-makership, co-producers, clusters, constellations, virtual relationships, community networks, extended enterprises and the list goes on. Indeed, throughout the book I use many of these words interchangeably. In short, don't get hung up on the labels but do get passionate about the practices, behaviours, mindsets and performance levels.

Traditionally, strategic alliances are relationships between two or more suppliers of like or unlike products and services, servicing the same customer base and/or different customers. For example, British Airways and Qantas are a classic example of a strategic alliance. In this case there is an equity share, with BA having a 25 per cent share in Qantas, but this is by no means a prerequisite for alliances or partnerships. Such alliances are common in the airline, automotive, transport, computer, communications, service, banking and pharmaceutical industries.

Strategic partnerships or partnering relationships are traditionally relationships between customers and suppliers. However, the world is becoming increasingly fuzzy and never before have customers, suppliers and competitors been so indistinguishable. In some cases a single organisation involved in a partnering relationship may play all three roles. Irrespective of the nature of the horizontal or vertical relationship in the supply chain, the principles, concepts and practices of alliancing and partnering are universal. They also apply to relationships internally and externally, regardless of the size of the organisation or whether it is manufacturing- or service-based, in the public or private sector.

Project partnering and alliancing are based on the same principles and many of the same practices as strategic partnering and alliancing but differ in scope and timeframe and are often linked into a narrower strategic focus, project scope and operational focus or intent. As the name implies, the focus is on a project such as the building of a hospital, major road, rail link, office block or manufacturing site. Organisations often use project partnering/alliancing, either a single project or a series of projects, as a stepping stone to strategic partnering/alliancing.

Here is my broad definition of strategic partnering and alliances:

> *The cooperative development of successful, long-term, strategic relationships, based on mutual trust, world class/best practice, sustainable competitive advantage and benefits for all the partners; relationships which have a further separate and positive impact outside the partnership/alliance.*

To gain a deeper understanding, this definition needs to be broken down into its component parts.

- *Cooperative development*: This is a cooperative, collaborative, continuous and breakthrough improvement, trustworthy 'development' based on shared vision and common goals/objectives for which individuals and joint teams hold themselves mutually accountable, as opposed to confrontational, adversarial 'development'.
- *Successful*: As measured against agreed Key Performance Indicators (KPIs). These measures of performance, normally in the form of a balanced scorecard or performance scorecard, will be a mixture of hard and soft, leading and lagging indicators, in many cases quite different from conventional measures (refer to Chapter 7 for more details). It is not just about the financials but a wide range of measures reflecting the broad outcomes achieved in the relationship. Along with ROI or financial success, performance will be measured via customer/stakeholder satisfaction, sustainable competitive advantage, world-class or best practice standards and processes, innovation and attitude.
- *Long-term*: Five years is a minimum term but this number is becoming increasingly less relevant as the true nature of the partnering relationship

becomes clear. Ironically, the best partnering and alliance relationships work effectively on the basis of 'no contract, no term'. Evergreen, performance-based relationships are a difficult enough concept for most organisations to understand, let alone practise. 'No contract, no term' does not mean no documentation. Good partnering will have all the appropriate require-ments (current and future), specifications and other information needed for the management and development of the relationship agreed and docu-mented. In putting the handshake back into business, the partnering/alliance relationship is based more on the upfront moral agreement between the partners rather than a legally binding and enforceable contract. These relationships are fundamentally linked to performance with supplier profit, gain or loss often openly and transparently put at risk, based on over- or under-performance against agreed KPI targets.

Increasingly, longer term relationships are coming into existence—I call them 'life of' relationships. For example, the Transfield Services Worley Joint Venture has an integrated services alliance with Woodside Energy providing all engineering, maintenance and construction services for the multi-billion dollar North West Shelf Gas Venture, for the *life of asset*. This covers a 25–30 year period. 'Life of mine' relationships in the resource sector, 'life of part' and 'life of model' relationships in the automotive sector (e.g. Chrysler, Honda, Ford) and 'life of service' relationships in the service and support industries are becoming more common. BOOT schemes (Build Own Operate Transfer) and DCO (Design, Construct, Operate) relationships over extended periods, in some cases 20–30 years, are occurring in the construction industry.

I am not suggesting here that all these relationships are partnerships or alliances by this definition, but rather indicating the changing and in many cases lengthening nature of 'term' relationships.

There are circumstances, however, where a traditional 'contract' docu-ment is unavoidable and appropriate—for example, where corporate, leg-islative, public sector or government requirements dictate that a formal contract and contractual process be entered into. My normal response is, 'If there are such requirements, then have a contract and have a term, but work towards and be able to demonstrate that the relationship works as if there was no contract and no term'.

Many relationships start with formal, lengthy contracts written and often driven by lawyers. Over time, as trust is developed, the legal contract gives way to more of a joint agreement capturing both the moral intent and the legally binding obligations of the stakeholders. Alternatively, what are often called 'bottom drawer' agreements evolve. The best contracts I have ever worked with remain in a secure but seldom-referred-to place and, in particular, become redundant for the purpose of resolving conflicts or litigation. The stakeholders already know what has to be done. Actions and behaviours become moral, common sense, practical understandings or imperatives well before they become legal or contractual requirements. As the relationship develops, the traditional contract becomes a safety net only, or irrelevant altogether. Many existing one- to three-year tender-based, competitively bid relationships are now moving to 10-year terms or five years plus extension options based on performance.

The other alternative that is finding favour and has real merit is effectively an evergreen agreement based on performance. Up front there is an agreed term (e.g. five years) but the relationship is renewed and extended or rolled over for another year, based on acceptable performance achieved at the end of each year. With poor performance, the term of the agreement can be shortened by one year. Significant or ongoing performance failings may even trigger disengagement. Outstanding or better than expected performance over the target may not only secure an effective contract/agreement extension but also attract additional profit over and above target expectations. There are many variations to this arrangement: for example, one year extensions based on a performance review every two years. On a five-year agreement, and based on good performance, the term would be extended to eight years. This approach avoids the potential for performance to drop off mid-term or the relationship to lose focus. It also gives up front the knowledge that, based on good performance, the relationship is sustainable and extendable.

Partnering or alliance agreements are quite different documents from the traditional contract in intent, language and format. They are positive, collaborative, interdependent, performance-based, continuous-improvement agreements, sharing risks and benefits via gain-sharing, pain-sharing mechanisms. Conventional contracts cannot adequately capture the complexity and ambiguity of genuine partnering and alliance relationships. The nature of partnering and alliance agreements versus legal contracts is discussed further in Chapter 6.

■ *Strategic*: These relationships are critical to the well-being of the partner organisations. There is a high degree of interdependence in that all partners have something fundamental to lose should the relationship break down and something fundamental to gain from success. These are customer/ supplier relationships in the broadest and fuzziest sense. They take into account reciprocal trade where the customer supplier role is reversed; complimentor relationships: internal relationships between divisions, operating units and regions as well as relationships between unions and management; relationships with competitors and co-suppliers; extended relationships up and down the supply chain involving clusters, networks and consortia.

- *Mutual trust*: Simply, without trust the partnership or alliance will not work. Within the agreed 'rules of engagement' for the relationship an unrestricted, unqualified and unconditional trust is developed between the alliance partners. This is a trust based on competence as well as the character of the people and the organisations. Understanding, documenting and communicating to all the stakeholders what trust looks like in terms of the behaviours, mindsets, practices, actions, principles and values expected will be critical to the success of the relationship. In short, it means doing what you said and having no secrets, telling no lies and delivering no unpleasant surprises.

  The concept of the trust charter is discussed in detail in Chapter 6.

- *World class/best practice*: The relationship is world class or best in class as jointly benchmarked against best practice. Initially, this may involve catch-up benchmarking opposite better organisations, competent competitors and more effective relationships or internal benchmarking across regions, business units and the like. Medium to longer term it is about setting the benchmarks and letting others play catch-up. Innovation, vision and the courage to act will lead this process. One of the ways that good partnering relationships avoid the tender system is continuously and jointly to test the marketplace together. Ford, Chrysler and Honda, for example, conduct joint tear-down exercises with their supplier partners on competitive vehicles to gain a better understanding of what the competition is doing and develop leapfrog innovation. The Mobil Oil and Transfield Services integrated services and maintenance alliance has a cross-organisational team in place to jointly benchmark best practice around the world. Benchmarking forums and joint visits to other best practice sites take place, improvements are implemented and their performance monitored. Refer to Case Study 2 on page 401 for further details.

- *Sustainable competitive advantage*: A modified Michael Porter definition would read something like this:

  Sustainable competitive advantage is all about generating sustainable value for the customer:

  1. beyond the cost of creating it;
  2. greater than the price the customer is prepared to pay for it; and
  3. superior to the competition.

  Attempting to partner in isolation from the marketplace and the competition is like training without ever playing a real game. The result is an exhaustive use of energy and time for no effective, measurable return or result and little understanding of your position in the competition table. 'Supercharging a piston engine is not good enough if a competitor has just invented a jet turbine engine.'[4]

■ *Mutual benefit for all the partners*: This is a mutually beneficial, win/win relationship with sharing of both the risks and the benefits. 'All the partners' applies to all customers and suppliers in the relationship in the case of multi-partner relationships and, as appropriate, other key stakeholders.

■ *Separate and positive impact*: The relationship produces benefits for the partner organisations that go beyond the partnership itself. A checkpoint for genuine strategic partnerships and alliances is that they are used as role models, reference points, benchmarks and centres of excellence for other customer/supplier relationships and other activities within and external to the corporation.

Agree up front on a common definition and thus a common understanding of what strategic partnering and alliancing means for the partner organisations. It doesn't have to be the same definition as detailed above, although I think this is a reasonable place to start, but it does have to be a common definition. It would be difficult to count the number of people who have said to me, 'I wish we had agreed that common definition 12 or 18 months ago. A crisis point has been reached because we now see the customer and supplier organisations have been talking and acting on two or more completely different understandings of what strategic partnering is really all about. There was never a common definition, and therefore a common understanding, agreed up front and that is what got us into trouble.' This predicament can also apply internally.

So agree up front what it means and what it looks like to have a strategic partnership or alliance. Then, ask the critically important question: 'Does it pass the handshake test?' That is, are the parties involved prepared to shake hands on this understanding and, in the event of issues, concerns or opportunities arising, prepared if necessary to fall back on the definition for clarification and direction? If the definition is any good it will hold up under such scrutiny. The definition above certainly does. I have put it to literally thousands of organisations and it is yet to fail under interrogation.

In passing the handshake test, of course, the partner organisations enter into a moral agreement and not only just a legal contract. This is a fundamentally important point for partnering and raises three questions. First, is a moral agreement important in business these days? Yes, I believe it is. Second, which do you act on first, the moral agreement or the legally binding contract?

Answer: the moral agreement. While there may be all sorts of legal obligations involved, as with any business or personal relationship, partnering is fundamentally about a moral agreement where the relationship is based on the spirit of the law rather than the letter of the law. The third question is, if the moral agreement is important and it is the first thing the parties act on, then what is it? You would be surprised at the number of people who cannot effectively answer this question. The trust charter (p. 201) and the Partnering/Alliance Charter (p. 216) are examples of moral agreements and usually appear as part of the partnering/alliance agreement.

I was facilitating a partnering workshop some years ago and we had just reviewed the definition above. I asked if everyone was happy with it so that we could continue with the agenda. Agreement seemed unanimous. I then asked: 'Does this definition pass the handshake test?' A senior member of the customer partner immediately asked for clarification: 'Are you asking us are we prepared to shake hands that this definition is going to be the basis of our understanding in the future?' My reply, 'yes'. His response: 'Okay, now I understand. But, on that basis, no, I am not in a position to shake hands. I have a few more questions and points of clarification.' For him, shaking hands was a symbol of his word and his word was his bond and this was not going to be given lightly. We spent the next thirty minutes discussing, clarifying and debating the details and eventually agreed that the definition passed scrutiny and the handshake test. This was a critically important thirty minutes. Common understanding was agreed, sign-off was achieved. Only then did we carry on.

So be wary of those who proclaim partnering success without substance. Although it's just applied common sense, the reality is that genuine partnering is anything but easy. Ask for a common definition, probe for the details. There are few organisations that fully embody the partnering approach being advocated here, although the numbers are growing rapidly. As with most best-in-class practitioners, whether in business, sport or life, modesty and humility often shade the success of the real partners. Their achievements to date are often overshadowed by their focus on the future.

THE EFFECTIVE BRINGING TOGETHER OF ENVIRONMENT, PROCESS AND PEOPLE

For strategic partnering to be successful, the three critical elements of environment, process and people must be understood and effectively integrated. This is shown diagrammatically in Figure 1.1. The environment sets the boundaries within which partnerships operate. This will be determined in large part by the culture, strategy and structure of the partnering organisations

Fig. 1.1 *Strategic partnering: the effective bringing together of environment, process and people*

and the marketplace in which they operate. Culture comprises the organisation's basic belief and value systems, with strategy and structure the mechanisms by which the organisation relates to the outside world. Explicit in the partnering strategy will be unconditional support and active participation from senior management.

Within the confines of the operating environment the strategic partnering process draws the road map by which customer/supplier partnerships are developed. It provides the balance between structure and flexibility and in turn enables reproducibility.

However, even with the right environment and an effective process in operation, success will not come without the right people involved, both as individuals and in teams. In particular, this applies to the role of the partnering and alliance managers. Their vision, skills and determination will be the rate-determining step to successful partnering.

0 to 10 RELATIONSHIP MANAGEMENT (0 to 10 RM)

Two partnering and alliancing myths
- *They are easy.*
- *They are for everyone.*

You can't be all things to all people but you can be the right things to the right people. Not all relationships are the same. If we are to understand partnerships and alliances, we also have to understand the other types of supplier/customer relationships that legitimately exist. Only a select group of your customers and suppliers will want to be, need to be or will be capable of being, true partners. Knowing with whom you do and don't want to partner, and why, is critical. In developing your future partnerships and alliances there will also be a need to understand the current state of the relationship as well as the desired future state. So where do the non-partners fit—those relationships unsuitable for strategic partnering but whose importance to the organisation is in no way diminished? The impact of a genuine partnership can have dramatic and beneficial effects on all customer and supplier relationships. An improvement in the quality of relationships with these customers and suppliers and in the way they are viewed within your organisation—and ultimately the improvement in return on investment (ROI) or financial success to the business—will be just some of the additional benefits.

Figure 1.2 puts strategic partnering and other customer/supplier relationships into perspective in terms of the outcomes: in other words, the degree of collaboration, loyalty, complexity, time involved, customer satisfaction, innovation, ROI/financial success and competitive advantage opposite the relationship type on the horizontal axis. We can classify customer/supplier relationships into three categories or segments—vendor, supplier, and partner relationships. The further the relationship moves to the right on the scale, the greater and more diverse the benefits will be.

Figure 1.3 shows the ten different relationships that make up the vendor, supplier and partner segments as well as relationship type zero. In terms of resource allocation, funding, strategy, training, internal and external relationship management, exploiting synergies and leveraging competencies, it is the entire 0 to 10 relationship scale that must be managed and coordinated effectively. While our focus in *The Strategic Partnering Handbook* is clearly on partnering/alliance and associated relationships, having an understanding of the other relationship types provides a critical set of milestones and benchmarks for relationship development and management generally.

The 0 to 10 scale is universal and captures all other relationships, business and personal. Internal and external, customers, suppliers, principals, contractors, service providers, complimentors, peer groups, support teams, employees, shareholders, sponsors, joint ventures, acquisitions, mergers, licensing, franchising and any other relationships will all fit somewhere on the 0 to 10 scale and into the 0 to 10 Relationship Management Matrix (Fig. 1.4). The relationship types are static but the relationships themselves are fluid, moving from one relationship type to another or integrating characteristics or aspects of several relationship types. This will depend on the associated attitudes, behaviours, practices deployed, the performance levels achieved, the marketplace and other external conditions prevailing.

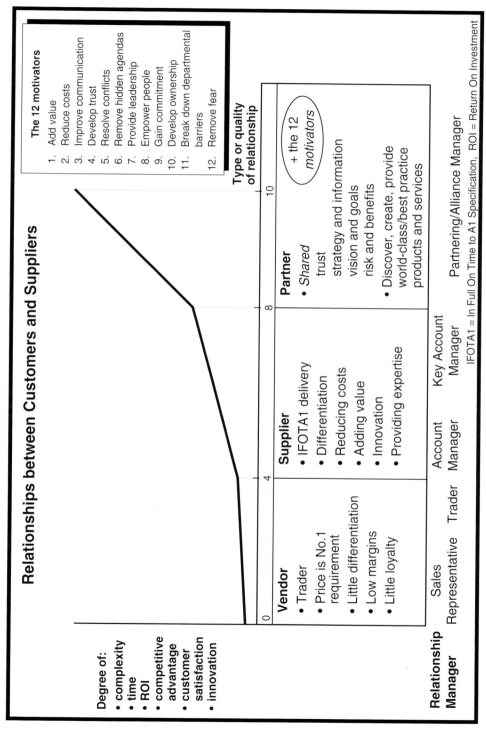

Fig. 1.2 *Relationships between customers and suppliers*

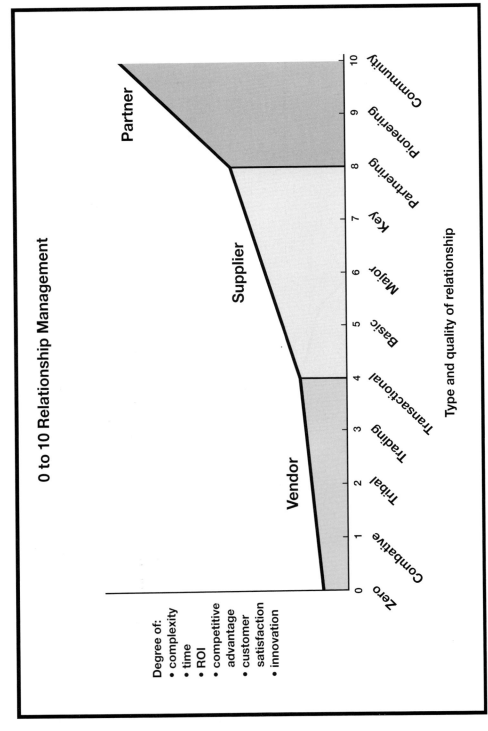

Fig. 1.3 *0 to 10 relationship management: relationship types*

Customers are the reason suppliers exist. If you don't have a customer you don't have a job or a business. Each customer and each supplier is linked via their relationship with people and associated products/services, supporting systems, technologies, primary and support activities. So how we manage and develop our relationships is critically important. Relationships in the context of 0 to 10 RM are those human associations, connections or interactions that have a goal or a purpose. As customer satisfaction is the driving force, relationship type will be determined from the customers' perspective but not necessarily by the customer in isolation. Ideally, there should be agreement between all the parties in the relationship as to the current relationship type, the desired future relationship approach, the optimum levels of performance to be achieved and a 'how to' action plan or strategy to achieve them. The 0 to 10 RM philosophy is summarised in Figure 1.4. In essence, the 0 to 10 RM matrix is surprisingly simple. Eleven relationship types on the horizontal scale and eleven performance levels on the vertical scale form a relationship type/performance matrix.

The horizontal axis, or x-axis, represents the 11 legitimate relationship types split into three segments (vendor, supplier, partner). Each relationship type represents the principles, practices, qualities, attributes, behaviours and mindsets that are deployed in the relationship. The vertical axis, or y-axis, is the performance scale and represents the results, effectiveness, impact of the deployment of those principles, practices, qualities, attributes, behaviours. That is, it represents the degree to which the desired outcomes have been achieved or the performance of the relationship has been successful. Depending on the relationship approach(es) taken, performance will be measured in different proportions or weightings, as a function of six components. They are:

- Return on Investment or Financial success;
- customer satisfaction or stakeholder satisfaction;
- sustainable competitive advantage;
- world-class achievements or best practice implementation;
- innovation;
- attitudes of people.

Sometimes it is just a matter of improving performance and not moving to another relationship type or approach; that is, doing what you are doing now, just doing it a whole lot better.

Understanding the type and quality of relationships and performance levels required up and down the supply chain and integrating the individual relationship strategies into the corporate strategy will be one of the keys to future success.

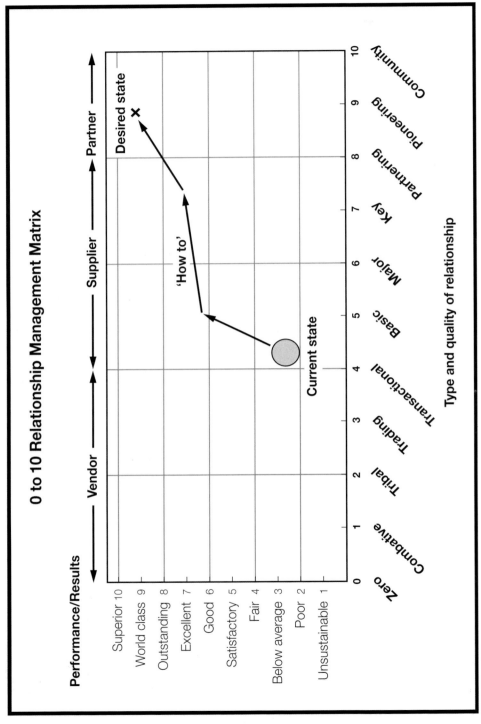

Fig. 1.4   *0 to 10 relationship management performance matrix*

The type zero relationship and each of the three relationship categories (vendor, supplier, partner) and their associated relationship types are explained below.

Type 0—zero relationships

As strange as it may seem, the zero relationship is legitimate. It needs to be part of the 0 to 10 relationship scale and also part of your business strategy. In a zero relationship the choice is made, deliberately and consciously, for good reason(s), not to have a relationship with the customer, supplier or competitor in question. For customer or supplier this could involve a potential new account, a lost account to be regained, a lost account to be left at zero, or a deliberately discarded account. Zero relationships could also involve other organisations with which, for ethical or commercial reasons or little or no strategic alignment, you choose not to do business. It may well be to your advantage that you leave these relationships to your competitors. Let them waste their time, money and resources on unproductive relationships.

Vendor relationship types (1–4)

Vendors normally have a cost-plus strategy and mentality, trading on thin margins with little or nothing differentiating them in a positive way from their competition. Price and/or cost is the driving force behind the relationship, with customer/supplier loyalty having a low priority. They occupy the horizontal scale from 1 to 4 depending on their ability to deliver the base customer requirements 'at a low price'. Relationships with suppliers are not necessarily strong with the focus more on risk transfer from customer to supplier than risk management. In fact, one of the qualities of a good vendor is the ability to change quickly from one customer to another, or from one source of supply to another, in the event of non-availability, lack of dependability or pricing problems. In the case of a trader it could be that the principal company changes agents, going direct to the customer, or the supply source dries up.

Good vendors, however, know their business—that is, their suppliers, customers and competitors, their products, services and costs and hence can have very successful, high-performing relationships. They have a low-cost base and don't pretend to be anything more than they really are. Depending on the strategy, the time and place, and the nature of the product or service, vendors can be competent and effective. A good vendor may cause many a reasonable supplier or a poor-quality partner to come unstuck. Good vendors, like good suppliers and partners, don't over-promise and underdeliver and they can be flexible and responsive in the right circumstances and when it suits them. They understand their limitations and match their capabilities against customer expectations. There are four relationship types in the vendor segment—combative, tribal, trading and transactional.

Type 1—Combative relationships

'You're not in business to make friends. If you want a friend, get a dog. Me, I'm not taking any chances. I've got two dogs.' A quote by the 'partner from hell'.

Uncooperative, confrontational, adversarial, aggressive and, on occasions, coercive and warlike are the words and behaviours that best sum up combative relationships. They are driven by a win/lose, master/slave control/compliance mentality, manipulation of facts, the need for secrecy and a short-term profit focus. This is a world of self-survival as much as it is about self-interest at the expense of others. The combatants in these relationships are reminiscent of schoolyard bullies, with communications often threatening and hostile. This creates an environment of intense competition and rivalry that stifles creativity, openness and honesty.

These are the mean, deceitful, vindictive, vengeful 'bad boys' of the 0 to 10 relationship scale. Lawyers are one of their largest expenses and the legal system and traditional contract process their playing field. Relationship management is seen as something of a blood sport. Tenders and the competitive bid process are commonplace and often associated with detailed, hard nosed, hard dollar and one-sided contracts.

Combative relationships are seemingly everywhere in our lives. They are what our legal system thrives on. Combative relationships can include hostile takeovers, mergers, acquisitions and joint ventures; many management/union relationships; competitors forced to do business with each other through legislation requirements or market forces; hard-nosed contractual relationships, for example, in the building and construction industry; rival company directors fighting it out in the courts for boardroom control; politics; relationships between feuding neighbours; the divorce courts; interdepartmental rivalry and a multitude of other business and interpersonal relationships. They range from the very large to the very small. Unfortunately, many large capital projects, for example, in the civil engineering and construction sectors, are still based on combative relationships. I knew a CEO who regarded his office as a trophy room, showing off on the walls the verdicts and associated publicity from successful litigation and courtroom battles.

I am not suggesting that combative relationships cannot be successful, but they demonstrate less sustainability. Many successful monopolies, semi-monopolies and bigger institutions, especially in banking, information technology, manufacturing, construction and tele-communications, still wave the combative banner. Risk is often transferred 100 per cent from customer to supplier or from one party to the other party, or at least there is an attempt to do so. This can often lead to some bizarre behaviours and practices. While it may appear to be so legally or contractually the reality is that it is impossible to transfer 100 per cent of the risk. First, even if it were possible, you would pay for the privilege and, second, there will always be some aspect that comes back to bite you, if only by affecting your reputation, credibility and future competitive advantage.

For example, a typical strategy or tactic in a combative relationship would involve one or more of the parties employing lawyers to scrutinise contracts (before, during and/or after they are signed or awarded) for potential loopholes. These loopholes are then used to introduce variations into the scope of work at a point in the contract timeline where it would be difficult if not impossible for the customer/principal to displace the contractor or vice versa, or at least renegotiate the outcomes.

Being type 1 on the 0 to 10 scale, combatants are the 'partners from hell'. Generally, relationships improve the further to the right you move on the scale. By default, then, this is as bad as it gets, certainly in terms of loyalty, collaboration, openness and trust. Often type 1 combative relationships can be a catch-all for other relationships that have gone wrong. Even with high performing combative relationships one or more parties in the relationship will make a comment something like, 'They do a good job but, damn, they are difficult to deal with'.

Type 2—Tribal relationships

> In the race of life, always bet on self-interest.
> Attributed to Paul Keating, former Australian prime minister

Tribal relationships are often spoken about as fiefdoms or organisational silos within which exist parochial, insular, protective, territorial groups resistant to change, with an intense suspicion or fear of outsiders. They occur internally between departments, functions and other operating groups and externally between customers, suppliers and other organisations. Tribal relationships also extend to political, union, sporting, suburban and family environments. For example, politics is a haven for vested interest groups and factions with its legendary 'turf wars' and intergroup rivalry.

Those involved in tribal relationships exhibit a willingness to protect and defend everything from territory, departments, markets, position and title, information and power, to profits and margins and are, therefore, often laden with hidden agendas. Within these normally hierarchical structures there is much back-watching, self-interest and finger-pointing with medium-to-high levels of loyalty to the group or tribe in question but little trust or loyalty towards the external environment. So called 'old boys' networks are commonplace. But even in this environment tribal relationships can pass the median performance standard, for example, state and federal governments from different political parties are forced to cooperate on specific issues. Many sporting, indigenous and vested interested groups are very successful in protecting and defending their culture and heritage for all the right reasons. Tribal relationships are often full of demarcations and boundary issues where control and influence is tightly managed. Managers and leaders are spoken about as effective 'warlords' in terms of the power they have over the people, business and activities they control.

Certainly, if provoked, participants in tribal relationships can quickly turn combative but their natural instinct is to take a defensive rather than offensive approach to the external environment.

Type 3—Trading relationships

Type 3 trading relationships exist in a world of opportunism and are all about negotiating, bargaining, bartering, doing the deal and getting/giving the order, predominantly at the best or lowest price. Quality and service aspects are normally to minimum required standards and often have a lower priority. This is the classic environment of low margins, little loyalty and little differentiation of products and services with more of a focus on performance against budgets and other short-term profit and financial targets. They tend to be shallow, short-term relationships where the speed and timing of decision making is critical. Therefore, one-time-only or irregular buying patterns are just as common as trading, ongoing, repeat business.

Intensely competitive environments, trading relationships are found everywhere from the share and currency markets, traditional commodity markets such as mining, oil and petroleum products, agriculture and chemicals and energy markets, through to traditional selling organisations, car and property sales, food, homewares and clothing markets. However, there is an opportunity to make a difference in any of these marketplaces. In the words of Theodore Levitt, 'every product and service is differentiable'.[5]

Trading relationships are often associated with tenders and competitive bidding, where one organisation is traded off against another for the best deal. Sales representatives, purchasing officers, traders and the like are the main points of contact.

Type 4—*Transactional relationships*

Traditionally, transactional relationships involve the straight purchase or sale of products and services over the counter, over the phone, by fax or via the Internet with little or no negotiation involved. This makes them quite different from trading relationships. If people are directly involved it is very much a sale of goods and/or services for a set price with point-of-sale payment or a predetermined set of payment terms and conditions. No lengthy discussion is entered into and no real personal relationship is built. Supermarket or retail shopping is a typical example, although transactional relationships can be found in every business sector, public or private.

Transactional relationships have become far more prominent over the last 10 years, especially with the advent of electronic communications and the Internet. In many cases they have become impersonal, system- or technology-based, at arm's length, and are often faceless and invisible. Conducting e-commerce on the Internet, working through sophisticated and often outsourced call centres, or doing all your banking transactions via an ATM (Automatic Teller Machine), a telephone or over the Internet, are typical images of modern-day transactional relationships. For many people this gives the perception, if not a reality, of a cold, clinical and impersonal relationship.

Transactional relationships can, however, be very effective and efficient. They can add value, entertain (in the case of the Internet), and be profitable. In fact, as the Internet expands its scope of activity and influence, transactional relationships will become far more dominant and have an impact on all the other relationship types. In 1994 the Internet was effectively a commerce-free zone. In the two months of November and December 1999, prior to Christmas, sales by the US Internet retailers reached $US11 billion. There is a message for us all here. But the ability of transactional relationships to differentiate and sustain a competitive advantage to date has been based more on the quality of the electronic interface than the quality of the relationship. Trust is built more through technology, systems and processes than through people. The question is 'Is this sustainable?'

Until a couple of years ago I bought and sold shares through stockbrokers that called themselves a non-advisory, discount broking firm. They would buy and sell shares on your behalf for a small, flat brokerage fee, irrespective of the volume and nature of shares, but that is all. No advice or information was given or, indeed, any service at all over and above the buying and selling of shares. But they did this very effectively. The service met my requirements as I had other avenues by which information and advice were gathered. They were fast, efficient and cost-effective. However, this type of transactional relationship has now developed into online Internet trading of stocks and shares.

The transactional relationship has now developed to the point where organisations sell sophisticated software packages that analyse market trends online instantaneously and make buy/sell recommendations. Then, with the press of a couple of keys on your PC, you can make the buy/sell transactions online, withdrawing or depositing the appropriate funds automatically from selected accounts.

Supplier relationship types (5–7)

Supplier relationships occupy positions 5, 6 and 7 on the relationship scale. Delivering products and services 'In Full On Time to A1 specification' (IFOTA1) becomes the base requirement for any reasonable supplier. Understanding the customer's requirements and then meeting and servicing them via cost-reduction and value-adding initiatives like technical service, product development, maximising synergies and responsiveness to special requests become a good supplier's trademark—all at a competitive price. Usually, but not always, these relationships normally involve tightly managed contracts, often detailed and associated with tenders and competitive bidding. The degree of innovation in these initiatives will determine the degree of differentiation achieved, and, in turn, the profit margin. In going from 5 to 6 to 7 on the relationship scale there tends to be a growth in size, complexity or importance of the relationship.

Many organisations think they are good suppliers and good customers positioned at 6 and 7 on the relationship scale, but in fact are nothing more than vendors at 1, 2, 3 or 4. Delusions of grandeur can lead to a trip down the well of mediocrity.

Most businesses today are striving to become good suppliers and to have good suppliers working for them. There is no shame in being a good supplier. The level of 6 or 7 on the relationship scale represents a very effective, competent, quality-driven and probably continuously improving organisation. Many outsourcing relationships are part of the supplier segment. For many customers and suppliers today, high-performance relationships in the supplier segment will be all they require to sustain a sound and profitable business and strong customer/supplier relationship.

Using the maintenance analogy, type 5 'basic' relationships involve mainly breakdown maintenance. Type 6 'major' relationships would involve reducing overall maintenance costs against an agreed baseline and type 7 'key' relationships would involve improving overall reliability and availability of plant and equipment and those activities further down and more imbedded in the customer's value chain, normally of higher impact, value or importance.

Type 5—Basic relationships

Basic type 5 relationships are low-impact, low-profile, low-priority, non-critical, independent, 'business as usual' relationships from the customer's perspective. Traditionally involving non-core activities or perceived non-core activities, type 5 relationships often involve service or trades activities, and simple or undifferentiated commodity-based products. Any improvements in products and services are either reactive or driven by general market trends. The major focus is on measured delivery of agreed requirements IFOTA1 and little or no focus on innovation or continuous improvement. Basic relationships are the first of the genuinely customer-focused and -serviced or account-managed relationships beyond the spot buying/selling and regular dealing of trading relationships and the often impersonal, faceless detachment of transactions. Still very competitive, often involving tenders and competitive bidding, they are normally contract, SLA (Service Level Agreement) or specification driven involving the delivery of an agreed set of requirements and expectations IFOTA1. A large focus is on price, basic quality and service maintenance or the beginning of total cost reductions. These relationships often comprise a large segment of a commercial organisation's relationships. They are normally small to medium-sized accounts where the products and services involved are not critical in application, or large in size or $ value to the customer.

There is continual pressure on basic relationships to become more cost-effective and go transactional, to be continually traded off on price against other competitors or somehow to differentiate, aggregate, expand in scope and importance and move up the 0 to 10 relationship scale.

Although combative and tribal relationships share some of the same contract and work-scope characteristics mentioned above, they are quite different from basic relationships. Basic relationships do not carry the same aggressive, adversarial, confrontational, threatening or hostile behaviours that typify combative relationships. Nor do they display the degree of territorial, protective or defensive attitudes or approaches that are so much a part of tribal relationships. This is a relatively simple relationship of low- to mid-range importance, and short- to medium-term focus, managing repeat business for small to medium-size accounts and projects. Basic relationships are serviced by an account manager, project manager, customer service manager or a similar person as the relationship manager, conforming to a predetermined set of requirements IFOTA1. A simple action plan is likely to be in place with Key Performance Indicators (KPIs) to measure performance.

Basic relationships are often spoken about as list price or small discount off list price, standard rates, 'no frills' relationships with proactive customer service and reactive product and/or service development.

Type 6—Major relationships

Major relationships are typified by an increasing complexity and importance of the products, services and projects delivered, and the supporting relationship. Conformance to requirements IFOTA1, together with a strong and proactive focus on total cost reductions, tends to overshadow true innovation and added value opportunities. Major relationships are the first of the real proactively managed, quality-focused, continuous-improvement relationship types. They are still, however, independent more than interdependent relationships with a minimum sharing of risk. The parties to the relationship would be sharing with each other their business goals, performance drivers and measures, and identifying where their individual corporate objectives complement and conflict. They may even conduct a joint SWOT (strengths, weaknesses, opportunities, threats) analysis within a medium- to longer-term perspective.

A formal differentiation strategy involving process re-engineering or new product or service development is in place but based more on total cost reductions against agreed baselines. Adding value in terms of new product and service development to improve the customer's margin, selling price, sales volume or market share tends to be more reactive than proactive. Major account managers, project managers, asset managers, procurement, supply and good contract managers actively manage and monitor the progress of these relationships, a job that would include regular reviews of the overall supplier performance. An informal, multilevel network of internal and external service providers would support them. Many outsourced relationships of non-core activities would be candidates for type 6 major relationships. In fact type 6 'major' relationships are often seen as the entry point for outsourcing—outsourcing being defined as the transfer of non-core competencies or activities from customer to supplier. Many would involve single or preferred supplier arrangements with medium levels of systems or process integration. On occasions type 6 and 7 relationships are seen as part of 'best of breed' strategies where the best parts, competencies and qualities are 'cherry picked' from suppliers, creating a patchwork effect on the supply of products and services.

Type 7—Key relationships

Key relationships are the most critical and important in the supplier segment of the 0 to 10 scale. Delivering products and services IFOTA1 is a prerequisite, a given. They are strategically important, complex and multidimensional products and/or integrated service relationships. Focused more on genuine value adding than just total cost reductions, these are quality driven, continuously improving, innovation-based relationships. Both the customer and supplier parties to the relationship provide expertise over and above the products and services given or received for which they are paid or pay. Organisations, departments, functions and teams use their strengths, skills and expertise to assist the other customers/suppliers. For example, this may involve areas of joint training, finance, information technology, IT systems, workplace reform, preventative, predictive or design-out maintenance techniques.

Key accounts are enlightened self-interest relationships based on long-term win/win outcomes for all parties. This involves detailed sharing of business strategies and other relevant information, minimising the areas of conflict and exploiting synergies between the parties in the relationship. They may well be associated with multifunctional support groups or customer focus teams working within a complex multilevel contact environment. However, management and responsibility for the relationship is still linked more to individuals and individual accountability than teams and joint accountability as with partnering/alliancing.

These relationships are the domain of key account managers, strategic supply and procurement managers, senior project and asset managers, business managers and mid- to senior-level relationship executives. Regular and formal business review and development (BRAD) meetings take place to review progress against the documented key account plan, objectives and requirements, and to discuss future opportunities. While growing in interdependence, this is still at heart an independent relationship.

Two key relationships we developed at ICI involved warehousing and distribution providers and our catalyst supplier. Effective and efficient warehousing and distribution were critical if we were to deliver literally hundreds of thousands of tonnes of plastics and petrochemicals per annum IFOTA1. Without the best catalyst the right chemical reaction did not take place in the reactors and the manufacturing process was stopped or impeded. Both these relationships subsequently developed into partnerships and alliances.

Partner relationship types (8–10)

There is a greater scope for relationship development than vendor and supplier relationships can offer. We are becoming more and more reliant on the quality, consistency, reliability and dependability of external skills, products and services to ensure we meet our own customer requirements. As the world becomes more complex there will be the need for much stronger, more enduring and more effective business relationships.

Alliance partners, apart from having all the qualities of the best 7+ key relationships, share visions, strategies and a wealth of information. They discover, create and provide world-class and/or best practice products and services. The quality of their relationships with upstream suppliers will be as good as, or close to, those with downstream customers and the partnerships themselves. Internal and external barriers will be removed and communication will be free and open. Above all, partners will share a mutual trust. They will also share mutual risk as well as benefits on the basis of the interdependence built between them. This is the most fulfilling target you could aim for. Achieving genuine partner status with selected customers and suppliers has far-reaching and positive implications for the organisation as a whole. The impact of the 'twelve motivators' (see Fig. 1.2), as I call them, will have an influence far wider than just the partnership and alliance itself. These motivators are looked at in detail when discussing the strategic partnering process in Chapter 6.

Partnering, pioneering and community relationships share the same principles, concepts and many of the same practices but their form, structure, level of complexity, 'fuzziness', and ambiguity can differ significantly. All three types are managed and led by the partnering or alliance manager(s) with the support of a core cross-organisational team(s) all of whom hold themselves mutually accountable and responsible for the long-term well-being of the relationship. *The Strategic Partnering Handbook* is all about partner and alliance relationship types 8, 9 and 10, so I will not elaborate on the details of these relationships at this point. The following is just a brief summary of partnering (type 8), pioneering (type 9) and community (type 10) relationships.

Type 8—Partnering relationships

Partnering or alliance type 8 relationships are, above all, about mutual trust. They are based on competence, character, interdependence, honesty and integrity in fair-minded and reasonable people working together, in good faith, as individuals and teams to achieve shared visions and common goals for mutual benefit. These relationships live in a world of transparency, seamless boundaries, frictionless commerce, performance-based remuneration and joint benchmarking, absence of tenders or competitive bidding in the traditional sense, leveraging core competencies around a broad balanced scorecard of performance measures. The win/lose options have been removed and the relationships are based on the management and effective allocation of risk rather than the 100 per cent risk transfer. Risk is allocated to those partners best able to manage the risk. Risk management and allocation are then linked directly to risk/reward and profit gain/painshare. This is the transition stage between the old and the new worlds, moving from phase 1 to phase 2 on the development curve (see Fig. 1.9) where paradigm shifts have changed from rough concepts to practical application.

Type 8 relationships would normally involve one-on-one or simple cluster relationships more than the virtual or extended networks and supply chains applicable to pioneering and community relationships. This is the transition point from being a traditional customer and supplier to being a partner. The great leap forward has occurred. These relationships are not only strategic but are seen as critical to the long-term well-being and success of the partner organisations. This is now a world of sharedness, not just sharing. The basis for this is having a shared vision, common goals and jointly agreed performance indicators for which the alliance partners hold themselves mutually accountable. There will be a formal relationship development process and strategy or action plan in place. Cross-organisational teams and not individuals manage the relationship with involvement, commitment and leadership from senior management and the executive teams.

The application of the moral agreement has taken prominence over, but not necessarily displaced, the traditional contract. In many cases they are one and the same. Paradigm shifts that fundamentally change the way business has been done in the past are developing or are in place. Twelve partnering paradigm shifts, together with current practices and case studies, are discussed in detail in later chapters.

Type 9—Pioneering relationships

Pioneering type 9 relationships capture those paradigm shifters and pioneers daring to seek new boundaries and break old rules. They are often spoken about as brave, bold and different relationships, and are at the next level of maturity, interdependence and complexity for partnerships and alliances. Sometimes called virtual relationships, virtual companies, co-producers, clusters and consortia networks, they are truly seamless and transparent environments in every respect, often involving public and private sector organisations. This is about going from phase 2 to phase 3 on the partnering development curve (see Fig. 1.9).

Some of the activities partnering paradigm pioneers involve themselves with include:

- shared ownership and management of assets;
- buy-back and lease of assets, products and services with remuneration linked to asset performance;
- integrated corporate strategies, not just 'one-off' relationships;
- expanding relationships globally across political, cultural and social boundaries;
- turning the alliance itself into a virtual company or organisation, equity or non-equity linked or a separate legal entity or joint venture;
- joint customer/supplier partner involvement in new projects and other long-term relationships;

- complex public/private sector partnerships and alliances, clusters or networks;
- the relationship owning the intellectual property for joint benefit, not individual alliance partners, based on self-interest;
- advanced multi-partner alliances;
- each partner waiving all rights to litigation in the event of any non-conformance other than for wilful default.

The Alcoa/Honeywell global alliance, the Transfield Services/Worley story and the Sydney Water journey are excellent examples of pioneering relationships and are looked at in detail as case studies in Part D.

Type 10—Community relationships

Community relationships are reserved for the extended networks, supply and value chains that we are starting to see develop in the airlines, business and financial services, computers and communications, pharmaceuticals, automotive, entertainment and leisure, healthcare and chemicals, energy and resource sectors and elsewhere. Still in the early stages of development, the One World Alliance and its competing counterpart, The Star Alliance, are just two examples in the airline sector of extended partnering networks and supply chains competing with each other. Sometimes called extended enterprise relationships, these communities share the same principles and concepts as type 8 and 9 relationships but are now extended up and down complex supply and value chains. People often talk about a 'sense of community', an interconnected and shared destiny or purpose, to express the common and shared bonds/objectives/goals of community groups. Community relationships come in various shapes and sizes (e.g. business cooperatives, emergency response communities, health communities, virtual communities).

These relationships will have social and political implications as well as economic implications for profit, non-profit, public and private sector organisations. This is not about individual companies, departments or internal functions competing or relating to each other but extended, interconnected communities, supply chains and internal organisational value chains.

Figure 1.4 looks at relationship types on the x axis and their associated performance levels on the y axis. Even within complex, multi-site, multi-business, multi-partner relationships there will most likely be a variety of relationship types to be managed. In summarising Figures 1.2, 1.3 and 1.4, there are three important points to make. First, it is not about shifting all your customer and/or supplier relationships to partnering and alliance relationships. It is about understanding the optimum mix of relationships (0 to 10 on the type/quality scale) and performance levels required to sustain your organisation's competitive advantage. It is not always the case that relationships need to move up or down the (horizontal) type scale, just that the performance levels of the current relationship need improvement. Second, it is estimated[6] that less than 50 per cent of partnerships and alliances are successful. That does not mean they are complete failures but rather that they fail to achieve their full potential. In large part this is due to lack of alignment between the organisations. Specifically, there is a misalignment in what I call the five fundamental relationship components of culture, strategy, structure, process and people. These components are discussed at length in the coming chapters. Third, partnerships and alliances are a fundamental part of an organisation's business plan. They will take time and resources and will impact widely on the organisation and other customer/supplier relationships. Thus, they cannot operate in isolation.

Understanding the 'current state' and potential 'future state(s)' of your relationship(s) and implementing a 'how to' plan to bridge the gap is the key to effective relationship management and therefore your future success (see Fig. 1.4). This applies to relationships internal and external to the organisation. I would encourage all organisations to complete this analysis. The results will be extremely useful and rewarding.

As appropriate to the operating environment and the organisational business strategy, any organisation or relationship, irrespective of size or market sector, relationship type or performance level, is capable of achieving partner status. Turning this vision into reality will depend largely on the quality of leadership from the top of the organisation and level of buy-in and commitment gained at the operating levels. Beware of those people who talk the language of alliance partners (types 8–10) but 'walk' elsewhere on the 0 to 10 scale.

It is often the case that a crisis—either imminent or current—between customer and supplier organisations is the reason for the low score on the 0 to 10 scale. This crisis is often the catalyst for fundamental change, generating a sense of urgency that drives the partnering process forward. Ironically, high-performing relationships/organisations at 6 and 7 on the scale often have the potential and capability but lack the sense of urgency to take them further. They have difficulty getting to 8 and beyond because they think they have never had it so good or that it can't get any better.

Partnering is a paradigm shift and not just a matter of doing the same things better. Going from 7 to 8 on the relationship scale is not about incremental change, reducing costs a further few dollars, improving customer service a notch, getting stock levels down a smidgen and products to market a few days earlier, or winning another percentage point of market share. It is about a fundamental change in attitude, mindset, performance and behaviour.

MANAGING VENDOR/SUPPLIER/PARTNERSHIP RELATIONS

The other important issue is the type and quality of the individuals who manage these relationships. Figure 1.2 shows five relationship manager types associated with the various customer/supplier relationships. They are:

1. Sales representative
2. Trader
3. Account manager
4. Key account manager
5. Partnering/alliance manager

This is by no means an exhaustive list but is meant to initiate a discussion on the types and qualities of people managing the organisation's relationships. This split of relationship management roles will prove useful in aligning people, skills and competencies with the types of customer/supplier relationships you currently have and the customer/supplier relationships you want to develop. Managing relationships is all about people and communication and there are probably no more important individuals than those who lead and manage the process.

What sort of business are you in? What sort of relationships are you trying to develop? What kind of people do you employ to manage these relationships? It is probably easier to discuss these questions from the traditional sales perspective, starting with the sales representative and working our way up to the partnership manager.

■ **Sales representatives**. Sales representatives are often associated with trading, transactional and many basic relationships. Sales representatives can be good operators for simple relationships but can quickly get out of their depth in higher order relationships. They can do a sound job, albeit task focused, given the right management and incentives. However, they can also be driven by self-interest, often based on commissions, limited in skills and large on ego, with short-term objectives that are at odds with the strategy of the business as a whole. Often difficult to manage and a nightmare to upskill, their renegade tactics focus more on 'doing the deal at almost any cost' than on developing a sustainable relationship or, at least, return business. They are the cause of many good tribal or interdepartmental battles among sales, planning, purchasing, production, marketing, and credit and collection.

- Good **traders** in full flight are a pleasure to watch. They know their business, their costs, the margins they require, the products and services they sell. Skilled negotiators, they work with the persistence of bull terriers and the cunning of water rats. The emphasis is on speed and price. Unquestionably, there is a place for good traders in the world, but they are not suited to partnerships and the long term.
- **Account managers** are the base from which your small, medium and some of your major customers are serviced. They will range from a mixture of young, ambitious tearaways, using sales as a stepping stone to marketing and senior management, to stable, seasoned veterans who have the respect of their peers throughout the marketplace. They are all totally professional and committed to professional selling and continuous improvement.
- **Key account managers** are specialists in the area of developing and maintaining relationships with key strategic accounts. These relationships are well developed at all levels by a strategic hands-on approach to professional selling and the use of strong communication, interpersonal and negotiating skills. The skills and market knowledge of key account managers are broad-ranging, and they are well respected among their peers, senior management, customers and competitors. If you are genuinely interested in a value-added, longer-term, professional approach to account management, it will pay to have one or more of these people on your payroll.
- **Partnership, partnering, alliance managers** are the 'top shelf'. Their business is the development, leadership and management of strategic, long-term customer/supplier partnerships that are of critical importance to the well-being of the organisation. Their marketplace is global and their focus on the short, medium and long term. Their skills are those of the best key account managers or business managers, teamed with the ability to understand and manage extremely complex environments from a technical, commercial, strategic and interpersonal point of view. They are unique individuals, highly sought after but rarely seen in business today. As professional troubleshooters they are without peer in the field of customer/supplier relationship management. The success or failure of the partnership will depend on their commitment, capability and skills.

We go into this aspect of relationship management in greater detail in Chapter 9. It is important first to understand what type of relationships you want to develop with your customers and suppliers, and why. Is it a vendor, supplier or partner relationship? This in turn will determine the quality of the individuals you employ and the associated skills required to manage those relationships.

NOT EVERYONE WANTS A PARTNERSHIP

Ask yourself the question: Where do you, your suppliers and your customers, especially the top twenty—or the top 20 per cent—sit on the 0 to 10 relationship management matrix (RM) (see Fig. 1.4)? Where do your competitors lie?

Critical to this understanding is the assumption that not all organisations, big or small, necessarily want to be partners. Their own vision and strategies, whether they are least-cost or value-added, will determine whether they want to engage in strategic partnering or be serviced by vendors and suppliers, or be vendors and suppliers themselves. We all have customers and suppliers who, for whatever reasons—cultural or commercial values, competitive or strategic impact—do not want to develop, or aren't willing and/or capable of developing, strong, long-term strategic relationships.

For example, the following reasons may be relevant:

- As a supplier or customer, you may be only a small part of their overall sale or purchase of raw materials or services. However, they may be a very large part of your business.
- As a supplier, you, or another division of your organisation, or an associated company, may be a downstream competitor. It is very difficult to share visions, strategies and other information under such circumstances. However, if the appropriate relationship/association is developed, there is no reason why it could not be a profitable and rewarding arrangement for all parties, even to the extent of scoring 7 for key relationship type on the 0 to 10 RM scale.
- The customer's own strategy is that of a vendor.
- Whether perception or reality, the customer sees your own strategy as being that of a vendor or poor supplier and does not regard your organisation as willing and/or capable of developing and sustaining partnerships.
- The customer's staff may not trust the people they have direct contact with in your organisation. Even though your firm may have what it takes to develop partnerships, if the main contacts the customer deals with do not have the appropriate skills, then this will be a major stumbling block.
- The concept of partnerships and alliances is totally foreign to the customer. A case of diminishing returns can ensue if development of the relationship is not handled carefully and a common understanding developed.
- The customer has a fundamental lack of confidence in your technology and processes and doubts your ability to be dependable and reliable in delivering continuously improving products and services.

Be extremely careful and thorough in your choice of a partner. Strategic partnering takes time, resources and, on many occasions, up-front expenditure, and while genuine and significant short-term benefits are almost always achieved, the real results of your labour become visible years, not months, down the track. However, the rewards of a successful partnership are enormous and go far beyond what would otherwise have been. Partner selection is discussed in detail as one of the twelve steps in the partnering process in Chapter 6.

THE BENEFITS OF
STRATEGIC PARTNERING/ALLIANCING

The full extent of the benefits of these long-term relationships will only become clear as the partnering process unfolds in the following chapters. At this point, however, it is useful to understand the broad scope of those benefits and the various aspects of the business they impact upon. There are two levels of benefits, the *base-level benefits* and the *higher-level benefits*. The base-level benefits are listed in Figure 1.5. The relationship between base-level and higher-level benefits is illustrated in Figure 1.6.

The **base-level benefits** are the shorter-term, more immediately tangible and more easily measurable results. Many or all of these base-level benefits would be applicable and advantageous in the course of normal customer/ supplier relationships. Both their performance and priority can change relatively quickly, depending on the changing nature of the prevailing environment. For that reason the list of base-level benefits is by no means exhaustive.

The **higher-level benefits** are the broader, longer-term leading and lagging indicators that both customer and supplier organisations have irreversibly changed for the better. They represent the degree to which change has occurred in the set of core values that the relationship is based upon. Ultimately, they are the real and lasting benefits that both parties are looking for. No doubt they are more difficult to measure and more difficult to achieve, but that is what partnerships are all about. These higher-level benefits are in fact the 'outcomes' of the strategic partnering process itself and are ultimately the reasons why the relationships exist. The six higher-level benefits will also appear as lead and lag outcome headings on the partnering/alliancing Balanced Scorecard which is discussed in detail in Chapter 7.

The current obsession with generating shareholder wealth exclusively, with denominator management[8] of Return on Investment (ROI) and Net Assets (RONA), and with the often used vehicles of implementation, downsizing, right-sizing, cost cutting and restructuring has little to do with outstanding

---

Customer base-level benefits

- Improved quality, fewer rejects, less waste
- Lower operational costs
- Reduced inspection time
- Customer complaints due to non-conformances dramatically reduced
- Lower prices in real terms (i.e. reduced total cost)
- Superior performance or effect at lower, equivalent (or even higher) prices (i.e. greater value for money)
- Improved productivity/efficiencies/process stability
- Shorter lead times
- Improved reliability, flexibility and dependability of supply
- Improved cash flows and reduced working capital costs
- Lower inventory and cycle times
- Reduced product/service development time
- Improved skills
- Joint training and skills development
- Fewer hassles and less frustration
- More time and resources available for downstream customers
- Increased margins (i.e. increased total value)
- Improved communication and people relationships
- Increase in market share
- Aggregate purchasing
- Supplier-managed inventories
- Improved/extended range of products and services
- Early supplier involvement in product/service development
- Elimination of waste associated with tenders, annual auctions and multiple suppliers
- Elimination of litigation and adversarial confrontation
- Improved development cycle times
- Improved time to market
- Joint planning
- Reduced capital and operational expenditure
- Improved safety performance
- Higher value, structured financing
- Simplification and/or integration of networks, processes and systems
- Leveraging off the global strength, brand and market knowledge of the partner(s)
- Influencing partner product/service development activities
- Full and effective engagement of resources
- Aligned incentives with performance and financial success directly linked
- Reduced or improved risk profile

Fig. 1.5 *The base-level benefits of strategic partnering*

Supplier base-level benefits

- Larger volumes of products and services (domestic and/or export)
- Longer-term stability of supply
- Greater stability of forecasts
- Improved production efficiencies/cycle times
- Higher quality at lower operational costs
- Lower costs in real terms
- Fewer hassles and less frustration
- Improved skills from joint training
- Increased margins
- Fewer customer complaints/less waste
- Improved communication and people relationships (internal and external)
- Price premium over the competition (i.e. greater value for money)
- Achievement of preferred supplier/preferred relationship status
- Increased market share and access to new markets
- The partnership becomes a benchmark for other customer/supplier relationships
- Greater responsiveness and flexibility in fulfilling customer expectations and resolving customer complaints
- Improved rate of product/service development
- Improved logistics and delivery systems
- Greater integration of activities between divisions/departments, etc.
- Fewer process steps and less complexity
- Early involvement in product or service development
- Scrapping of the dreaded tender system
- Elimination of litigation and adversarial confrontation
- Cross-company secondments
- Co-location, cross-company secondments
- Greater transparency and openness
- Improved safety performance
- Reduced capital and operational expenditure
- Co-location of people and assets
- Cross-company secondments and people exchange programs
- Greater levels of innovation
- Reduced or improved risk profile

Fig. 1.5 *The base-level benefits of strategic partnering* (continued)

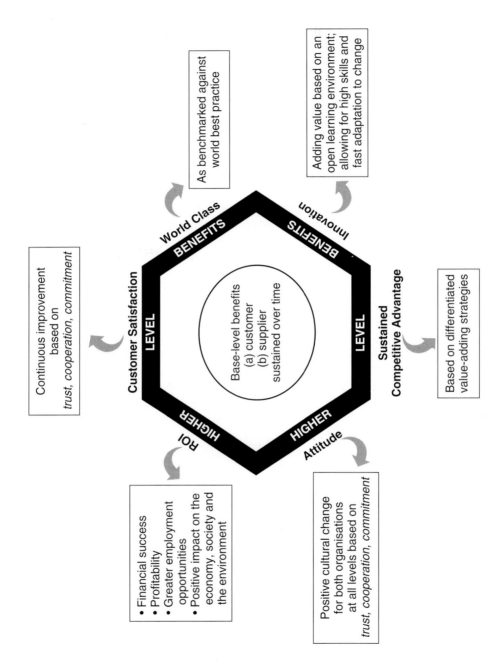

Fig. 1.6   *The relationship between base-level and higher-level benefits*

partnering and alliancing. That is not to say these initiatives are not appropriate or useful, but their indiscriminate application and ineffective implementation have caused many indifferent company results and a resultant loss of jobs. Genuine partnerships and alliances are about growth strategies and generating wealth and other benefits for stakeholders, not just shareholders. Stakeholders include customers, suppliers, employees, community and the environment as well as shareholders.

My experience and observation of base-level benefits in strongly performing partnering and alliance relationships is that you get more of them more often to a greater degree than would otherwise be gained via other relationship approaches.

PARTNERSHIPS: THE LOGICAL EXTENSION TO EXISTING REFORMS

Most innovation in the future will demand that historically adversarial relationships—(1) between many functions in the firm, (2) between labour and management, (3) between suppliers and the firm, (4) between the firm and its distributors/customers—be replaced by cooperative relations.

Establishing new relationships requires listening, creating a climate of respect and trust and coming to understand the mutual benefits that will ensue if partnership relationships are firmly established.

Tom Peters[9]

Partnerships involve the bringing together of:
- strong, focused management and leadership;
- successful (or in the process of succeeding) workplace reform;
- a total quality environment;
- technology and process capability;
- a simple yet workable partnering process and the people to operate it; and, of course,
- suppliers and customers of like minds.

Figure 1.7 outlines the breadth and depth of involvement required. Partnerships are the logical extension of workplace reform and the total quality movement, both of which will have produced tremendous benefits for those organisations that have followed them through. The next steps involve the integration of these initiatives within the organisation and all its functions

Strategic partnering: a combination of ...

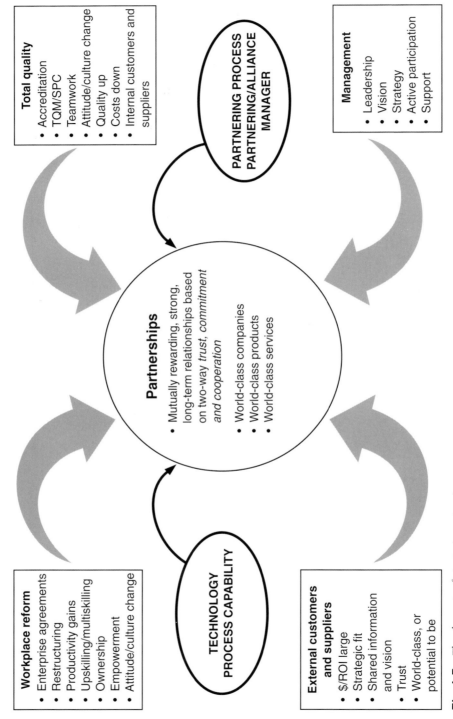

Total quality
- Accreditation
- TQM/SPC
- Teamwork
- Attitude/culture change
- Quality up
- Costs down
- Internal customers and suppliers

PARTNERING PROCESS PARTNERING/ALLIANCE MANAGER

Management
- Leadership
- Vision
- Strategy
- Active participation
- Support

Partnerships
- Mutually rewarding, strong, long-term relationships based on two-way *trust, commitment and cooperation*
- World-class companies
- World-class products
- World-class services

Workplace reform
- Enterprise agreements
- Restructuring
- Productivity gains
- Upskilling/multiskilling
- Ownership
- Empowerment
- Attitude/culture change

TECHNOLOGY PROCESS CAPABILITY

External customers and suppliers
- $/ROI large
- Strategic fit
- Shared information and vision
- Trust
- World-class, or potential to be

Fig. I.7   *The elements of strategic partnering*

and then throughout the supply chain of customers and suppliers. There is no short-cutting here. This is one of the reasons strategic partnering takes so much time and is ultimately so rewarding. However, a certain level of maturity and development is required within your own organisation as well as in external customers and suppliers if these relationships are to be successful and sustainable.

It is impossible to overstate the importance of the effective use of a total quality approach and workplace reform in the development of partnerships. It is absolutely critical that, within your own organisation, the right environment is in place, the right attitudes prevail and the right level of skills has been developed. This enables the organisation to compete effectively on the world stage, based on world best practice and doing business with world-class companies. Whatever form it takes to achieve this, whatever action is appropriate—enterprise agreements, restructuring, renegotiating awards, accreditation, TQM programs—DO IT. You cannot hope to develop and then sustain strong, long-term relationships with external customers and suppliers, based on trust, commitment and cooperation, unless the same types and quality of relationships exist with internal customers and suppliers; that is, your own people.

There is a direct comparison in the relationships being built between the two traditional adversaries in workplace reform, management and workers, and the partnerships we want to build between customers and suppliers. The desired outcomes are the same and the qualities that both relationships require include:

- courage
- trust
- calculated and skilled risk taking
- innovation and initiative from management and workers
- the development of skills and competencies
- leadership
- shared vision and common goals
- resolution of conflict and removal of hidden agendas
- communication
- commitment
- a long-term perspective
- hard work
- greater responsibility and accountability at the shop-floor level

In many ways the quality and progress of your workplace reform will be an indicator of how successful you will be in forming partnerships with customers and suppliers. That is, how well management treat their employees and how well the employees respond will be an indication of how management will treat the principles and practice of strategic partnering and how satisfactorily the employees are likely to respond to customer and supplier partners. The same logic applies to the implementation of total quality reform. Partnerships are the logical extension of total quality reform, applying the same principles but now focusing them externally, up and down the supply chain, on customers and suppliers.

The Business Council of Australia got it absolutely right in their book, *Managing the Innovating Enterprise*, when they said:

> *The Study Commission found that sustained innovation in the leading group of enterprises has much more to do with enterprise–employee relations and much less to do with technology-driven activity than is widely understood. Building competitive innovating enterprises requires a great deal of sustained effort by people at all levels in enterprises. That task strongly connects the three themes of high-quality management, employee relations and applied technical development. Moreover, the outcome of productive employee relations is higher sustained performance standards, not lower incomes.*[10]

In the final analysis and after breaking away all the layers, at the heart of competitive advantage are *people*. It is people, skilled and committed, who will do the innovating, who will determine, develop and implement the technologies, and who will provide the leadership in teams and as individuals to achieve common goals. Without people, the entire process of partnering/alliancing cannot exist.

The challenge awaits everyone throughout the organisation but in particular management, who must have the courage and foresight to instil the spirit of discovery and change, not only in the workers but also in themselves. They must actively participate in the process and not just abdicate this responsibility under the guise of delegation and empowerment. The old view of imposing control to achieve compliance simply does not work. The alternative is to elicit commitment, participation and ownership via effective leadership and the building of trust in order to form partnerships.

PEOPLE AND THE PROCESS OF CHANGE

> *The definition of insanity:* 'Doing the same things and expecting different results.'

In other words, 'If you always do what you have always done, then you will always get what you have always got!' Strategic partnering is fundamentally a process of change. It will require some extraordinary people to lead, manage, participate in and even survive such a change. Some, in fact, won't! It is important to realise that not everyone is in the same change mode with the same degree of intensity or focus. In partnering it will be the managed change of many, as well as the uncontrollable and dynamic change in a few, that will ensure success.

We are talking here about a **paradigm shift**. The futurist Joel Barker,[11] in his *Discovering the Future* series, talks of paradigms as 'patterns of behaviour and the rules and regulations we use to construct those patterns'.

He further states: 'In almost all cases we measure our life's success by our ability to solve problems within our paradigms. In science, in business, in politics, in education, in our lives—changing a paradigm means fundamentally altering the way things are done.' Paradigm shifts can be big or small but, nevertheless, they are all fundamentally important for those people practising the prevailing paradigm. They are not only about the world being round and not flat, the Earth revolving around the sun and not being the centre of the solar system or being able to travel faster than the speed of sound. A paradigm shift can be as simple as moving from a 'base salary plus overtime' component linked in large part to a rework and breakdown environment to an 'annualised salary' work environment based on high productivity and reliability. Entering a two-way, open-book, performance based, transparent and trusting relationship and not a closed-book, low-trust, non-transparent relationship is still a paradigm shift for many organisations. Strategic partnering is about fundamentally altering the way we approach and manage our relationships with customers and suppliers.

In his book *Relationship Marketing*, Regis McKenna says that 'social-science researchers have noted that people can be divided into four categories according to how quickly they adopt new products and beliefs'[12]—that is, how quickly they adapt to change. The four categories are innovators of change, early adaptors to the change, late adaptors and laggards. Says McKenna: 'According to one book on the subject, about 2.5 percent of the public are innovators, 13.5 percent are early adaptors, and 16 percent are laggards.' This leaves late adaptors at 68 per cent of the population. While the percentages will vary from one study to another, the numbers allow for a useful and relevant comparison. To make the point of people, partnerships and change more dramatic, I have substituted *followers* for late adaptors and *terrorists* for laggards: followers, at 68 per cent, are the majority and doing exactly that—following; and terrorists is a more descriptive term to describe those individuals who actively, overtly or covertly, oppose or deliberately undermine the change process. They are the gatekeepers, roadblockers and filters in the business context; in respect of partnering they will ignore the principles and reject the process. You cannot ignore them, however, for they can stall or impede the progress of even the best of partnerships.

The four categories are shown diagrammatically in Figure 1.8. One of the objectives of partnerships and, indeed, all good businesses must be to encourage and lead the change profile towards the **innovators**. Adaptability to change will be one of the key success factors into the 21st century, certainly for strategic partnering. Encourage and empower your innovators, for they will provide the activation energy to overcome many of the hurdles and explore many of the opportunities. They are your champions and leaders of the partnering process. They will not only imagine the future but play a critical part in creating it.

Early adaptors will keep the momentum going. They are the first non-innovators to commit themselves to the change process. However, they are not above questioning, modifying and improving the change as required in order to accommodate the greater majority more effectively. In this way they genuinely add value to the innovation/change process. They will also stop the followers from losing sight of the innovators. They provide the bridge. The classic early adaptor statement is 'Wow, what a great idea. I wish I had thought of that'. Encourage, coach and lead them. The earlier they catch on, the quicker the 'pull-through' effect and the faster your progress.

Joel Barker[13] also talks of 'paradigm pioneers', a special group of people who drive the paradigm shift from rough concept to practical application. They have the intuition, the courage and the long-term perspective to make the vision a reality. They can be found anywhere in the organisation, at any level, in every function. They can also be third party trustworthy independents. It will be among your innovators and early adaptors that these **paradigm pioneers** will be found, developing, creating and discovering.

Followers are the vast majority. They know a good thing when they see it and their enthusiasm to support strategic partnering will depend directly on the quality of the argument and the delivery of results. I mean in no way to denigrate followers. In good organisations they are highly skilled and committed

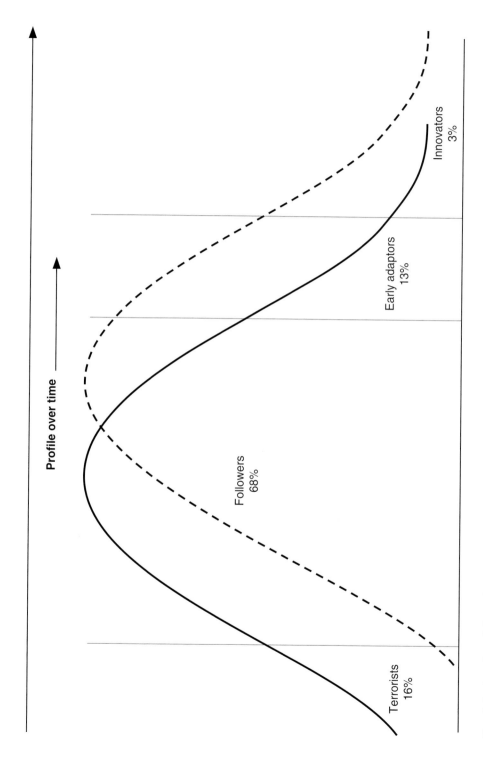

Fig. I.8 *People and their ability to adapt to change*

individuals doing a good job, but they are not innovators or early adaptors. One of the real tests of how well your partnership is going is to what degree the followers are on side. How committed are they and to what extent are they participating in the partnering process? It is not the innovators or the early adaptors that you have to be concerned about; they are already there. And there should be no reason why followers and early adaptors can't move up the scale to become early adaptors and innovators respectively. It should be one of the partnership objectives that they do so.

Terrorists are a different animal altogether. They have to be dealt with in one way or another. That is, manage them up or manage them out, or at the very least have them in a position where they can do no harm, (e.g. 'special projects!'). Many, however, will just 'drop off' as the change will be too great for them to handle. This is where tribalism and fear reside and is the perfect breeding ground for power-hungry, self-motivated individualism, complacency and arrogance. I am not saying you should sack them all. In fact, quite the opposite. If the terrorists can be coached and led out of their ignominious state up through the ranks to innovators, these individuals will become your greatest champions. I have seen it happen on many occasions and it can be one of the partnership's greatest and most rewarding achievements. The similarity between innovators and terrorists is that both groups are made up of passionate, stubborn and unreasonable people. It is these very qualities, focused in the right—or wrong—direction, that cause them to have either a constructive or destructive effect on the change process. From my experience terrorists are not stupid people. They just have the wrong attitudes and approach, but there is nothing worse than smart people coming to work with a bad attitude.

This change model applies to all levels of the organisation and indeed to organisations themselves. Hamel and Prahalad[14] describe NEC, Schaarb, Glaxo,

Canon and Honda as unreasonable organisations, unreasonable in their ambitions and unreasonable in their creativity in getting the most from the least.

Middle-level executives who have the will and the way but not the sanction or the freedom often ask me, 'What do we do if a senior manager(s) is a downright terrorist?' Senior manager terrorists may reside either within the organisation or among customers and suppliers. Although I have seen some inspiring leaders over the last few years at the vanguard of the partnering process, this terrorist scenario is still all too often the predicament middle and shop-floor employees find themselves in. The options are several.

First, get a senior manager sponsor(s) who is supportive, inspirational and courageous to help in removing the roadblocks and empowering the innovators, early adaptors and followers. These sponsors could come from anywhere—internal, customers, suppliers, even independents like community leaders and high-profile business or sporting identities. Second, take outrageous risks. Muster every ounce of passion, courage, emotional and intellectual commitment and put yourself and probably your job on the line. Without authority, without any direction but your own vision of what is possible, utilising all the resources and support you can gather, prove it possible to the nay-sayers. Third, if terrorism, closely followed by a large group of unenthusiastic followers, is so well entrenched at the top then maybe you are working for the wrong company. There are better and more satisfying places to sell your services.

Unfortunately, we tend to deal with terrorists as they treat us. That is, we often try to:

- isolate them
- withhold information
- go over, through or around them
- ignore them
- confront them and get aggressive
- lie
- develop our own hidden agenda
- sack, dismiss or make redundant (sometimes there is no alternative)
- silence them

These tactics seldom work as the terrorists are normally better at them than we are. The alternative is to get buy-in, involve them, provide data, build openness and transparency, inform them, seek cooperation and commitment—in effect, the reverse of many of the common unsuccessful practices listed above. But if they don't come on board with the change process, think about the old cliche 'If you can't change the people, change the people'.

In summary, understand who are the innovators, early adaptors, followers and terrorists. Their development will provide the inspiration and the substance to continue.

THE PARTNERSHIP DEVELOPMENT CURVE

Partnerships and alliances are both fascinating and inspiring phenomena. They happen for all sorts of reasons, progress at different rates and ultimately succeed or fail for an even greater variety of reasons. Before we get into the detail of partnerships—their operating environment, the process and the people involved—it is important in terms of their development to understand the different stages, milestones and possible time frames involved.

One thing is certain: partnerships don't just happen. They are not a vaccination for commercial good health and a successful future. You don't get an injection of strategic partnering and alliancing and wait for the benefits to follow. Partnerships and alliances involve directed and focused attempts to improve the customer/supplier relationship over an extended period. That is, there is a process. In terms of continuous improvement, their development is certainly not linear over time. Partnerships and alliances are dynamic living things whose rate of progress and direction can be changed by myriad internal and external factors.

Just like a marriage, business partnerships go through phases. Figure 1.9 outlines the general progression of partnerships and their possible impact over time on some of the more important performance criteria, such as competitive advantage, ROI, adding value and quality of relationship. This time frame and rate of change are indications only and partnerships can take longer or shorter times to develop, depending on the circumstances. The sequence of events and the time frames involved in Figure 1.9 are largely based on a very successful partnership between ICI Plastics and Tetra Pak Australia, in which I was involved as the Partnering Manager. However, the principles discussed, from my experience, are totally consistent with partnering and alliance relationships in general. For example the development of the very successful Alcoa/Honeywell global alliance, although different in time frame, followed exactly the same path as in Figure 1.9. The details are given in Case Study No. 1.

Customers and suppliers generally embark on strategic partnering because they wish to achieve improvements of some kind. We can safely assume, then, that the point prior to strategic partnering is not where they want to be and that there are some or even many impediments to an improvement in the relationship. The problems could be related to quality, technology, commercial and market-related issues, process, systems or people. There may even be a

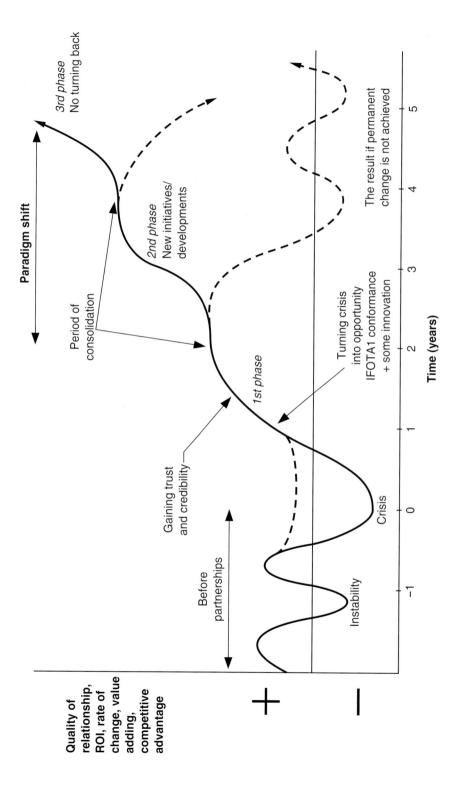

Fig. 1.9 *Partnering/alliance development curve*

crisis, quality-based or otherwise, that threatens the very future of the relationship unless a significant and visible change can be achieved. In some cases, both parties drift from one problem or complaint to another. In between these problems and complaints are periods of relative calm but little progress. As we will see, these periods can also be typified by a great deal of confrontation and a largely adversarial approach to getting things done. This can go on for years, indefinitely in many cases, until the supplier loses the business or the supplier and/or customer go out of business.

In Figure 1.9 let us assume that time zero represents the lowest point in the relationship development. This is often the point of crisis, to which there is no return. Actions from here onwards will determine the fate of the relationship into the foreseeable future. It may be that business has already been lost and there is one last opportunity for the relationship to stay alive. However, not all partnerships start in this manner; some would be situated at a point to the right of time zero on the development curve.

Alternatively, some smart organisations are pre-empting the oncoming crisis through preventative, predictive and design-out initiatives. These short-circuit strategies are represented by a broken line running above the crisis point before and after time zero. The challenge is how to generate a sense of urgency in advance of the incipient crisis before the relationship is yet again propelled into unrelenting hostility and, most likely, poor performance. The perception at the high point before the fall into crisis is that the relationship has never been so good. Telling people at the height of their success that they must change or risk failure is not an easy task. The fallback is a well-managed crisis, the subsequent solutions from which can be the required catalyst for change. Also ask yourself: Is the crisis half-full or half-empty? The real crisis may not be the height of the fall into the trough but rather the distance between the current level and the mountain you have to climb.

In the case of strategic partnerships and alliances it will most likely take years, not months, to turn crisis into opportunity. Building trust and credibility on the basis of conformance to requirements, and delivering genuine innovation to indicate that a real change has occurred, will take time. With crisis point at year 0, the customer will notice a significant and measurable change at around eighteen months. This is the first phase. This rate of change will continue for another six months before a period of consolidation is reached at year 2.

From my experience there comes a point where both parties pause to take a breath, to understand and consolidate what has happened and plan for the next steps. This can also be a period for others not so familiar or enthused with the process to catch up. Don't forget the followers and the terrorists. Turning crisis into opportunity can be a time of intense change in both attitudes and processes. Some people need more time to change and come on board than others. In this example, I have allowed six months for this period of consolidation. I should emphasise that this is not a period of standing still. It is the rate of change that has temporarily subsided, not change itself—which will be continuous. Unfortunately, it is also the point at which apathy, complacency and arrogance can creep in if the process is not managed effectively. People feel they have done a great job and effectively the end point has been reached. There is no more to be done. Strong leadership and a clear vision will be required to avoid slipping back to the comfort zone or, even worse, back to before time zero with all its instability and variation. In Figure 1.9 this is indicated by the broken line that begins just after year 2. Creating a more attractive, achievable and common vision for the future is then paramount if the alliance partners are to jointly develop the new rules of engagement. People, relationships and organisations, their past practices and beliefs, will not change unless the future represents a compelling alternative to the past. This will involve continuous and breakthrough improvement.

At time 2.5 years into the partnership and all being well, we start to enter the paradigm shift. All the easier problems have been solved and the associated opportunities implemented. Only the toughest problems from the old paradigm remain. New opportunities are being discovered and new problems will be solved via the incoming partnering paradigm. The second phase of the change in growth and development, from 2.5 to 3.5 years, takes the partnership from a focus of meeting current requirements to a goal of exceeding requirements and meeting future requirements. This is the period when principles and process are consolidated, a time when innovation outweighs the importance of fulfilling requirements In Full On Time to A1 specification (IFOTA1). Meeting requirements IFOTA1 is now taken for granted. At this point, relationships between customer and supplier are strong, broad and deeply based on a high level of trust and mutual commitment. This allows for extensive and world-class or best in class innovation and the delivery of the other higher-level benefits. The 12 paradigm shifts for partnerships and alliances are listed on page 317 and discussed in detail throughout the book.

There is a second period of consolidation at 3.5 to 4 years. Reasons for this could include changes in key personnel, the need for catch-up time for others, and the building of new technology. Again, watch out for pockets of apathy, arrogance or complacency.

A third-phase change is now entered into at a point four years beyond time zero. This will carry through to five years and beyond. The process is now virtually self-motivating and self-perpetuating, with the partnership robust enough to handle almost any circumstance. A genuine and sustainable partnership is now in place. The cycles of growth and consolidation will continue for as long as both partners desire. It is my view that once the third phase has been reached, irrespective of the time involved, both customer and supplier have changed and improved so significantly that they are beyond the point of no return. Irrespective of what happens in the future, once the benefits and the trust have been experienced, there can be no going back to the 'bad old days'. *Exercise:*

If you feel the partnership development curve is applicable to the relationship(s) you are involved with, or are developing, carry out the following exercise. First, agree where the relationship is currently positioned on the development curve, what phase or period of consolidation and substitute your own timescale if appropriate. Second, list on the curve the activities, initiatives and milestones that got the relationship to where it is. Third, ask where the relationship is going on the curve, in what time frame, and what goals, strategies, activities and milestones will enable the relationship to get there. In particular, you are interested in what is the next paradigm shift that will take the relationship from one phase into another. You will find this exercise an enlightening reality check.

BUILD IN TWO-WAY SYNERGY, NOT ONE-WAY DEPENDENCE

> *Facing complex, multi-year development challenges, companies are recognising that it is impossible to 'go it alone'. Vertical integration, and a concern for keeping all components and competencies inside, no longer makes sense. 'Virtual integration' is replacing vertical integration. The relationships among the partners are not transaction-oriented; they are long-term. One often sees in these relationships interdependence without ownership or legal control.*
>
> *Gary Hamel & C.K Prahalad[15]*

A friend once told me that the only regrets we have in life are about the risks we don't take. Successful people, as with successful organisations, normally have few regrets. For them, failure from risk taking is just confirmation of more successful alternatives. These risks may well be calculated, educated and informed but, nevertheless, decisions are made that involve a considerable downside should they prove to be incorrect. Successful partnerships are no different. Risk here involves mutual dependence, or interdependence. Both buyer and seller have something of great value to gain or lose should the partnership succeed or fail.

I am convinced more than ever that interdependence is a fundamental prerequisite for successful partnering and alliancing. Yet it is one of the most misunderstood concepts and one of the most difficult to apply in practice. Microsoft and Intel are a good example of two organisations who can no longer do business without each other.[16] The world's largest and most successful computer chip and software manufacturers are now inextricably linked, not by legal contracts but by a mutual hunger for success based on innovation, a shared vision of the future and the need for continuous improvement. Proctor & Gamble and Wal-Mart are an example of an interdependent partnership in the retail sector.[17] Wal-Mart needs P&G's brands and P&G needs Wal-Mart's access to customers. This benchmark manufacturer–retailer relationship has been built up over a ten-year period and represents approximately 10 per cent of P&G's total revenues at more than $3 billion, with Wal-Mart being its largest customer.

Figure 1.10 outlines the dependence alternatives between customers and suppliers. An imbalance either way may cause a breakdown in the relationship. It is essential to build in two-way synergy and mutual risk/benefit, not a

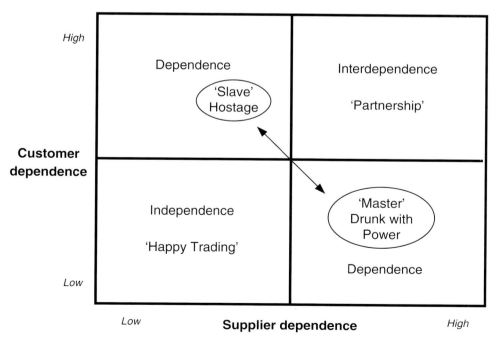

Fig. 1.10 *Relationship dependence*

one-way dependence. The two high/low one-way dependence quadrants are often spoken of as the master/slave or 'hostage' and 'drunk with power' scenarios. Independence is about trading, low-reliance relationships but can often be a retreat position from a previous win/lose or lose/lose one-way dependence experience. Often unhappy with the lack of results of this independence over time but unwilling to go back to the dependent bad old days, organisations look to a more cooperative, interdependent relationship for their success.

For those in the more dominant position, are you prepared to level up control, power and influence to build interdependence? To give something now to gain a greater mutual benefit at a later date is a sign of smartness, not weakness.

PARTNERSHIPS ARE EVERYWHERE

It is extraordinary that we find the concept and application of partnerships so difficult in our business lives when, in the broader sense, genuine and successful partnerships are all around us in our personal lives. People everywhere and of all ages are involved in partnerships that are based on the same principles as strategic business partnerships and often use similar techniques. The most common and obvious is the institution of marriage. A direct analogy to building strategic partnerships with customers and suppliers in business is the everyday partnership of marriage.

After all, what is a good marriage all about? It's certainly about the long term: 'Till death do us part.' It's about hard work, a lot of hard work: 'Through good times and bad, for better or for worse, in sickness and in health.' It is not a fair-weather friendship. Fundamental to a strong marriage is trust, a common set of values, good communication, commitment to the long term, shared information, the ability to resolve conflicts and remove hidden agendas amicably. A good marriage involves developing the right attitude. It's about having a vision, a common set of goals and the courage, skills and commitment to go forward and make it happen. Is this starting to sound familiar? A successful ten-year marriage is a successful ten-year partnership.

Partnerships, whether business or personal, are about people. Understanding what makes a successful personal relationship will provide an insight into the qualities required of a successful business relationship.

I have found a surprisingly simple exercise that generates a paradigm or mindset shift in the ability of people to understand the true nature of partnering. It is a logic sequence of five forced-choice questions that will test personal values and bring together the concept of applying partnering at both a business and personal level. The answers with explanations are given on pages 60–63. The five questions are:

Question 1

What is more important to you:

(a) your marriage (formal or informal/de facto), family, health, your personal life *or*

(b) your business/job, your business life?

Question 2

Is your marriage (formal or informal/de facto), family, health, your personal life based on:

- trust
- shared values
- common goals
- open and shared information
- long-term commitment
- cooperation
- hard work
- resolving conflicts
- removing hidden agendas
- adding value (i.e. personal development, education, etc.)
- leadership (family, children, role model, education, local community, sport, etc.)
- interdependence (e.g. In marriage, formal or informal, where children are involved and all parties have something fundamental to lose or gain should the relationship fail or succeed?)

(a) Yes

(b) No

Question 3

As a generalisation, is it true in business that you can't manage what you can't measure?

(a) Yes

(b) No

Question 4

How do you measure the success or failure of the most important relationship or priority in your life? The most important priority in your life is the answer you gave to question 1 (a or b).

Question 5

For those people who are or have been married (formally or informally)—do you have a formal, legally based pre-nuptial agreement? For those people who are not married—would you consider a pre-nuptial agreement in the event of getting married?

(a) Yes

(b) No

THE ROLE OF MANAGEMENT

> *There is a difference between leadership and management. Leadership is of the spirit, compounded of personality, vision and training. Its practice is an art. Management is a science and of the mind. Managers are necessary, leaders are indispensable.*
>
> Admiral J. Moorer USN[18]

Much will be said about the role of management and leadership throughout this book, so I will not dwell on the matter here. By their action or inaction, management can make or break the partnership culture, the process and the partnerships themselves. They set the vision and broad strategies for the organisation in line with the external environment and the organisation's internal structure, capabilities, potential and their personal values. Then, by their support, active participation, leadership, vision and inspiration, they create an environment that 'makes it happen'. While there are many roles for management to play, I see five major objectives for strategic partnering and alliancing:

1. Set a world-class and achievable vision, a broad strategy and standards opposite partnerships that inspire all in the organisation from the CEO to the shop floor. Effective leaders will have a genuine long-term focus.
2. Lead and coach others in creating a learning environment based on continuously improving skills and competencies, on the delivery of superior performance, and on trust—an environment where individuals and teams are encouraged to perform, empowered and committed to their full potential.
3. Suitably reward and recognise high performance and outstanding achievement in skills development, innovation and leadership, whether individual or team-based. This is not about a twice-monthly salary slip or annual bonus, but about creative and flexible remuneration that generates loyalty to the organisation and personal satisfaction for the individuals and their families.

4. Create an environment where people enjoy coming to work: a place where they are challenged by the expectations and the opportunities; where risk taking is not only condoned but encouraged, and honourable, courageous and intelligent failure is rewarded; where the barriers and obstacles to effective communication and performance have been removed.
5. Support and actively participate in the strategic partnering process. In the words of Keki Bhote:

> There are several attributes of leadership that successful CEOs have in common: vision, deeply held personal values that become corporate values and permeate the entire organisation; an ability to inspire and fire up their people with enthusiasm; a willingness to listen and pay attention to employees and give them a sense of worth and involvement; and the desire to encourage entrepreneurship as an antidote to bureaucracy.[19]

WHICH COMES FIRST—PARTNERSHIPS WITH CUSTOMERS OR WITH SUPPLIERS, AND ARE THEY DIFFERENT?

Customers, customer focus and customer satisfaction should be the primary driver for all businesses today and into the future. The thrust or push in the customer/supplier value chain must be forward towards the end customer or consumer, not the reverse. Quite simply, customers are the reason suppliers exist. If you don't have a customer, you don't have a job. To that end I have looked primarily at the strategic partnering process from the perspective of a supplier proactively pushing forward and leading the partnership to the customer.

However, the supplier/customer partnering process, if it is to be successful throughout the supply chain, must be fundamentally the same for both customer and supplier, irrespective of which way the partnering and alliance relationship is being driven. That is, there should be no difference between the process of a supplier forming a partnership with a customer downstream and that of a customer forming a partnership with a supplier upstream. This same logic and practice also applies internally within the organisation.

A SHORT HISTORY OF PARTNERING AND ITS BENEFITS

> *. . . as you stare at the ceiling at two in the morning, unable to sleep, guts churning, Malox bottle empty, think of the time you are wasting being an adversary. Give partnering a try. Trust me.*
>
> Michael B. Murphy[20]

While at first sight partnering and alliancing may seem more suited to an Asian culture and philosophy, in terms of its structured process and a formally practised principle it originated on the North Sea oil platforms and in the United States' construction industry in the 1980s. For example, the US construction industry was plagued by a growing number of claims, overuse of litigation and an operating environment built around confrontation and legal relationships as opposed to win/win working relationships. Government contracting in particular had become an increasingly adversarial and unrewarding process for contractors and federal employees alike.

In the words of Charles Cowan: 'We have witnessed an escalation of onerous documents and contracts focused on punitive measures to enforce performance. Consequently we have seen a dramatic increase in litigation, which is expensive and counterproductive to everyone's efforts to produce quality projects on time and within budget.'[21] The industry decided to take another approach—partnering. It was called 'putting the handshake back into business', going back to the old way of doing business where people's word was their bond and honesty, respect, integrity and trust were the most valued items.

Initially, it was the efforts of DuPont Engineering and Fluor Daniel (as the contractor), who took a TQM approach towards partnering.[22] They realised that increasing communication, employing a better definition of shared risk and clarifying measurement criteria would lead to a greater contract success rate opposite foreign competition.

There are seven key elements in partnering for the construction industry:[23]

1. **Commitment** from the top management of all related parties with the jointly developed Partnership Charter seen as a symbol, not a contract.
2. All stakeholders having equal **equity** in the relationship, jointly creating mutual goals, satisfying each other's requirements and focusing on win/win outcomes.

3. **Trust**, without which there can be no teamwork, development of personal relationships or effective communication; trust results in a synergistic relationship.
4. **Mutual goals/objectives** that are overlapping and specific to the nature of the project, developed in a workshop environment.
5. The **implementation** of mutual goals via stakeholders' jointly developed strategies and agreed techniques for conflict resolution.
6. Review of progress of goals and objectives via **continuous evaluation**.
7. **Timely communication and responsiveness** to avoid disputes and save time, money and resources.

Although different from strategic partnering in time frame and scope, the early results of the United States experience indicate that this project partnering approach has been extremely successful. For example,[24] the United States Army Corps of Engineers, a major public sector client in the construction industry, found that both major and minor projects had resulted in:

- an 80–100 per cent reduction in cost overruns
- virtual elimination of time overruns
- a 75 per cent reduction in paperwork
- all project goals being met or exceeded
- millions of dollars saved
- significantly improved site safety performance
- no outstanding litigation, and
- improved morale within the organisations involved

Associate Professor Thomas E. Uher[25] of the University of New South Wales has also documented partnering successes in the United States.

> It appears from the published information that partnering has so far been highly successful. Schreiner (1991) studied eighteen partnered projects over the last three years involving Brown & Root Corp. and Union Carbide Corp. Schreiner concluded that the productivity of the partnering projects was around 16% to 17% or better.
>
> According to the Construction Industry Institute: . . . partnering has helped the clients reduce cost by 8% and shorten schedules by 7%. Contractors have reported that they have improved profitability by an average of 10%. In addition, our survey results of realised improvements showed engineering (design) costs were reduced by 10% and administrative costs reduced by 6%.

Partnering in Australia is still relatively new. However, there is a growing number of examples in both the private and the public sectors where strategic partnering and alliancing has delivered significant benefits. Australian-based companies such as Transfield Services, Worley, Alcoa, Honeywell, Mobil, BP, Baxter Healthcare, CS Energy, Sydney Water Corporation, Hazelwood Power and many others are developing successful strategic partnerships and alliances. Case studies presented in Part D of this book explore specific details. In all cases the emphasis is on cooperative teamwork in an environment of good faith, fair dealing, trust and world-class skills, products and services.

As a result of the New South Wales Royal Commission into Productivity in the Building Industry, the New South Wales Government has developed its own set of partnering guidelines and policies.[26] As with the North American experience, the Royal Commission found that project outcomes in the construction industry in New South Wales were heavily influenced by the quality of relationships. Further, it found that relationships had severely degenerated into a destructive and costly approach characterised by mistrust, lack of respect and an ever-present threat of litigation. The challenge was to change to a more cooperative approach that would sustain and fund the cultural change required. Partnering is seen as a moral contract, not a legal one.

SELF-TEST ANSWERS (to questions on pp. 55–6)

1. (a) your marriage (formal or informal/de facto), family, health, your personal life

If there is difficulty in determining the right answer put yourself in the following position. You are a dedicated, hard-working, long-term employee in a job you have always wanted. Your family, in this case a wife and two children, often argue that you spend too much time at work and travelling and not enough time at home. It has been a particularly difficult and busy couple of years and just recently you have found the pace is getting to you. Odd things have been occurring over the last month—headaches, slurred speech, difficulty with coordination—but, being the loyal dedicated employee you are, you have pressed on regardless. A visit to your local doctor and then a specialist reveals that you have an inoperable, malignant brain tumour which the doctors believe has been brought on by the stress of the job, a heavy workload and excessive travel. The prognosis: without extensive radiotherapy and chemotherapy, and a complete change of lifestyle focused on the family and good health, you will be dead within six months. It is your choice to live or to die. The answer should now be obvious.

This is not only a true story but many similar stories have come out of discussions about this exercise.

2. Yes

Having been happily married for over 20 years I believe there is a direct overlap between the qualities, values and characteristics involved in the personal context and those required in a business context. This applies particularly in the context of a relationship, formal or informal, where children or extended family are involved.

3. Yes

This is a fundamental principle of Total Quality Management.

4. The assumption is you choose (a) from question 1 (refer explanation above). The short answer is it's a 'feel good' experience, a mixture of hard and soft indicators, leading and lagging in their timing, recognition and importance. Are the financials and assets important, e.g. the bank account balance, the income and expenditure sheets, the size of the house and the number of cars in the garage? Sure they are, but is that all there is to it? Is that the reason the relationship exists? I don't think so. There are the hard indicators like:

- the financials
  —bank balance
  —debts
  —cash available
  —income
  —investments (real estate, shares, etc.)
- assets acquired, e.g. house, car, boat, furniture, jewellery

There are also the soft indicators like:

- happiness
  —love and respect for your partner
  —similar (not necessarily the same) likes and dislikes
  —number of, location, or time associated with, holidays/vacations per year
  —how often you say or receive the comments 'You make me laugh'/'You make me happy'/'I love you'
  —having fun
  —number of special events and/or surprises

—your love-life
—setting and achieving goals as individuals and a family
—being a good listener
—number of conflicts (few) and how they are resolved (win/win)
—future plans and expectations
—the absence of greed and jealousy

■ trust
—maintaining confidentiality
—fidelity
—being supportive at all times, good and bad
—commitment to the long term
—no lies or hidden agendas
—honesty and integrity
—open communication
—saying what you feel
—doing what you say

■ similar and consistent values
—equality
—respect
—fairness
—service to others

■ education for self, partner, children
—programs completed
—knowledge, skills, competency gained
—full potential achieved

■ health and fitness
—diet/weight
—vital signs, e.g. heart rate, blood pressure
—number of days of sickness, time lost from work
—you feel 'good'
—low stress/anxiety

■ personal development
—self-confidence, esteem, respect
—new skills learnt

■ religion and spiritual well-being

■ quality and number of external relationships, i.e. friends, neighbours, relatives, service providers (e.g. family doctor, plumber, builder, restaurants, mechanics)

■ riding through the tough and difficult times together, e.g. financial, health

■ celebrating the success of others

This is not an exhaustive list and will vary from relationship to relationship, which is entirely appropriate. The same will occur in business. Try this exercise for your own personal circumstances; you will find it a rewarding experience. Of course, the overlap with business partnering and alliances is direct. Too often our focus is just on the financial and asset-based indicators. In business too there will be a mixture of leading and lagging, hard and soft indicators applying.

Lead indicators will be those performance drivers agreed up front to measure the progress towards achieving ultimate goals or outcomes as measured by lagging indicators. For example, a weight loss and fitness program are two lead indicators in achieving an ultimate outcome or lagging indicator of better health.

5. My experience is that most people (>99%) will say 'no', there is no prenuptial agreement in our relationship, be it formal or informal. This is a simple question but in the spirit of partnering not trivial. The most important relationship in your life, based on exactly the same partnering principles that apply in business, operates on the basis of trust and 'no contract, no term'.

REFERENCES

1. Chairman, Motorola Inc. In the Foreword to Keki Bhote, *Strategic Supply Management*, American Management Association, 1989.
2. Tetra Pak, *Power of Partnership—The Integrated Approach*, Ruter Press, Sweden, 1994, p.43.
3. Tom Peters, *Liberation Management: Necessary Disorganization for the Nanosecond Nineties*, Macmillan, London, 1992.
4. Gary Hamel & C.K. Prahalad, *Competing for the Future*, Harvard Business School Press, 1994, p.170.
5. Theodore Levitt, *The Regis Touch*, Addison-Wesley, 1986, p.35.
6. Andersen Consulting, Annual Alliance Best Practice Survey, 1998.
7. W. Edwards Deming, *Out of Crisis*, Massachusetts Institute of Technology, 1982.
8. Hamel & Prahalad, op.cit., p.9.
9. Tom Peters, *Thriving on Chaos*, Pan Books, London, 1989, p.278.
10. Roderick Carnegie & Matthew Butlin, *Managing the Innovating Enterprise*, Business Council of Australia, 1993, p.xxxvi.
11. Joel Barker, *Paradigm Pioneers—Discovering the Future* series (video), 1991.
12. Regis McKenna, *Relationship Marketing*, Addison-Wesley, Canada, 1991, p.114.
13. Barker, op.cit.

14. Hamel & Prahalad, op.cit., p.170.
15. Hamel & Prahalad, op.cit., p.213.
16. *Fortune* magazine, July 1996, p.33.
17. *Harvard Business Review*, Nov–Dec 1996, p.102.
18. Admiral J. Moorer, USN (Chairman JSC 1970): from a quotation given to the author by a friend.
19. Keki Bhote, *Strategic Supply Management*, American Management Association, 1989, p.33.
20. From a letter by Michael B. Murphy, Vice-President: Donald B. Murphy Contractors Inc., 1991. MBA workshop notes, 1992, p.70.
21. Charles Cowan, from Master Builders Construction and Building Association of Australia workshop notes, September 1992, p.3.
22. David Johnson, Senior Council for Contracting and Environmental Compliance, Portland District, US Army Corps of Engineers, in a paper titled 'Public Sector Partnering' given at an MBA workshop, September 1992, p.56.
23. Cowan, op.cit., p.70.
24. 'NSW Government's Partnering Guidelines', *ACLN*, Issue 33, December, 1993.
25. Thomas E. Uher, 'What is Partnering?', *ACLN*, Issue 34, p.44.
26. 'NSW Government's Partnering Guidelines', *ACLN*, Issue 33, December 1993.

CHAPTER 2

Organisational structure

In *Strategy and Structure*, a book that influenced two generations of managers, Harvard business historian Alfred Chandler argued that organisational structure should take its form from a firm's chosen strategy. I understand Chandler's reasoning, but I think he got it exactly wrong. For it is the structure of the organisation that determines, over time, the choices that it makes about the markets it attacks.

Tom Peters[1]

STRUCTURE IS IMPORTANT

Strategy should determine structure. Tom Peters' statement above suggests that the reality for many organisations, knowingly or unknowingly, is unfortunately quite the reverse. Don't even think of trying to form a customer/supplier partnership unless you have, or are on the way to having, a customer-service-based culture, and a restructured enterprise-based workplace functioning on a TQM philosophy. I remember a work colleague, a process operator, saying to me in relation to a customer partnership we had spent over two years developing: 'This could never have happened four years ago prior to the enterprise agreement. We would not have even let you guys on the plant, let alone have plant people visit customers outside of work hours and work on partnering teams, customer focus teams or any other teams. The environment just wasn't right. It was all about confrontation with management, defending "our" turf and little to do with teamwork and customers.'

Structure will be as important as strategy. Strategic partnering demands a ruthless dismantling of the old structures. Traditional hierarchical monoliths with all their inefficiencies, inconsistencies and double standards are no longer accept-able to customers and will certainly not survive partners. Open and instant lines of communication will need to be created. Information technology will have to start adding value for customer and supplier. Intranets, extranets, shared websites and other Internet applications, telemetry-based stock management systems, complete systems re-engineering and other electronic linkups will be the order of the day. Attitude manifested in a willingness to share information and achieve common objectives will be the driving force behind reducing layers, removing roadblocks, developing a network of teams and involving people historically far removed from the front lines. This will be revolution for most, and strong and visionary leadership will make the difference between success and failure.

To understand the organisational structures (or lack of them) required of partnerships, we need a broad understanding of the structures involved with other customer/supplier relationships. Figure 2.1 outlines the structures of the five types of customer/supplier relationships. I have called them:

1. Traditional (freight and baggage class)
2. Basic multilevel sell (economy class)
3. Advanced multilevel sell (business class)
4. Partnerships (world class)
5. 'Fuzzy' partnerships (future class)

Within any organisation there will be a moving state of equilibrium among these structural types as people change, strategies change and attitudes change. No organisation today, I suspect, fits precisely into any one of these structures but in reality is made up of a mix of several structural types. Never-theless, these structures and their inherent characteristics represent the pro-gression from the very worst to the very best of organisations.

To look specifically at how they operate, I have categorised each cus-tomer/supplier relationship and its structure under the following headings:

- internal relationships
- external relationships
- management
- organisation
- quality, service and measurement
- cost and value for money

In reading through the following pages I have no doubt you will recog-nise the various parts of your own organisation in their varying stages of development. There may even be an opportunity to predict the future.

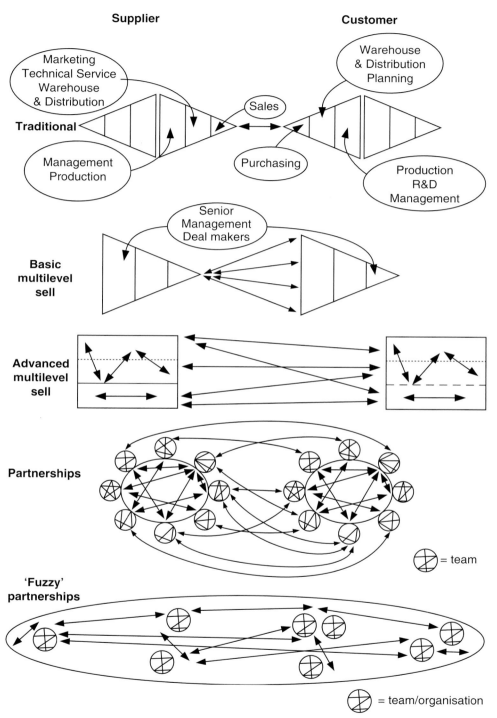

Fig. 2.1 *Customer/supplier structures*

TRADITIONAL RELATIONSHIPS (FREIGHT AND BAGGAGE CLASS)

> *While it is frequently observed that the purpose of marketing is 'getting and keeping customers', there tends in practice to be more attention focused on the 'getting' and rather less on the 'keeping' and yet it may cost as much as five times more to get a new customer than it does to keep an existing one.*[2]

Traditional relationships are generally the way businesses used to work (see Fig. 2.2). Anyone who has been in business more than ten years will know this way of operating was common from the 1950s to the 1980s. Unfortunately, there are still many examples in operation today. In the 0 to 10 Relationship Management context and as a generalisation they represent 'unsustainable' to 'less than satisfactory' performing vendor relationships.

Internal relationships

At best, internal relationships in the traditional structure are non-existent with little or no effective internal communication. At worst, they are tribal, adversarial and destructive. Self-interest and self-survival are paramount, with middle management the all-powerful and ultimate gatekeepers and filters

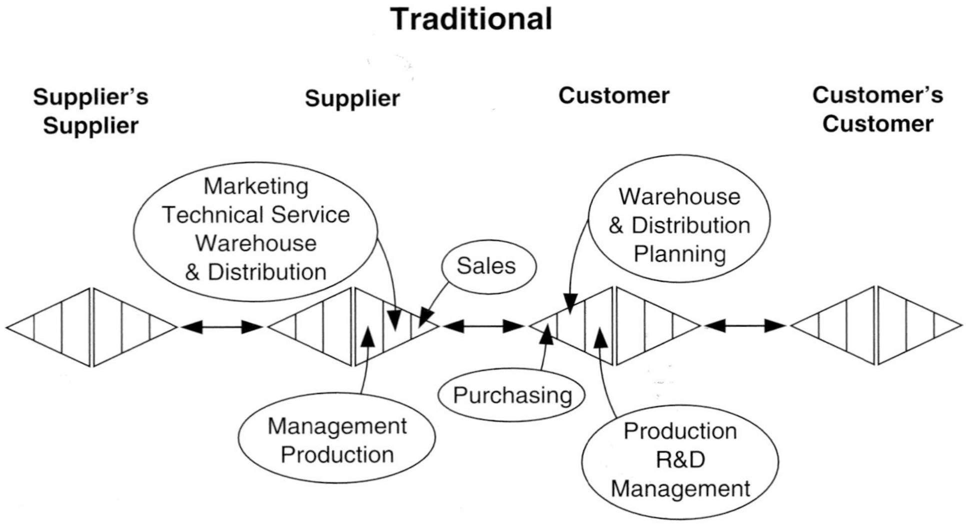

Traditional

Fig. 2.2 *Customer/supplier structures: traditional*

of information. They work on a simple philosophy. The more information they have and the more that others don't have, the stronger their position. Their departments and functions work on a 'them and us' mentality, with battles between production, distribution, sales and marketing a commonplace occurrence.

Sales are not totally blameless in this environment, either, with their attitude of 'I worked damned hard to get this order and now you tell me you can't make it on time or to the right specification'. They have absolutely no understanding of what goes on in other areas of the business and little interest in knowing. Information about such things as the problems encountered, the rate-determining steps in the process, the lead times on raw materials and services or the importance of forecast accuracy does not concern them.

Production and operations, on the other hand, take the approach that 'they [sales] are captive customers who can't go anywhere else in the event of poor quality or service'. This attitude is directed not only towards the sales team but often towards the external customers themselves. Production workers have no idea about the environment outside the factory, and little concern for it. This is understandable to a certain extent because they have never met an external customer and don't even know who they are. They have never seen a list of the biggest to the smallest customer for turnover, volumes or contribution. Nor have they seen a comparison of the products they produce, service or deliver opposite the products or services the customers produce. No one has ever taken the time to explain the business strategy to them, let alone involve the shop floor in its development. There is no understanding of the customers' processes and the importance of conformance to an agreed specification on quality. Probably, there *are* no documented customer requirements—they have not been discussed. This is truly a production-led, product-push environment. You sell what you make, as opposed to making what you can sell.

In this traditional business environment there has been little or no workplace reform; many demarcations still operate and strikes, or the threat of strikes, are commonplace. Productivity and quality are low as measured by volume/dollar output, first-pass efficiencies, high overtime levels and high scrap or waste levels. Stock levels are high and labour turnover is higher. The abuse of sick leave is rampant and those workers who are at work are generally underskilled, with little enthusiasm or incentive to improve. A commitment to customer service and customer satisfaction doesn't exist. This is truly an environment of entitlement and blame as opposed to continuous improvement. Good people in particular find this a difficult environment in which to work and eventually they leave, feeling bewildered, angry and frustrated.

I was involved with many organisations during the 1980s where management encouraged the workers to 'leave their brains at the gate' when they arrived for work. Workers were told what to do by their managers and supervisors during their shift, be it day or night. They would then 'pick up their brains' at the same place when they went home, probably after some unnecessary overtime. The irony is that many of these same people then went home and utilised their skills to take on prominent leadership roles in their communities. Marketing and senior management in these organisations were dinosaurs, but more of them later.

External relationships

Sales and purchasing are the only real points of contact between customer and supplier and generally the relationship between these two functions is based on low skills, low commitment and low levels of trust. It's a very shallow existence. Any direct senior or middle management involvement is no more than a check-up on the sales rep or a meaningless 'fireside chat' that adds little or no value to the relationship.

The scope for involvement from the support functions—technical service, finance, design, R&D, credit and collection, production, marketing—is minimal. They are kept well away from customers for fear of 'spilling the beans' and encroaching on traditional sales turf. Similarly, at the customers' end, purchasing officers want to enhance their own position by allowing little contact with other departments, such as quality or production, for fear of diminishing their own control, position or power base. In short, there is 'one door in and one door out', a single point of contact. There is little product or service development, or innovation, with both customer and supplier generally content with the status quo. Negotiations are regular and mostly confrontational and adversarial. Purchasing officers often trade one supplier off against another, sometimes with facts but often with fiction. Tendering and competitive bidding are rife. There is a greater emphasis on sales representation as opposed to account management.

The situation for the suppliers' suppliers is worse; they are not taken into consideration at all, but treated like mushrooms and kept in the dark. Suppliers on the other hand scrutinise contracts for loopholes around which they can introduce variations at a later date. As with customers, tendering and the competitive bid process is commonplace and often associated with one-sided, detailed contracts based on lump sum or fixed fee arrangements with up to 100 per cent of the risk transferred to the supplier. The result is a continuation of this hard-line and aggressive approach back up the supply chain.

This is truly an environment of under-promise and under-deliver.

Management

If you want to know how such an environment is created and sustained, look no further than management. In the main, they will be autocrats with a dominant and coercive power style, ruling by fear rather than respected leadership—individuals of little vision and a lot of blame, rather than team players. Information for these managers is power. The more they have of it, and the less that others have, will determine their level in the hierarchy. Control and regulate the information flow and you have the power.

Traditional managers have an amazing ability to focus solely on short-term profitability and monthly budgets. They represent the antithesis of quality and good statistical process control (SPC), reacting always to the 'last point on the curve' and deliberately inducing unnecessary variation so as to be seen to 'challenge' the system. They will deliberately set up conflict and confrontation between individuals and departments on the premise that this is good competition and healthy for both company and individual. They have a complete lack of understanding of the difference between healthy and unhealthy competition, and of the value of teamwork.

Trust and the building of long-term relationships have no place here. And while they are prepared to set individuals against each other in order to generate change, they are extremely unreceptive to change themselves, especially if it's not their idea.

Organisation

Such firms are top-heavy, multi-layered hierarchical monoliths where middle management dominates. Fearful and often tribal departmental competition reduces the effectiveness of the organisation to a minimum. Divisional, functional and departmental territories are fiercely fought over and protected as if the laws of the animal kingdom prevailed.

Quality, service and measurement

Stockouts and quality and service complaints are not only a common occurrence but an accepted occurrence. Because the culture of such an organisation is based on an absence of teamwork, lack of cooperation and poor communication, people not only do not care about such problems—most of them don't even know they exist.

If any measurement takes place at all, it is done mainly to apportion blame. The concepts of systems analysis, process stability, delivering In Full On Time to A1 (IFOTA1) specification, and continuous improvement have not as yet seen the light of day. Statistical process control is either not believed in or unknown and the names Deming,[3] Juran[4] and Crosby[5] have little or no meaning. In most cases, product or service specifications will be vague or arbitrary and bear little resemblance to customer requirements. Inspection and 'fire-fighting' are the major forms of quality control. This quick-fix environment is sustained by an oversized, underskilled service department where frustration is surpassed only by a lack of enthusiasm and commitment.

Cost and value for money

The primary focus for both supplier and customer is price, price and more price. Daylight is second, with quality and service a long way third and fourth. Because there is no trust, negotiations are mostly acrimonious, tough and drawn out far beyond the bounds of reasonableness. This is the world of 'don't get mad, get even'. Win/lose or lose/lose are the only games in play. We have not even reached the stage of the classic 'aim high, fall back' negotiating strategy, with trade-offs and concessions. Opening positions are virtually ambit claims, due to a fundamental lack of understanding of each other's business, product and process requirements.

You will often find that these customers have a deliberate multisourcing supply policy. First, they want to trade off against the lowest price, purposely avoiding a differentiated product or service. This, of course, completely stifles any new development or innovation. Second, because of the way people and organisations are treated, the customer cannot trust any one supplier to deliver the product or service In Full On Time to A1 specification. They need the second, third and fourth suppliers to cover for the inevitable stockouts or quality non-conformances. Third, they probably don't know themselves what their real requirements are or their customers' requirements. The outcome is the acceptance of second-best so as to minimise the overall cost. In many cases this policy, based on short-term convenience, leads to ongoing problems. Customers buy imported competitive products at a higher price and then lie to the local supplier that they have product at a cheaper price that needs to be matched if the local supplier is to get the business. Sounds crazy, doesn't it?

The overall package of price, terms, conditions, service, quality, dependability, reliability, availability, technical support and product/service development is rarely if ever considered.

Summary

As you can probably tell, I am not a fan of the 'traditional relationship' organisational structure. They don't come any worse than this. This sort of structure and supporting mindsets, behaviours and attitudes will be totally unsustainable and unacceptable in the future. These outmoded organisations are unlikely to survive. If the competition doesn't get them first, their own people will. This is *freight and baggage class.*

BASIC MULTILEVEL SELLING (ECONOMY CLASS)

The basic multilevel selling structure of customer/supplier relationships is illustrated in Figure 2.3.

Internal relationships

Internal relationships are effectively no different from those of the traditional organisation—still very much departmentalised and tribal and on occasions combative. From the customers' perspective the supplier appears more inquisitive and questioning but no more effective in the delivery of quality or service. There is, however, a recognition within the supplier that change must occur internally for improvements in customer satisfaction to be sustained. The problem is a lack of understanding as to how it will happen. The benefits of teams and effective teamwork are just starting to develop. Workplace reform is also seen as essential to survival, but little has been achieved at this stage and no contact with external customers by other areas of the business (e.g. production) has occurred yet.

External relationships

A commitment, even a sense of urgency, has come down from management from their recent readings, seminars or inspired vision. 'We must get closer to the customer.' But how? Multilevel selling, that's how! Sales will build on their current relationships, but outside their normal areas of contact, namely purchasing and materials handling. They will understand customers better by building stronger, broader and deeper relationships throughout the customer organisations. This will generally lock customers in more effectively and make it more difficult for them to purchase elsewhere.

Several problems can arise when building this new-found trust and commitment. The customer is somewhat sceptical, based on past performance, and is not sure whether this new approach is not just rhetoric or, at worst, downright trickery. Because little has changed internally in the supplier's process, culture or people, there is a tendency to over-promise and under-deliver. This same tendency may also be seen in the supplier's suppliers, who as yet have not been considered in the whole equation. Other functions are becoming more involved on a call-up basis—technical service, for example. Their involvement could be classified as active and committed firefighting. Unless improvement occurs and firefighting turns into innovation, this initial enthusiasm will degenerate into frustration and disillusion. There still exists a poor understanding of the internal relationships within both customer and supplier organisations, with little creativity or calculated risk taking and therefore little return for their efforts.

However, bridges are being built and broader relationships are developing over time. Negotiations become a little easier and less confrontational as the account manager acquires a better understanding of the customer's business.

Management

Management are certainly more visible. There is a sudden surge in customer visits and a tendency to listen more to what the customer is saying. In fact, the rhetoric is sounding rather good but, effectively, culture and attitudes remain unchanged and so the performance stays the same.

Management are thinking about a TQM program and accreditation and how to implement these. Although the mindset is developing, the skills are absent and the organisation still tends to operate in blame mode as opposed to teamwork and continuous improvement mode.

This is also the place and time for the senior management 'deal makers'. They are not unique to basic multilevel selling but this is where they are more prominent and probably most successful. Deal makers are influential individuals within the customer/supplier organisations. They are normally senior in title with legitimate authority and, virtually to the exclusion of all around

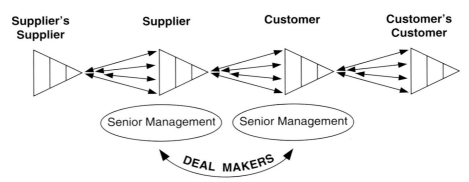

Fig. 2.3 *Customer/supplier structures: basic multilevel sell*

them, negotiate agreements that have a large impact on both the buyer and seller organisations. These agreements could include joint ventures, acquisitions, large supply agreements and machinery purchases. There will be support staff as appropriate but their involvement is subservient and clandestine.

Deal makers may also act as circuit breakers for major quality, service or commercial crises. Autocratic in style and domineering by nature, their personal drive and competitiveness are unrelenting. Depending on their cunning and foresight, they can be true and successful entrepreneurs or ruthless dictators. Should they mature in their outlook and broaden the involvement of others in developing long-term customer/supplier relationships, they can play a major role in leading their organisation to the next step.

Unfortunately, because on many critical issues deal makers work in virtual isolation in terms of effective communication, the long-term success of their deals or agreements is often difficult to ensure. Decisions tend to be agreed at the senior level but poorly communicated to those who have to implement and manage the ongoing details.

Organisation

The structure is still hierarchical, top-heavy and departmental, but change is on the way. Recognition of the need for change is sometimes driven out of crisis or driven by survival, sometimes out of a change in management or a management consultant's review.

The important thing to note here is that the people who actually manufacture the products or services are still as much in the dark as ever. This will be a fundamental impediment to progress if not taken up with urgency. The middle management power base still dominates.

Quality, service and measurement

Feedback from customers, either informally from new-found relationships or formally from surveys, suggests that quality and service are important and identifies the reasons why. This gives an idea how the organisation is performing against both the competition and customers' expectations. The importance of prevention and delivering the product or service In Full On Time to A1 specification first time and every time is clearly evident. The 'how to' is still unclear.

However, the vision of a whole new world is starting to appear. Quality accreditation is now an important and even urgent issue for the future. 'We must have it to survive' is the cry and the 12–18 month approval program begins. Most people in the organisation, especially management, sales and marketing, still don't appreciate that even with accreditation you can still make and sell 'rubbish'. You just do it in a 'quality' way. Management are also starting to think seriously about a TQM program for all in the organisation, such as that described by Crosby,[6] Deming[7] or the like. This is a watershed period for the organisation. Change and change agents will initially be driven by a quality improvement imperative which, if effective, will have a lasting effect on systems, people, plant and equipment and, not least, on customers and suppliers. Many hurdles will be placed in their way, some by design, some by accident. They must be overcome if success is to ensue.

Cost and value for money

Price is still the driving force but the importance of both quality and service comes a clear and close second. Things have clearly changed. Suppliers are now starting to talk about 'the package', adding value and differentiation, and customers are starting to listen. But lack of real commitment, little backup or support, and average delivery are still real issues to be tackled. It's the 'wolf in sheep's clothing' dilemma. Customers see a change but don't quite understand if it's real and of benefit, or just a mirage.

The relationship is still based on tough negotiations albeit a little less adversarial. However, the approach has changed from focusing purely on price to selling the overall benefits, often at an overinflated price. Arrogance and complacency, especially at the commercial level, are being replaced with facts and logical argument.

Summary

The basic multilevel selling structure is a change for the better but still one-way traffic from supplier to customer. It is to be hoped there is a major crisis during this stage that will shake both parties to their foundations. This will provide the major catalyst for change. 'No big pain, no fast gain', to quote a phrase. This is *economy class*.

ADVANCED MULTILEVEL SELLING (BUSINESS CLASS)

> *The point is, managers still talk about the people who 'report' to them, but that word should be stricken from management vocabulary. Information is replacing authority... To build achieving organisations, you must replace power with responsibility.*
>
> *Peter Drucker[8]*

Figure 2.4 illustrates the advanced multilevel selling structure of customer/supplier relationships.

Internal relationships

Real change has taken place with internal functional and departmental barriers breaking down to varying degrees. Functional teams are operating effectively with both support and active participation from management. They may be corrective action teams (CATs), product development teams, improvement or benchmarking teams, for example. Teams composed of members of different functions and departments are no longer an impossibility, and in selected areas are starting to work effectively. There is also more effective communication between senior managers of the various departments and functions about the next steps in the customer/supplier relationship-building process.

Advanced multilevel sell

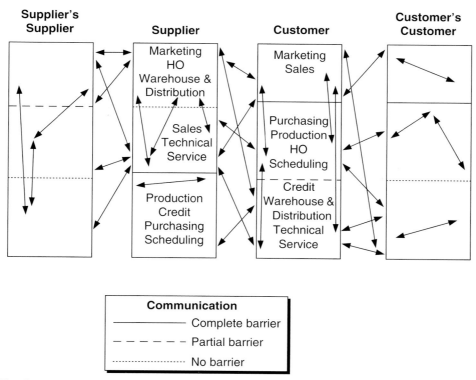

Fig. 2.4 *Customer/supplier structures: advanced multilevel sell*

Workplace reform is well under way and the rewards and benefits associated with the hard work are being realised: improved quality and productivity; reduced second grade, waste and scrap levels; overall stock levels down; reduced overtime and sick leave; and a dramatic reduction in days lost due to industrial disputation. People at the coalface in all areas are starting to make effective decisions based on good information and sound logic. This new way of working frees up time for more rewarding work goals as well as additional time with the family.

Salespeople now get to meet the traditional enemy, production shift workers, and find to their surprise they aren't bad people. All agree there is no substitute for good communication and understanding at first hand each other's requirements and problems. This unaccustomed camaraderie and teamwork is a revelation to all. Recognition is given and the snowball of enthusiasm, empowerment and involvement begins to grow more quickly.

People, particularly middle management, now start to listen and discuss, not tell and demand. A fundamental change in attitude has occurred for the better.

External relationships

Regular and effective two-way contact at many levels between customer and supplier is now a reality. The customer has found that there is more to the supplier than just the sales rep or account manager and the occasional dose of technical service. IFOTA1 focus is bringing rewards, evidenced by fewer stockouts and improved quality. The phrase 'over-promise and under-deliver' no longer applies. Internally, the systems, procedures, attitude and overall culture are in place so that requirements can be met (mostly) first time and every time. This has come about through a far better understanding of customer requirements and a genuine commitment to their fulfilment.

The *key account* management philosophy is in place. The overall customer base is now looked at more strategically and segmented on the basis of current size, potential, fit with the marketing plan and the degree of mutuality developed. Customer visits by production people and others who were traditionally barred from any external customer contact are proving greatly rewarding and useful. In fact, if the situation gets any better there is the potential for real trust and genuine relationships to develop both ways.

Similar improvements are being seen with suppliers, with improved quality, service, flexibility and dependability having a significant and positive impact on downstream operations and relationships. As these relationships develop there is a realisation by some, hopefully from both customer and supplier, that the relationship can be even stronger and more effective on both sides—that this is, in fact, just the beginning. It will be these innovators and early adaptors who will take the relationship to the next stage. Watch out for them, nurture and encourage them.

Management

The likelihood is that some new managers have come onto the scene as *change agents*. Some old ones will have a new and positive outlook on life. For others, the going will be tough and the change too difficult and they will leave. The end result, however, will be a new and enlightened approach towards customers, suppliers and internal personnel. 'Get me involved if it will add value. Otherwise, get on and do it—you are empowered,' they will cry. The appropriate training/skills programs are also in place to support this empowerment. Management will set the strategy and the vision and they will get involved with customers and suppliers where they can add value. Less blame and more cooperation and teamwork is clearly evident.

Management by walking around (MBWA) is more prevalent, and is proving effective in putting names to faces and in personally answering questions that in the past would never have been asked. Those roadblocking middle managers are starting to find this open and shared information policy quite hard going. They are either retreating to their respective bunkers and preparing for the final showdown or coming out of their shells and contributing to the process. TQM and benchmarking now constitute a major focus in improving customer service and reducing costs, which in turn delivers greater shareholder wealth and bottom-line profits. A vision of becoming world class is perceived and action plans at all levels are drawn up to achieve it.

Organisation

The organisation is flatter, more fluid and accepting of change. The brick walls have been replaced by pinewood with open doors, and front-line people are starting to make a real contribution and play a part in strategy development.

Quality, service and measurement

Accreditation has been achieved and the TQM program is well under way. SPC charts appear everywhere, measuring everything. Unfortunately, they are not always fully understood and they don't always measure the right things in the right way. Nevertheless, process measurement is taking place. The enthusiasm and commitment is there and lessons are continually being learnt. Efficiencies and cost savings from reduced process variation are starting to be felt, and this has management thinking about the next steps. Corrective action and troubleshooting teams are measuring the frequency and cost of non-conformances. Some staggering figures are beginning to appear, showing the cost of not getting things right the first time—many millions of dollars in some cases. *Pareto charts* appear and terms like *prioritisation*, *quick fixes*, *root causes*, *permanent solutions* and *cause and effect diagrams* become part of the everyday language. Cultural and attitudinal changes are happening because of this quality push.

It is very important not to let momentum slip at this point, as the bad old ways can return remarkably quickly. Recognition and reward structures are in place but mistakes are still being made by targeting individuals rather than the teams. It is discovered very quickly that rewarding people can also be destructive and demotivating if not done in absolutely the right way. It can result in increased internal competition, which brings on the return of tribes. This is a temporary setback to the process. One significant change from the past is that sales and purchasing within the same organisation are not only talking to each other but often *working* together on joint negotiations and customer/supplier initiatives. They find there is no substitute for seeing first-hand how the other half lives. Rather like production people visiting the customers, it's a real eye-opener for both sides.

A positive spin-off is fewer suppliers delivering better quality at a cheaper overall total cost—a win/win situation for both parties at last.

Cost and value for money

Win/win, value-added strategies are starting to emerge, and both parties like them. Benefits on both sides with genuine cost-downs and improved value-added margins are made possible by genuine product and service developments. Negotiations are no longer sordid, drawn-out affairs. A less hostile pricing policy is rewarded with greater stability in forecast and usage. You may recall the days when the pricing strategy from Head Office was to up the price to breaking point, then withdraw at the last moment; remember how the customer hated that? The days of brinkmanship are gone. You are on the short list for preferred supplier status and it feels good.

Summary

Reaching the advanced multilevel selling structure is a critical point in the organisation's history. Do you stay where you are and survive, or is there a hunger to push the boundaries even further to achieve something better? This is *business class*.

PARTNERSHIPS (WORLD CLASS)

> *Today businesses grow through alliances, all kinds of dangerous liaisons and joint ventures, which, by the way, very few people understand.*
> Peter Drucker[9]

Internal relationships

Life is basically very simple when all the barriers and facades are removed. Common sense has become common practice. It has all resulted from trust, communication and the other initiatives we have mentioned, and a partnership is where it all comes together. Internally, everyone talks to everyone about everything. There is complete transparency, honesty and openness, with no internal barriers causing miscommunication or conflict. Information about profits, pricing, variable and fixed costs, marketing strategies, operational systems and procedures, and so on is freely available and spoken about. Hidden agendas are a thing of the past. Relationships are now circular, not vertical (see Fig. 2.5). Teamwork is in, tribalism is out. There is not only trust here but real friendship and camaraderie.

Workplace reform, whether via formal enterprise agreements or internal

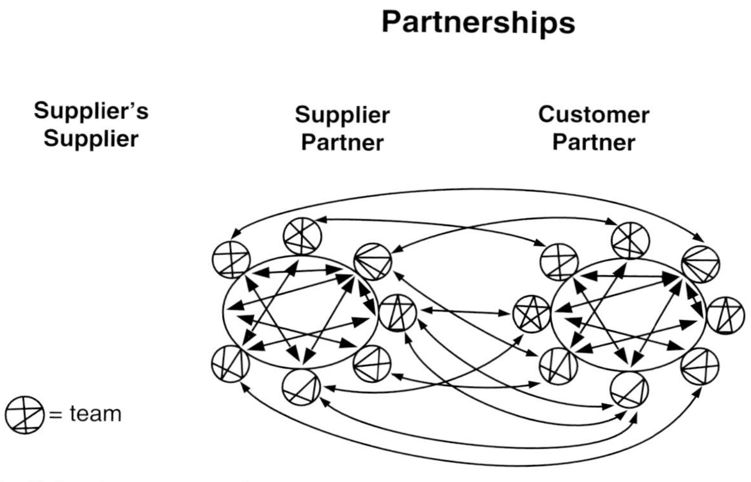

Partnerships

| Supplier's Supplier | Supplier Partner | Customer Partner | Customer's Customer |

⊕ = team

Fig. 2.5   *Customer/supplier structures: partnerships*

structural and cultural change, has brought real and consistent benefits in improving attitudes, communication and skills levels. It is seriously starting to affect bottom-line profitability via improved quality and service levels and other value-added initiatives. Self-managed work teams—whether production, sales, technical service or finance, or a combination thereof—now dominate the organisation. Not only are they skilled and empowered and accept totally their accountabilities and responsibilities—they want more!

Partnering teams, made up of people from all parts of the business, effectively manage the partnering/alliance relationships in every aspect. They, in turn, are linked with the leadership team, partnering/alliance board and other teams of different sizes and composition, such as customer focus teams, supplier focus teams (SFTs), project teams, product rejuvenation teams, corrective action teams and waste reduction teams. There is little involvement here from middle management (if they still exist) and senior management get involved only where necessary. This is a learning environment made up of committed, multiskilled, cross-functional employees as well as customers, suppliers and others, freely exchanging ideas and developing new products and services.

Training as an outcome is a thing of the past; skills, competencies and self-learning are values now entrenched in the corporate culture. The organisation now comprises well-rounded business people with specific areas of expertise who participate widely, as opposed to individuals with specific skills pigeonholed according to department or location.

Internal and external customer and supplier requirements are well understood and all the preventative systems are in place. There are just no stupid mistakes made any more. Processes are such that IFOTA1 is taken for granted—it is the way business is done. Process variation is understood and in control. Prediction and designing out are the steps currently being managed in the relationship. Add to this a clear understanding of future requirements and a plan to achieve, and you are talking about a world that traditional management could not even imagine.

External relationships

Everyone talks to everyone about everything. This sounds like the situation within the organisation and, in fact, it is. There now exist, effectively, no boundaries between customer and supplier. The relationships within and between the two organisations have become truly seamless and transparent. There is a free exchange of ideas, people, resources, strategies and visions. Formal and informal links exist in both directions, taking a variety of forms: simple, long-term commitment; equity participation; joint ventures; technology exchanges; secrecy agreements; joint business strategies; world-class innovation from product and service developments; joint operations; people-exchange programs; electronic linkups of all kinds; and so on.

All the relevant resources of the supplier partner are being utilised to meet and, as appropriate, exceed customer requirements. This process is being managed by the partnering team/s, with joint customer and supplier participation. The Partnership Manager is now a key player in directing the strategic partnering process. In strategic selling jargon, one of the many customer coaches is the *economic buyer*, that is, the person who makes the final buying decision. There is also a far greater involvement with the customer's customers and their requirements and future developments. Direct links are developed further up and down the supply value chain.

There are 1001 small things going on to make the partnership successful. Reciprocal site visits, joint strategy reviews, joint participation on teams and true multilevel contact are commonplace. At this point the partnership process is well understood and all levels of both customer and supplier are committed to it. As with customer partners, selected supplier partnerships and alliances are also in place, with the relationships just as strong, the same principles applying and similar benefits evolving.

In a word—*trust*. There is total and absolute trust both ways, earned and maintained based on competence to deliver and the strength of character to do what you said you would do.

Management

The kind of management that was associated with the traditional structure no longer exists—that is, self-centred, egotistical megalomaniacs whose personal ambition was surpassed only by their insensitivity to those around them. In most areas of the business, middle management, as we used to know them, have disappeared. The traditional roles of sales managers, credit managers, logistics managers, product managers, supervisors of all types and most marketing managers will have changed for ever. There is no need for them in their traditional roles, as the skills, ownership and commitment to make it happen are now at the coalface. Old-world middle management is now an obstacle to the smooth running of the organisation.

Senior management have provided a clear and effective vision and the resources to make it happen. An environment has been created where change is not only welcomed but expected, and where risk taking is encouraged. The role of management has changed to that of facilitator and coach in many cases. Otherwise, managers are just members of the team, contributing on a needs basis in their own particular fields of expertise. In terms of the customer/ supplier partnering process, they are active and willing participants, whether directly involved in partnering teams, or elsewhere in the partnering process.

The traditional organisation chart no longer applies. The organisation is made up of people with various roles too numerous to mention and contacts too numerous to list. Effectively, the organisation chart is circular and team-based with no top, no bottom, no power base, boundaries or demarcations. You are respected for what you do and how you do it, not for the title on your business card. It is a matter of skills and competence.

The critical role for management in this environment is managing human imagination and creativity opposite the vision and goals and, ultimately, the performance of the organisation.

Organisation

I am reminded of the Tetra Pak Australia objective and their words 'One Team, One Goal'. Departments and functions are completely fluid, all with the common focus on customers and customer satisfaction, all with a common goal. A free exchange of people and skills occurs between customer and supplier partners. There is no organisation in the traditional sense. Any sub-structure is circular, not layered. The entire environment is based on a team approach, not a hierarchy.

Quality, service and measurement

Quality in everything that is done is now a way of life, so much so that it appears initially that the urgency and focus on quality have gone. Of course, this is not so. It is just that the principles are so well-entrenched, understood and practised that attention is now focused on other things, such as relation-ships, partnerships, strategy, innovation and the future. And the future is all about sustainable processes, technologies and services that will meet current and future requirements. Customer quality control on incoming raw materials is a thing of the past. When dealing with total quality organisations there is no need for duplication. JIT, EDI, kanban, Internet and intranet communication, and supplier stock management programs are everyday strategies.

TQM, SPC principles and process re-engineering are being used through-out the organisation. Variation is being continually reduced and systems changes via best practices, attitude and technology shifts are now frequent. Both customer and supplier are jointly and separately benchmarking against the world's best, and winning.

Cost and value for money

Negotiations on price, terms and conditions no longer occur. Jointly agreed and mutually beneficial decisions are made on the basis of shared information. Reviews occur on a regular basis with the entire package of quality, service, innovation and teamwork being considered. SPC, process stability and reducing variation are just as much features of the commercial process as they are fundamental parts of the production and quality process.

The customer partner is actively seeking to make the supplier partner more profitable, and the supplier partner is able to give the customer partner genuine value-adding innovation and/or continuous cost-downs in real terms. Not only are win/win value propositions and common goals in place but individual partner organisation objectives and business drivers are aligned. This is driven by a shared risk/reward remuneration model where the supplier partner can gain additional profit or lose part or all expected profit opposite agreed targets based on the over or under performance against agreed Key Performance Indicators. This risk/reward approach provides the key link between performance, measurement, behaviour, attitude, risk management, risk allocation and remuneration.

Summary

The partnership situation is truly a win/win relationship, benchmarked against the best in the world and totally committed to continuous improvement. Genuine and sustained global competitive advantage is the outcome for both customer and supplier partners. This is truly *world class* and best practice.

'FUZZY' PARTNERSHIPS (FUTURE CLASS)

> *You see things and you say why, but I dream of things that never were and say why not.*
>
> *George Bernard Shaw*

The word 'fuzzy' is taken from the term *fuzzy logic*. These are the pioneering and community relationships that we spoke about in Chapter 1. Imagine an entire marketplace where there are no boundaries between customers and suppliers, internally or externally; a market where the whole supplier/customer supply chain is in fact one partnership, a genuinely seamless and transparent environment. Sustaining such a market requires social and political change as well as organisational, technological and cultural change, so that partnerships between organisations (profit and non-profit) and the community are as common as customer/supplier partnerships.

A 'fuzzy' partnership is illustrated in Figure 2.6.

Internal/external relationships

Internal and external relationships are now one and the same. There are no boundaries, only people and relationships. There is a total integration of strategies and activities across the marketplace, covering all links in the customer/supplier chain. There is a constant people and skills exchange covering all functions. You may work for three or four organisations in a short space of time or, indeed, be working for three or four at the same time. Not only are there roving individuals but roving teams that are highly skilled and empowered, launching themselves from one organisation to another, improving, problem solving, benchmarking, listening, talking, thinking, imagining, creating, innovating.

They are also *destroyers*. They annihilate apathy, gatekeepers, complacency, arrogance, bureaucracy and poor quality wherever they go. Such teams could be cross-company, cross-functional, customer/supplier customer focus teams, product and service development teams, legal teams, special project teams, innovation teams, finance teams, engineering teams, production teams, process re-engineering teams, problem-solving teams, quality improvement teams, and so on. This is an incredibly exciting and stimulating environment with total openness and full exchange of information. People are reinventing their own roles, their teams and even the organisation itself on a monthly, weekly, daily, hourly basis.

'Fuzzy' partnerships

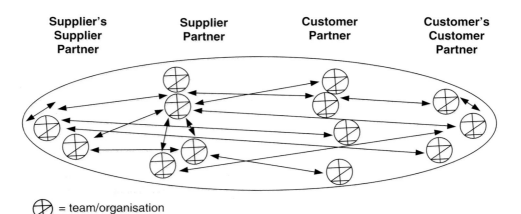

Fig. 2.6 *Customer/supplier structures: 'fuzzy' partnerships*

The use of subcontractors and outsourcing is rife. Permanent part-timers, part-time permanents, job sharing, skill sharing and home offices are commonplace. Demarcation is no longer a part of the language. Industrial disputation is nothing but a distant memory. There is no longer a 'them' and 'us', only 'we'—one team, one direction, common goals. Individual skills have reached extraordinary levels through working in a learning environment with an insatiable drive to improve.

Wherever possible, the customer/supplier chain is now made up of single preferred suppliers at each link who have formed long-term partnerships up and down the supply chain. Where single preferred supply arrangements are not possible, three-way or greater partnerships, clusters and alliance networks are common. Cooperative or co-supplier benchmarking is standard practice between competitive and non-competitive suppliers. When it comes to the common good of the interdependent partnering supply chain, traditional adversaries and organisational troglodytes will do surprising things to learn from each other, to improve together and to cooperate.

This new paradigm will not be sustained without world-class processes and technology. We are right at the edge and beyond. 'Fuzzy' partnerships don't learn from history—they make it.

Management and organisation

Flat, one layer: 'All men and women are created equal.' That's not to say everybody is paid the same amount or in the same way. Reward and recognition are related to the degree of effective leadership, innovation, commitment, ownership and skills. With multiskilled workers, a complete fluidity of people and job roles, and the incredible pace at which this environment moves, there is no possibility of having an organisation in the normal sense. You could not possibly have a traditional organisation chart—it would have changed by the time you had written it up. It wouldn't tell you anything, anyway. There may be a directory or database of people, skills and current projects being worked on and where/how they can be contacted. It will surprise you how many people you know in this environment, having either met them personally or communicated with them via phone, email or fax. It doesn't matter how big or small the organisations or the marketplace. You are forced to communicate and to share.

Traditional middle management has been extinguished. This is a learning environment that is genuinely based on skills and competencies. Strategic alliances, joint ventures, equity participation, shared investments and profit sharing are standard practice.

It will take extraordinary courage and vision from management to implement and sustain such an experience. The leadership here is undoubtedly inspiring and world class. This is the future.

Quality, service and measurement

Total quality is no longer a priority. Like workplace reform, culture and attitude, it simply exists. Throughout the supply chain, JIT, totally integrated stock management and IT systems, and so on, are a way of life. Innovation and learning are now the keys. Those involved in these initiatives are insatiable and unstoppable.

Cost and value for money

It is now the entire supply chain that is subject to improved total costs and total value, not just a single customer/supplier partnership. Designing out via world-class innovation is now the mode of operation. Step-change improvements in productivity, process control and technology mean a continuous reduction in real costs and a continuous improvement in quality and value-adding benefits.

As with partnerships, negotiations in the traditional sense don't happen. It's all about mutually agreed decisions based on shared information for mutual benefit.

Summary

A 'fuzzy' partnership is an unbelievably stimulating and successful environment. This is **future class**—the ultimate in competitive advantage.

Clusters, hubs and spokes, and consortia networks

> *Almost every large company today has a spaghetti bowl of alliances, but there is seldom an overall logic to the set of partnerships in that there is no distinctive, underlying point of view about industry futures and no conscious attempt to assemble the companies that have the complementary skills to turn that conception of the future into reality. Thus, although many companies have a wide variety of partnerships, the individual partnerships are often disconnected, each serving an independent and unrelated purpose.*
>
> *By way of contrast, what we have in mind are multilateral partnerships that possess a clear 'cumulative logic'.*
>
> *Gary Hamel & C.K. Prahalad*[10]

There are many variations on the 'fuzzy' theme. Managing the diversity and complexity of multi-partner networks is creating structures old and new. The most appropriate structure or combination of structures is only limited by the nature of the alliances, the make-up of the supply chain and the imagination of those entrusted with their development. Clusters, hubs and spokes, consortia and networks involve the concept of multiple organisations like alliance partners (customers and suppliers) and co-suppliers (competitive and non-competitive) joining forces to exploit synergies, leverage core competencies and benchmark best practice for mutual benefit. A sample of structures is shown in Figure 2.7.

Although the hub and spoke model has successfully worn the test of time as an organisational form, it is no less appropriate to partnerships and alliances today and for the future. The principle is simple. There is a 'hub' or dominant organisation at the centre connected to surrounding 'nubs' or satellite organisations. The nature of the connections will depend on the quality of the relationships, the scope of products and services provided and the degree of cooperation employed between the network partners.

Ford Australia has initiated a cluster of its major suppliers to work together as a core group. With 70–80 per cent of the cost of the motor vehicle residing with external suppliers, building outstanding and cooperative relationships with suppliers is essential.

Extended partnering networks and supply chains are now commonplace within the airline industry. It is all about maximising synergy, efficiency and share of the global marketplace. For example, Qantas and British Airways have further expanded their alliance to include code-share services between major and regional centres in the UK and continental Europe. They have developed an extended airline partner network, the One World Alliance, including American Airlines, US Air, Canadian Airlines, SAS, Air Pacific and a number of Australian domestic carriers. The partnering network also includes a raft of hotel groups (e.g. Marriott, ITT Sheraton, Hilton, Holiday Inn, Inter-Continental), car partners (e.g. Hertz, Thrifty, Carey Limousines, CitiCar) and other service partners such as American Express and Telstra. It does not take too much imagination to see these relationships extending themselves to aggregate purchasing arrangements, operational activities like maintenance and reliability, and the synergistic and leveraging use of other core competencies.

'We are increasingly bidding and working in consortia, where there are high levels of interdependence', says Frank Theophile, Research Fellow at the Serco Institute, which tracks outsourcing trends for global, task management

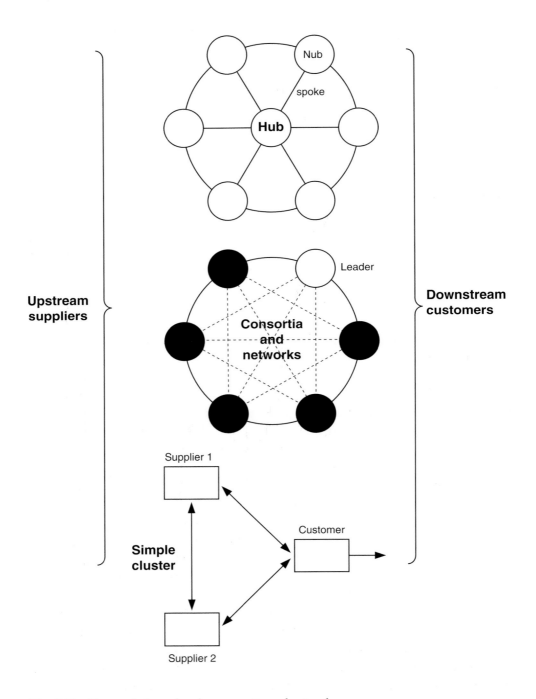

Fig. 2.7 *Clusters, hubs and spokes, consortia and networks*

contractor Serco. He adds, 'it is not enough just to bring a "brand name" for inclusion in a proposal. Each of the parties in the bid relies on the other parties bringing their specialist skills to bear, in order for the operation to be successful. For example, Serco teamed with P&O Australia (POAL) for the nationwide and, in some cases, overseas provision of a comprehensive range of port services and support craft for the Australian Navy. Serco brought expertise in change management, an in-depth understanding of the Navy and their requirements, and a strong "service culture" oriented towards flexibility and responsiveness. POAL brought deep and broad experience in the maritime industry, expertise in ship procurement and management, and well-developed procedures for regulatory compliance and risk management. The combination of the partners' complementary business networks, both nationally and globally, was also essential in meeting the diverse and geographically dispersed requirements of the customer.'

The multinational drug company Rhone-Poulenc Rorer has assembled, under a single organisational umbrella known as RPR Gensell, a hub-and-spoke network of thirteen biotechnology and research institutions specialising in gene and cell therapy. As the hub, Rhone-Poulenc Rorer is investing nearly $0.5 billion in the effort and devoting several hundred internal scientists to gene-therapy research. Says Robert Cawthorn, Chief Executive at the time of RPR Gensell's inception:

> *It is clear that a variety of technologies—a tool box, if you will—is needed if we are to conquer diseases such as cancer, Alzheimer's and cardiovascular disease. Our answer is RPR Gensell, an integrated network of external and internal scientists that will share the tools and expertise necessary to build successful cell and gene therapeutics on an accelerated time scale. It is the world's first broad biotechnology network.*[11]

Sega, the Japanese video game company, is at the centre of an alliance partner network that includes AT&T, Time Warner, TCI, Pioneer, Yamaha, Hitachi and Matsushita.[12] Sega's aim is to become a world-class entertainment company. Through this alliance network Sega will access technology required to download computer games over a cable television network, produce life-like graphics for video games and a lot more.

Chrysler came back from the edge of extinction through an outstandingly successful and well-documented partnering strategy.[13] The reporting of a fourth-quarter loss of $644 million in 1989 proved to be the catalyst for change and a strategy of building long-term, cooperative relationships with suppliers was initiated. This was in stark contrast to the adversarial, non-productive and unrewarding relationships that existed previously. Through a complex network involving over 150 key suppliers, Chrysler as the hub improved its profitability per vehicle from approximately $250 in the 1980s to $2110 in 1994 and has had the highest return on assets among US automakers since 1992. As an example of the cooperative, open nature of the relationships, Chrysler has over 300 supplier engineers working directly within its factories designing component systems.

Lotus Development Corporation, in the development and marketing of its *Notes* software, used hub-and-spoke alliance networks extensively. 'We just couldn't get *Notes* to market quickly enough, nor could we provide all the support *Notes* demanded,' says Steve O'Neill, Lotus vice-president for alliances.[14] 'For every $1 of *Notes* business, there is probably $15–20 worth of ancillary business—everything from providing the hardware, training, support, right down the line. We simply couldn't provide that. We needed to find partners who could.'

AT&T provided the telecommunications platform for *Notes*, hardware makers like Sun and Apple bundled *Notes* to their machines and also provided marketing, sales and customer support, and systems integrators like EDS and Unisys provided consulting and computer integration services—in total, over 20 major and strategic alliance partners.

'I am convinced that it [the alliance strategy] ended up working so well that one of our partners, IBM, decided to pay a big premium to acquire us,' says Hemang Dave, Lotus's first vice-president for strategic alliances.

Michael Porter, the guru of strategy, says: 'Whereas once the scale of the firm was important, now the scale of the cluster—the network, the infrastructure—is important. A firm's scale can be smaller if there are many good suppliers and supporting companies around.'[15]

As their popularity grows, these fuzzy webs of cooperative competence will mature and become increasingly complex and rewarding. Ultimately these networks and integrated supply chains will displace the traditional competitive arena between individual companies.

The 'inside out' partnering development model

In a seamless, transparent environment the same approaches, the same rules apply, from personal through to internal work relationships, to external customer/supplier relationships and then on to the extended supply chain networks. This is the 'inside out' partnering model at work (see Fig. 2.8). True fuzzy partnering with all its benefits then pervades the entire spectrum of personal and

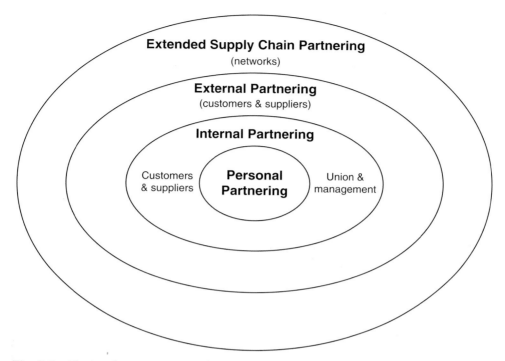

Fig. 2.8   *The 'inside out' partnering development model*

business relationships. Effectively managing the 'inside out' partnering model will not only deliver a better business but an improved personal quality of life.

In our personal lives we have many and differing relationships with all types of customers and suppliers. They include supermarkets, motor mechanics, doctors, pharmacists, builders, teachers, sports coaches, friends and family. All these relationships need to be managed to varying degrees of quality and performance. The 0 to 10 Relationship Management model discussed in Chapter 1 applies equally well to these relationships in our personal lives as it does to business relationships.

For most people, the largest financial commitment of their lives involves either the building or renovation of a house. How many of us have treated builders as low-level, untrustworthy (0–4) vendors, effectively tendering out the business on the basis of the best of three quotes and won on the cheapest price. All too often, the results fall short of expectations and on occasions end up in the courts. On how many occasions would we like to have the time over again with relationships that have gone off the rails, to take a different approach? It is easy with hindsight to turn confrontation into cooperation. The life skill, as well as the business skill, is to get it right the first time.

THE FOUR STAGES OF RELATIONSHIP MAINTENANCE

Engineers are clever people. For decades they have had a very effective system for looking at the various categories of maintenance of plant and machinery. The four categories are:

1. Breakdown maintenance
2. Preventative maintenance
3. Predictive maintenance
4. Design-out maintenance

They are self-explanatory when it comes to engineering and maintaining the well-being of moving parts. But this system is also a very useful way of looking at relationships and how we maintain them. Figure 2.9 outlines the major features of the four types of maintenance as they apply to relationships. It will be in the areas of prediction and designing out that real competitive advantage lies. Preventing non-conformances is quickly becoming a minimum requirement for staying in business. Prevention will keep you in the competitive pack; prediction and design-out strategies and relationships will keep you ahead of it. Again, innovation will be the key.

A simple example will illustrate how this works from an engineering perspective and how it can then be compared with relationship maintenance. Take a large gearbox and set of bearings turning a shaft on a compressor. The compressor is a vital piece of equipment in maintaining high pressures to a chemical reactor. The gearbox and bearings are lubricated by oil that is circulated via an oil-cooling system. However, because of some design deficiencies with the oil-cooling system there has been greater wear on the gearbox and bearings than would normally be expected.

Breakdown maintenance

The first attitude you can take to maintenance is to run the gearbox and bearings to failure. In other words, don't touch them until they break down. In our example that could be very expensive, as the failure of the gearbox and bearings would cause the compressor to stop and the reactor to come off-line. Repairing or replacing the gearbox and bearings could also be very expensive and the lead times long. As any plant manager will tell you, unscheduled maintenance can be the stuff nightmares are made of. There is no such thing as a pleasant surprise in the case of unscheduled maintenance. Breakdown maintenance is a short-term and ultimately unprofitable way to approach the situation.

The Four Stages of Relationship Maintenance

1. *Breakdown (the quick fix)*
   - The traditional way
   - 'Firefighting' culture
   - High cost and/or little value adding
   - Poor customer/supplier relationships
   - Focus on the short term
   - Reactive vs proactive to complaints/problems/developments

2. *Prevention (rather than cure)*
   - TQM approach
   - Value adding and/or cost reducing
   - Medium/long-term focus
   - Quality supplier/customer relationships

3. *Prediction (rather than prevention)*
   - Creates competitive advantage through innovation and differentiation
   - Value adding and cost reducing
   - Long-term approach to strategic relationships and partnerships
   - Beyond TQM

4. *Design out (a systems change)—Paradigm shift*
   - World-class innovation and 'everything else'
   - Long-term strategic focus outside the traditional frame of reference
   - Process re-engineering is the norm
   - The outcome of successful partnerships
   - Reinvention of people roles, processes, organisations
   - Doing things fundamentally differently.

Fig. 2.9 *Relationship maintenance: four stages*

How many times have we seen relationships managed on the basis of the breakdown maintenance principle, focused on the short term? We have all heard the expression 'management by crisis', or 'we manage from one crisis to another'. This is the world of breakdown maintenance, a world of reactive complaints resolution as opposed to a proactive search for opportunities or solutions. It's a tough way to run a business, unrewarding and frustrating for those at the coalface. It can also be very costly from a customer service perspective.

Preventative maintenance

The next alternative is prevention rather than cure. It sounds simple, and it is. All it requires is a policy from management that we will look at things before we have to. In our gearbox and bearings example this means that, at regular, scheduled and convenient intervals, the gearbox, bearings and the lubricating oil system are shut down, inspected for wear and repaired or replaced if necessary. No unscheduled downtime, no costly repairs or impact on the customers.

Prevention in relationship maintenance is the basis of quality and the best way to approach a good relationship. Prevention is as much an attitude as a physical reality, a mind set with a medium- to longer-term focus that says: What can I do to ensure certain things don't happen? Because it is a mindset issue, prevention also needs management and leadership skills if it is to be implemented effectively. An example is the decision made by the customer to introduce a bar-coding system on raw material stocks to avoid or prevent stockouts.

Predictive maintenance

With our gearbox, bearings and oil lubrication system, predictive maintenance means that we either buy in the expertise or upskill our own people in condition monitoring and vibration analysis. This will include an upfront investment in some computer hardware and some quite sophisticated software. Condition monitoring and vibration analysis is a clever and powerful predictive tool that will not only tell you the condition of the gearbox and bearings while they are still running, but will also predict under varying conditions the time to failure and the rate of deterioration to that point. This ability to predict breakdown allows for a managed long-term maintenance program to be planned and implemented.

In relationships, this is the world of real innovation and creativity. People at all levels are thinking about the next steps, adding value, predicting and implementing tomorrow's initiatives today. This is the first step beyond total quality, a proactive approach to thinking 'outside the square'. Skills and leadership are critical here as this is life in the fast lane, with a genuine long-term perspective. Using a bar-coding system for prevention of customer stockouts could also be the means of transferring ownership and responsibility for stock management from customer to supplier. Combined with SPC techniques, this becomes a predictive tool for the supplier in forecasting and managing the customer's future off-take. The step change in the level of empowerment and trust required to make this happen is obvious.

Design-out maintenance

Design-out maintenance would involve a radical redesign of the whole lubrication system and parts of the gearbox and bearings, giving a virtual guarantee of breakdown-free running over a long period, say 20 years. Then, under normal running conditions, there is no need for maintenance. In this example, the savings over the period of 20 years can be enormous.

Designing out in relationships can be just as significant and rewarding. This is about innovation at its best, where process re-engineering is normal practice and world best practice is the benchmark to improve upon. This is the step change that everyone is looking for. In the future, though, these step changes will be required far more frequently if businesses are to become world class and stay that way. Management and shop floor are continually reinventing their roles and processes, even their organisations. This is where partnering and alliance relationships will ultimately hold their rewards. They will create the environment whereby such initiatives and innovations are achievable and sustainable. For example, the Internet with its potential for interactive multimedia activities will provide the step change for many organisations to achieve the next level of competitive advantage.

Tetra Pak, world leader in processing, packaging and distribution systems for liquid food, talks about the shop-controlled factory of the future.[16] The potential for designing out and strategic partnering is awesome.

> *In the future it might also be possible to connect the dairy's automation system directly to the shop's computer, making ordering completely automatic.*
>
> *When the storage level begins to near the critical point (the system can take into account the time of day, e.g. three hours before closing time), the shop's computer calls the dairy's automated system and places an order. The automated system receives the order, ensures that the desired products are produced, plans the distribution and makes sure the goods are packed and placed on the transport vehicles.*
>
> *When the products arrive at the shop, the computer checks off the delivery and sends a confirmation back to the dairy's automation system which then prints out an invoice.*

Imagine the skills, technology, leadership, trust and teamwork required to integrate such complexity of both hardware and relationships. Is this where your organisation is heading? If the answer is no, think again!

REFERENCES

1. Tom Peters, *Liberation Management: Necessary Disorganization for the Nanosecond Nineties*, Macmillan, London, 1992, p.148.

2. Martin Christopher, Adrian Payne, David Ballantyne, *Relationship Marketing*, Butterworth-Heinemann, Oxford, 1991, p.157.

3. W. Edwards Deming, *Out of Crisis*, Massachusetts Institute of Technology, 1991.

4. J.M. Duran, *Juran on Leadership for Quality*, The Free Press, New York, 1989.

5. Philip Crosby, *Quality without Tears*, McGraw-Hill, New York, 1984.

6. Crosby, op. cit.

7. Edwards Deming, op. cit.

8. Peter Drucker, in an article by T. George Harris, 'The post-capitalist executive: an interview with Peter Drucker', *Harvard Business Review*, May–June 1993, pp.114–24.

9. Drucker, op. cit.

10. Gary Hamel & C.K. Prahalad, *Competing for the Future*, Harvard Business School Press, 1994, p.207.

11. *Alliance Analyst* magazine, 28/10/96.

12. Hamel & Prahalad, op. cit.

13. Jeffrey H. Dyer, 'How Chrysler created an American Keiretsu', *Harvard Business Review*, July–August 1996, p.42.

14. *Alliance Analyst* magazine, 11/12/95.

15. Michael Porter, 'Creating advantages', *Executive Excellence* magazine, Executive Excellence Publishing, Dec 1997, p.18.

16. Tetra Pak, *Power of Partnership—The Integrated Approach*, Ruter Press, Sweden, 1994, p.93.

CHAPTER 3

Partnerships, competitive advantage and the fit with strategy

> *Survival depends on winning ... losing means extinction ... There is no alternative to partnership—but I submit that our expectation level of how that partnership must work, and the results it must yield, must be raised by an order of magnitude. Our involvement with each other—trust and respect for each other—must be magnified. Nothing else is acceptable—because nothing else will win the ball game.*
>
> Bill Weisz, Vice-Chairman, Motorola[1]

Based on the 80:20 rule, take the annual turnover, contribution, profit (or whatever measure is appropriate) of the top 20 per cent of your customer and/or supplier base and multiply this figure by five (i.e. five years). In the partnership business, five years will be the minimum period. If you end up with what you regard as a large number, then you will need to consider customer/supplier strategic partnering/alliancing as being critical to your future success and a fundamental part of your future strategy.

Also consider those customers and suppliers you currently don't have but who will be critical to your future success. Determine if you are going to be a trader, a customer/supplier to those organisations, or a partner with them. Add these partnering numbers into the above calculation.

Remember that your large customers/suppliers (current or potential) who have not been given partnership status are also important. You will need clear strategies for them as well. It is the management of the entire 0 to 10 relationship scale (see Figs. 1.2, 1.3 and 1.4) that is critical, not just the 8 to 10 partnering section.

In this book I am not telling you how to write your business strategy. Clearly, you know best what your core competencies are and which market sectors and customers you wish to target. External forces, controllable and uncontrollable, will vary from market to market. The effects of reducing tariffs, deregulation, dumping, microeconomic reform, workplace reform and changing legislation are variables we all need to consider to varying degrees when putting together the business strategy. What are the growth rates and future trends of the product, company and industry sectors? In terms of picking winners, which companies (hopefully your current or future customers and suppliers) have the most effective strategies for the future? Strengths, weaknesses, opportunities and threats, supply/demand balances, reinvestment strategies and variable/fixed costs are all critical points to consider, but beyond the scope of this book. What I can give you is a clear set of principles, guidelines and tools on how to develop, maintain and improve on your partnering and alliance relationships, on how best to select the right partners.

I can tell you, too, that partnering is extremely time- and resource-consuming, but also incredibly rewarding for those organisations that do it well. For strategic partnering to work you must have a world-class, best in class, value-added, customer-service-based strategy, focused as much on people and communication as on plant and equipment. A cost-plus strategy may be appropriate in certain markets or for specific customers but it cannot sustain the cost and time required to develop long-term strategic relationships. Clearly, written into your strategy must be an unambiguous statement to all in the organisation that the company is totally committed to customer satisfaction and the development of strategic partnerships and alliances with selected customers and suppliers. The strategy must also support all those involved and empower them to do whatever is necessary to ensure success.

Just as important is the corporate culture. Partnering cannot sustain tribalism, departmentalism, miscommunication, lack of trust or hidden agendas. The process simply collapses. Partnering needs a strong effective vision from the top of the organisation, effectively communicated and implemented throughout the organisation and owned at all levels by dedicated, skilled and creative teams and individuals. Tom Peters calls these creative people 'curious'. Support from senior and middle management and their active participation in the process are also essential if those at the coalface are not to think it is just another flavour-of-the-month exercise.

STRATEGY AND PICKING WINNERS

Partnerships, competitive advantage and strategy are inevitably closely linked, otherwise the entire principles and process of partnering and alliancing could legitimately be questioned. Partnerships cannot work in isolation from the strategy and activities of the organisation. First, they require high resource utilisation in people, hardware and software that will need to be prioritised in response to the rest of the activities of the organisation. Second, successful partnerships will have a strong and positive influence on other internal and external customer/supplier relationships.

Strategy sets the direction and time frame while partnerships play a fundamental part in the execution of that strategy by generating sustainable competitive advantage for the customer/supplier organisations. Extend this process up and down the supply chain and you develop an integrated set of partnership organisations, all pursuing effective and synergistic strategies based on delivering products and services superior in value in terms of their performance and effect. This then becomes a very powerful platform by which an entire supply chain can become competitive on a global scale.

Integral to the success of partnerships and sustainable competitive advantage will be those critical elements of leadership, workplace reform, quality and innovation. It is now well understood and documented that innovation will play a critical role into the new millennium in successful organisations wishing to achieve competitive advantage. From its study, the Business Council of Australia states:

> *Among the chief characteristics of strong enterprises is their ability to innovate and thereby improve performance. Strong, globally competitive enterprises are the natural vehicles for industrial and business innovation.*[2]

For enterprises that are following a value-adding differentiated approach, innovation will play a critical role in the formation and implementation of strategy. This, together with the achievement of sustained competitive advantage, will most certainly lie at the heart of successful partnerships.

SUSTAINABLE COMPETITIVE ADVANTAGE

Business is about achieving that delicate balance between the seller's cost of producing and delivering a product or service at a price the buyer is prepared to pay. Both parties require value from the transaction—the seller in terms of a margin and return business, and the buyer in terms of the subsequent margin achieved from the performance or effect of the product or service. Remember, in most cases the buyer doesn't actually gain value until payment is received, via the subsequent sale of the modified original product or service, unless some benefits are gained in the process that reduce costs or improve efficiencies.

Fundamental to any strategy will be the desire to achieve competitive advantage, but what is it exactly? Michael Porter[3] talks of competitive advantage as 'growing fundamentally out of value a firm is able to create for its buyers that exceeds the firm's cost of creating it. Value is what buyers are willing to pay [for], and superior value stems from offering lower prices than competitors for equivalent benefits or providing unique benefits that more than offset a higher price'. Porter argues that there are two basic types of competitive advantage: cost leadership and differentiation.

Cost leadership

Cost leadership results from the cost advantage an organisation achieves by conforming to customer requirements at a lower cumulative cost and a lower delivered price than its competitors. Organisations can achieve cost leadership in a number of different ways:

- clear vision and achievable strategies
- economies of scale
- occupacity
- internal integration of related business functions and activities
- high level of multiskilling combined with the development of a *learning* environment rather than a *training* environment
- a high degree of association and integration with suppliers
- workplace reform combined with TQM programs to give associated productivity and efficiency improvements
- a favourable location
- external factors, such as government regulations, tariffs, financial incentives and duties
- process/technology chosen, independent of scale (e.g. faster cycle times or throughput rates)

Sweating assets versus cash cows

As with any good customer/supplier relationship, partnerships must pursue efficiency and productivity gains. In particular, cost reductions in areas of non-differentiation must be an ongoing objective, but this cannot be at the expense of adding value or innovation. There is a phrase, *sweating the assets*, which means making the assets work harder for you. In the context of maximising the use of resources, capacity utilisation, improving skills and gaining greater competency, finding and going beyond existing limits is an ambitious and laudable objective, one that strategic partnering will gain much value from.

If sweating the assets, however, is just a euphemism for *cash cow*—that is, milking the assets to maximise short-term profits with little or no consideration for reinvestment—then clearly this is a least-cost strategy. This may be appropriate in certain circumstances, but not if partnerships are involved.

Differentiation

Differentiation, on the other hand, occurs when an organisation provides unique products and/or services that are valuable to buyers beyond simply offering a low price. It is achieved when value-adding benefits, whether perceived or real, are delivered to the customer. These value-added benefits are based on the superior performance and/or the effect of the product or service beyond that of the competition.

Porter[4] states that, opposite the competition, differentiation allows the selling organisation to (1) gain a price premium, (2) sell more of its product or service at an equivalent price, or (3) gain additional benefits such as customer loyalty or long-term commitments. The price premium achieved is greater than the cost of benefits delivered. For the customer it is a question of the price premium asked by the supplier being less than the value of the benefits gained. In reality, there will be a compromise somewhere between the two positions. This does not imply in any way that organisations following a differentiated strategy should not pursue appropriate cost reductions, particularly those that do not impact directly on areas of differentiation.

The drivers of differentiation will be similar to those for cost leadership but different in interpretation, application and order of importance. They are:

- clear vision and effective strategies and leadership
- linkages within the value chain
- supplier linkages
- favourable location
- technology
- skills, effective workplace reform and implementation of total quality
- effective communication
- economies of scale

- external factors, such as government regulations, tariffs, financial incentives and duties
- integration of related businesses and activities

To achieve sustainable differentiation, an organisation must examine each of its areas of uniqueness or competitive advantage and identify the underlying driving forces. Uniqueness in itself, however, is not a recipe for success in the short, medium or long term. It must produce genuine benefits that have the effect of either reducing costs or improving performance. For partnerships based on a differentiation strategy, the real test of success will be if sustained premiums are achieved from well-informed and happy customer partners. Uniqueness can also be applied back up the supply chain to suppliers. For example, by working with a supplier you, the customer, may be able to develop a unique competitive advantage that generates benefits for you and a price premium or improved margin for the supplier.

Understand the value propositions

A differentiation strategy provides the platform for understanding the value proposition(s) for the relationship. Value propositions comprise those opportunities to be developed and the benefits to be gained beyond just price and cost. In the case of partnering and alliance relationships the value propositions will reflect the opportunities and benefits to be gained for all the partners. Value propositions could include:

- Easier and faster access and transition to new technologies
- The ability to leverage off or have access to partners' 'global' reach, capabilities, brand, market knowledge and networks
- Removal of complexity and lower total operating costs
- Improved speed to market for new products and services
- Increased revenues, additional profits, increased margin through risk/ reward linked, performance based remuneration
- Greater integration, simplification and efficiency of operations
- Improved brand and reputation
- Significant improvement in risk management or significantly reduced or improved risk profile/s

STRATEGY AND PARTNERSHIPS

Strategy sets the direction and the framework of the business in regard to how it will relate to its external environment, usually within a three to five year time frame. Strategy documents look critically at the prioritised market sectors to be developed and forecast the expected market share and growth rates over the period. The key customers are targeted. The external economic indicators that are likely to apply and the allocation of required resources are discussed. There will be a review of technology relating to both current and future requirements. All these factors will be taken into account in terms of an expected volume, cash and profit stream that is projected throughout the period. All senior management concerned sign off on its content and play an important role in the review of progress against the plan. Individual objectives and principal accountabilities would then be drawn up in line with the direction that has been set.

It should be no surprise, then, that the business strategy should legitimately have a powerful and controlling influence over the organisation in every aspect and at every level. It is the base working document for the organisation, in line with and supporting the vision and values statement as set by the Board of Directors and senior management.

Fundamental to the strategy will be senior management's views on customer service and the importance of satisfying customers' current and future needs. In short, it comes down to whether the approach and direction of the organisation is one of a least-cost or a value-added differentiation. With rare exception, the two approaches are incompatible. Pursuing alliance and partnering relationships under the umbrella of a least-cost strategy will be fraught with difficulty and will ultimately fail. A least-cost strategy may be appropriate in certain markets but it cannot sustain the cost, time and resource commitment required in developing long-term strategic relationships.

Genuine long-term strategic customer and supplier partnerships will usually exist within a five to ten year time frame and beyond. These long-term relationships will involve the organisation's most important and strategic accounts, whether current or potential. Managing such relationships will be concerned with the day-to-day activities of ensuring In Full On Time to A1 specification (IFOTA1) of product or service, as well as the medium- and long-term value-adding and differentiating initiatives. A crucial feature of this process will be the commitment and active participation of all or most business functions within the organisation. The selected involvement of external resources and suppliers will be critical. Support and active participation will also need to come from senior management, the same individuals who set the strategic direction for the business as a whole.

Every organisation has areas of expertise, often unique and sometimes world class, that can directly or indirectly benefit the customer. But, for some reason, these centres of excellence have not been effectively utilised. Understanding the entire value chain and integrating partnerships with the business strategy gives you a better appreciation of where your organisational resources and areas of expertise can be of most service or benefit.

Even just within your own organisation, strategic partnering and alliance relationships will need to survive two or three business/marketing strategies and probably one complete rewrite of the corporate vision and values not to mention the occasional takeover/buyout, merger and acquisition. In many cases this will provide the partnerships with some of their greatest challenges, so it is inconceivable that partnerships could operate outside the normal framework of strategy development.

As well as being a fundamental part of the organisation's strategic plan, specific partnerships and alliances will also need to be supported by, and appear in, the customers' and/or suppliers' strategic plans. Strategic partnering is a fully integrated process between customer and supplier in a mature environment and affects the entire value chain. Clearly, this level of commitment will not happen overnight. One of the key performance indicators of partnership success will be the development of a joint business strategy, or when recognition of the importance of the relationship appears in your partner's strategy documents. However, this commitment to the success of the relationship and your partner's own strategic direction will also need to be based on a world-class, value-added, differentiated strategy as opposed to a least-cost approach.

The partnership will be unsustainable if one party is focused on reducing prices/costs and the other on adding differentiated value. If the relationship involves a least-cost customer requiring an undifferentiated product or service, and a value-adding supplier, the result will be a frustrated supplier being pressured for lower prices while trying to pursue an improved, higher-value product or service. Alternatively, a value-adding customer will be continually at odds with a least-cost supplier; inevitably, there will be problems in the delivery of continuous improvement with regard to the development of new products and services and the basic IFOTA1 activities.

Strategic partnering between selected customers and suppliers can no longer be ignored in the strategic planning process. The quality and number of strategic partnerships and alliances will be one of the key success factors for world-class organisations in the future.

THE VALUE CHAIN AND CONTINUOUS IMPROVEMENT

Both cost leadership and differentiation strategies are based on a clear understanding of the buyer and seller value chains. The value chain is made up of the activities a firm performs in designing, producing, marketing, delivering

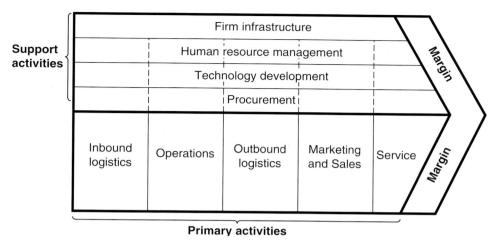

Fig. 3.1   *Michael Porter's generic value chain*

and supporting its product or service. Michael Porter's generic value chain[5] (reprinted with permission) is shown in Figure 3.1.

Strategic partnering and alliancing relationships must be based on a world-class or best in class, differentiated, value-adding, continuous improvement strategy. This will involve an integrated approach by the primary activities and the support activities of the organisation. Primary activities are those activities involved in the physical creation of the product or service and its sale and transfer to the buyer, as well as after-sales assistance. Support activities, on the other hand, support the primary activities and each other by providing purchased inputs, technology, human resources and various firm-wide functions. We will pursue in more detail this whole aspect of functional/ departmental integration and the benefits to be gained when discussing the partnering process in Chapter 6.

In the context of partnerships and the time frame involved, competitive advantage must also be sustainable; and unless buyer and seller are operating in a completely closed and static market this must involve continuous improvement. Assuming a no-change strategy results in a state of ever-diminishing competitive advantage. Continuous and breakthrough improvement, then, as part of sustainable competitive advantage for partnerships is non-negotiable.

PICKING WINNERS

It is logical to assume that an organisation's strategic direction should revolve around those customers and suppliers that the organisation believes will be most successful in their chosen marketplace, who will be leaders in their field, world-class even. Everyone wants to pick winners and be a part of their success rather than dumping losers and feeling the pain of failure.

Make no mistake: strategic partnering and alliancing is about picking long-term winners. Smart organisations will analyse their entire supply chain, both forward and back, not just their immediate customers and suppliers. After all, there is no point in having strong, long-term relationships with immediate customers and suppliers only to find there is a missing or weak link, current or potential. One of the characteristics of the partnership-based supply chain is the ability and commitment of partner organisations to assist other 'weaker' organisations, within and associated with the supply chain, to improve their performance. This could involve skills and people exchange, joint training, technology, IT linkages and the sharing of all kinds of experiences, best practices and other information.

STRATEGIC PARTNERING AS A CORE COMPETENCY

Core competencies[6] are those groups of activities, skills and technologies that a firm does well (ideally, world class) and which add direct value for the customer. In so doing, these competencies clearly advantage and differentiate the firm from its competitors, allowing the firm to extend itself into new markets, products and services. Understanding and developing core competencies is fundamental to any organisation striving for market leadership. At Canon, for example, the core competencies are precision engineering, fine optics, microelectronics and electronic engineering; at Honda it's small engines and powertrains; at Sony it is miniaturisation; at SKF (bearings) it's anti-friction and precision engineering; at Motorola it is wireless communication; at Federal Express it is logistics management. These core competencies, of course, take time to develop, up to five, ten, fifteen years and beyond. In many cases, it will need a not dissimilar time frame to develop the partnerships and alliances they will impact upon.

With global markets and competition now a reality, faster access to new technologies, products and service development will be crucial in a world of dramatically reducing life cycles. The building of strategic and cooperative customer/supplier relationships and supply-chain networks will be fundamental to a firm's competitive advantage. Relationship management and, specifically, strategic partnering and alliances as a core competency will be a clear differentiating indicator for world-class organisations in the future. Chrysler, Motorola, Honda, Marks & Spencer, Alcoa, Honeywell, Transfield Services, Worley are just some organisations with a track record of successful partnering that, it could well be argued, approaches core competency status.

The distinction must then be made between outsourcing and partnering. They are not the same. There is no argument that the transfer of non-core competencies from customer to supplier in outsourcing can be an important part of partnering or alliance strategy. However, while taking over part of a customer's business no doubt assists in building closer ties, sharing information, reducing costs, improving efficiencies and the like, it is still a far cry from a fully cooperative, interdependent, innovative, continuously improving, world-class alliance/partnering relationship. But when the core competencies of the outsourcing supplier impact positively and fundamentally on the core competencies of the customer, in conjunction with partnering principles and behaviours, then partnering and outsourcing become close cousins. For example, 70–80 per cent of the cost of a motor vehicle for Chrysler, Ford and Honda is outsourced. Canon buys more than 75 per cent of its copier components. All these organisations have strategies for being best in class. This just isn't possible without selected world-class alliances and partnering relationships. In moving from *vertical* integration to *virtual* integration, suppliers, alliance partners, and network, consortium and cluster members could contribute one or more core competencies each to the overall package of products, services and relationships required for the supply chain to be successful. Successful partnerships and alliances are not just about exploiting synergies but leveraging core competencies.

Frank Theophile, Research Fellow at the Serco Institute, sees a trend towards outsourcing products and services of increasing impact and importance to the customer. 'In terms of customer/contractor relations, we are seeing the outsourcing of activities that are much closer to core. For example, Serco currently operates the United Kingdom National Physical Laboratory (NPL) under contract to the United Kingdom Department of Trade and Industry. NPL is responsible for developing and maintaining national measurement standards such as the standard metre and the second. It is one of the world's major centers for precise measurement research and represents the first time that an entire government agency has been outsourced in the United Kingdom. A consequence of greater task criticality is an increasing focus on "value" and its creation or improvement, rather than downsizing and cost reduction (although efficiency continues to be important). By implication, this means collaborative, rather than arms-length confrontational working relationships. So accordingly, Serco has identified relationship management, partnerships and alliances, as a future core competence for the organisation.'

Building partnering as a core competency will not be a one-step process. In essence, it is what this book is all about.

STRATEGIC PARTNERING AND EXPORT STRATEGIES

In the past Australian companies have developed an appalling reputation as exporters. Their strategies have largely been dominated by 'spot', short-term, one-off business opportunities. Alternatively, strategies are based on a 'bottom-slicing' approach where export customers are the first to be cut off when the traditionally higher-value, more secure domestic markets pick up. Export markets have provided the buffer against the rise and fall of domestic markets in achieving maximum capacity utilisation of plant, equipment, people and services. In strategic partnering this approach is simply not acceptable, although there is no question that the reputation of Australian exporters has improved in recent times, due mainly to waterfront and other microeconomic reforms and a generally higher focus on export markets, particularly South-East Asia and the Far East.

Irrespective of the focus of your exports, the basis for export partnerships must be trust, quality, reliability, dependability and innovation. A partner is a partner. The principles and process do not alter between countries, organisations, strategies or anything else.

SIZE IS NO LIMITATION TO PARTNERING

In terms of big or small there is no discrimination as to who is the most suitable candidate for partnering. Large companies, diverse, international, multi-divisional, multi-site organisations can all be slow to move, inflexible and arrogant. But they can also provide critical mass. With the right leadership, culture, people, infrastructure and resources they can be a formidable force.

While smaller organisations can be fast moving, entrepreneurial, risk-taking and innovative, they often don't have the economics of scale and critical mass, the long-term vision or the financial resources to focus on sustainable partnerships. However, any enterprise is a potential customer or supplier partner. The determining factors are not size, technology or financial backing but rather leadership, vision, a compelling set of value propositions, competence and a high degree of commitment to the process at all levels.

No surprises, then, that with the right partnering combination of large and small, significant synergies, efficiencies and competitive leverage can be achieved. In particular, small to medium-size organisations can maintain their size with all their inherent strengths, yet achieve the scale and other benefits of the multinational conglomerates. In many ways this is a distinct advantage for smaller organisations. It is easier for smaller organisations to look and act bigger than it is for large organisations to look and act small. The irony is that all too few small to medium-size enterprises (SMEs) take advantage of this position. Fear of acquisition and merger, combined with an often fierce and hard-won independence, cause SMEs to shy away from potentially very effective and profitable strategic alliances and partnerships.

Many SMEs wrongly confuse the dependence associated with command and control relationships with the interdependence of genuine alliance partners. From the late 1980s, the software development company Lotus linked itself with a series of small entrepreneurial firms in the hope of locating ingenious new product ideas. The most famous example was Iris Associates, which developed the core technology for Lotus *Notes* back in the late 1980s.

Chemical giant, ICI, developed a strategic alliance with a key, but far smaller, supplier of catalysts to its plastics and petrochemical processes. The development of unique catalysts delivered significant process efficiencies and unique product qualities for both ICI and their downstream customers. The catalyst itself represented only a fraction of the cost, but was of critical importance to the process. The chemical reaction simply would not take place and the product could not be produced without it. It was the added value of the performance and effect of the catalyst that made the difference, not the price.

Queensland-based Clyde Babcock Hitachi (CBH) are leaders in the construction and maintenance of large boilers for electricity and power generation. They also design, construct and maintain industrial boilers in the sugar and process industries. Employing around 200 full-time people Australia-wide, they draw on a loyal, part-time, skilled and semi-skilled labour force. They have secured their future by building successful partnering relationships with Queensland Alumina Limited (QAL) at Gladstone in Queensland, the world's largest alumina refinery; NRG Gladstone Operating Services Pty Ltd, one of Australia's largest privately owned power stations; and Queensland government-owned power corporations, CS Energy, Tarong Energy and Stanwell Corporation. The success of these relationships has given CBH both the confidence and the credibility to compete effectively for business in the United States and elsewhere.

Numerous other small and medium-size organisations are joining together as alliance networks and consortia to secure public and private sector business opportunities.

COMPETITIVE ADVANTAGE AND PARTNERSHIPS: PERCEPTION VERSUS REALITY

It would be such a predictable and successful world if everything went to plan. Unfortunately, this is not the case. Somehow, messages and signals are miscommunicated or misinterpreted. The perception does not match the reality.

A mismatch of information, feelings and interpretations is generated and results in people making decisions that are unexpected and do not match the other party's view of reality. Not only can this often lead to loss of business but—just as important in partnerships—a loss of trust.

Successful partnerships are based on trust, shared information and the long term and, if they are to prosper, perception must equal reality. If it does not, then two things can be inferred:

1. There has been a breakdown in communication leading to incorrect interpretations or assumptions. This must be remedied, as good communication lies at the heart of good partnerships.
2. There is genuine deception taking place. This is not what partnerships are about.

For other customer/supplier relationships (see Fig. 1.2), it can be quite acceptable to gain a differentiated premium based on perceived benefits as opposed to, or as well as, real benefits. However, if you are dealing with well-informed professional buyers, the premiums gained are likely to exist only in the short to medium term. A smart buyer's perception will eventually match the reality and the advantage will be lost unless further benefits are given or the perception changes.

In any relationship, perception is just as important as reality and must be dealt with accordingly. In partnerships it is crucial to talk to people regularly to seek out misperceptions about the functioning of the partnership, and to take action to correct them. This will be an ongoing process even with existing, strong, long-term partnerships. As always it comes back to people and communication. The perception in most cases does not equal the reality because of poor communication.

MONOPOLIES AND PARTNERSHIPS

At first sight, monopoly relationships would appear to be the ultimate in competitive advantage. What could be more attractive in terms of profitability and general environment in which to work than an organisation that has captive customers and no direct competition? Nothing could be further from the truth. Monopolies provide probably the most difficult environment for partnerships to work. It could well be argued that, rather than having the ultimate in competitive advantage with monopoly supply, there is no competitive advantage at all. With no competition, there is no direct benchmark by which customer and supplier can judge and measure performance. I cannot think of a monopoly situation where the customers have not thought the service too poor and the prices too high.

Because of this lack of competition there is little incentive to improve, innovate or generally add value to customer relationships. There is probably no more stifling environment for creativity and imagination. Monopolies are the ideal situation for breeding arrogance and complacency, and for generating waste, inefficiencies and poor productivity. Management in particular tend to be insensitive to customers' changing needs and oblivious to the welfare and development of their employees. These deficiencies and the lack of a price benchmark in the form of a competitor normally result in high prices and inferior quality. This exploitation and abuse of the monopoly position will often impact on profitability and, ultimately, on the viability not only of the immediate customers but also of the entire supply chain. Paradoxically, monopolies would in most cases be more profitable if in fact they had competition.

The most extreme examples of monopolies and their effects on the value chain and the general environment could be seen with the opening up of Eastern Europe. For decades the communist regimes of the eastern bloc ran huge monopolies in both their heavy and light industries—in steel, chemicals, petrochemicals, automotive, textiles and even agriculture. The results were devastating, with both manufacturing and service sectors characterised by poor productivity, low skills levels and inferior quality. The effects on the wealth and well-being of society at large were disastrous, and factories created horrendous pollution problems that will continue to impact on the environment for many years to come.

There are three options for monopoly environments:

1. The monopoly position continues; in the medium to longer term this can have adverse implications for the entire supply chain.
2. Cheaper, direct substitutes in terms of performance and effect are developed, ultimately forcing the supplier to change strategy or go out of business. Few markets exist where it is not possible to introduce substitute products or services.
3. Direct competition is developed if the market is sufficiently attractive, usually more efficient, based on better service, producing more benefits and certainly cheaper in price.

This is why monopolies are normally involved in vendor-type relationships, to which they are more suited.

THE VALUE:COST/PRICE RELATIONSHIP

Sustained competitive advantage in partnerships is about managing the relationship between value, price and cost: that is, the price to the buyer and the cost to the seller. While generating value for customers beyond the cost of creating it at better than competitive prices, or with greater benefits at similar prices, may be desired, it is not always achievable, even in partnerships and alliances. Depending on the environment and the forces and variables operating within it, there may be a number of options available relating to value, price and cost. These are shown in Figure 3.2. Understanding their nature and possible implications will assist in the development of the relationship and the maintaining of competitive advantage.

Option A is a straight cost-down approach with little or no change in value. This can occur in the traded commodity markets due to:

- straight price pressures from the customer, or general supply and demand competitive pressures from the marketplace;
- cost improvements in economies of scale, productivity, efficiencies, new technology or other innovation that can be passed on to the customer or shared;
- low price/cost related to increased volume offtake by the customer partner.

Option B is a joint differentiation/cost-down approach. This is an extremely difficult position to sustain. Michael Porter[7] argues that differentiation and reducing cost strategies can take place simultaneously only where:
- a firm has not been fully exploiting all the opportunities to lower cost (in areas where the benefits and effects of differentiation are not sacrificed);
- being unique in an activity was formerly judged to be undesirable;
- a significant innovation has occurred which competitors have not adopted, such as a new automated process or integration that both lowers costs and improves quality.

This latter situation is common in the automotive, electronic, computer and manufacturing industries.

In **options between C and D**, for every unit of value gained there is less than a unit of cost or price incurred. That is, the value generated is greater than the cost of producing it for the supplier, and greater than the price paid by the customer, provided the angle is less than 45°. Beyond that point the price/cost is greater than the value gained. This is a genuine win/win position for both buyer and seller and the preferred option for maintaining or enhancing competitive advantage. In reality, products and services go through a life cycle of growth, stability and decline.

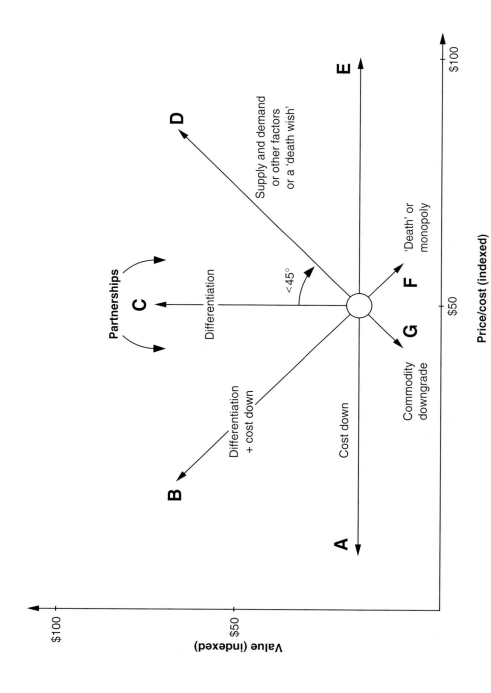

Fig. 3.2 *The relationship between price/cost and value*

While a product or service may live in the area of C to D for some time, with future innovation and new products and services the eventuality is that its value and hence its price are likely to diminish.

The Internet and communications, pharmaceutical, tourist and entertainment industries are examples of marketplaces continually searching for value beyond the cost and/or price. *Titanic* (the movie) cost over $200 million to produce and was the most expensive film in history at the time of release. It is also the most profitable movie ever made. This is a value return for the makers, 20th Century Fox, and value for the general public, over the cost incurred by the makers and the price paid by the viewing public. This, of course, will not stop *Titanic* from ending up in the local video store within six months.

Option E puts prices up with value relatively unchanged. This will only be achievable if:

- a shift in supply and demand allows for a rise in prices;
- other factors come into play, such as exchange rates, tariffs and government legislation, which can affect the prices that can be charged.

Otherwise, there is a strategy or a 'death wish' to price the product or service out of the market.

Option F, where prices are up and value down, indicates an abnormal development in market conditions such as a change to a monopoly position. Otherwise, commercial suicide is the only alternative. It would be extremely unusual to see this position sustained.

Option G indicates a change has occurred, reducing the quality required, or there has been a downgrading in the value of the product or service which in turn has caused prices to fall. This is a regular event in the electronics and computer industry with superseded models.

FOCUS ON TOTAL VALUE AND TOTAL COST, NOT UNIT PRICE

> *Any idiot can reduce a price by 10 per cent to become more competitive, but if you can offer an electric power transmission cable under the Baltic one year earlier than your competition, that is of tremendous value to the customer, and your competitor can't touch you.*
> *Percy Barnevik, Chairman Asea Brown Boveri*[8]

Sufferers of migraine did not initially begrudge paying up to $35 for a single tablet of Glaxo's Imagran to remove the acutely painful and debilitating headache. They, more than most people, appreciate the relationship between total value, total cost and unit price. The high upfront unit price of the tablet is insignificant compared with the total value gained from removing the pain and not incurring any lost work or leisure time. It is a simple issue of quality of life versus cost of living.

Figure 3.3 depicts the basic relationship between total value, total cost and unit price. In this generic example, supplier 1's unit price (SUP1) for its product/service is $10 or 10 per cent of the customer's total value (TV: $100) or selling price for its product/service. Total cost (TC) is the sum of all the supplier unit prices (i.e. SUP1 + SUP2 + SUP3 . . . SUPx) plus internal costs (fixed and variable, direct and indirect) associated with the primary and support activities of the organisation's value chain. Internal costs could be everything from the cost of the sales force to head office, R&D, warehousing, distribution and production.

In partnering and alliance relationships, total cost will almost certainly include the collaborative efforts of suppliers working and benchmarking together, exploiting synergies and leveraging core competencies to lower costs and add value. In Figure 3.3, total cost amounts to $80 or 80 per cent of total value. The difference between total value and total cost is the margin—that is, the difference between the value the market will pay and the cost of producing it. Margin will be made up of a wide variety of components depending on the nature of the products and services, their performance or effect. Innovation, uniqueness, flexibility, availability, competitive parity pricing, demand and criticality of application could be just some of the components that will ideally link back in large part to core competencies. As with total cost in partnerships and alliances, both the customer and its suppliers will contribute significantly to the margin through cooperative and integrated links. This is not an exercise in accounting so we will not concern ourselves with the vagaries of tax, interest, depreciation and the like.

Putting aside for the moment the process of how it is done, let us assume supplier 1 can deliver a 1 per cent (i.e. $1) increase in total value and a 1 per cent decrease in total cost (i.e. $0.80) to the customer. This is the equivalent of an 18 per cent decrease (i.e. $1.80/$10) in supplier 1's unit price or a 9 per cent ($1.80/$20) improvement in the customer's margin. Of course, the output numbers in this exercise will vary according to the input numbers, but the general principle holds true. That principle is: a focus on total value and total cost will yield a far better and more lasting result than an obsession with lowering supplier prices. Being 'penny wise and pound foolish' by focusing on the unit

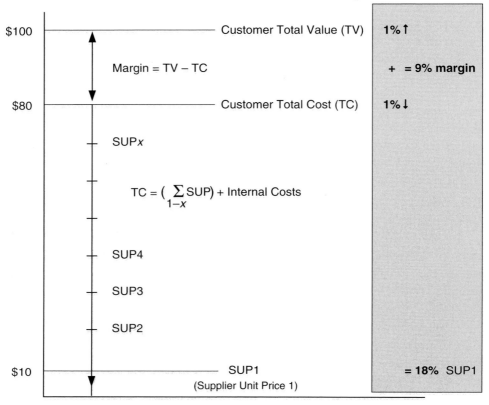

1% up in TV = $1.00 = 10% SUP1
1% dn in TC = $0.80 = $\underline{8\% \text{ SUP1}}$
18% SUP1 or 9% customer margin

$100 — Customer Total Value (TV)   1% ↑

Margin = TV – TC   + = 9% margin

$80 — Customer Total Cost (TC)   1% ↓

SUP*x*

$$TC = (\sum_{1-x} SUP) + \text{Internal Costs}$$

SUP4

SUP3

SUP2

$10 — SUP1   = 18% SUP1
(Supplier Unit Price 1)

Fig. 3.3 *Total value/total cost vs unit price*

price will not only ensure lost opportunity in the marketplace but increase the *angst*, frustration and miscommunication and decrease the performance and quality of the external and internal, customer/supplier relationships. Ultimately, it will have a negative impact on the margin.

While our customer could demand a smaller price decrease across all suppliers to gain equivalent savings initially, the suppliers are unlikely to see this as anything but a blatant act of aggression to gain a one-sided short-term advantage—a situation they will correct with interest at their earliest convenience. The result is a spiralling lose/lose outcome on the back of a degenerating relationship. The tragedy is that most good suppliers are just dying to open up with ideas that will add value. Mostly they are either not asked or ignored. Others are not proactive in offering ideas for fear of being played off

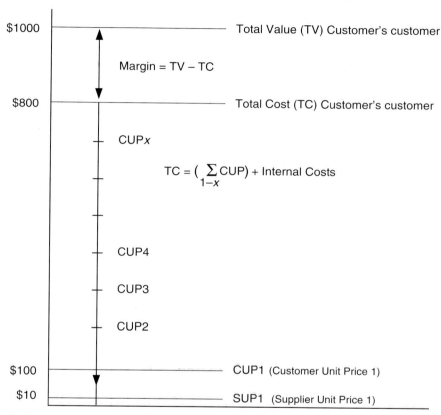

1% up in TV = \$10 = 100% SUP1

1% dn in TC = \$ 8 = 80% SUP1

180% SUP1 or 90% CUP1 margin

$1000 — Total Value (TV) Customer's customer

Margin = TV – TC

$800 — Total Cost (TC) Customer's customer

CUPx

$$TC = (\sum_{1-x} CUP) + \text{Internal Costs}$$

CUP4

CUP3

CUP2

$100 — CUP1 (Customer Unit Price 1)

$10 — SUP1 (Supplier Unit Price 1)

Fig. 3.4 *Total value/total cost vs unit price*

against other suppliers or having the unproven benefits taken as given and therefore justification or trade-off for immediate price decreases.

The extrapolation of this exercise (see Fig. 3.4) to the next step in the supply chain reinforces the additional positive impact of a more integrated supply-chain approach. Let us assume our supplier (SUP1) can impact on the next step in the supply chain (i.e. the customer's customer) by the same amount (1 per cent total value up and 1 per cent total cost down). Keeping the same proportions, the customer's customer total cost is $800, with total value at $1000. The results are a dimensional difference, producing savings equivalent to 180 per cent (i.e. $18/$10) of SUP1, 90 per cent of the customer's margin (i.e. $18/$20) or 9 per cent of the customer's customer's margin.

If you think this is just a whimsical academic exercise, insert your own organisation's numbers and understand its relevance. Brisbane-based computer software company Mincom[9] is developing the software that will allow Caterpillar to manufacture fully automated mine-site vehicles.[10] The benefits for Mincom, Caterpillar and its customers are enormous. Imagine a Caterpillar machine at a remote location, detecting, independently of the machine operator, current and potential problems via preventative and predictive diagnostics. These diagnostics—made up of software, hardware, sensors and other electronic wizardry inside the Caterpillar machine—either adjust the operating conditions of the machine to self-repair or send an electronic signal to a Caterpillar or dealer field technician for immediate response. Within hours of the initial alert the technician can be repairing the machine. On completion, the technician electronically updates the machine's history into a database, the information from which can be used in future design improvements, then prints out an invoice and receives payment by credit card. The impact on machine reliability, efficiency, uptime and hence the mine-site's productivity is enormous. Mincom's involvement is adding significant value for the downstream supply chain to the extent that Caterpillar have taken an 11.5 per cent equity in the company.

Chrysler is another example of how changing the focus from unit price to total value, and from confrontation to cooperation with suppliers, can significantly affect the performance of the organisation for the better and probably forever. 'Partnerships with suppliers have helped Chrysler improve performance significantly by speeding up product development, lowering development costs, and reducing procurement costs, thereby contributing to increases in Chrysler's market share and profitability,' says Jeffrey Dyer, Assistant Professor of Management at the University of Pennsylvania.[11]

In 1989 the giant US automaker was in financial crisis. With a record fourth-quarter loss of $664 million it had fallen to fifth place in the American car market. This parlous state was built on a $4.5 billion unfunded pension fund and a projected $1 billion budget overrun on their newly launched LH program (Chrysler Concord, Eagle, Vision and Dodge Intrepid) which was to be Chrysler's answer to the popular Ford Taurus. Relationships with suppliers had been very traditional up to this point. Short-term (two years), competitively bid contracts based on the lowest unit price were the driving force behind adversarial, unsupportive, low-involvement, low-feedback, low-return, task-based relationships.

A paradigm shift had to be found if the company was to survive. A significant event occurred in August 1989. Robert Lutz, Chrysler's President of Operations and part of the newly formed top-management team, made a speech at the Detroit Athletic Club to executives from twenty-five of Chrysler's largest suppliers. He explained the company's desperate state and the need to lower the costs of both Chrysler and its suppliers, and he wanted their assistance and their ideas to do it. His simple words were, 'All I want is your brainpower, not your margins.' Out of this meeting developed the famous Chrysler SCORE program (Supplier Cost Reduction Effort). The rest, as they say, is history, a well-recorded history of cooperation, partnership and joint success. The SCORE program captures and tracks, online, the ideas for improvement from suppliers. Cross-organisation, multiskilled, cross-functional, vehicle development teams or platform teams then review, select and implement the agreed initiatives and, via the SCORE process, track their progress through to completion.

The Chrysler savings alone have been remarkable. In the five years to December 1995 more than 5300 ideas generated in excess of $1.7 billion in annual savings. In 1996 there was an average of 137 suggestions per week of which two-thirds were approved and implemented, generating $1 billion in value. The vehicle development cycle has reduced from 54 months in the 1980s to 37 months in the mid-1990s. The new sedans from the 1998 Chrysler Concorde and Dodge Intrepid range took 31 months to develop, seven months less than the original versions in 1993. Over this ten-year period the cost of producing a new vehicle has plunged by an estimated 20–40 per cent.

In the spirit of equity and mutuality the savings and benefits from SCORE are then either shared equally with the initiating supplier or reflected in the supplier's larger offtake from Chrysler's growth and increased market share. The choice is up to the supplier. Chrysler regards the SCORE program as the most important method of building trust, lowering system-wide costs, improving communication and not hurting but enhancing supplier profitability. As a result of SCORE and the partnering strategy opposite suppliers, Chrysler improved its profitability from $250 per vehicle average in the 1980s to a record for all US automakers of $2110 per vehicle in 1994. This momentum has been maintained with profit per vehicle in 1996 still running at $2060. The principle of being interested in suppliers' ideas and not their margins, in total value and total cost not unit prices, paid off in a big way for Chrysler and continues to do so.

Rubber giants Michelin and Goodyear have been working with their suppliers and the automakers to develop run-flat tyres.[12] These tyres don't deflate but run for 80km if punctured, without ruining the wheel trim. They are the next step beyond self-sealing tyres. Michelin North America has introduced a run-flat tyre for such medium sedans as the Mazda 626, Ford Mondeo, Saab

900 and Honda Accord. Goodyear supplies run-flat rubber as standard equipment for the latest Chevrolet Corvette. At initially two or three times the price of conventional tyres, it is not just quality, convenience and safety as opposed to unit price per tyre that will make them successful. Goodyear has achieved a run-flat so reliable that the vehicle doesn't need to carry a spare, a key goal for all tyre manufacturers. This is a blessing for designers of sports cars and 4WDs in particular, freeing up new design options and available space and avoiding the dilemma of where to put the fifth tyre—on the tailgate, inside the vehicle or underneath the body. The point is, the impact of tyre development extends beyond the wheel trim and into car design, lower total costs and ultimately the added value the car owner is prepared to pay for. Focusing on value, not unit price, provides benefits up and down the supply chain.

Based on a world-class value-adding strategy, partnerships and alliances should be focused on their ability to increase the margin by lowering total cost and increasing total value. The fascination with downsizing, right-sizing, restructuring, price cutting and cost cutting has led to an unbalanced focus on lowering supplier unit prices at the expense of total value and total cost.

GETTING PAID ON PERFORMANCE OR EFFECT

If you're going to focus on total value and on improving the margin, why not get paid on the same basis? The really clever organisations, and therefore many partnering organisations, get paid not on the basis of unit price at all but on value, in the form of performance or effect of the products and services delivered. For example, selling aircraft tyres on the basis of dollars per landing, not dollars per tyre; companies like Honeywell (Home & Building Control Division) getting paid a percentage of the customers' energy savings, not dollars per hour of engineers' time to achieve those savings; the maintenance company that gets paid for every hour plant and equipment is running, not $/hour to get it running when it breaks down; or the same maintenance company getting paid a percentage of plant hourly output. It's all about getting paid on the basis of performance or effect, not unit price. The simple principle of getting paid on uptime, not downtime, still eludes many maintenance and manufacturing companies.

In my manufacturing days I worked with some outstandingly clever PhD engineers, delivering genuine, unique and differentiated value-added services and getting paid a meagre hourly rate ($100 per hour) for their efforts. I told them they were selling themselves short. The hourly rate, or unit price, totally eclipsed the value of the outcomes they were delivering. In many cases this value amounted to millions of dollars.

Orica Explosives (formerly ICI Explosives) developed a unique form of value and basis of payment. Originally, they sold ammonium nitrate-based explosives in dollars per tonne. This was a simple and effective strategy but limiting in its ability to differentiate them from the competition. Blast technology, both hardware and software, was then developed that allowed ICI technicians to determine the location and quantity of explosives required and the most effective blast sequence to deliver what the mine operators were really interested in. That was a specific particle size distribution of blasted rock within agreed environmental limits that would make for more efficient operation and higher output of the treatment plants. The result is greater profitability for Orica Explosives and reduced overall production costs for the mine operations. For a significant part of their business, Orica Explosives now gets paid not on the basis of dollars per tonne of explosives delivered to the mine site (i.e. unit cost) but on dollars per tonne of broken rock delivered to the treatment plant. Through what is known as the 'Rock on Ground' strategy, they are now truly getting paid on the basis of performance and effect of the explosives delivered rather than their unit cost. A genuine win/win position.

The examples are almost endless: the conveyor belt company that gets paid not on $/metre of conveyor belt delivered but $/hour of conveyor belt operation; the grape grower who gets paid by the wine company not on $/tonne of grapes delivered but percentage of sugar content in the grapes; doctors who are paid for keeping people healthy rather than getting them healthy; lawyers earning a percentage of winning outcome rather than an hourly/daily fee; equipment suppliers being paid per hour of operation not upfront unit sale; suppliers being paid a percentage of customers' profitability, ROA, ROI. The extension of this discussion is putting profit or revenue at risk, to gain or to lose above or below agreed targets based on the over- or under-performance achieved opposite agreed Key Performance Indicator (KPI) targets. Profit gain/pain sharing is discussed in further detail in Chapter 7.

In summary, understand your own core competencies and the core competencies of your supply-chain partners. Focus those core competencies on improving the margin via total cost and value management, and wherever possible get paid on the performance and effect of the products and services delivered. This will require an extensive sharing of information. Alliance partners will initially need to understand where and how their independent corporate and/or internal functional strategies conflict with or complement each other. Only then can an interdependent and joint partnering/alliance strategy be effectively implemented based on shared visions and common goals.

Understanding the real point of differentiation

There may be many points of differentiation beyond the direct product or service delivered. Partnerships in particular involve a long-term package of products and services plus the other tangible and intangible benefits that make up a relationship. These 'other benefits' may involve areas that are strategic, material or personal in nature. They may have no direct bearing on the immediate delivery of the product or service. Combined, however, they may have an enormous influence on the customer's short-, medium- and long-term buying decisions and ultimately on the quality of the relationship itself. Quality, industrial relations, IT solutions are just a sample of areas for consideration. Competitors are at a distinct disadvantage if they fail to recognise these 'other benefits' and the positive effects they have on the customer/supplier relationship. Confusion can often be the result, due to their inability to build strong commercial and personal links, coupled with poor commercial decisions.

REFERENCES

1. Vice-Chairman, Motorola Inc., Supplier Conference 1986. Quoted in Keki Bhote, *Strategic Supply Management*, American Management Association, 1989, p.70.
2. Roderick Carnegie & Matthew Butlin, *Managing the Innovating Enterprise*, Business Council of Australia, 1993, p.xxxiv.
3. Michael E. Porter, *Competitive Advantage: Creating and Sustaining Superior Performance*, The Free Press, London, 1985, p.3.
4. Porter, op. cit., p.3.
5. Porter, op. cit., p.37.
6. Gary Hamel & C.K. Prahalad, *Competing for the Future*, Harvard Business School Press, 1994, p.223.
7. Porter, op. cit., p.129.
8. Jordon D. Lewis, *The Connected Corporation*, Free Press, 1995, p.106.
9. *Business Review Weekly*, 14 July 1997, p.35.
10. Donald Fites, *Harvard Business Review*, April 1996, pp.84–95.
11. Jeffrey H. Dyer, 'How Chrysler created an American Keiretsu', *Harvard Business Review*, July–August 1996, pp.42–56.
12. *Sydney Morning Herald*, 30 January 1998, Drive Section, p.3.

CHAPTER 4

Corporate culture

> *Unlocking the creativity of the people in the workplace is a key source of improvement. This is one of the reasons why employee relations is so important to developing an innovating culture in Australia's enterprises, and why the current environment contains the seeds of a major new opportunity for many enterprises.*
>
> Business Council of Australia [1]

WHAT IS CORPORATE CULTURE?

Corporate culture can be defined as the deep-rooted values, beliefs and underlying assumptions of an organisation that determine how it functions and how it interacts with both its internal and its external environment. It is the heart and soul of the organisation, its personality and character, and is often spoken about in the context of 'the way we do things around here'. It is what causes people to think the way they do, say the things they say and do the things they do when involved with the organisation and its customers and suppliers. Every company and organisation has a culture, be it strong or weak. It will be based on many factors, ranging from the history of the organisation, values, beliefs, symbols, myths and heroes to the influence of the national or regional culture.

At its heart, though, corporate culture is about people—whether the great corporate icons whose feats of daring, intellect or discovery set the direction and shape of an organisation for decades, or the new managers of new corporations implementing first-time visions and business strategies, or middle management and the employees on the shop floor. People behave in ways that are guided by the basic vision and strategy of senior managers. If those visions and strategies are successful over a period of years then a culture emerges that reflects those visions and strategies and the experiences people had in implementing them.

It is not surprising, then, that there is a direct link between corporate culture and leadership. Strong and successful organisations have distinct corporate cultures and produce strong leaders, not only at the top but throughout the organisation. In their book, *Corporate Culture and Performance*, Kotter and Heskett[2] analyse the nature of this relationship. They state:

> *Moreover, when describing how the cultures of the better performers had influenced their results, interviewees often referred to qualities such as leadership, entrepreneurship, prudent risk taking, candid discussions, innovation and flexibility. Those were seen as cultural traits that helped firms do well in a changing business environment. In other words, they saw a causal link going from cultures that value leadership and the other qualities mentioned above to superior performance—an assessment that is entirely consistent with the adaptive culture's viewpoint.*

In talking about customer/supplier partnerships it is necessary to understand the importance and the impact that both the right and the wrong corporate cultures can have on their success. Strategic partnering involves an effective cross-fertilisation of people, skills, functions, departments, suppliers, locations, ideas and innovation. The importance of these base values and beliefs to the people involved and their effect on the success of the partnership over time is obvious. Managing these varied relationships and cultures as well as their rate of change is one of the great challenges for strategic partnering. Successful corporate and partnering cultures of the future will require intense curiosity mixed with a large amount of humility.

Deal and Kennedy,[3] in their book *Corporate Cultures: The Rites and Rituals of Corporate Life*, outline four generic culture types. Their development was based on the relationships between the degree of risk associated with companies' activities and the speed at which the companies and their employees received feedback on whether those decisions or strategies were successful. This is risk as a function of capital, consequence and probability. The four cultures are shown in Figure 4.1.

1. The **tough-guy, macho culture** (high risk/fast feedback)
   Fortunes and failures can be made overnight in this world of high risk and quick feedback. For example, while it might take a year to make a

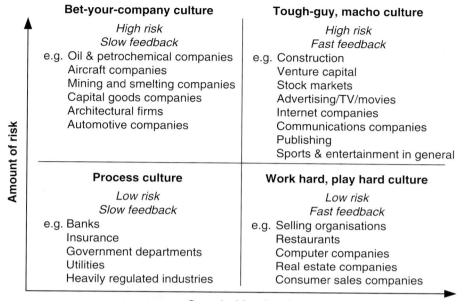

Fig. 4.1 *A simple culture quadrant*

feature-length movie at a cost of tens of millions of dollars, it may need only a couple of weeks at the box office to determine its success or failure. These are the high rollers, the true entrepreneurs, risking all for high returns. Construction, stockbrokers, venture capital companies, advertising, television, movies, the entertainment industry, computers and Internet companies in general fall into this category.

Quick decision making, action-oriented, aggressive, individualistic, temperamental, short-sighted and superstitious are the terms that best describe this culture type.

2. The **work hard, play hard culture** (low risk/fast feedback)

This is the culture of the super salesperson. The primary values of this culture centre on customer service. While this is true of any sales department, in the corporate sense it refers to sales-oriented organisations. Typically, they will be the service industries, computer companies, restaurant chains, McDonald's, and retail organisations and distributors. This is a world of small risks where no one is going to lose their job over a lost sale, but the feedback is fast. You have the sale or you don't. High activity, initiative, a work hard/play hard mentality, a volume orientation, and the quick fix rather than the permanent solution describe this culture type.

3. The **bet-your-company culture** (high risk/slow feedback)
    Oil companies, aircraft designers and manufacturers, and petrochemical and mining companies would fit this culture type, where large investments and therefore high risk are associated with returns over a long period. In many cases it may be three to five to ten years or more. In this situation it is not so much 'careers on the line', as with the tough guys, but the downfall of entire corporations or business units in the event of only a couple of failures. The values of the 'bet-your-company' culture focus on the long-term future and the importance of investing in it. Maturity, respect for authority, age and experience, a long-term perspective, and measured and deliberate decision making are typical traits.
4. The **process culture** (low risk/slow feedback)
    This is a world of bureaucracy where actions, initiatives and creativity get lost in the paper trail and the hierarchy. Because of the lack of feedback, employees tend to focus on *how* they do a task rather than on *what* they do. Banks, insurance companies, government agencies, utilities and heavily regulated industries would normally live here. Protective, cautious, orderly, formal, procedural, departmental, hierarchical and paying attention to detail would be typical characteristics. Deregulation and privatisation are moving many of these organisations out of their comfort zones and into a world of earning and accountability and therefore a higher-risk, faster-feedback environment.

Of course, no organisation fits neatly into any one of these categories. The variety of culture types that usually exists in any organisation is one of the major challenges for all its employees, particularly where partnerships are involved. To manage the many different culture types that will be found among divisions, functions and departments will require exceptional skills. All four culture types are quite likely to be found in the one organisation.

Take, for example, an existing petrochemical company making a new investment. From a strategy point of view the culture would most probably be 'bet-your-company', as petrochemicals are highly capital-intensive with a long-term return on investment perspective. A world-scale ethylene cracker plant or plastics plant could cost $250 million, each with lead times from conception to startup of three years or more. The earliest pay-back period is probably two to five years after that. Yet the existing business, particularly sales, marketing and production, would most probably have a 'work hard/play hard' culture, whether commodity or differentiated products were involved. And finance and administration would probably fit the bureaucratic mould of a process culture. In fact, it could be said that the best performers are organisations that have successfully blended the best elements of the four culture types and are able to adapt appropriately when the environment around them inevitably changes.

Why look at corporate cultures in this way, and what is their connection with strategic partnering? First, while Deal and Kennedy first proposed this model in the early 1980s, the categories and characteristics are still very relevant today. Second, it is inconceivable to me, or at the very least defeatist, to think that strategic partnering is not applicable to all four generic culture types and could not be successfully implemented in each of them. There is no reason why both the principles and practice of partnerships should not be equally applicable to oil companies, mining companies, construction companies, advertising companies, computer companies, restaurant chains, insurance companies, government departments or any other company or organisation. These organisations may be at various points on the learning and development curve but all have customers and suppliers of varying size and importance. The very best of these organisations are world class or striving to be. And all but the very worst of performers see the connection between world best practice, overall performance and customer satisfaction.

Successful partnering will depend on the flexibility of the partnership process and the variation in application appropriate to the focus and nature of the organisation and its business environment.

So, is there a partnership culture overlaying these four generic cultures, a culture that is compatible and will also improve upon what, in reality, will be a mixture of these generic cultures for any one organisation? The answer is yes, and it should be no surprise that the partnership culture I am suggesting here is similar to, and completely synergistic with, the corporate cultures pervading today's leading organisations.

THE CORPORATE CULTURE OF PARTNERSHIPS AND ALLIANCES

I have detailed the characteristics of the partnership culture under nine headings.[4]

1. **Autonomy**: the ability of individuals to exercise initiative in their jobs. Initiative is directly connected with innovation, ownership and commitment, all of which hold high office in the world of partnering and alliancing at both a personal and a team level. There is no need for prompting here. High performance through the effective application of skills has earned the right and the desire to exercise initiative. Initiative here is also

associated with calculated and educated risk taking and the ability and willingness of individuals to think 'outside the conventional square'.

2. **Control**: the nature of the coordination procedures used in the organisation. Individuals and teams can show initiative because there are few restrictions on communication and decision making. Partnerships are a place for leaders, not managers. People are well aware of their roles and responsibilities and those of others. The problems associated with hierarchies and roadblocking, procrastinating middle and senior management have given way to flat organisations where empowerment, accountability and leadership at every level are encouraged. The role of management is critical here in creating such an environment and allowing it to improve and develop via clear vision, effective strategies and active and constructive participation. Management are the source of inspiration, not perspiration.

3. **Recognition and reward for performance**: the behaviours that are valued and rewarded in the organisation. Skills development, initiative, innovation, leadership qualities and their successful implementation opposite internal and external customers and suppliers are the qualities most valued and rewarded in the world of strategic partnering. The logic is quite simple, really. Applying genuine skills both as individuals and as groups leads to competence and high quality. Competence, associated with initiative on the right technology base, leads to innovation and competitive advantage. Strong and effective leadership from all levels allows for good communication, effective teamwork, quick resolution of conflict and the removal of hidden agendas and departmental barriers. Strong and effective leadership combined with innovation and competitive advantage gives the organisation a sustainable and high level of return on investment. A high level of return on investment allows the organisation to reinvest to achieve higher returns, to employ more skilled and committed people who are happy in what they do and who they work for. This state of affairs is to the benefit of customers in general, the customer partners in particular, other stakeholders and the general economy and society at large.

    Financial rewards are based on performance achieved against a mix of financial and non-financial goals and objectives and are not linked to short-term, self-interest based financial targets.

4. **Change tolerance**: the willingness and capability of the organisation to change. Because of the nature of the people employed and the environment that has been developed, both the willingness and the capability to change are ever present. Partnerships are highly flexible and responsive places. They have to be. Partnerships can only survive in a world-class, best practice environment. They lie at the leading edge of innovation and

competitive advantage. Change is not something this culture lives with but something it continually creates and adapts to.

5. **Conflict tolerance**: the manner in which conflict arises and how it is managed. Because of the quality of leadership and a total quality approach at all levels, together with an absence of rivalry between departments and functions, when conflict arises it is handled quickly and effectively on a win/win basis. The same approach exists externally with customers and suppliers. This can occur because of the open environment based on shared information, trust and mutual respect. Partnerships and alliances are not about blame or confrontation but embrace constructive feedback and teamwork.

6. **External coping**: the manner in which the organisation understands and responds to its external environment. It is the external environment—and primarily satisfying current and future needs of customers and potential customers—that drives the partnering culture in the first place. 'Customers are the reason suppliers exist' and 'If you don't have a customer you don't have a job' are philosophies that pervade the culture. By necessity, this leads to a proactive approach in understanding and developing unique benefits opposite competitors. Working with suppliers, in some cases as partners, will create the same advantage. Flexibility and responsiveness within an atmosphere of total quality management are the drivers to the external environment.

7. **Internal organising**: the nature of collaboration and cooperation within the organisation. Cross-functional/interdepartmental, integrated teamwork based on trust, skills, leadership and cooperation, all focused on the external environment, is the key to the success of the internal organisation of partnerships. Tribalism is out and self-directed, self-managed teamwork and integrated project teams are in. This is all driven by the clear vision and effective strategies of the senior managers; strategies that are shared with all in the organisation and are well understood and supported by them. This cohesive state is assisted by a flat organisation where communication is open and easy.

8. **Identity**: the manner in which employees identify with the organisation. Employees identify with the company vision with pride and a sense of commitment. They are proud to be associated with the organisation, not only for what it has achieved but for how it has been accomplished. They also feel, quite rightly, that they have played a significant part in that success. Self-confidence and high levels of self-respect and self-esteem typify employees in a partnering culture, and this carries over very much into their personal life as well. In many respects the organisation is an extension

of their family, with a great deal of social activity taking place with work associates.

9. **Communication**: the pattern and extent of information exchange within the organisation. Communication is completely open, direct and based on shared information. The paper trail of endless memos and reports that clog up and frustrate the system doesn't exist. This is mainly because the degree of ownership that individuals have in the decision-making process requires less asking and telling and more doing. Their view is that it is better to seek forgiveness than to ask for permission. People talk to each other a lot more, particularly face to face, and this direct contact builds up confidence and trust. Communication like this results in things being done without the need to ask people to do them and then having to supervise their progress. Electronic communications and computing skills also play a significant role in improving the productivity of communication and avoiding duplication of effort.

How will this extraordinary environment be developed and sustained? Robert Porter Lynch, in his book *Business Alliances Guide*, gives us a hint when he says 'creation is given birth by people in a perpetual state of enlightened dissatisfaction'.[5] An ongoing sense of urgency within individuals, teams and the organisation, in search of improvement and excellence, will be the driving force. Judith Bardwick[6] talks about the bell curve relationship between productivity (y-axis) and anxiety (x-axis) in her book *Danger in the Comfort Zone*. Low productivity is related to low or high levels of anxiety, which produce an environment of what the author calls 'comfort zone' entitlement or fear, respectively. High productivity is delivered by mid-level (top of the bell curve) anxiety or an appropriate level of discomfort. This is an environment of earning for the individual, team and organisation. Continually maintaining this state of discomfort and 'enlightened dissatisfaction' with the status quo will be the key to producing the required creativity and innovation to take the relationship through the phases of the partnership development curve.

PARTNERING AND ALLIANCES—PRINCIPLES, VALUES, CONCEPTS AND PRACTICES

Figure 4.2 outlines the elements that make up the principles, values, concepts and practices that apply to partnering and alliances. For partnering relationships and alliances, there is a difference between principles and values.

Principles are those undeniable, self-evident and fundamental truths that are immutable and non-negotiable. They are, or should be, universal and

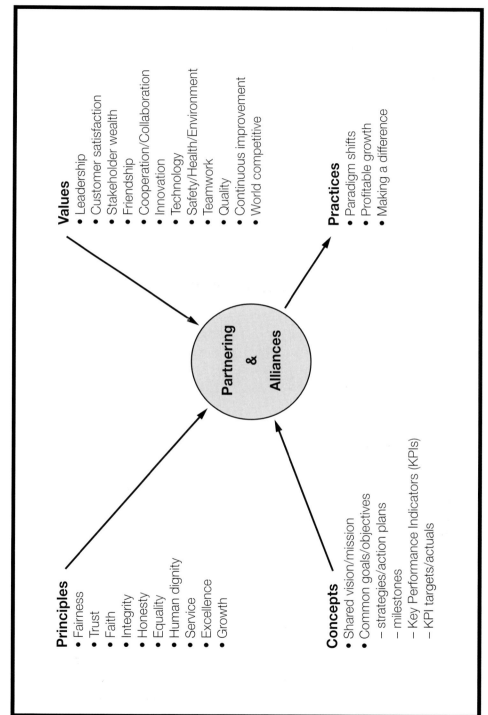

Principles
- Fairness
- Trust
- Faith
- Integrity
- Honesty
- Equality
- Human dignity
- Service
- Excellence
- Growth

Values
- Leadership
- Customer satisfaction
- Stakeholder wealth
- Friendship
- Cooperation/Collaboration
- Innovation
- Technology
- Safety/Health/Environment
- Teamwork
- Quality
- Continuous improvement
- World competitive

Partnering & Alliances

Concepts
- Shared vision/mission
- Common goals/objectives
  – strategies/action plans
  – milestones
  – Key Performance Indicators (KPIs)
  – KPI targets/actuals

Practices
- Paradigm shifts
- Profitable growth
- Making a difference

Fig. 4.2 *Partnering and alliances: principles, values, concepts and practices*

non-specific to any faith, culture, country or business sector. Specifically, think what a partnering relationship would look like if it were based on the opposites of the principles listed in Figure 4.2. Not an attractive proposition, I'm sure you would agree.

Values are those human qualities or characteristics used to achieve the vision and mission of the organisation and hence are often seen in mission and vision statements. They will vary in degree and application from one organisation to another. In the words of Stephen Covey[7] 'a gang of thieves can share values, but they are in violation of the fundamental principles'.

The concepts or ideas as applied to partnering are based on sharedness. Not only sharing strategy, information and the like, but having a shared or joint vision, common goals and performance indicators and therefore a shared future for which the partners hold themselves mutually accountable. The practices revolve around doing something fundamentally different rather than small variations on business as usual. That is, gaining benefit from displacing as appropriate the prevailing paradigms and replacing them with new paradigms based on new rules, new boundaries, new problems to solve and new opportunities to take advantage of.

It is not difficult to see how the partnering principles, values, concepts and practices are directly linked to the culture of the organisation. Understanding the degree of alignment or misalignment of cultures between the alliance partners then becomes critical to the long-term well-being of the relationship.

THE RELATIONSHIP BETWEEN BUSINESS CULTURE AND COUNTRY CULTURE

Some would argue that the two major types of culture, that is, country (national/regional) culture and business culture, are quite different and should not be confused. After several years of working in the Far East, my view is that the two are inextricably linked. The country culture is born out of hundreds, even thousands, of years of history. The basic values and beliefs of the society have been shaped by religion, climate, geography, politics and time. It is impossible to imagine that these influences will not flow over to business in various forms. After all, it is people who lie at the heart of business, not machines. The culture of the organisation must in some way reflect the culture of its surroundings.

I was working in South Korea during the mid-1980s with ICI, looking at acquisitions, joint ventures and the licensing of technology. One particular joint venture that we were negotiating was a large, 200 000 tonnes per annum, $300 million petrochemical project with a Korean company. Negotiations—often drawn-out and even hostile on occasions—had been going on for nine months. We were at the stage where a 200-page document had been produced and serious discussions were taking place on management participation and control, profit shares, plant design and layout. Our Korean partner was also talking to a Japanese manufacturer about a similar investment. It is well known that there is no love lost between the Japanese and the Koreans (as a short reading of history over the last 100 years will testify) so all of us on the ICI team were feeling very comfortable with progress to date.

At the end of a particularly long meeting in London, I asked: 'All things being equal, wouldn't you rather deal with ICI than the Japanese company?' President Kim responded: 'All things being equal, there is no question we would always do business with the Japanese.' Somewhat surprised, I asked why. He answered: 'Well, we understand them and we have very similar cultures. Basically, while we don't like the Japanese from an historical perspective, we understand them better than the western culture. We think the way they do!'

The end result some months later was that our Korean partner and the Japanese company formed a 50/50 per cent joint venture. The size of the JV document was twenty pages (not 200). That joint venture still stands today as a successful ongoing operation.

The point is that it was the quality of the relationship and the similarity of cultures and thinking that were of primary importance to the Koreans, not the financial, management and other technical details.

THE NATURE OF LOW-PERFORMANCE CULTURES

It is useful to understand the main characteristics of low-performance cultures. Unfortunately, we have all seen them at one time or another and even today they are all too familiar. Kotter and Heskett studied the relationship between poor performance and culture in twenty large organisations in the United States. They came up with the following conclusions.

1. Managers tended to be arrogant.
2. Managers tended not to place a high value on customers, stockholders or employees.
3. These cultures were hostile to values such as leadership or other engines of change.

There was a similarity among these firms in that they had been initially propelled—either by good leadership and strategy, or good luck—into a position of market dominance and economic success. The rest of the story I quote directly from Kotter and Heskett.

This dominance, or lack of competition associated with it, brought these firms great success in terms of both growth and profitability over a period of years during which they experienced little real adversity. But sustained growth created huge internal challenges: more and more employees were hired; the organisations grew larger and larger; day-to-day operations became more and more complex. To cope with the internal organisational challenges, executives sought, hired, developed and promoted skilled managers who were not necessarily leaders—that is, people who understood structures and systems and budgets and controls much better than they did vision and strategies and culture and inspiration. In time these individuals became top executives. With the changes in personnel, the relative ease with which these people were able to create revenue and profit growth, given the strong market position, and the behaviour of top management, any collective sense of why the firm was successful in the first place was lost along the way.[7]

Do not underestimate the importance of culture in the development of customer/supplier partnerships.

FROM CRISIS TO OPPORTUNITY

A crisis always brings out the best and the worst in people. In situations of war, marriage and sport, as well as business, how many times have we seen victory being snatched from the jaws of defeat? How often have we seen teamwork, loyalty, skill, guts and determination lead to success and be rewarded by undying respect and trust from friends, family and peers? Relationships in business are no different. The quickest and probably the easiest way of developing a good relationship with a customer or supplier, based on all the right qualities, is to solve an immediate problem. The bigger and more urgent the problem, the better, especially if it is solved in a quality way, namely:

1.   Define the problem.
2.   Put a quick fix in place.
3.   Determine the root cause.
4.   Implement corrective action.
5.   Evaluate and follow up.

Permanent solutions to seemingly insurmountable problems are very impressive things. Unfortunately, they tend to be treated as one-off events rather than opportunities, and hence a feeling of relief rather than excitement when the problem is resolved. A culture must be developed where employees actively seek out crises and problems, whether caused by their own organisation or not. Problems and crises occur every day in areas within and outside the domain of your organisation's product or services.

You will find you have areas of expertise throughout your organisation that you never knew existed, expertise that often your customers and suppliers don't have. Create an inquisitive environment and train your people to seek out problems and solve them, turning crises into opportunities. This will require very specific training and coaching—communication and problem-solving skills, observation and questioning skills, analytical and SPC skills, computing skills, teamwork and leadership skills.

I'm not talking just about crisis management here, but crisis recognition. My experience is that major and urgent problems occur on a daily basis outside the usual involvement with your customers or potential customers. But we are not trained to act upon the indicators. Take advantage of these unique opportunities to 'show your stuff', consolidate the relationship and further your competitive advantage.

THE 'BIG PICTURE' FOR CUSTOMERS AND SUPPLIERS

To summarise: what is the connection between culture, strategy, structure, process and people across the three relationship types of vendor, supplier and partner? The 'big picture' is shown in Figure 4.3. *Vendor organisations* have a vendor culture, a least-cost, lowest-priced based strategy, a traditional limited contact selling/supply structure and a basic selling/transaction process, and are serviced by sales representatives, traders and other 'deal makers'. *Supplier organisations* have a customer-focused, continuous-improvement, total-quality culture, a differentiated strategy based on cost or value or a combination of both, and a multilevel selling structure; they operate within a complex selling and buying process where the accounts are serviced by account managers, good project managers or key account managers, depending on the quality and size of the relationship. *Partnering organisations* operate under a highly flexible, empowering partnership culture with world-class or best practice, value-adding strategies, a team-based structure and a process of relationship management; they are managed by the partnering/alliance manager acting as coach to the self-managed partnering and alliance team(s). Understanding the degree of alignment between customers and suppliers opposite these five relationship components of culture, strategy, structure, process and people, across the 0 to 10 relationship management scale, will be critical for the management of all important relationships, not only partnerships and alliances.

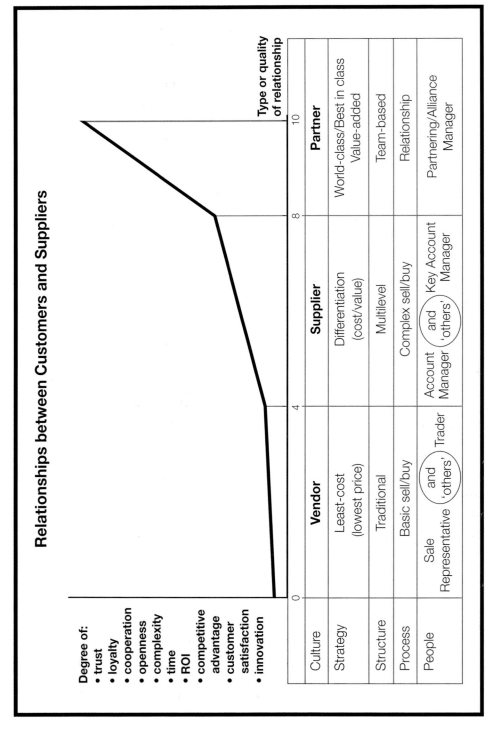

Fig. 4.3　*Relationships between customers and suppliers and the five relationship components*

Of course, it is extremely unlikely that any one company will be built around a customer/supplier base of purely vendors or suppliers or partners. In reality, especially with larger organisations, a spread of vendor, supplier and partner relationships will be required. The question then is: how can you have a mixture of cultures, strategies, structure, processes and people, within the one organisation, that can effectively manage such a wide range of relationships? The answer is that organisations capable of higher-level relationships are quite able to adapt and modify their operations and behaviour to suit lower-level relationships.

An organisation does not have to take on 'multiple personalities' in order to service this wide range of customers and suppliers effectively. Supplier organisations will more than adequately be able to adjust their culture, strategy, structure, process and people to manage vendor relationships. Likewise, partner organisations will have the flexibility and be developed to the stage where they can adapt themselves easily and effectively to supplier and vendor relationships. This is possible because of the level and quality of skills, technology and processes that have been developed and the maturity, knowledge and experience of people at the higher levels.

For example, meeting customer product and service requirements In Full On Time to A1 specification will have the same meaning for vendors as it does for partners. It will be the level of complexity, innovation, resources and skills that will increase up the relationship scale. Often, it also happens that customer/supplier relationships develop progressively from vendor through supplier status to partnership. Lessons and skills learnt through practical experience are seldom forgotten.

The reverse position, however, does not apply. Vendor organisations will not be capable of forming effective supplier or partner relationships. Even at a level of 7 on the relationship scale (see Fig. 4.3), a supplier will be unable to sustain the requirements of a genuine partnership. It is possible to come down the scale to manage relationships. It is impossible to go up the relationship scale unless the appropriate environment, processes and people have been developed. It is easy to see why partnerships cannot operate in isolation from the rest of the business, and how the benefits of a genuine partnership can have a positive influence on the lower-level relationships. The average quality of all customer/supplier relationships will be seen to be raised.

Again, the reality will be that no organisation will fit neatly into any single category of vendor, supplier or partner. Culture, strategy, structure, process and people will be at different stages of development. So don't think that skills in trading, project management, account management and key account management are not important. Even the best organisations, genuinely focused on strategic partnering and alliancing, will require a mixture of these skills. There is no doubt, though, that it will be the partnering and alliance managers and all those associated with the relationship who will determine the rate of progress for world-class, best in class organisations in their search for excellence and best practice.

We learn more about the nature of the partnering processes, the twelve partnering steps and the people who operate them in the following chapters.

REFERENCES

1. Roderick Carnegie & Matthew Butlin, *Managing the Innovating Enterprise*, Business Council of Australia, 1993, p.21.
2. John P. Kotter & James L. Heskett, *Corporate Culture and Performance*, The Free Press, New York, 1992, p.47.
3. Terrence Deal & Allen Kennedy, *Corporate Cultures: The Rites and Rituals of Corporate Life*, Penguin, Harmondsworth, 1988, pp.107–27.
4. Gattorna Chorn, *Strategy Spotlight*, vol. 2, Nov. 1992, Gattorna Chorn Business Strategists.
5. Robert Porter Lynch, *Business Alliances Guide*, John Wiley, 1993, p.279.
6. Judith Bardwick, *Danger in the Comfort Zone*, AMACOM, 1993.
7. Stephen R. Covey, *The Seven Habits of Highly Effective People*, The Business Library, 1990, p.35.
8. Kotter & Heskett, op. cit., p.70.

PART B

THE STRATEGIC
PARTNERING PROCESS

CHAPTER 5

Introduction: motivators, steps and outcomes

> *Strategic partnering and alliancing is a process, not an event; a journey, not a destination.*

AN OVERVIEW OF THE STRATEGIC PARTNERING PROCESS

The strategic partnering process is the basis on which customer and supplier partners are chosen and the relationship developed, managed and improved upon. It is the mechanism enabling all the available internal and external resources and skills to be put to effective use, as appropriate to the time, place, people and organisations, in order to achieve the desired outcomes. It applies to all organisations (big or small) and to all areas, whether service industries, manufacturing, public or private sector organisations. The partnering process is also applicable to customer/supplier relationships internal to the organisation, between teams, departments, functions, business and other operating units.

To make partnerships work, you need a simple yet sustainable quality process that is flexible enough to allow for plenty of creativity and imagination yet provides the structure for measurement and reproducibility. The process should provide a structure that enables people to think 'outside the square' as opposed to rigid 'belts and braces' procedures that so often confine or force people to think conventionally. The key word is guidelines. The partnering process is really a set of guidelines. You interpret and implement these guidelines in the way that best suits your own environment.

As strategic partnering and alliance relationships are about long-term and never-ending continuous improvement, there can be no finish to the partnering process. It is ongoing. It also applies to every part of the business chain—raw material suppliers, manufacturers, converters, distributors, wholesalers, retailers, trades and services. Environments, strategies and tactics will change but the same fundamental principles and process steps will apply. All parts of the business chain face similar imperatives.

The entire process of partnering upstream with suppliers and downstream with customers is summarised in Figure 5.1. Irrespective of the partner's position in the supply chain the principles, processes and practices are exactly the same. As discussed in Chapter 1, the process of customers partnering with suppliers upstream in the supply or value chain is exactly the same as suppliers partnering with customers downstream in the supply or value chain. Both logic and commonsense dictate this must be so. Openness and transparency based on shared vision and common goals for long-term mutual benefit require the consistency and simplicity of a single approach. The process can be looked at in three sections which I have called *motivators*, *steps* and *outcomes*.

THE TWELVE MOTIVATORS

The twelve motivators are the driving forces behind the process. They provide the reasons and the motivation to propel the partnership continually forward. It is from the motivators that innovation, creativity and the freedom and ability to think and act are born. In terms of cause and effect, the motivators are the cause and the outcomes are the effect. The motivators then become the basis for reward and recognition of the partnering process. Any significant change or improvement should be capable of being traced back to the motivators. Within a true partnership, the motivators will not only impact on the specific customer/supplier relationship but contribute significantly to the overall well-being of the customer/supplier organisations. I have personally witnessed the positive and negative impact of each of the twelve motivators physically and emotionally and from a bottom-line perspective.

In moving from one step to another, the motivators are prompted in the process by the question: 'Will the next step . . . ?'

Will the next step . . . ?

1. Add value
2. Reduce costs
3. Improve communication

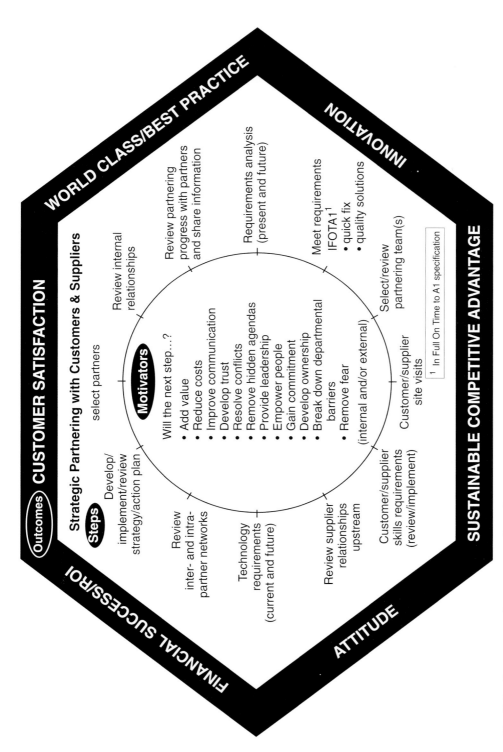

Fig. 5.1 *Partnering with customers and suppliers*

4.   Develop trust
5.   Resolve conflicts
6.   Remove hidden agendas
7.   Provide leadership
8.   Empower people
9.   Gain commitment
10. Develop ownership
11. Break down departmental barriers
12. Remove fear

It is important that there is a common understanding of what the motivators mean. The definitions I have used in the partnering context are as follows.

Add value

In terms of differentiation within the partnership supply chain, does the adding of value provide something unique that is of value to buyers and sellers beyond a lower price? This will also be the basis for the value proposition. Are the benefits achieved in the performance or effect of the product or service greater than the cost of creating them for the seller and greater than the premium paid by the buyer? Will more of the product or service be sold at the same price, or will other benefits such as greater customer loyalty, referred business or longer-term commitments be gained? The adding of value could also involve the provision of products and services beyond the original products and services for which the supplier is being paid and the exploitation of synergies between the partner organisations. Are the benefits produced and delivered going to be sustainable?

Reduce costs

For the buyer and/or the seller, do the activities performed produce a lower total cost in the process, product or service?

Improve communication

Communication includes anything that helps individuals, groups and teams—internal or external—to relate more effectively to each other, irrespective of their level or role in the organisation; to have a clearer understanding of what other individuals, groups and teams do, and to participate in those activities that will add value for the business. Sharing information in an open, honest, accurate and timely manner, a helpful, open attitude, and respecting and trusting others will be the keys to good communication. Communication comes in all forms—verbal and non-verbal, face to face, and long-distance by using any or all of the available technologies.

Develop trust

Trust, in the context of strategic partnering, is based on a value system involving confidence, competence, reliance, interdependence, respect, strength of character, honesty, integrity and openness. It requires a firm belief that people, whether individuals or groups, will act as they say they will. On that basis, others are prepared to undertake risk and make decisions or specific recommendations.

Resolve conflicts

Will the partnership/alliance be able to resolve the problems of confrontation, miscommunication and misunderstandings of an adversarial nature to the mutual benefit of all parties concerned—a win/win, 'no blame, high accountability' philosophy?

Remove hidden agendas

Hidden agendas are issues, views, opinions or intentions that individuals or groups deliberately wish not to be brought out into the open (for reasons best known to themselves) and which differ from their publicly held views or statements. These hidden issues, which differ from the public or general perception, are the real cause of why people speak and act the way they do. Removing hidden agendas will be one of the cornerstones of improving communication in particular and assisting the other motivators generally. Unfortunately, hidden agendas can exist at any level of the organisation. Seek them out and remove them. They are destructive and debilitating.

Provide leadership

How can the relationship and associated business activities give genuine leaders the chance to lead and potential leaders the opportunity to learn? The ability to create and lead a vision, to lead by example and inspire others to follow, and the strength of personality and character to get the job done, typify good leadership. Colin Powell, US Secretary of State and an outstandingly successful leader of demonstrated ability, says in his autobiography, 'Leadership is the art of accomplishing more than the science of management says is possible.'

Empower people

Broaden people's responsibilities and accountabilities. Delegate to the shop floor and increase their levels of authority. Allow people to make more of their own decisions. Encourage calculated and educated risk taking. Applaud failure when genuine creativity and innovation have been implemented but have been unsuccessful due to factors beyond control. Reward success when the boundaries have been pushed back. The level of empowerment achieved will only be effective if the appropriate training is implemented and the necessary skills and competencies developed. Empowerment builds confidence, competence and, therefore, trust which in turn will deliver results over and above what would otherwise have been.

Gain commitment

Do the activities generated by the partnering process gain the unwavering support of others who would otherwise be less supportive or would not normally have been involved in the process and who will follow the activities through to completion?

Develop ownership

Developing ownership begins with giving employees recognition for successful outcomes and the personal commitment involved in achieving them. It is about people and teams successfully handling responsibilities, tasks and accountabilities as if they were their own design or creation. This will also involve strong elements of leadership and empowerment.

Break down departmental barriers

Departmental barriers between business functions are roadblocks to effective communication and the doing of good business within and between organisations. The barriers can be real or perceived, physical or non-physical, and due to reasons that may be historical, cultural, personal, technological or organisational. Fundamentally, however, it comes down to poor management and leadership. As with hidden agendas, departmental barriers can be particularly destructive and debilitating and they must be sought out, broken down and removed. They can lead to organisational silos, factions and fiefdoms. Their legacy can be higher costs, duplication, lower productivity and efficiency, poor communication, reduced effectiveness and increasingly frustrated employees.

Remove fear

Edwards Deming says:[1] 'Fear takes a horrible toll. Fear is all around, robbing people of their pride, hurting them, robbing them of a chance to contribute to the company. Replace fear with freedom and security.'

Fear manifests itself in many forms: fear of asking questions; of making mistakes; of taking risks; of challenging the system; of losing your job; of failing to meet management budget targets; of the appraisal/performance system; of new technology; uncertainty about the future.

John McConnell,[2] a Deming devotee, says in his book, *Safer than a Known Way*: '. . . fear is negative and destructive. It destroys morale and teamwork, it corrupts data; it damages quality and thus productivity. I do not believe any management theory can work in a company driven by fear, let alone a theory that requires fundamental change in attitudes and methods.'

THE TWELVE STEPS

The **twelve steps** provide the vehicle and structure by which the motivators, as the drivers of the process, can be realised. As with any successful process there must be a balance between structure and flexibility. Critical to successful implementation is the understanding that the steps are not necessarily sequential; they can be done in any order that is appropriate to the organisation and environment. As well, more than one step can and should be undertaken at any one time. The process is continuous and never-ending. A summary of the twelve steps is given below.

Select a partner

Choosing a partner will initially be based on your business strategy, general operating environment and a strong understanding of the competition—then understand, from the customer's perspective, the relationship between strategic value and commercial value, that is the impact, criticality or importance of the products and/or services delivered and their $ value. Once this is understood, determine each partner's or potential partner's willingness and capability to form strong, long-term partnerships and alliances. Place the most important relationships on the 0 to 10 Relationship Management Matrix (see Fig. 1.4), noting both the current and desired states. Also take the opportunity to rank or categorise where the non-partner, customer/supplier relationships sit on the 0 to 10 Relationship Management Matrix and agree how these relationships are to be resourced, managed and, as appropriate, improved.

Review internal relationships

A review of internal relationships should be carried out to ensure that your own organisation is capable of developing and sustaining partnerships. Earning trust, sharing information, resolving conflicts, removing roadblocks and improving internal communication will be the key issues. It's all very well wanting to build open and transparent, trusting, high performance relationships externally with customers, suppliers and complimentors but if your own organisation cannot meet the same or similar standards, is not willing or is not capable, then it is going to be a very difficult and potentially unfulfilling journey.

Review process with partner and share information

The purpose of initially reviewing the partnership process with your partner is to share the principles and process and associated practices of strategic partnering and alliancing, your vision and strategies, and information generally. You also need to determine how, when and by whom these reviews are going to take place. Your partner must be equally committed and supportive of the process if success is to be achieved. The partnering/alliance workshop will be one of the major and most effective forms of review.

The initial workshop will most likely involve reaching agreement on the current state of the relationship, shared vision, common goals and joint key performance indicators and generally signing off on the 'rules of engagement' for the relationship. Ongoing reviews or workshops will involve such things as review of performance, opportunities for improvement, celebration and recognition of success, general education, reaffirming or renewing the shared vision, goals, strategies and performance indicators and the general rules of engagement.

Analyse requirements (present and future)

It is impossible to embark on a journey unless you know where you are going and how to get there. An analysis and documentation of requirements or the scope of the relationship both current and future is fundamental to a total quality approach and the basis from which a strong relationship and future innovation will develop.

Ensure In Full On Time to A1 specification (IFOTA1) conformance to requirements

(a) *The quick fix*

There is no point talking about strong, long-term relationships and future opportunities unless the basic day-to-day requirements are being met first time and every time. This is the 'quick fix' section. Permanent solutions via prevention and other quality systems development must follow. Focus on the hourly, daily and weekly detail must not be lost if the future is to be proactively and creatively searched for, and credibility maintained.

(b) *Ensure IFOTA1 (quality solutions)*
Delivering product and service In Full On Time to A1 specification first time and every time is one thing. Doing it in a quality way may be entirely another. The cost of customer satisfaction and, in turn, the cost of the partnership can be exorbitant if the quality culture and processes are not in place. This step is about attending to the detail of ensuring that innovative solutions and the right systems and procedures are in place to eliminate non-conformances and develop sustainable and stable processes.

Select and review partnering and alliance team members

Successful partnerships are about successful teamwork and good governance. Develop, coach and empower a core group(s) of people, selected for their skills and ability to meet and exceed customer needs and meet future expectations. They will in turn sponsor other individuals and other teams from customer and supplier, and from other support organisations, in delivering continuous improvement. This will involve understanding the roles, responsibilities and accountabilities of the partnering/alliance leadership teams and operational/management teams.

Carry out customer/supplier site visits

Site visits are essential if you are to become familiar with plant, equipment and services, the way the exchange of information is handled, and to understand the people issues at first hand. Equally important is the chance to meet and befriend the people and to understand the culture and 'soul' of each other's organisations. Genuine friendship based on trust, respect and common goals is a difficult bond to break, and removes the likelihood of deception or misleading behaviour. Site visits make this happen.

Review and implement customer/supplier skills requirements

World-class/best practice companies in world-class/best practice relationships will require people with world-class skills where competence, not training, is measured and a learning environment is developed, encouraged and supported. Skills and competency requirements must be under constant review to drive the ongoing innovation that sustains the partnership and the organisation's competitive advantage. In this step, the organisation's culture and leadership style is as important as training and skills development.

Review relationships with supplier(s) upstream

Irrespective of whether your organisation is the customer or supplier in the relationship, how effective you are at partnering will depend on how you treat and selectively partner with your suppliers upstream in the supply chain. Are your dealings with them good, bad or indifferent? You are only one link in the chain and all links must be strong if success is to be realised. Don't forget that your customer sees you as a supplier, not a customer. How well do you treat your suppliers? Understand the opportunities and benefits of joint benchmarking and collaboration between selected suppliers as well as customers.

Discuss technology requirements (current and future)

If applied effectively and developed selectively to reduce costs and add value, technology will be critical in achieving world best practice and securing sustainable competitive advantage. This step is about understanding the opportunities that exist between customer and supplier partners for making changes in technology and agreeing on their implementation.

Review your inter- and intra-partner networks

Partnerships and alliances are underpinned by relationships internal and external. Once you understand the relationships within your own organisation, you can then look at the number, quality/type and performance levels of relationships between and within the customer and supplier organisations and agree with the partner(s) what future relationships need to be developed. Managing changes in personnel through effective succession planning, people exchanges, secondments and skills development will also be critical.

Develop, implement and review a strategy/action plan

As part of the strategic partnering/alliance process there will be a strategy/ action plan that brings together the strategy and activities of the other eleven steps and monitors their progress. It will also provide an opportunity to fill any activity gaps, innovate further and generally challenge the ongoing effectiveness of the process. The Partnering/Alliance Manager, together with the partnering/ alliance team(s), will lead and coordinate this step as appropriate, depending on the scope and complexity of the relationship. The strategy/action plan will be directly linked to the shared vision, common goals and guiding principles in the partnering/alliance charter as well as the measures of success as detailed in the KPI Balanced Scorecard.

THE SIX OUTCOMES

The **six outcomes** are the result, effect or performance of implementing one or more partnering steps which in turn are driven by one or more of the twelve motivators. Outcomes don't happen by themselves but are the result of the motivators operating within the structure of the partnering steps. While they represent the outward and visible manifestation of success, the real champions and heroes are the people and teams behind the successful realisation and implementation of the motivators. The outcomes are not an end in themselves but a part of the cause-and-effect relationship development and measurement process and are a visible indicator of the rate of progress of continuous improvement. There are six outcomes which, you may remember, come from the discussion on higher-level benefits in Chapter 1 (Fig. 1.6).

Customer satisfaction

There are no surprises here. Customer satisfaction should be the desired outcome from all business relationships, not just partnerships. For many public sector relationships, complex public/private sector relationships and other selective private sector relationships, customer satisfaction can be extended to comprise stakeholder satisfaction—stakeholders being third parties with a key or vested interest in the relationship success (e.g. shareholders, employees, regulators, community and environmental groups).

Innovation

Innovation in the business context can be defined as:

> *Something that is new or improved done by the enterprise to create significantly added value either directly for the enterprise or indirectly for its customers. Innovation can be in the form of either:*
> - *an innovating thrust that develops existing strengths in a business unit through continuous incremental improvement and the occasional discontinuous change; or*
> - *a strategic leap that creates a totally new business unit unrelated to existing activities.*
>
> *Business Council of Australia[3]*

Sustained competitive advantage

Partnerships and alliances cannot exist in isolation. Achievement of 'Relationship of Choice' or 'Partner of Choice' is the reward for sustainable competitive advantage based on a strategy of differentiation and world-class value adding. Sustainable competitive advantage is about delivering sustainable value for the customer, beyond the cost of producing it, beyond the cost the customer is prepared to pay for it, and which is superior to the competition. Competitive advantage is discussed at length in Chapter 3.

Understanding and jointly agreeing what 'sustainable competitive advantage' looks like for all the relationship partners is fundamental to long-term success. It is surprising how often this is not fully considered when putting together the KPI performance scorecard. $ referred business, term extension, increase in percentage of available business, percentage of non-bid business, percentage of business bid for successfully and improved market share are just some of the measures of sustainable competitive advantage.

World class/best practice

World class is about becoming internationally competitive as benchmarked against world best practice and is critical for those organisations competing on a global stage. Not every organisation or every partnering/alliance relationship is necessarily focused on 'world class' in the literal sense but is more interested in best practice in terms of its own operating environment. This is best practice in terms of practices, systems, standards within a defined area of influence (e.g. industry, market, geographical segment). Best practice may also apply internally to the organisation across geographical and business unit boundaries.

Benchmarking against world class is sometimes unnecessarily difficult and time and resource consuming. In other areas 'apples for apples' benchmarks don't exist. The point is, there should be an agreed standard or level of performance jointly set by the partners by which the relationship effectively and sustainably benchmarks its achievements.

Financial success/return on investment (ROI)

'Business must run at a profit ... else it will die. But when anyone tries to run a business solely for profit ... then also the business must die, for it no longer has a reason for existence.'

Henry Ford[4]

Nan Stone, editor of the *Harvard Business Review*, commenting on the success of 100-year-old 'Living Companies', states that 'earning profits (in business) was like breathing in human beings: essential for survival but not the purpose of life'.[5]

Apart from the traditional measures like return on assets, return on share-holders' funds, and profitability measures, there will need to be a far broader appreciation of what financial success and return on investment really means for partnerships and alliances. The ability to employ more people and the positive impact that these business partnerships can have on the economy, society and the environment at large are some of the other returns on investment that need to be considered. I am reminded of Edwards Deming's quality philosophy[6] (see Fig. 5.2), a philosophy that leads to a higher return on investment.

Deming goes on to say: 'This chain reaction was on the blackboard of every meeting with top management in Japan from July 1950 onward.' The principle is still applicable today. World-class/best practice companies, now and in the future, have an obligation to look beyond the traditional narrow definitions of return on investment.

Good partners talk about building a legacy for the organisations, society and the environment. Genuine partnering and alliance relationships are all

Fig. 5.2 *The quality philosophy of W. Edwards Deming*

about generating stakeholder wealth (i.e. customers, suppliers, employees, shareholders, community, environment) as opposed to shareholder wealth alone. In the long term, being successful is about profitable growth, whether business or personal. Profitable growth and sustainable competitive advantage is about creating a better society in which all the citizens enjoy an ever-improving standard of living and quality of life, in harmony with the environment. They better themselves through the attainment and successful application of knowledge and learning and by assisting others to do the same. They join together as groups, communities and organisations and enjoy the synergy, benefits and well-being that result from the pooling of experiences. This principle lies at the heart of partnering and alliances and will therefore need to be reflected in the measures of the return on its investment.

Attitude

Attitude is about behaviours, mindsets and attitudes that are present and around the relationship. Attitude is also about happy, skilled and committed people doing a first-class job and wanting more. It is a bringing together of the individual's values and the organisation's culture. People have pride in themselves, they take pride in what they do and they have pride in the organisation they work for. Attitude will come out of strong leadership, trust, good communication and the removal of the traditional confrontational and adversarial work practices and barriers between management and workers, customers and suppliers. Attitude is keeping faith in the partnering and alliance principles, staying focused on common objectives and compelling value propositions, enjoying the partnering and alliance journey and having some fun.

THE PARTNERING PROCESS OPERATING RULES

1. *Where you start and the choice or sequence of subsequent steps is completely flexible.* It will depend on the requirements of your customer/supplier partner(s), your business strategy and the general operating environment. Read through all the partnering steps before deciding on the best place to start for your situation.
2. *More than one step can, will and should be worked on at any one time.* In a mature or complex partnership or alliance, as many as eleven steps could be in the process of being worked upon at the same time, assuming the step of selecting a partner has been completed. Even in partner selection most, if not all, of the other steps will be discussed or worked on. Implementation of each step is prompted by the question directed at the twelve

motivators, 'Will the next step . . . ?'. The various activities will need careful monitoring and documentation, but it is vital that you do not regard the steps as discrete entities that can only be attempted one at a time. It will become apparent how one step links into another, and starting points for other steps will appear as the process gets under way.

3. *There is no end.* This is a continuous improvement process. As the relationship develops, the steps unfold and the partnering process becomes continuous. Each of the twelve steps will be discussed in detail in the next chapter.

REFERENCES

1. Mary Walton, *The Deming Management Method*, Mercury Books, London, 1989, p.72.
2. John McConnell, *Safer than a Known Way*, Delaware Books, Sydney, 1988, p.224.
3. Roderick Carnegie & Matthew Butlin, *Managing the Innovating Enterprise*, 1993, Business Council of Australia, pp.3–4.
4. Frederick F. Reichheld, *The Loyalty Effect*, Harvard Business School Press, 1996, p.16.
5. Nan Stone, editorial, *Harvard Business Review*, April 1998, p.14.
6. Dr W. Edwards Deming, *Out of Crisis*, The Massachusetts Institute of Technology, 1982, p.3.

CHAPTER 6

A process for partnering/alliancing with customers and suppliers: the twelve steps

Selecting a partner

Objective

To select the right customer and/or supplier partner(s) who are willing and capable, based on an understanding of the general operating environment, the strategies of your own organisation, competitors, customers and suppliers and the value propositions/key objectives for the relationship under review.

Key points

1. Agree the scope of work activities, products and services involved, document the value propositions or business drivers for the alliance/partnering relationship(s) to be developed and understand the link/relevance/synergy/fit with the broader corporate strategy.

2. Agree and implement a partner evaluation process and selection roadmap linked directly to the value propositions and based on the four areas of evaluation focus:
   - strategic value to be gained
   - commercial value to be gained
   - willingness to partner
   - capability to partner

3. Understand the nature and quality of the supply chain involved. Understand the fit on the 0 to 10 Relationship Management scale of other (internal and external) customer/supplier/stakeholder relationships that are not under direct partner evaluation but are associated with the work scope activities, products and services.

4. Know whether you are taking a proactive or reactive approach, that is, whether the selection is crisis-driven and which party is leading the process (customer(s) or supplier(s)).

5. Make the selection by using a multifunctional team that covers a cross-section of the organisation. Include frontline people and others who have an understanding of and a vested interest or prior involvement in partnering and alliance relationships. Some of them will be involved in the transition and implementation stages.

6. Consider the impact this partnership/alliance will have on servicing the existing customer and/or supplier base.

7. Understand your competitors' strategies with regard to your chosen customer/supplier partner(s) and connected organisations in the supply chain.

Partner selection: getting it right the first time

This step is predicated upon understanding the relationship types that need to be developed and the value propositions and key objectives that need to be delivered to ensure the business/organisation strategies are achieved. Evaluating and selecting a strategic partner assumes that developing an alliance/partnering relationship is the right thing to do in the first place.

The clear and simple message with partner selection is 'get it right the first time'. The consequences of poor partner selection can be time and resource consuming, expensive and can diminish the appetite to try partnerships again. Poor selection also provides a fascination for spectators and self-satisfying vindication for the cynics, sceptics, nay-sayers and terrorists of the partnering/alliancing approach.

On the other hand, successful strategic partnering and alliance relationships can often have a direct and positive influence on the profitable growth and sustainable competitive advantage of an organisation through their sheer size, performance, influence and referral potential. They can impact on share prices, can redirect the organisation's future strategies and supporting structures, and can impact on culture (attitudes, mindsets, behaviours, practices), systems and processes, people, personal development and career potential. So in terms of partner selection the viable alternatives to getting it right the first time are few.

Keeping the partnering/alliancing faith is about having an immutable belief it is the right approach for the right reasons. It is a part of the development curve to share learning and experiences and to learn from mistakes, otherwise we are destined to relive them. With partner selection the paradox is, 'Pioneers don't always get it right the first time but good pioneers, like good partners, rarely make the same mistake twice'.

Evaluation techniques can range from simple checklists to complex models, depending on the operating environment, market sector, nature and size of the relationship to be developed, the products/services and organisation(s)/people involved.

There are a number of different aspects/viewpoints/combinations that may cause variations in the selection process and roadmap taken. For example:

1. Is this a new relationship which may or may not be initiated via market testing and a successful down selection process?
2. Is this an existing relationship where it is recognised that (a) the current approach and performance levels are not delivering best value for money and/or where the relationship has significant potential for improvement or (b) the current relationship has maximised in performance opposite the current relationship approach and partnering/alliancing is the next logical step? The relationship may have undergone review and a new approach been mutually agreed to. At this point the relationship activities may or may not be put out to market for competitive review and down selection. The term of the current agreement or contract may also be approaching renewal/expiry.
3. Is the process customer led or initiated, with or without market testing?
4. Is the process *supplier led* or initiated? This may or may not precipitate a market review process via a call for competitive proposals. It may seem counter-intuitive but the incumbent supplier(s) may feel they have a timely opportunity or competitive advantage in having their new and/or innovative model tested fairly in the market place.
5. Is there a *market testing*, competitive down selection process in place to identify the preferred partner(s)? If the process is done well the market is tested fairly and equitably, from both perception and reality perspectives. The process will then determine the best value for money partner(s) at minimal cost and in optimum time.
6. Is partner selection via an *in-house strategic review*, where the relationship has not formally gone to the market place for competitive down selection? This can occur where there is an existing relationship, there are limited players in the market place and/or the players' willingness and capability is clearly understood, or where the approach is driven/initiated by the incumbent supplier and a down selection process is not appropriate.
7. Is a *long-term, strategic* partnering/alliance relationship proposed?
8. Is the relationship *project based* with defined scope, cost and non-costs objectives and milestones (e.g. quality, schedule, safety, community, environment)?
9. Is the relationship *internal or external*?

Although there are a number of combinations that can occur, there are several common themes that allow for both flexibility and consistency in partner evaluation and selection. It is also useful to approach or review the process from the other party's perspective.

There a number of reasons and business drivers for taking a partnering approach over other alternatives on the 0 to 10 RM scale. They are:

- There are significant and compelling value propositions behind the formation of the relationship or project.
- There is an unclear, unpredictable risk profile for the project or relationship (i.e. many unknowns/variables).
- Risk is to be shared and not transferred among the partners.
- The relationship/project scope is not well defined or open ended.
- The relationship is long term and of critical importance (e.g. for the life of the asset).
- High levels of innovation are required, both incremental and breakthrough.
- Total openness, honesty and transparency is required.
- There are critical time deadlines to meet.
- There are unprecedented or challenging stretch targets on safety, quality and cost.
- Significant community or environmental issues require broad partner and stakeholder ownership, commitment, communication, consultation, engagement and involvement.
- The strategic value and commercial value is high, requiring a high degree of interdependence between the organisations (e.g. technology development, critical and/or ongoing operational activities, innovative integrated financial models).
- There is a leveraging of core competencies required between partner organisations.
- Changing political environment requires committed, inter-dependent partners.

Understand the value propositions/business drivers for the relationship

Irrespective of whether you are in the position of customer or supplier or whether the relationship is new or existing, there needs to be clarity on the strategy and value propositions to be delivered and agreement that partnering/alliancing is the best relationship approach and best method of delivery.

As we saw in Chapter 1, there are eleven legitimate relationship types and associated performance levels. The assumption at this point is that the strategy discussion has been completed and internal agreement reached that alliancing/partnering is the right strategy and the right relationship approach to take. Further, as discussed in Chapter 3, partnering and alliance relationships cannot operate in isolation or outside the umbrella of the corporate or business strategies. Relationships, and in particular partnering and alliance relationships, are the cornerstones for successful strategy implementation.

Value proposition(s) are the value added and/or other total cost benefits to be gained and the opportunities to be developed. These go beyond a cheaper price or a lower input/unit cost. In other words, value propositions are the key business drivers as to why the relationship exists or is to be developed. The partnering/alliancing approach is then the relationship vehicle by which the benefits are sustainably achieved. As general examples it could be argued value propositions comprise many of the 'base-level' benefits listed in Figure 1.5 (pp 36–37). Also refer to page 104 for additional examples of value propositions.

Telecom New Zealand, the largest telecommunications provider in New Zealand and a major player in Australian telecommunications via the wholly owned company AAPT, and Alcatel, one of the world's largest designers, developers and builders of communications equipment, reached agreement in June 2002 to develop a long-term strategic partnering relationship to manage the development and integration of Telecom's trans-Tasman 'Next Generation Network' (NGN).[1] It is regarded as a new model for the telecommunications industry.

For Telecom and Alcatel and, in turn, the downstream customers, the value propositions needed to be clear and significant. In the words of Rhoda Holmes, the Telecom General Manager for Network Investment, 'The company currently invests around $NZ300M in capital expenditure per year on its network in New Zealand. We envisage that over time, a large slice of this expenditure in New Zealand will go to Alcatel.' The Next Generation Internet Protocol network means that Telecom will be able to:

- combine voice and data on the same line;
- deliver multiple services with ease;
- roll out new services much faster and more cost effectively;
- continue to provide integrated solutions for voice, video and data;
- simplify Telecom's network and achieve substantial efficiencies.

And for Telecom's customers it means:

- end-to-end service management to the desktop;
- greater data speeds for many customers;
- a flexible 'plug and play' IT and T environment;
- lower overall costs for IT and T services.

These benefits will be directly linked to more efficient operational models, generating lower (total) costs and increased revenues through access to Alcatel's global knowledge and expertise. The relationship will also be a vehicle for employees of the partners to have a widened sphere in which to operate and advance their careers, particularly in the area of Research and Development.

For Alcatel the partnering relationship will, in the words of Mark Giles, Managing Director of Alcatel New Zealand, have significant benefits, apart from the significantly increased revenue stream: 'This partnering relationship supports Alcatel's strategy of being a leader in the NGN space and increases our brand reputation as an enabler of change and sustainable growth'.[2]

Be very clear, not only on your strategy and relationship approach but also in the specific value propositions around which benefits will be gained. They are the basis upon which partner evaluation and selection takes place.

Application importance and organisational trustworthiness: the four areas of evaluation focus

As a first pass evaluation it is often very useful and effective to look at the relationship between application importance and organisational trustworthiness as shown in Figure 6.1. Application importance is the relationship between strategic value and commercial value for the partnership, and organisational trustworthiness is the relationship between willingness to partner and capability to partner. The evaluation technique applies equally to customers, suppliers and complementors. Complementors are those organisations that complement the customer/supplier relationship through synergy of their people, products, services and the leveraging of core competencies. Within the complementor relationship the complementors themselves can have changing customer/supplier roles, depending on the nature of the products and services they are delivering and their associated responsibilities. They could take the form of JV partners; virtual partners; network, consortia or community partners. For example, Transfield Services has a core competency in operations and maintenance support services and facilities management. Their complementor partner in the strategic alliance with Mobil at their Altona oil refinery is Worley, whose core competence is engineering services. There is a high level of synergy between the two organisations and together they deliver a better result than would otherwise be. See the Transfield Worley case study on pages 401–425 for further details. The discussion below applies to complementors equally as well as it does to customers and suppliers, and they can take on both roles.

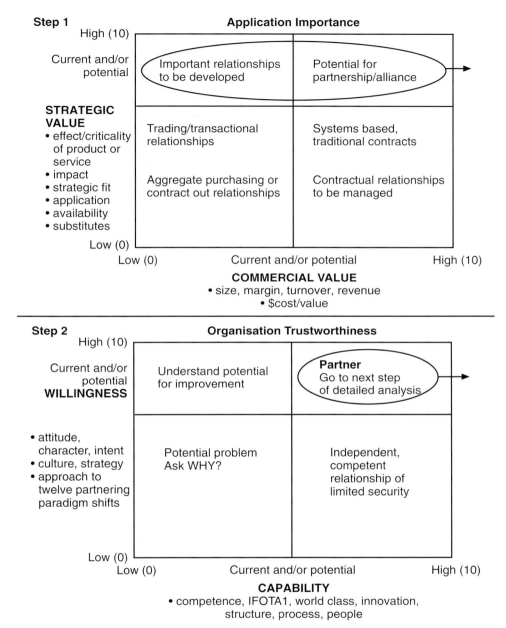

Fig. 6.1 *Partner selection process*

Strategic value is the extent to which the products and services associated with the potential partners' proposals under evaluation and their application have a positive impact on the short, medium and longer strategic well-being of the organisation.

Commercial value is the financial and associated commercial benefits gained from the application of the products and services in regard to the value proposition(s) under review.

Willingness is the level of commitment from the potential partners that they have changed or are prepared to positively change practices, attitudes, behaviours and mindsets as required to unlock the value from the value propositions, including changing organisational structures and aligning people's incentives.

Capability is about the ability and competence to work together to deliver the value propositions.

A non-exhaustive summary of characteristics that can be associated with each of the four areas of evaluation focus is shown in Figure 6.2.

The first step in evaluation looks at application importance: the relationship between strategic value and commercial value. As customer satisfaction is the driving force in this process, step 1 is looked at from the customer's perspective, both now and in the future. That is, does the customer see the impact, criticality, strategic fit and so on of the supplier's products and services as low, medium or high on the zero to ten scale? From the customer's perspective is the commercial value of the supplier's products and services low, medium or high on the zero to ten scale?

The organisations/relationships that fall into the high impact quadrants, that is, high impact/high dollar value and high-impact/lower-dollar value, are then looked at in terms of organisational trustworthiness. This is step 2. It involves understanding the relationship between willingness and capability to undertake partnering and alliance relationships now and/or in the future. Willingness is all about attitude and intent to develop partnering and alliance relationships. It is also about the flexible, responsive and empowering culture and the value based strategies required to make paradigm shifts and breakthrough improvements a reality. Capability is about competence, IFOTA1 product and service delivery or better—the ability to innovate and deliver on world-class, best practice agreed standards as well as structure, processes and people.

Step 2 is looked at from your own organisation's perspective as well as the perspective of the other organisations in the relationship. Where does each organisation sit on the willingness/capability scales? It is the organisations that rank highly on capability and willingness that make up the partner short list for detailed evaluation. The remaining firms or relationships are then categorised according to the 0 to 10 relationship types in Figure 1.3. 'It takes at least two to tango': that is, irrespective of the strategic and commercial value, there is no point in one organisation going down the partnering/alliancing path when the other organisation(s) are either unwilling and/or incapable. This is determined through discussion and agreement by the selection team, which will have cross-functional representation.

Step 2, organisational trustworthiness, is also an important opportunity to review the performance of non-partner relationships and implement improvement plans as appropriate. Organisations for future partnering and alliance relationships may very well be on this list, but they may need to make significant, and in some cases urgent, improvements. This applies in particular to organisations and relationships shown to be high on willingness but low on capability.

As strategic partnering and alliance relationships are time and resource consuming this exercise will also give you an idea how much time and resource should or can be given to non-partner relationships. It may well be counter-productive to form partnering/alliancing relationships at the expense of important key, major and 'other' accounts.

I am often asked what is the ideal mix or ratio of partner/alliance to non-partner/alliance relationships. The answer is, whatever is appropriate for your business. I know of an organisation in the engineering services sector which has a vision to partner with 60 per cent or more of their customer base within three to five years. Another large Australian based manufacturer sees only a small percentage (<2 per cent) of its supplier base as being true alliances or partnerships. Both organisations are right for their circumstances.

The key to effective partner evaluation/selection will be aligning/linking a clear set of value propositions with the four areas of evaluation focus: strategic value, commercial value, willingness and capability.

The evaluation/selection process roadmap

There is a base theme around the steps involved in partner evaluation and selection, and some distinct differences from traditional 'competitive bid', tender based evaluation. A typical roadmap is detailed in Figure 6.3 but there are many variations and the order of the steps can change. For example, Telecom New Zealand, in their search for a network service provider partner, instead of the half-day interviews had a small team of senior staff travel around the world to meet the Head Office senior executives from the short-listed service providers. The discussions themselves still took on average half a day but it became very clear, very quickly the level of commitment Telecom New Zealand were putting into the relationship.

A brief explanation of each of the steps in Figure 6.3 is outlined below. You will find there is some overlap with some of the steps and the partnering steps discussed in the next sections. The partnering steps can and will be used many times throughout the life of a partnering/alliance relationship and even in the evaluation/selection process.

Strategic value
- Strategy alignment/fit
- Effect, criticality, impact of the products and services under evaluation
- Growth potential (e.g. market share, referred business)
- Technology migration
- Customer care/satisfaction
- Enhanced brand leverage
- Potential for innovation
- Uniqueness of application
- Availability of products and services
- Availability of substitute products and services
- Global links
- Compatibility, synergy with existing customer/supplier relationships
- Ability to leverage core competencies
- Speed to market for new products and services
- Reliability/availability

Commercial value
- Profitability
- Margin
- Revenue
- Pricing
- Cash flow
- Total costs
- Unit costs
- Cost of capital
- Capital expenditure
- Operational costs/expenditure
- Financial engineering flexibility
- Strength of balance sheet

Willingness
- Cultural fit/alignment
- Strategic alignment
- Level of trust and trustworthiness now and potential for the future
- Management/leadership/negotiation styles
- Willingness to enter a performance based relationship
- Willingness to put profit at risk based on over/under-performance against agreed KPIs

Fig. 6.2 *Four areas of evaluation focus*

- *Degree of flexibility and responsiveness in approach*
- *Willingness to work with third party organisations*
- *Quality and level of information sharing*
- *Commitment to the long term*
- *Approach to breakthrough thinking and changing paradigms*
- *Willingness to leverage core competencies*
- *Openness and transparency in communications and information sharing*
- *Approach to risk management/allocation*
- *Willingness to embrace alliance/partnering principles*
- *Support at all levels for the relationship*
- *Willingness to strive for outstanding outcomes*

Capability

- *Technical*
- *Financial strength (balance sheet), access to capital*
- *Financial management*
- *Competence (e.g. leadership, relationship management, communications, technology migration/commercialisation, product/service development, service/support delivery)*
- *Communications and language*
- *Track record of doing what they said they would do*
- *Organisation/relationship governance/management structure*
- *Product/service differentiation*
- *Product service support*
- *R&D capability*
- *Product/service life-cycle management*
- *Transition plan credibility*
- *Management of legacy technology*
- *Previous partnering/alliance experience*
- *Ability to work with first and second tier third parties/ sub-contractors*
- *Brand credibility*
- *Management team partnering/alliance competence/capability*
- *Availability and quality of resources*
- *Quality of existing partnering relationships and alliances*
- *Conflict with existing commercial relationships*
- *Supply chain management*
- *Risk management*
- *Innovation capability*

Fig. 6.2 *Four areas of evaluation focus* (continued)

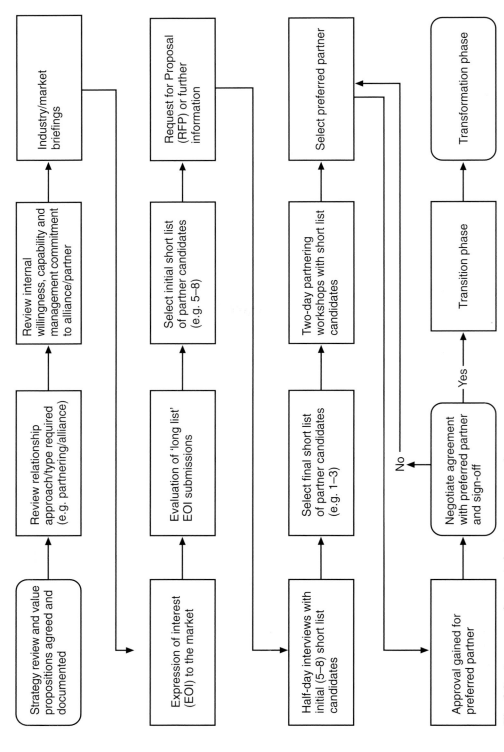

Fig. 6.3 *Partner evaluation/selection process roadmap*

Depending on the industry sector, the organisation and corporate policies, the process may also involve a probity auditor or similar role, or an independent third party, coach or facilitator to ensure that all steps are conducted effectively and from a perception and reality perspective, without conflict or prejudice. This is often the case in the public sector, for example in defence, water and energy utilities.

Strategy review and value propositions agreed and documented

Understand the business drivers and agree the value propositions in line with the broader business strategy. Conduct an analysis of strategic value and commercial value underpinning the strategy.

Review relationship approach/type and performance levels required (e.g. partnering/alliance)

Agree that partnering/alliancing is the correct relationship approach to take. Conduct a 0 to 10 relationship management strategy review to identify the most appropriate relationship type and performance levels to develop (refer to Fig. 1.4).

Review internal willingness, capability and management commitment to alliance/partner

It is all very well to have the strategy in regard to the external market place identified and the value propositions documented but is the organisation willing and capable to carry it off? This will require considerable internal reflection and due diligence to see if there is in place or there is the potential to have the right culture, strategies, structures, systems, processes and people to support such a relationship and not tribalism, internal rivalry and demarcation.

Industry/market briefings

Before going out formally to the market place a briefing(s) can be very helpful in setting up the right environment and explaining, in a joint forum with questions and answers, the principles, process and roadmap under which the partner evaluation will take place. Industry or market briefings can also take place at the short-list stage.

Expression of interest (EOI) to the market

This tends to be a relatively short document explaining the purpose or intent of the document, overview and background, the strategic objectives and value propositions for the relationship, the scope, the relationship approach/rationale, proposal requirements, desired outcomes, EOI conditions/requirements, evaluation/selection process, criteria and milestones.

Evaluation of 'long list' EOI submissions

This can be done as a desktop evaluation by using the application importance (strategic value and commercial value) and organisational trustworthiness (willingness and capability) models as previously explained, or the long list can be evaluated more analytically and formally via the evaluation process detailed on pages 180–181. Depending on the scope of activities involved, the 'long list' can be quite large. I have seen EOI where 30 to 50 submissions have been presented. A simple, less quantitative screening process is often more appropriate to reduce the time, cost and resources involved in short-listing. At this point only enough information and detail will be required to screen effectively and to short list the best partner candidates for the next stage in the process. A further request to the market (e.g. RFP/RFT) for specific and detailed information can be issued as part of the next steps.

Select initial short list of partner candidates (e.g. 5–8)

The initial short list number will vary depending on the quality and quantity of the EOI submissions. On occasions the down selection may lead straight to a final short list (2–3 partner candidates) from which a Request for Proposal (RFP) can be issued, further information gathered or workshops initiated. Alternatively a 'longer' short list may be required to evaluate fairly the best candidates.

Request for Proposal (RFP)/Request for Tender (RFT) or request for further information

Like the EOI above the RFP/RFT tends to be a relatively short document explaining the purpose or intent of the document, overview and background, the strategic objectives and value propositions for the relationship, the scope, the relationship approach, proposal conditions/requirements, desired outcomes, evaluation/selection process and milestones. Alternatively, there may just be a request for further information, often requesting a greater level of detail (e.g. on technical capability, commercial aspects, previous partnering/alliancing experience). The industry briefing discussed above may also be done prior to the RFP/RFT step rather than the EOI step. There is no prescription here and number and sequence of the steps will depend on the size and nature of the relationship being evaluated and what is considered by the participants to be the best approach.

Half-day interviews with initial (5–8) short list candidates

Half-day interviews or something similar are used as face-to-face opportunities for both parties to ask questions, share information, gather further information, uncover gaps or close gaps from the EOI/RFP/RFT submissions. The discussion can be technical, financial or commercial but is often focused on the partnering/alliance relationship aspects. For example, questions related to partnering/alliance principles, resourcing, risk/reward remuneration, value generation, governance, people competencies, cultural alignment, issue resolution and sustaining the relationship are often discussed.

The interviews are normally conducted in an open, relaxed and conversational environment, often without electronic slide-ware and other mechanical or electronic hardware and software. It is about meeting the people involved in the process now and those that will be in the future. One of the criticisms of traditional evaluation based purely on written submissions is that the best 'essay writers', not the best partners, sometimes get the business. The interview and workshop process helps to understand the people and the faces, the intent and capabilities behind the submissions, as well as how both the interviewers and the interviewees interact as a team and the way each approaches the other as a prospective partner. It also helps to gain the next level of commitments required. In that regard both parties are under the spotlight in terms of how they will behave and act and the competencies and experiences each brings to the relationship.

Select final short list of partner candidates (e.g. 2–3)

The final short list is made by the evaluation team, based on joint discussion of the information gathered and discussions held to this point and the use of an evaluation model or spreadsheet to score and rank the short list candidates. The evaluation spreadsheet involves weighted selection criteria and a scoring mechanism which, based on the information and discussions held, ultimately delivers a ranked outcome of best to worst scores (i.e. from the most successful candidate to the most unsuccessful candidate). Again there are no hard and fast rules here. If, from the analysis, there is one and only one outstanding candidate then that is the preferred partner put forward for approval.

Two-day partnering workshops with short list candidates

The two-day workshops are seen as a continuation of the half-day workshops in terms of face-to-face opportunities for both parties to build on the existing relationship, ask questions, share information, gather further information, uncover gaps or close gaps that exist in areas technical, commercial, financial or relationships in order to be in a position to make the next level of commitment. More specifically, the workshop can cover the following:

- Establish a shared vision, common goals and operating principles for the relationship (i.e. a draft partnering/alliance charter).

- Build on the foundation of trust and integrated team work to understand what trust looks like for the partnering/alliance relationship.
- Gain commitment to shared success, mutual benefit and win/win outcomes.
- Identify technical, commercial, financial and relationship gaps and share ideas and information.
- Achieve understanding of the degree of alignment of the partners on culture, strategy, structure, process and people.
- Explore innovation opportunities.
- Build a draft Performance or Balanced Scorecard of KPIs, which are linked directly to the vision, key objectives and value propositions for the relationship. Further information on the Performance Scorecard or Balanced Scorecard approach is given on pages 323–328.
- Agree on a draft partnering/alliance agreement framework, guiding principles and, as appropriate, supporting details associated with each of the main headings. For example:
  —Partnering/alliance relationship vision, key objectives, operating principles
  —Value proposition, strategic business objectives
  —Scope of relationship
  —Term (fixed, fixed + extension(s), evergreen)
  —Governance, structure, expected roles, responsibilities and accountabilities
  —Issue resolution/escalation
  —Performance measurement and evaluation, benchmarking, performance indicators
  —Risk management, risk sharing and risk allocation
  —Insurance and indemnities
  —Remuneration (e.g. performance based, risk/reward gainshare/painshare based)
  —Joint business planning
  —Intellectual property
  —Termination and rules for disengagement
  —Contracting parties
  —Communications
  —Transition plan
  —Health, safety and environment
  —Others matters as agreed

There is also some similarity between this two-day workshop, which is specific to the evaluation/selection process, and the more general application one- to two-day workshop agenda detailed in the step 'Reviewing process with partner and sharing information' on pages 206–207. This agenda has wider application and can be used internally or externally, driven from either a customer or a supplier perspective, and does not have to be part of a market bid process.

Each of the workshops with the respective partner candidates is conducted on the assumption that each partner candidate will be chosen as the preferred partner and all workshop participants are encouraged to think, contribute and actively participate with that mindset. The workshops are interactive, informal, collaborative in style and are a genuine test for all participants, at a personal and organisational level, as to the willingness and capability to partner, in particular the approach to openness and transparency in all areas of evaluation.

Select preferred partner

The preferred partner is then selected by the evaluation team from the outcome of the workshop(s) and the information/opinion gained from the previous steps. The performance of each possible partner is ranked using the weighted scoring spreadsheet process or similar, as discussed on pages 180–181.

The agreed ratings/scores opposite the selection criteria will be carried forward and adjusted up or down depending on the outcome of discussions at each step in the evaluation/selection process. The final scores then represent the basis for the evaluation team's recommendation of the preferred partner.

Approval gained for preferred partner

Most times the selected preferred partner is then put to an executive team, board of directors or review panel for recommendation and approval. In some cases this step is irrelevant (e.g. where the executive team is in fact the evaluation team or equivalent, or the evaluation team comprises some team members who have the authority to approve the decision of the evaluation team). On other occasions the team is initially empowered to run the process and make the decision and/or an independent probity auditor(s) is present throughout the process, allowing an effective by-passing of this step. On still other occasions this step occurs after the negotiation has successfully taken place or a second approval step may also occur at that point.

Negotiate agreement with preferred partner and sign-off

One aspect to this process that is very different from the traditional, hard-nosed, hard-money, competitive contest is the approach to negotiating the commercial arrangements and the details of the partnering/alliance agreement. At this point, because of the process and approach taken, there will be a significant amount of trust between the parties, based on similar attitudes and mindsets and the collaborative, open and transparent, win/win level of agreement already reached on technical, financial, commercial and relationship issues.

The negotiation is conducted via a series of workshops and meetings over whatever time frame is appropriate, with the preferred supplier only. There is no 'parallel negotiating' in the traditional sense. Depending on the size and nature of the relationship and the commitment, willingness and approach of all the parties, this could take days, weeks or months. If the negotiation is ultimately unsuccessful then the customer partner has the right to close down discussions and restart the negotiation process with the second-placed organisation from the original selection process. The aim is to conduct the negotiations in an atmosphere that fully supports and promotes partnering and alliance principles, concepts and practices. All too often so-called partnering and alliance relationships are born out of very traditional, hard-nosed, win/lose negotiated positions, leaving many of the players involved bitter, frustrated and itching for revenge. At best this will generate a poor start.

All being well at this point there are few surprises, fewer secrets and certainly no lies to be caught out on. Many of the details of the partnering/alliance agreement will have already been discussed in the interview/workshop phases, and in many cases the negotiation will be about filling in the details behind the commitments already entered into or broadly discussed.

Specific aspects that need to be finalised at this point are:

1. the specific wording of the agreement (see the discussion points listed above for the two-day workshop as a guide);
2. the details of the general commercial and, if appropriate, risk/reward arrangements agreed to (e.g. performance based, risk reward based KPIs and targets; direct cost, overhead and profit definitions, framework and percentages; risk/reward curves—risk/reward modelling is discussed in detail in Chap. 7);
3. the approach to benchmarking/measurement to ensure the relationship is delivering best value for money and/or delivering agreed performance levels against financial and non-financial KPIs and targets;
4. the details of the transition plan to ensure an effective startup or transition to full delivery/operation;
5. the governance process and the membership of the various partnering/alliance teams (e.g. the leadership team, management teams, project teams) plus team member roles and responsibilities;
6. resource/people requirements and allocation;
7. the involvement of area or industry experts to assist in the finalisation of the agreement and the ongoing development and performance of the relationship generally (e.g. technical, financial, legal, partnering/alliance coaches/facilitators);
8. other issues, gaps, opportunities that have arisen out of the process to date.

Transition phase

The reason the transition phase is part of the evaluation/selection process is that some organisations are guilty of walking away to other projects or opportunities, assuming that signing-off on the agreement is the equivalent of automatic success. It is not! The 'A' team cannot now be replaced by the 'B' team. While the formal aspects of the selection process are completed many would agree the real work now begins. This may involve people relocation, co-location, business case or project plan development, concept and design activities, systems integration or development, cultural alignment and induction training (e.g. safety, technical, process/operations, partnering/alliancing). In some cases an interim partnering/alliance agreement or MOU is entered into for the transition phase.

Transformation phase

The relationship is now in full operation. The evaluation/selection phase is complete and the delivery/implementation/improvement or transformation phase begins.

Selection process: overview and general observations

Figure 6.4 looks at the relationship between the agreement, charter, Performance/Balanced Scorecard and remuneration. It includes the following:

1. An amicably negotiated partnering/alliance agreement detailing both the spirit and intent of the relationship, the scope of activities, governance and remuneration, as well as the legally binding obligations for all the parties involved and, of course, the general terms and conditions.
2. A signed Alliance/Partnering Charter detailing the shared vision/mission for the relationship, key goals/objectives and the guiding principles.
3. A performance based or Balanced Scorecard of KPIs that measures current relationship performance, predicts future performance and assists in the management and leadership of relationship improvement. The scorecard will include both risk/reward-based KPIs linked directly to the remuneration model and non risk/reward-based KPIs which are used to monitor, manage and improve relationship performance. The scorecard then links directly to associated action plans or strategy documents.
4. A clear link between relationship performance, measurement and remuneration, often via a risk/reward, gainshare/painshare remuneration model.

All these components are brought together by the right people and clearly articulated value propositions at the centre of the figure. This will provide a solid platform for understanding and allow the relationship to enter the transition, implementation and transformation phases.

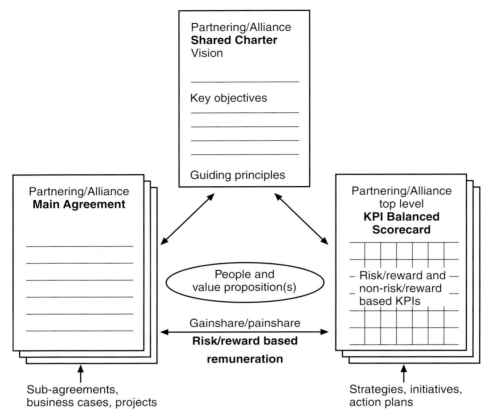

Fig. 6.4 *Partner evaluation and selection: the key components*

Having been involved in the process many times, I can make some extra observations here.

1. Involve in the process people who understand or have experience in alliancing/partnering.
2. The workshops are fundamental in understanding how the partners will behave and react in the actual relationship, as real partners. They are also a lot of fun and very stimulating. Conducting only desktop reviews for the selection will, in all but rare cases, not be good enough.
3. Commitments for which the parties will be accountable can be made as the process progresses.
4. While the commercial arrangements need to be agreed early on from a value for money perspective, most times it is not until the final stages, and not until the preferred partner has been chosen, that the commercial details are completed and the risk/reward models agreed. This is quite different from the traditional tender approach.

5. The process is time and resource consuming but, if done well, will produce the right result.

6. Probity auditors can be used to ensure that the process is running as planned from both perception and reality perspectives. This often occurs in the public sector where links to the political process, internal stakeholders, external community groups and other vested interest groups can be direct. On first thought the use of a probity auditor may seem contrary to the principle of partnering and alliancing but if their role in the process is carried out well their participation can eliminate unnecessary intervention from stakeholders or other interested groups/individuals whose intentions are less clear or well intended.

7. The use of an independent facilitator can be very useful in coaching and guiding the workshop forward at the right pace while still delivering the workshop objectives.

The partner evaluation/selection process: the principles and mechanics

There are many variations on a theme with evaluation/selection processes. What is presented here is a general model that can be modified and adapted to any circumstance to effectively and fairly evaluate and select a partner from an initial long list and subsequent short list(s) of candidates. Any model implemented should be logical, transparent, quantitative and consistent with the principles/ values of the organisation, the business strategy and value propositions.

It is the quality of the discussion by the evaluation team that generates the scores—this is not a purely analytical, faceless, impersonal exercise that delivers numbers which then generate a discussion. Ultimately it will be people who make the decisions, not software or spreadsheets.

The mechanics of the evaluation process are relatively simple, involving evaluation criteria, allocated/agreed weightings, and actual and weighted scores. In the example in Figure 6.5 there are four value statements. These are, in effect, value propositions for the relationship. The value statements are weighted according to their overall impact/importance and risk profile and in total add up to 100 per cent. Each of the value statements can be broken down into delivery statements, which reflect the various aspects of the value statement that need to be scored. Each of the delivery statements associated with a specific value statement is then weighted and the total adds up to 100 per cent. Each delivery statement is then evaluated through the four areas of evaluation focus (strategic value, commercial value, willingness and capability). The four areas of evaluation focus are also weighted for each delivery statement and total 100 per cent. Once this framework has been completed, the written proposals,

Definitions:

%WA = % weightings for value statements
%WB = % weightings for delivery statements
%WC = % weightings for evaluation focus
%TW = %WA × %WB × %WC = Total weighting A × B × C

Scoring (0–10 performance Scale)

1 = Unsustainable	6 = Good
2 = Poor	7 = Excellent
3 = Below average	8 = Outstanding
4 = Fair	9 = World class
5 = Satisfactory	10 = Superior

A. Value statement	%WA	B. Delivery statement	%WB	C. Evaluation focus	%WC	%TW	Company X		Company Y		Company Z	
							Raw score	Weighted score	Raw score	Weighted score	Raw score	Weighted score
1. Improve safety, health and environmental performance.	15%	1.1 Effective safety, health and environmental systems and management practices in place.	40%	1.1.1 Strategic value	30%	1.8%	9	0.16	8	0.14	9	0.16
				1.1.2 Commercial value	25%	1.5%	8	0.12	7	0.11	8	0.12
				1.1.3 Willingness	15%	0.9%	7	0.06	5	0.05	7	0.06
				1.1.4 Capability	30%	1.8%	8	0.14	6	0.11	6.5	0.12
				Total	100%	6.0%						
		1.2 Evidence of a strong commitment to and outstanding performance in providing a safe and healthy workplace.	30%	1.2.1 Strategic value	25%	1.1%	9	0.10	8	0.09	9	0.10
				1.2.2 Commercial value	25%	1.1%	8	0.09	7	0.08	8	0.09
				1.2.3 Willingness	25%	1.1%	7	0.08	5	0.06	6	0.07
				1.2.4 Capability	25%	1.1%	8	0.09	7	0.08	8	0.09
				Total	100%	4.5%						
		1.3 Demonstrated commitment to and strong achievements in protecting the environment.	30%	1.3.1 Strategic value	25%	1.1%	9	0.10	5	0.06	6	0.07
				1.3.2 Commercial value	25%	1.1%	8	0.09	7	0.08	8	0.09
				1.3.3 Willingness	25%	1.1%	7	0.08	6	0.07	7	0.08
				1.3.4 Capability	25%	1.1%	7	0.08	6	0.07	7	0.08
				Total	100%	4.5%						
			100%	Total: safety, health, environment		15.0%		1.20		0.98		1.13
2. Deliver sustainable and superior value which supports the broader business strategy.	30%	2.1 Demonstrated understanding of customer requirements and strategy expectations.	20%	2.1.1 Strategic value	25%	1.5%	7	0.11	6	0.09	7	0.11
				2.1.2 Commercial value	20%	1.2%	8	0.10	4	0.05	5	0.06
				2.1.3 Willingness	25%	1.5%	7	0.11	4	0.06	4	0.06
				2.1.4 Capability	30%	1.8%	8	0.14	5	0.09	4	0.07
				Total	100%	6.0%						
		2.2 Credible plans/milestones for transition phase, ongoing product/service development and delivery operations and maintenance.	10%	2.2.1 Strategic value	30%	0.9%	8	0.07	5	0.05	5	0.05
				2.2.2 Commercial value	25%	0.8%	9	0.07	5	0.04	5	0.04
				2.2.3 Willingness	20%	0.6%	8	0.05	9	0.05	9	0.05
				2.2.4 Capability	25%	0.8%	7	0.05	5	0.04	5	0.04
				Total	100%	3.0%						
		2.3 Demonstrable track record of delivering best value for money performance.	10%	2.3.1 Strategic value	25%	0.8%	9	0.07	5	0.04	6	0.05
				2.3.2 Commercial value	25%	0.8%	8	0.06	6	0.05	6	0.05
				2.3.3 Willingness	20%	0.6%	8	0.05	7	0.04	8	0.05
				2.3.4 Capability	30%	0.9%	8	0.07	6	0.05	6	0.05
				Total	100%	3.0%						
		2.4 A commercial arrangement that ensures the best value for money/total cost outcomes.	50%	2.4.1 Strategic value	20%	3.0%	8	0.24	5	0.15	5	0.15
				2.4.2 Commercial value	50%	7.5%	9	0.68	5	0.38	5	0.38
				2.4.3 Willingness	10%	1.5%	8	0.12	5	0.08	5	0.08
				2.4.4 Capability	20%	3.0%	8	0.24	5	0.15	5	0.15
				Total	100%	15.0%						

	Item	Weight	%	Score	Value	Score	Value	Score	Value
2.5 Strength of Balance Sheet (10%)	2.5.1 Strategic value	35%	1.1%	8	0.08	5	0.05	5	0.05
	2.5.2 Commercial value	35%	1.1%	8	0.08	6	0.06	5	0.05
	2.5.3 Willingness	10%	0.3%	8	0.02	5	0.02	5	0.02
	2.5.4 Capability	20%	0.6%	8	0.05	5	0.03	5	0.03
	Total	100%	3.0%						
	Total: value for money	100%	30.0%		2.45		1.55		1.56
3. Establish a role model partnering/alliancing relationship which is performance based, risk/reward linked, open, transparent, collaborative and mutually beneficial. (30%)									
3.1 Understanding of partnering/alliancing principles and practice. (25%)	3.1.1 Strategic value	20%	1.5%	9	0.14	5	0.08	6	0.09
	3.1.2 Commercial value	20%	1.5%	8	0.12	6	0.09	5	0.08
	3.1.3 Willingness	30%	2.3%	9	0.20	6	0.14	7	0.16
	3.1.4 Capability	30%	2.3%	8	0.18	4.5	0.10	4.5	0.10
	Total	100%	7.5%						
3.2 Demonstrated partnering/alliance capability. (20%)	3.2.1 Strategic value	20%	1.2%	8	0.10	6	0.07	6.5	0.08
	3.2.2 Commercial value	20%	1.2%	8	0.10	6	0.07	5	0.06
	3.2.3 Willingness	30%	1.8%	9	0.16	6	0.11	7	0.13
	3.2.4 Capability	30%	1.8%	8	0.14	4	0.07	4.5	0.08
	Total	100%	6.0%						
3.3 Commitment to working in a performance based, risk/reward linked, open, transparent, collaborative, mutually beneficial relationship. (30%)	3.3.1 Strategic value	20%	1.8%	9	0.16	5	0.09	6	0.11
	3.3.2 Commercial Value	20%	1.8%	8	0.14	6	0.11	5	0.09
	3.3.3 Willingness	30%	2.7%	8	0.22	6	0.16	7	0.19
	3.3.4 Capability	30%	2.7%	9	0.24	4.5	0.12	7	0.19
	Total	100%	9.0%						
3.4 Ability to work collaboratively with and manage 3rd parties. (25%)	3.4.1 Strategic value	20%	1.5%	8	0.12	6	0.09	6	0.09
	3.4.2 Commercial value	20%	1.5%	8	0.12	5	0.08	6	0.09
	3.4.3 Willingness	30%	2.3%	9	0.20	7	0.16	7	0.16
	3.4.4 Capability	30%	2.3%	9	0.20	4.5	0.10	7	0.16
	Total	100%	7.5%						
	Total: partnering/alliancing	100%	30.0%		2.55		1.63		1.84
4. Deliver world-class and/or best practice innovation through continuous and breakthrough improvement. (25%)									
4.1 Demonstrated track record of delivering successful innovation and improvement. (60%)	4.1.1 Strategic value	20%	3.0%	8	0.24	7	0.21	8	0.24
	4.1.2 Commercial value	20%	3.0%	8	0.24	8	0.24	8	0.24
	4.1.3 Willingness	20%	3.0%	10	0.30	9	0.27	10	0.30
	4.1.4 Capability	40%	6.0%	9	0.54	5	0.30	7	0.42
	Total	100%	15.0%						
4.2 Commitment to leverage partners' global capability and fully engage partner resources in the development and delivery of products and services. (40%)	4.2.1 Strategic value	30%	3.0%	8	0.24	7	0.21	8	0.24
	4.2.2 Commercial value	50%	5.0%	8	0.40	8	0.40	8	0.40
	4.2.3 Willingness	10%	1.0%	8	0.08	7	0.07	8	0.08
	4.2.4 Capability	10%	1.0%	9	0.09	6	0.06	7	0.07
	Total	100%	10.0%						
	Total: innovation	100%	25.0%		2.13		1.76		1.99
Value statements 1 to 4	**TOTAL**	100%	100%		**8.33**		**5.92**		**6.52**

Fig. 6.5 *Strategic partner evaluation spreadsheet*

the workshops and other discussions can be analysed, discussed, evaluated and scored opposite the value statement, delivery statement and four areas of focus. Associated with each of the delivery statements there may be specific questions that are the minimum requirements for the participants to address. They would be detailed in the EOI and RFP/RFT documents.

As discussed in the previous section, the agreed ratings/scores will be carried forward and adjusted up or down depending on the outcome of discussions as each step in the evaluation/selection process proceeds. The final scores then represent the basis for the evaluation team's recommendation of the preferred partner.

The scoring system can also vary. A 0–10 scale and associated word descriptions are shown on Figure 6.5. For simplicity and consistency it is the same 0 to 10 performance scale from the relationship management matrix (refer to Fig. 1.4). The actual scores are then weighted and totalled to ultimately produce a single number result ranked for each organisation/proposal under evaluation. As stated earlier it is the quality of the discussion that generates the score and not the score that generates the discussion. This will be based on a shared understanding of the value proposition(s) or business drivers for the partner organisations. If there is not a reasonable differential between first and second candidate (e.g. less than 3–5 per cent), then the process can be re-evaluated. Typically, the selection process takes longer than the traditional tendering process which is often skewed with a large weighting on price. Partnering/alliance partner evaluation is very different. A lot more time is spent up front in getting the right partner before talking through and negotiating the commercial details. In this example, company X, with a score of 8.33 out of a possible 10 is clearly the successful partner candidate, based on the discussion and associated scoring that would have taken place.

Partnering/alliancing 'upstream' and 'downstream' with customers

In practical terms, who (i.e. customer or supplier) is leading the partnering/alliancing approach, whether the relationship is new or existing and what its current state is will determine the detail required in the selection process and the roadmap used. This step will be handled differently, depending on whether you are selecting supplier partners upstream or customers/complementors downstream.

Understand which direction in the supply chain the approach is coming from. For suppliers evaluating customers, the lead will most likely come from business development, marketing and sales and senior management. For customers evaluating supplier partners, the lead will mostly come from procurement, operations/maintenance and senior management. In both cases senior management play a critical role in sponsoring, guiding, and often directing and leading the process.

Project partnering/alliancing

Beyond the defined scope and time frames associated with specific projects, the differences between strategic and project based partner selection are few. The value proposition, business drivers or key objectives for the project need to be clear and articulated. If a project partnering/alliancing approach is taken, there will be partnering/alliance agreement for the delivery of the project, a project charter comprising shared vision, common goals and guiding principles, a KPI Balanced Scorecard and probably a profit at risk gain/pain share model based on performance against key objectives. Most likely the objectives will not be as broad or long term as for strategic relationships and will revolve around quality, cost, schedule, safety, community and environment because of the defined scope of the project and its time frame. Project partnering/alliancing, as with strategic partnering and alliancing, can apply internally or externally to the organisation, to any market sector, the public or private sector and to large/medium/small organisations.

If partnering and alliance relationships take time to develop, the challenge for many project-based organisations and relationships is, once having selected the right partners, to get the relationships up to speed and high performance quickly. The statement often made about strategic partnering and alliance relationships is that they take time, years in many cases, to build and imbed the cultural characteristics; deliver on the strategies; put in place the supporting structures, systems and processes; and get the right people to perform to their full potential. With projects you often don't have the luxury of time and pressured deadlines are a fact of life. In many cases people/organisations are working together before the agreement is signed. Good project partners involve themselves with some or all of the following initiatives:

1. Bundling of activities/smaller projects to provide a critical mass of work and revenue that attracts the right partners who can take advantage of the scale, synergy and efficiencies associated with larger projects.
2. A short list of preferred supplier/project partners or a pre-qualified panel of partners who have the willingness and the capability to engage early and effectively in the project partnering/alliancing.
3. Early engagement of partners, if possible and where appropriate, in the broader strategy development, project concept and design phases.

4. Partnering/alliance workshop(s) as part of the evaluation/selection process: a 'foundation' workshop at the beginning of the project and ongoing review and improvement workshops throughout the project.
5. Clear governance and management structures involving leadership teams, project management teams and integrated project teams which have clear responsibilities and accountabilities and meet regularly.
6. Clear goals/objectives and a Balanced Scorecard or Performance Scorecard of Key Performance Indicators (KPIs) with which to monitor, manage, and measure the progress of and improve the relationship(s) and project.
7. Effective issue resolution/escalation processes.

Often strategic partnering and alliance relationships are based on the bundling of projects large, medium and small over an extended period. Long-term commitments are made up front to engage strategic partner(s) and, based on performance against agreed measures of success, the relationship will continue from one project to another.

Avoid 'best of breed' at the strategic level

A 'best of breed' strategy, where the best provider for a defined product or work scope is chosen with little concern for circumstances or trends outside the scope boundary, will still support successful partnering/alliance projects. However, at a strategic level a 'best of breed' strategy often presents itself as multiple, independent relationships delivering varying value, based on customised or proprietary products, services and technologies. Telecommunications, petrochemicals, oil and gas, manufacturing and other sectors often have 'best of breed' legacies due to past relationship and procurement strategies. These relationships are often based on events or procurement opportunities that can in the long term deliver layers of debilitating complexity, which in turn inhibits speed to market and product and service differentiation. A 'best of breed' strategy is unlikely to support a long-term strategic partnering/alliance approach. I'm not suggesting a 'best of breed' approach cannot be successful but it is more appropriate for vendor (0 to 4) and supplier (5 to 8) relationships. The market is changing and organisations are having to reorganise their long-term relationships and commitments, and their allegiances.

Is the selection crisis-driven?

Crises can be a real threat to the existence of the business or provide a genuine opportunity for change. They can show your ability to solve a major problem in a professional and quality way, be it of your making or otherwise. There is nothing better than a good crisis that threatens the loss of a large and important customer to shake a business to its foundations. Crises have been known to wrench organisations out of their comfort zone of arrogance and complacency. If you recognise it as a wake-up call and it isn't too late to respond, then it can certainly provide the catalyst for change.

It is important to decide whether there is a genuine crisis that can be used as a catalyst for the development of a long-term partnership. Or is it just a case of a problem that no doubt needs to be fixed, but which presents no opportunity for pursuing a partnering strategy? Don't be fooled—many problems are just that, problems which should never have happened in the first place and for which solutions need to be found just to maintain the relationship.

To be a genuine catalyst for permanent change, a crisis and its solution(s) need to be carefully managed and the outcomes used for further development, with a sustained and effective focus on the customer/supplier relationship as a whole. You need to become skilled in recognising and resolving crises, wherever the responsibility for them may lie. Then study the results of their solution and determine whether they can be built upon.

Who should select the customer/supplier partner?

Traditionally, this would be left for senior management to debate and argue about behind closed doors and then filter the decision down to the lower ranks. The reasoning and logic behind the decision, and the strategy for implementation, were often not effectively transmitted to those at the operating levels who would actually do the work. If you want commitment and ownership from the front line, from the individuals who will actually deliver on the detail, involve them in the big picture from the start.

The selection of a customer/supplier partner will no doubt involve senior and middle management to give legitimate authority to the process and its outcomes, and a group of front-line people who will have a vested interest in the partnership succeeding. They could be from production, operations, warehousing and distribution, technical services, and so on, depending on where the current and future focus areas for the partnership will be.

Understand your competitors' strategies

Strategic partnering cannot operate in isolation from the rest of the business strategy or from your competitors. In almost every situation there will be some form of competition—superior or inferior, major or minor, innovative or static, fast or slow moving, synergistic or aggressive. Good competition can stimulate continuous innovation, learning and overall improvement. Bad competition—apart from not providing the catalyst for fast and effective change—can actually be destructive, affecting the reputation and performance of products, markets and companies up and down the supply chain.

Competitors will provide one of the benchmarks by which you manage, develop and innovate within the partnership. Good, strong, professional competitors will ultimately be more effective and rewarding than weak, inconsistent and unprofessional combatants. Understand their current and future strategies, technology (product and process) and, in particular, their intentions towards your customer partner and their customers. Note the number, nature and quality of relationships they have developed with the customer partner and compare these with your own networks.

Just as we assessed potential partners in Chapters 2, 3 and 4, understand the culture, strategy, structure, process and people associated with your competitors. Where do they lie on the relationship matrix shown in Figures 1.2, 1.3 and 1.4? How does this competitor analysis compare with your own organisation and the potential customer partner? Where is the alignment or misalignment, strengths and weaknesses, and where can improvements be made? It may be that your competitor is developing a similar partnership with your customer's competitor. In effect, one supply chain is competing with another. This will demand cooperative efforts in order, ultimately, to produce world-class results.

Multi-partner relationships

Can you partner with two or more customers or suppliers of like products or services—that is, partners who are direct competitors of each other? The short answer is yes. There may be various and legitimate reasons for having two suppliers, or multi-supply arrangements, where partnerships are involved. These may include:

1. The customer partner's volume requirements for the product or service may be such that no one supplier can adequately and effectively deliver.
2. The business may be split by geographic regions or markets. On a global scale this could involve countries and continents.
3. The competitor plants may be in different locations or using different technologies, thus offering local advantages.
4. One supplier may offer certain advantages in its products and services over the other suppliers. These benefits could attract dollar premiums, additional volumes, other commitments or a combination thereof.
5. There may exist strategic alliances between the supplier organisations that allow for effective and mutually beneficial dual supply arrangements; for

example, technology exchanges, joint ventures, licensing, joint distribution, packaging arrangements.

6. The customer partner has requested closer working relationships between suppliers, on the basis of:
   ■ critical mass to be achieved for the product or service
   ■ improved logistics regarding dependability and reliability of supply
   ■ improved product/service consistency and reduced variation
   ■ joint product/process developments
   ■ future customer requirements that need the joint efforts of others

7. There has been a formation of clusters (i.e. three-way, or more, joint ventures), consortia and extended supply chain activity between the customer and suppliers.

8. Single-source dual-competition strategies are being employed where similar products and services are supplied by preferred supplier partner organisations for the customer partner's different models and functions, and are used as benchmarks for joint cooperation, continuous improvement and mutual benefit. For example, this often occurs in the automotive industry.

For similar reasons, supplying two or more competitive customer partners is also possible, with the same levels of complexity, confidentiality and sensitivity to be managed. Imagination will be required in structuring the relationship to cater for these issues. The options can range from the highly cooperative to the totally segregated. Qantas and British Airways cooperate in both customer and supplier roles and with their global alliance partners.

In other cases, separate joint venture structures are formed to separate the competing relationships, both physically and legally. The reality is, of course, that most organisations already deal with customers and suppliers who are competitors of each other. This is just normal business. The issue with partnerships and alliances is that the quality of the relationships being developed is clearly of a higher calibre. It is entirely appropriate to develop an 8+ partnership and in turn have a legitimate relationship lower down the relationship scale (e.g. 4, 5, 6, 7, see Fig. 1.2) with your partner's competitor. This would be for reasons of alignment or misalignment in the areas of culture, strategy, structure, process and people.

REFERENCES

1. Telecom New Zealand, *Telecom & Alcatel complete innovative network partnering agreement*, media release 14 June 2002, <http://www.telecom-media.co.nz>
2. ibid.

Reviewing internal relationships

Objective
To determine whether your organisation has what it takes internally to develop, maintain and improve upon customer/supplier partnering and alliance relationships.

Key points
1. Draw up internal communication and relationship maps using an understanding of your organisation's 'primary and support' value chain activities.

2. Analyse the quality of communication within the organisation.

3. Goal:
   - to earn trust
   - to document what trust looks like—a Trust Charter.

4. Focus: sharing information.

5. Actions: communicate/listen
   - resolve conflicts
   - clarify roles
   - bring out hidden agendas
   - develop internal willingness and capability

6. As appropriate, implement an internal partnering strategy between subsidiaries, associated companies, divisions, functions and departments.

The best enterprises unite their people around a common purpose. Innovating enterprises have developed a highly productive means of creating common purpose. They have broken through the internal barriers which divide parts of enterprises, including their leadership. Many of them have developed formal processes to coordinate the interactions of their people around particular common purposes, such as development of new products and services, or the provision of certain extra customer values. Most innovating enterprises have started creating a general climate of common purpose at the shop floor.
Business Council of Australia[1]

This is probably the single most difficult step in the partnering process and may even come before selecting the customer partner. This is where you get to look closely at the people within your organisation and their relationships with each other. It needs to be determined very early in the process whether your organisation, its structure, its culture, its systems and its people are capable even of starting, let alone sustaining, strategic partnering and alliance relationships. You can't hope to develop strong, long-term strategic relationships with external customers and suppliers unless there exists strong, long-term internal relationships, supporting and developing world-class or best of class products and services.

'Over-promise and under-deliver' is the trademark of the company that does not have its internal relationships right. Remember the analysis in Chapter 2 of the traditional and the basic multilevel selling customer/supplier relationships. Figure 6.6 outlines the possible networks within supplier (A) and customer (C) and also shows the connections between the two companies (B). What happens is that the supplier tends to over-promise in area B, making commitments to the customer that can't be kept, and then under-deliver in area A because of poor internal communication and/or process capabilities. All the focus has been on the inter-company customer/supplier relationship networking, multilevel selling and promising, with little attention being paid to internal relationships or the need to understand customer requirements and the ability to meet them.

This is the classic case of the salesperson returning from the field of battle with a bonus winning order, joint project or product development opportunity only to find—for reasons he or she does not understand or refuses to understand—that the business can't deliver. Some possible reasons could be:

- Production is at full rates. 'Sorry, can't fit it into the current schedule.'
- 'You should have told us earlier.'
- Low stock levels or no stock.
- The order has not been forecast.
- Lack of feedstocks or other raw materials.
- Plant breakdown, notification of which was not circulated.
- Cannot deliver on time because of freight delays.
- The process cannot make to this specification. 'The spec limits are too tight.'
- 'We don't have the technical, operational, project or R&D resources at this time.'
- 'This customer has a low-priority status according to the business plan. We will do our best to meet the revised schedule but that is all.'
- 'Sorry, but this does not fit with the strategy.'
- 'To fulfil this requirement, we're going to have to drop somebody else off the program.'

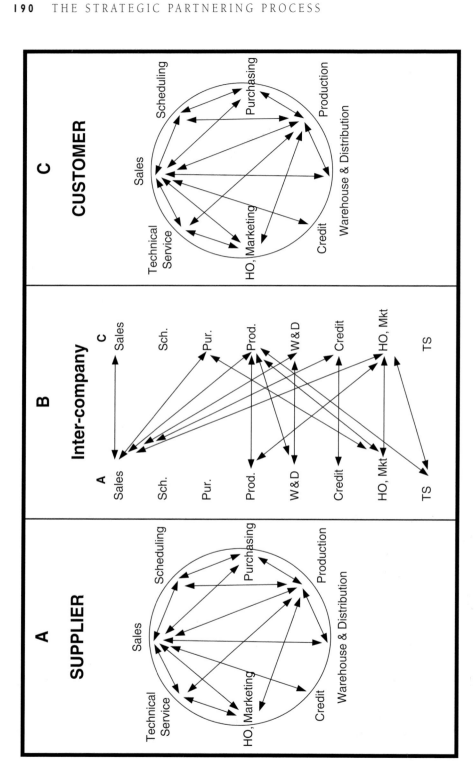

Fig. 6.6 *Supplier/customer networking*

- 'You just missed out. Somebody else came in just before you and made a similar request.'
- Production doesn't like salespeople because of a current personality clash or historical perceptions of them.

And we wonder why we can't make good our promises. Internal customer/supplier relationships are as important as the external customer/supplier relationships, not only in making alliances and partnerships work but in any customer/supplier relationship.

There is no question that you will use this step many times to determine and review the quality of your organisation's internal communication flow. Irrespective of strategic partnerships, this step will have a beneficial effect on your customer and supplier base as a whole.

The objective is to analyse the number and quality of relationships within your organisation to determine if there are any roadblocks to developing and/or sustaining partnerships. You need to develop trust, share information, resolve conflicts if they exist and clarify the individual's role if there is confusion.

My experience is that most problems or shortcomings within an organisation can quickly be traced back to communication and people. It doesn't matter whether the problems involve systems, procedures or equipment— they are merely the symptoms. The root cause is always people. These 'people problems' can have many causes:

- lack of good leadership
- lack of vision, clear strategies/objectives, compelling value propositions
- lack of focus on the important issues
- lack of information and involvement
- lack of skills or training
- lack of commitment/ownership
- lack of effective teamwork
- lack of the 'prevention, prediction and design out, rather than cure' approach in everything from maintenance to capital expenditure to relationships
- lack of trust
- fear and hidden agendas

All these causes involve people, not plant or machinery. How do you locate the good and bad relationships within your organisation, and identify the good and the poor lines of communication and the reasons for them? Answer: draw some maps.

Figure 6.7 shows the classic Crosby quality approach to customer/supplier relationships, with each organisation within the customer/supplier chain

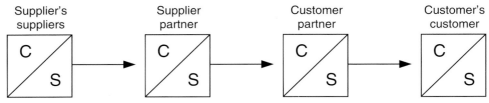

Fig. 6.7 *The customer/supplier chain*

being both a customer for goods and services and also a supplier of goods and services. There are, of course, processes within processes and we could expand these customer/supplier relationships within an organisation to an almost infinite degree. That is, in fact, what we want to do: to take the *supplier partner* box and expand on it to determine the quality and extent of relationships involved. Figure 6.8 shows how this can be done. Your organisation may be quite different in structure but the principle is the same.

Relationship mapping

First, brainstorm and document what good communication looks like for your organisation and the partnering relationship. For example, 'Good communication looks like:

- open, honest, timely, accurate and relevant sharing of information
- no unpleasant surprises
- talking before you write
- proactive resolution of issues and identification of opportunities
- not over-promising and then under-delivering
- doing what you said you would do'

Second, complete an internal value chain for your organisation (see p. 107). Then the steps involved in relationship mapping are as follows:

1. *Draw up a relationship map*, indicating all the functions/departments in your organisation (see Fig. 6.8).
2. *Involve a wider group of people* in the exercise, with at least one person from each of the major areas of influence on the customer, plus the partnering/ alliance manager and some of the original group that selected the customer/ supplier partner. Then draw relationship lines between all the departments/sections that communicate with each other. A solid line indicates a good relationship or strong line of communication. A broken line indicates a poor relationship or an ineffective communication link that requires

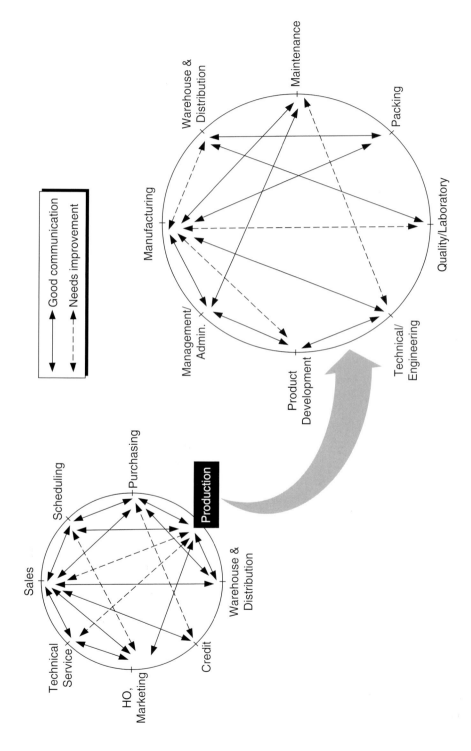

Fig. 6.8 *Relationship mapping: communication links*

improvement or corrective action (Fig. 6.8). Then document the issues needing corrective action under the headings of the twelve motivators (see Fig. 6.9). Cross-check this information by walking around and asking open, upfront questions.

This action list is very important and must be seen as a positive step forward in improving relationships, not a stick that you subsequently use to beat people over the head. The perception is just as important to deal with as the reality. The aim is to use the action list as a vehicle to communicate and listen to people more effectively, to understand their concerns and frustrations better, to hear their ideas and suggestions for improvement and then to act on what they have said. People not only want to be heard, they also want to be responded to. This may involve direct change, reclarification or further sharing of information. Good lines of communication are about the ability of two or more parties to share information openly by a mutually agreed means that is timely, accurate and relevant, and allows one or more of those involved to do a more effective job.

3. *Share the information on the action list with as many people as possible* to confirm or refute the initial findings. The aim here is again to communicate and listen; to resolve conflicts, clarify roles and bring out the hidden agendas; to develop both the willingness and the capability to build relationships internally and in turn support the partnership development process externally. This will undoubtedly create concern, questioning and, in some cases, retaliation and animosity within certain people and departments. There will also be a great deal of positive confirmation. Those with an open mind who are willing to participate constructively in the partnership process will have nothing to fear and everything to gain. On the other hand, those gatekeepers of information, those with hidden or political agendas and the poor communicators will be facing the light of day. This is where you start to see whether you have the right stuff for partnerships.

You will need the support of senior management to ensure effective solutions are put into place. You will also need to conduct a training audit for those whose communication skills and other soft and hard skills need improving. Training in conflict resolution will be another area requiring development. If you don't already have an effective TQM program in place, you would be well advised to set one up; otherwise, you are going to have problems.

TQM provides the essential skills/tools and a common language for developing your people, systems, products and services to differentiate your organisation and gain competitive advantage.

4. *Understand why* there are good relationships and *who* makes them work. They will be your ambassadors and their relationships your case studies.

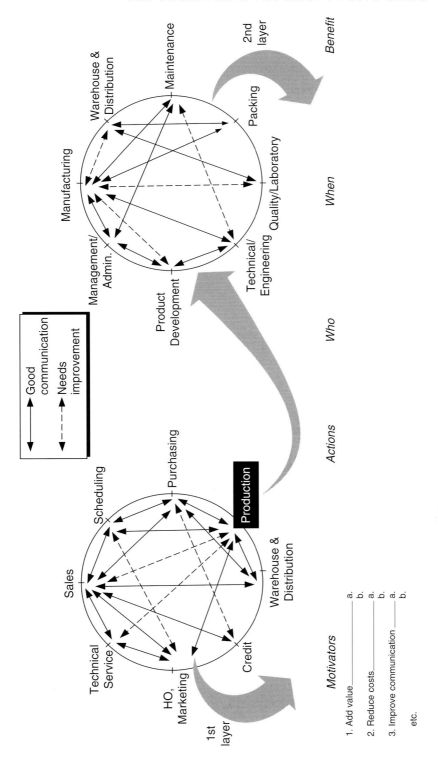

Fig. 6.9   *Documenting issues needing corrective action*

5. For departments that are particularly complicated, such as production, or where special problems exist, *draw up a second-layer relationship map* (see Fig. 6.8) and repeat steps 1 to 4 above.

The relationship mapping exercise can be applied equally well to teams and will indicate how effectively your cross-departmental/functional activities are working. Team analysis can be done as a separate exercise or included in the major departmental/functional maps. Depending on the size and complexity of the organisation, third- or fourth-layer relationship maps can be drawn up. The aim is to reach the shop-floor or coalface level, where individual relationships and roles can be understood and improved upon.

When doing these exercises it would also be useful to consult an organisation chart to cross-check that the official reporting structure and the relationship structure are in harmony. It may be that the reporting structure of the organisation itself is the problem. The ultimate aim is to reduce layers dramatically and to implement cross-functional participation, thereby eliminating the need for the conventional organisation chart.

Communication between departments is one thing, but real complications occur when there is interaction across sites, divisions and even subsidiaries, each with its varying degrees of autonomy and responsibility. This is the real test for management: to supply the right structure, empower the right people and provide the right environment, such that good communication and strong internal and external relationships can occur.

The customer partner should see one common face of your organisation. Internal combative and tribal relationships are unsustainable if external partnering and alliance relationships are being developed. Also, you can't have one part of the organisation involved in a partnership when another division or subsidiary is also a supplier or vendor type but with different priorities. To one division, they may be a partner. To another division, where the volume and/or dollars may be smaller, they may be one of the 'other' accounts, although the product or service may be no less critical in its application. From my experience, this is a major problem and must be solved. While the divisional structure can be maintained there must be a common strategy and commitment. The internal relationship maps become more complex but more critical in these situations, as does the will and active participation of management and the rest of the organisation to make it work.

There also needs to be a single partnering or alliance manager who has overall responsibility for the relationship. This really does turn the traditional company structure on its head. I have seen as many as five salespeople from the one company, but from separate divisions, calling on the same customer, all with their differing strategies and priorities. This is completely unworkable if you are looking at strategic partnering.

We shall return to Figure 6.6 in the step 'Reviewing inter- and intra-partner networks' to look at the broader scope of customer/supplier relationships and the people networks that need to be developed.

Sharing information

> *The Toyota secret was, finally, no secret at all. Treat both white and blue collar workers with respect, encourage them to think independently, allow them to make decisions and make them feel connected to an important effort. Combine that culture with a good car and quality parts, and the results are obvious.*[2]

If trust is to be developed it is critical that information be shared. How much information? Whatever it takes to enable people to feel they are part of the partnering/alliancing process, actively participating and making informed decisions based on accurate and up-to-date information. Basically, this means sharing everything. There can be no secrets here. Whether people take it all in is another question. That is a function of quality of environment and the level of skills and attitude prevailing. Information and the ability and legitimate authority to use it to competitive advantage is the basis of power. Power in the hands of a few can be a manipulative and destructive weapon. Power in the hands of many is ownership and empowerment, generating a creative environment in which individuals and teams are prepared to act and push beyond normal boundaries to achieve their full potential.

In particular, discuss and share information about the partnering principles and process, with the aim of gaining active support for the next steps. Workshops are a most effective technique for getting people out of their normal environment and placing them among others they would not normally have contact with.

Share information about your own organisation, the supporting value propositions, your customer partner(s), their customers' products and services, your suppliers and supplier partner(s), your competitors and the external environment. Figure 6.10 outlines the type of information that can be shared. Who to share it with? Anyone who is the slightest bit interested. Much of this information should be common knowledge, anyway, if the organisation is truly progressive.

Use this data as the basis of a gap analysis on the information you currently have and the information you need to have. Then set about filling the gap. Similar modified profiles can be done for suppliers and competitors.

Customer profile (updated: month/year)

Customer Name:

Address:

Phone/Fax No:

Prepared by:

Corporate structure: ownership, company type, organisation chart(s). Who are the decision makers? What decisions do they make that will have an impact on your business? What is their business style, leadership style, personality, likes, dislikes? What are the relationship maps between and within the two customer/supplier organisations?

Financial performance: profitability, return on assets, ROI, financial ratio analysis, the latest balance sheet and profit and loss statement.

Business done with other parts of your organisation:

Reciprocal business:

Current business and potential opportunities with your partner:
- Product/service name(s).
- Application/effect/end products.
- Your organisation's performance rating in the eyes of the customer.
- Previous sales (volume and $ value) in previous 12 months, plus the volume/value trend over previous years since commencing business with them, plus projections for the future. This can be done in the form of SPC control charts that will also indicate system stability and the amount and effect of process variation, including explanations of special events.
- Prices, credit terms and conditions. Up-to-date status of commercial terms and conditions.
  - prices
  - credit terms and conditions and performance against
  - rebates and the nature of
  - incentives (product, price, promotion, export, import replacement, etc.)
  - other
- Projected growth rates, into which markets, and why.
- Current prices/contribution. How does this compare with product/service contribution with other partnerships, and key and major accounts?
- Competitors (products/prices/volumes/application/effect). Their performance rating as a supplier and why. Competitor SWOT analysis.
- Buying criteria/requirements.

Fig. 6.10　*A customer profile*

Your customer partner's business in detail:
(a) Marketing
- their mission/vision statement
- corporate objectives and enabling strategies
- division objectives/strategies
- product group objectives/strategies
- key issues (internal and external)
- development plans/opportunities and your current involvement
- their competitive advantage
- their strengths, weaknesses, opportunities and threats

(b) Sales
- product and services
- application/effect
- from which division, manufacturing or distribution site
- sales volume/$ turnover
- the market sectors they serve and their market share
- key/major customers, plus customers' customers
- percentage of your product used (volume and value)
- growth rates
- their major competitors (names/market sectors/market share)
- exports (volume/value/percentage)

(c) Manufacturing/service infrastructure (by site)
- relationship maps within and between other functions and departments
- plant and equipment (type, capacity, age, flexibility, condition, etc.)
- process description
- support facilities (QC, training, technical service, R&D support)

In terms of your organisation's performance opposite your supplier partner:
- What does your customer partner see as your strengths, weaknesses, opportunities and threats?
- What do you see as your strengths, weaknesses, opportunities and threats?
- What is your customer partner's perception of your performance opposite your competitors'?
- Where and what are the gaps?

Note A similar profile can be done for suppliers and competitors.

Fig. 6.10 *A customer profile* (continued)

Goals: to earn trust and document what it looks like

You can't have more empowerment than trust. Stephen Covey[3]

You can only empower people as far as they are aligned with your vision, values, strategies and goals. The alternative (empowering with poor alignment) leads to anarchy. The development of trust will be the key goal of this partnering step: trust in people's abilities, competencies, their objectives and intentions, systems and processes, all based on shared, open and honest information. Build confidence that they are playing a part in, and making a valuable contribution to, the process, the partnership and all that it involves. People's confidence and their level of empowerment will depend on how little fear and how much trust they have in management, peers, suppliers, customers, technology, process, vision and strategy.

Trust is closely linked with strength of character and is therefore something that is earned over a period of time, not given on demand. Strength of character is associated with conviction in personal beliefs and values: the strength and conviction to stand up and sometimes fight for what is believed to be right, and to help others during times of difficulty. There is no room for deception with trust. It is a most powerful and sustaining quality.

Develop a trust charter—a single-page document of the intent and practice surrounding trust for the relationship being developed. There are five steps to building a trust charter.

1. Agree with your customer/supplier (internal and/or external) that trust is critically important to the development and well-being of the relationship.
2. Define trust. Stephen Covey[3] refers to trust as a function of competence as well as character.
3. Brainstorm the question: 'What does trust look like specifically for this relationship?'
4. Agree on an appropriate short list (5–20 items) through joint discussion.
5. Sign off on the trust charter and live by it.

Figure 6.11 is an example of a project trust charter. Trust is not just about the intangibles and will manifest itself in real bottom line affecting initiatives, attitudes and behaviours. The trust charter is applicable to relationships internally and externally to the organisation and can form the basis of the moral agreement between the partners. Ask the 'Trust looks like' question at every level of your organisation. You will be surprised at the openness and quality of responses.

Internal partnering

Partnering principles and practice will travel seamlessly across organisational boundaries, internal and external, and eventually into the extended supply

Trust Charter

Trust is the basis upon which this project will be successfully completed for all parties. Trust is a function of competence as well as character.

Trust for this project looks like the following values, attitudes and performance levels:

- quality coming first
- value for money, *not* the cheapest price
- proactive, not reactive, response to problems and issues
- progress payments paid In Full On Time
- doing what you said you were going to do
- being earned, not given on demand
- agreeing targets, goals, milestones that are SMART* and then sticking to them
- letting others know as early as possible, and proactively, when these targets, goals, milestones can't be reached
- win/win, positive approach and outcomes to resolving conflicts and problems
- open, honest sharing of information and ideas (i.e. good communication)
- our success is your success
- referring on for new business (i.e. other jobs)
- friendship and having respect for each other
- conformance to Safety, Quality, Schedule and Cost requirements
- sound commercial outcome for all parties
- developing a similar understanding with other suppliers and customers
- elimination of duplication

(The signatures of all the people involved in the development of the Trust Charter should appear on this document.)

*SMART = Specific, Measurable, Achievable, Relevant, Trackable

Fig. 6.11   *Trust charter*

chain. Organisations are just beginning to realise that what they are implementing externally can be just as effective between internal customers and suppliers—that is, subsidiaries, associated companies, divisions, functions and departments. This involves implementing internally the total partnering process of twelve steps/motivators and outcomes. 'Getting your own house in order first' is the principle that drives this initiative, thereby avoiding the over-promise and under-deliver syndrome. In facilitating external partner seminars and workshops it often becomes apparent that the participants, while keen and enthusiastic, lack the internal capability and competence for partnering.

Achieving internal alignment on culture, strategy, structure, process and people is just as critical to partnering success as external alignment. A parallel partnering strategy can be implemented internally while at the same time developing external relationships. Open/honest genuine external partners will share information, build on strengths and assist each other in minimising weaknesses in both internal and external relationships.

Corporatisation/commercialisation and privatisation of government departments and utilities has produced huge organisations that are often ill-equipped to compete in today's commercial environment. Traditional internal fiefdoms must now work cooperatively for common goals and customer satisfaction like never before. Displacing the process and entitlement cultures that are often endemic in the public sector can be just one of the major achievements of an internal partnering strategy.

I have worked with many organisations in the public and private sector where it has become clear early in the planning and implementation stages that, unless partnering is considered internally, then the external initiatives are likely to produce less than optimum results. Allowing marketing, sales and supply to make naïve, external promises that can't be kept by uninformed, uninvolved and uncommitted employees does not make good commercial sense. This also extends to the relationships between management and unions. The same principles, concepts, practices and behaviours apply.

REFERENCES

1. Roderick Carnegie & Matthew Butlin, *Managing the Innovating Enterprise*, Business Council of Australia, 1993, p.21.
2. Dave Garwood & Michael Bane, *Shifting Paradigms*, Dogwood Publishing, Marietta, GA, 1990, p.14.
3. Stephen Covey, presentation at Sydney Opera House, May 1994. Author of *The Seven Habits of Highly Effective People*, Simon & Schuster, New York, 1990.

Reviewing process/progress with partner and sharing information

Objective

To share the principles, process and progress of strategic partnering/alliancing and general information and to gain your partner's initial and ongoing support, commitment and involvement.

Key points

1. Involve the customer(s) or supplier(s) in the process to ensure commitment and support and a *win/win* long-term partnering/alliancing philosophy.

2. Assist the integration of strategic partnering/alliance principles and practice throughout the partner organisations and associated supply chains and imbed measurement systems to monitor and manage performance and to drive improvement.

3. Share information on strategy, vision, goals, objectives, the marketplace and other areas of mutual interest and benefit. Identify areas of conflict and opportunities for improvement.

4. Understand the value of:
   - partnering/alliance workshops
     - —partnering/alliance charter
     - —shared vision, mission, common goals/objectives, guiding principles
     - —developing trust, trustworthiness and teamwork
     - —aligning relationship performance to measurement and remuneration
   - general partnering workshops involving customers and suppliers
   - ongoing reviews
   - informal reviews
   - partnering and alliance agreements

5. Use the 'wait and see' approach, if appropriate.

6. Have an agreed fallback strategy in case the potential partner says no.

7. Don't forget the benefits of surveys.

8. Understand that traditional tenders are not compatible with partnering/alliance relationships.

Reviews will be one of the main measures of the progress and success of the partnership. They are the mechanism by which customer and supplier partners initially gain support for, and participation in, partnering/alliancing. Reviews can subsequently be used to reconfirm this support and participation. It is on these occasions that measured performance against agreed objectives and opportunities for future improvement are discussed, and where due recognition is given to those who have participated in the process. Partnering is a cooperative/collaborative process based on an open and transparent sharing of information, agreeing common goals and objectives and then, within an environment of trust, shared principles and teamwork, making those goals and objectives a reality. Initial and ongoing reviews are an important part of that process.

The partnering workshop

Once you have selected a customer/supplier partner and probably reviewed internal relationships (to ensure that your organisation is capable of sustaining the process), the next logical step will probably be to review the process and the partnering principles with the partner themselves. The most important result of this step will be a successful partnering/alliance workshop lasting one to three days, depending on the size and complexity of the relationship. Workshops are held not only at the beginning of the relationship but also at regular intervals (e.g. 6–12 months). This would apply to partnering/alliance based projects as well as ongoing strategic relationships.

The workshop is attended by all the stakeholders from both customer and supplier organisations who take part in the relationship activities with the aim of understanding the principles and process of partnering/alliancing, and then form a commitment to the concept and practice. Joint activities also build the foundation for teamwork and the development of personal relationships. The workshop plays a critical role in the education process. There are three stages to the workshop:

1. Pre-workshop activities
2. The workshop itself
3. Post-workshop activities

1. Pre-workshop activities

Initial commitment from senior management

Senior management from both organisations should meet first to discuss the broad nature of the desired relationship and jointly agree their senior-level commitment and participation. There must be unequivocal ongoing support for the principles and process of partnering/alliancing from senior management at this point or the partnership will be doomed from the start. The details surrounding the partnering workshop should then be discussed. The agenda, location, list of participants and the role of an independent third-party facilitator should be agreed upon and a team given the task of coordinating the pre- and post-workshop activities and responsibility for running the workshop itself. This team should include people from both organisations. Senior management must be involved for the duration of the workshop.

The role of a facilitator

Although not critical to the process, especially if one or both organisations are seasoned partnering/alliancing campaigners, a neutral, trustworthy and independent facilitator can be very helpful in organising the workshop agenda and participating, not as workshop leader, but rather as a coach, providing training, insight, experience and direction as required. The facilitator's experience and general listening and communication skills can prove useful in making participants comfortable with what, for many, will be a new way of doing business. The facilitator can also assist with the development of the workshop outcomes, such as the Partnering/Alliance Charter, Balanced Scorecard of Key Performance Indicators, the process to be followed, methods of communication and conflict resolution.

The ideal facilitator will be industry-neutral with a basic understanding of business activities, backed by strong organisational and interpersonal skills. Someone with previous experience as a partnering/alliance manager would also prove extremely valuable. Senior management and the coordinating team should meet the facilitator before the workshop to agree on the facilitator's role and extent of involvement.

Workshop location

If possible, the workshop should be run at a neutral location far removed from day-to-day work influences and respective corporate cultures. The location should be conducive to free and lateral thinking with plenty of room for work groups, brainstorming and team-building activities.

The agenda

The content and timing of the agenda should be carefully considered. It is the logical roadmap by which commitment and interest will be gathered. A sample two-day workshop agenda is shown in Figure 6.12. For some people the definition of logical is 'a systemic way of getting things wrong with confidence' and therefore

Day 1	Agenda item	Objective	Outcomes
8.30–8.45	1. Introduction and opening remarks	To set the scene: ■ Background to the day ■ Overview of process to be taken and desired outcomes ■ Introduction of participants to each other	
8.45–9.30	2. Opening statements on vision, strategies and objectives from partners' senior manager(s)	■ Presentation of the vision, strategy and objectives from senior executives of the partner organisations ■ Q&A response from participants to share information	■ A better understanding of the business priorities and value propositions for the relationship ■ An appreciation of the need for the workshop and the role the participants can play
9.30–12.15 (Break 10.15–10.30) (Lunch 12.15–1.00)	3. Review of Strategic Partnering/Alliance principles, concepts and practices and the 0 to 10 Relationship Types	■ Agree on common definition of partnering/alliancing ■ Achieve a common understanding of the principle, concepts, practices and broad objectives involved ■ Linking performance measurement and remuneration to outcomes ■ Understanding the role of partnering champions, key influencers/doers, sponsors	■ Documented agreed partnering/alliance definition ■ 'What does trust look like for this relationship' documented ■ Joint agreement to proceed to the next steps
1.00–2.30	4. Partner organisation alignment —Relationship Alignment Diagnostic (RAD): an intuitive analysis	■ To understand the degree of alignment between the partner organisations on culture, strategy, structure, process and people ■ Understand the 'Current State' position i.e. current requirements and expectations, milestones and performance against ■ Understand the future 'Desired State' position i.e. future requirements and expectations and capability of delivering ■ Conduct gap analysis based on current and desired states and/or SWOT analysis	■ Completed Relationship Alignment Diagnostic (RAD) ■ 'Current State' position documented and agreed ■ 'Desired State' position documented and agreed ■ Opportunities for improvement documented ■ Completed SWOT analysis
2.30–4.45 (Break 3.15–3.30)	5. Development of Partnering/Alliance Charter	■ To understand the principle and intent behind the partnering charter ■ Review/develop partnering charter —Vision and/or mission statements —Key objectives (6–12) —Guiding principles ■ Understand the links to finance and organisational structures	■ A signed Partnering/Alliance Charter and the joint commitment and ownership to implement successfully
4.45–5.00	6. Review of the day and close	■ Also outline day 2 activities	

continues

Fig. 6.12 *Partnering/Alliance workshop agenda*

Day 2	Agenda item	Objective	Outcomes
8.30–9.15	**7.** Discussion of personality indicator e.g. Myer-Briggs Type Indicator (MBTI) (optional)	▪ To have all participants complete the personality indicator prior to the workshop ▪ To understand their own personality type ▪ To appreciate partnering is a relationship/people-based process	▪ Participants understanding their own personality type and the difference and similarities to other types ▪ The impact of personality type on individual, team and therefore partnering performance
9.15–12.15 (Break 10.15–10.30) (Lunch 12.15–1.00)	**8.** Develop (draft) partnering/alliance Key Performance Indicators (KPIs)	▪ To understand that KPIs are different for alliances and partnerships (how/why) ▪ Review existing KPIs ▪ Agree on future KPIs (or draft) for the partnering relationship in Balanced Scorecard format ▪ Review and/or develop associated strategies and Action Plans for achieving key objectives and associated KPI targets and identify barriers to implementation	▪ Documented existing KPIs if appropriate ▪ Agreed (or draft) Balance Scorecard of partnering/alliance KPIs ▪ Strategy/Action Plan(s) (draft) and barriers to implementation
1.00–3.00 (Break 3.00–3.15)	**9.** Agreeing on some details	▪ Agree on the commercial and organisational structure for the relationship ▪ Relationship governance ▪ The role of the Partnering Manager and leadership and/or management partnering team(s) ▪ Individual/team roles and concerns ▪ Agreement on an issue-resolution process ▪ Communication process ▪ Training/skills requirements	▪ Agreement on all issues and document as appropriate
3.15–4.15	**10.** Prioritise the major issues, opportunities and concerns for the relationship	▪ Brainstorm the major issues, opportunities and concerns ▪ Prioritise via an impact/urgency matrix ▪ Assignment of owners to ensure implementation and completion	▪ A completed impact/urgency matrix or action plan
4.15–4.30	**11.** Sign off on the next steps and close Summary session with senior managers	▪ Via consensus agree on the next critical steps i.e. 'where do we go from here' ▪ Confirm participants' support and commitment for the next steps and their roles from this point on as champions and ambassadors for partnering/alliancing ▪ Review of the value gained from the 2 days	▪ Agreement and documented actions on who/how/when/why to proceed ▪ Support for and commitment to the next steps ▪ One Team, One Direction, Common Goals

Fig. 6.12 *Partnering/Alliance workshop agenda (continued)*

the agenda should be flexible in both content and timing to allow for improvements, modifications or changed environment. This is where a partnering facilitator with previous experience will be helpful to senior management and the coordinating team. If additional time can be made available, activities such as Myer-Briggs team-building exercises are very useful for personal development, creating a strong teamwork environment and improving communication.

Completion of a Relationship Alignment Diagnostic (RAD)

It is extremely valuable to have an understanding of the degree to which the partner organisations are aligned (or misaligned) in their approach to the relationship and the desired performance levels achieved. The intuitive 'self-assessment' RAD is a simple diagnostic tool based on three questions with reference to the 0 to 10 Relationship Management matrix (see Fig. 6.13).

The three questions are:

1. How do 'we' currently approach this relationship?
2. How do 'they' currently approach this relationship?
3. What is 'our' desired future approach to this relationship?

After independent discussion each organisation separately places the numbers 1, 2 and 3 (corresponding to questions 1, 2 and 3) at the appropriate position on the 0 to 10 Relationship Management matrix, capturing the reasons why the three numbers are where they are on the matrix. The partners then get together as a full group and overlay the results and discuss the patterns the numbers produce, the degree of alignment/misalignment and the reasons why. The next step is to understand and agree how the gap will be bridged between the current state and the desired future state.

Regarding the degree of alignment there is a simple cross-check with this intuitive diagnostic tool: your question 1 is mirrored by your partner's question 2 and vice versa—their question 1 is mirrored by your question 2. Linking questions 1 and 2 will give a feel for the current state of the relationship and question 3 will give the desired future state and approach. Support or secondary approaches sometimes occur when the relationship is under pressure or stress or special projects/tasks are being implemented. Questions 1, 2 and 3 can be answered prior to or during the workshop. The answers are then analysed in a joint discussion held at the workshop. The degree of compatibility of the results will determine the ease or difficulty the two organisations will have in developing and maintaining the partnership.

The RAD itself looks only at the single customer/supplier relationship and not the entire customer/supplier base or the organisation as a whole. However,

RAD—Relationship Alignment Diagnostic

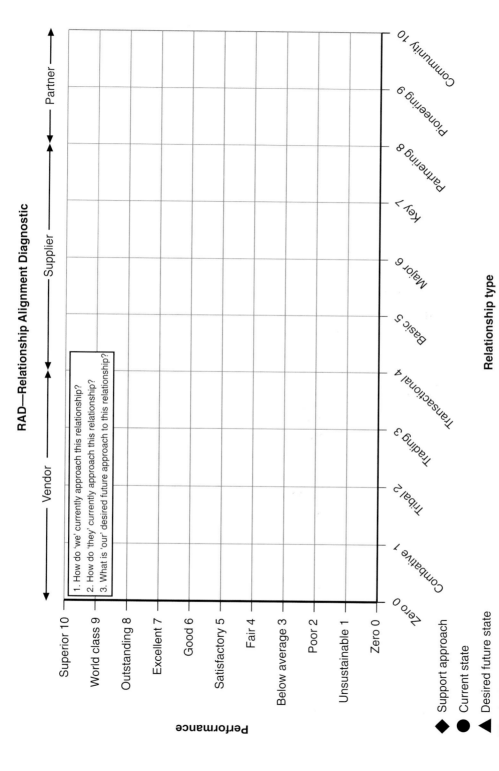

1. How do 'we' currently approach this relationship?
2. How do 'they' currently approach this relationship?
3. What is 'our' desired future approach to this relationship?

Performance

Vendor ⟶ Supplier ⟶ Partner ⟶

Superior 10
World class 9
Outstanding 8
Excellent 7
Good 6
Satisfactory 5
Fair 4
Below average 3
Poor 2
Unsustainable 1
Zero 0

Relationship type

Combative 1
Tribal 2
Trading 3
Transactional 4
Basic 5
Major 6
Key 7
Partnering 8
Pioneering 9
Community 10
Zero 0

◆ Support approach
● Current state
◀ Desired future state

Fig. 6.13 *Relationship health check: self-assessment*

the results of the RAD will shed much light on the nature of the customer and supplier organisations in general. It should be completed by the workshop participants, either individually or as a group.

This information will prove helpful in understanding the strengths and weaknesses of the partner organisations in the context of partnering/alliancing and give an indication of which areas need to be worked on. The RAD can then be used as an independent measurement tool to track regularly the progress and development of the partnership and the organisations themselves over a period of time. The RAD can also be used independently on internal customers and suppliers, where it would be useful in understanding the relationships between internal functions, departments, divisions and businesses.

List of participants

All the stakeholders who play a critical role in maintaining and developing the relationship and those people with a vested interest in ensuring its success should attend the workshop. These people will range from senior management to the shop floor. They will be a mixture of innovators, early adaptors, followers and the occasional terrorist (see Chap. 1). Their selection is important as they will be the ambassadors and champions for the next steps. They will need to take back with them to their own workplaces not only a sound understanding of the partnering/alliance principles and the actions arising from the workshop, but also their enthusiasm and new-found commitment. The success of the workshop will in part be measured by the desire of others to get involved with the process voluntarily.

Agree desired outcomes

Understand the minimum outcomes required of the workshop and tailor the agenda and workshop activities accordingly. The list may include:

- Jointly share vision and strategies and exchange information.
- Establish a joint Partnering/Alliance Charter detailing the shared vision/ mission and common goals/objectives and guiding principles for the relationship/project.
- Build the foundations of teamwork and trust.
- Complete SWOT analysis.
- Identify opportunities for improvement and barriers to implementation.
- Establish joint commitment and participation of all partners.
- Review degree of alignment.
- Understand the current state between the partners and the desired future state for the relationship.

- Establish a communication framework, i.e. what, why, how, when, to whom.
- Define individual roles/concerns.
- Agree methods of issue resolution/escalation.
- Agree on performance measurement methodology, KPIs (Key Performance Indicators) and milestones.
- Agree on the partnering/alliance manager(s) and partnering/alliance integrated lead team and management team members, or a process and time frame for choosing them.
- Agree the next steps and timing of the next workshop.

2. The workshop itself

Senior management must participate and lead the workshop agenda. The participants must be given enough time to ask plenty of questions and to think over what is being discussed. For most, it will probably be a foreign way of doing business and senior management and those on the coordinating team should be watching for confusion, doubt or mistrust. The activity must not be seen as just another flavour-of-the-month exercise. This is very much the occasion for active leadership.

There is a particularly important team exercise at the end of day 2 that involves identifying and then prioritising common issues/opportunities/problems via an impact/urgency matrix. The exercise is shown in Figure 6.14. Understand the number and spread of issues within the matrix, in particular the areas rated 'high' for either impact or urgency. The associated action plan should provide the basis for the next steps.

Agree at the workshop that, in the future, conflicts and issues will need to be resolved at the lowest possible level and at the earliest possible opportunity. To that end Figures 6.15 and 6.16 are examples of simple issue escalation, issue resolution processes. The operating principles that support the processes are as follows:

- All issues are to be resolved within the alliance/partnering relationship.
- Unresolved issues are to be escalated by both partners, in an agreed timely manner, prior to causing project delays, cost increases or other negative effects.
- Issues are to be resolved at the lowest level.
- There will be no jumping levels of authority.
- Ignoring the issue or making no decision is not acceptable.
- Decision time may be extended with the agreement of a level above the point of indecision.
- An issue can be escalated earlier than the process time frame by mutual agreement.
- Complete the feedback loop to the issue initiator.
- No one has the right to 'screw up' the agreement or the relationship.

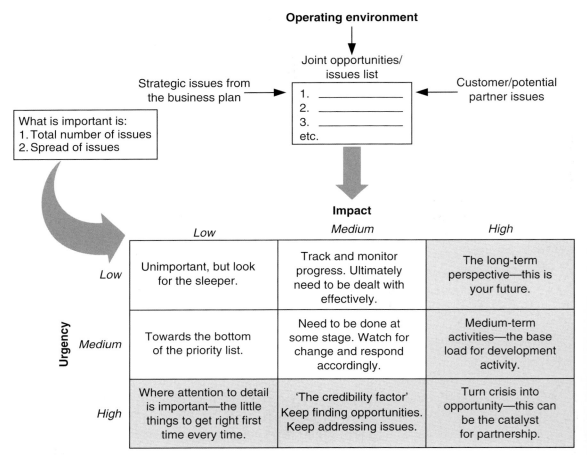

Fig. 6.14 *An impact/urgency analysis*

3. Post-workshop activities

Evaluation and follow-up will be one of the key activities of a successful workshop. The momentum from a successful workshop can be enormous and must not be lost. A follow-up letter from a senior manager should go to all participants thanking them for their participation. Distribution of notes and action lists from the workshop or a workshop report should go out promptly. A debriefing session should be held between senior management and the coordinating team to table feedback and agree on any subsequent role for the coordinating group. Alternatively, this can be done by the leadership team or the relationship management team.

Workshops should be held regularly (e.g. every 6–12 months), though not too frequently. Suitable times will become apparent as the steps are worked through.

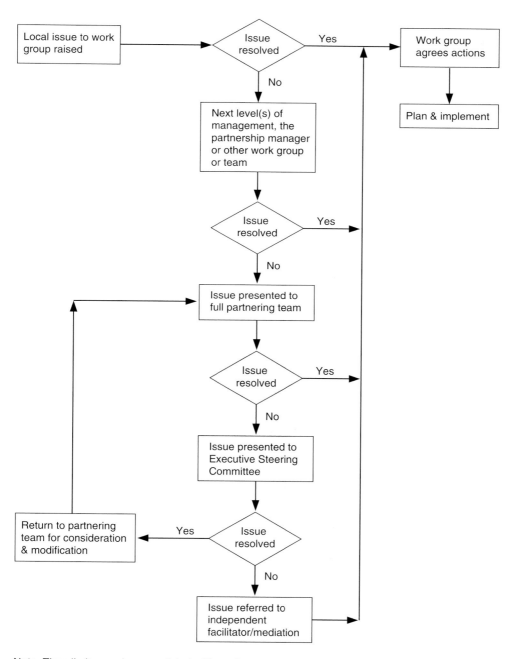

Note: Time limits can be associated with each step as appropriate.

Fig. 6.15 *Issue resolution process (sample)*

Level	Organisation A	Maximum time to resolve or escalate	Organisation B
1			
2			
3			
4			
5			
6			

Fig. 6.16   *Issue resolution/escalation process (sample)*

There are several reasons for holding workshops:

1. They are an important part of the education process of partnering/alliancing.
2. As the partnering/alliance relationship matures and enters different phases, new skills, people and ideas will be required. Workshops can be the vehicle by which information is exchanged, consensus decisions reached, ideas brainstormed and joint actions implemented.
3. They are a valuable avenue for training and personal development.
4. They are a revitalisation mechanism when momentum slows down.
5. They can be used as an avenue of recognition and celebration when milestones are reached.
6. They are an essential tool for performance measurement and relationship review.

The success of the workshop can be measured by the quality of actions implemented and the delivery of results in the short, medium and long term.

The Partnering/Alliance Charter and Partnering/Alliance Agreement

> *Stage 4 is Nirvana. Both sides have earned full trust through translating the goals of partnership into tangible results. Legal contracts have given way to a handshake.*
>
> *Keki Bhote*[1]

There are many variations but basically the Partnering/Alliance Charter consists of a jointly agreed vision and/or mission statement, a list of 8–12 major objectives or critical success factors (CSFs) and guiding principles for the relationship.

Richard Whitely[2] defines a vision as a 'vivid picture of an ambitious, desirable future state that is connected to the customer and better in some way than the current state'. The vision will have wholeness and integrity and embody the values and long-term aspirations of the partnership. The mission statement is more specific in time frame and intent. Usually in no more than one or two sentences, it outlines what is to be done, broad goals, and who is to achieve them. The main objectives or CSFs transform these goals into specific aims of the partnership. The key performance indicators (KPIs) are then developed from these main objectives/CSFs. The principles are those fundamental and self-evident truths by which the relationship will be guided.

Ideally, the Partnering/Alliance Charter is signed by all workshop participants, or all those who had to do with its development. This will certainly include senior management. It becomes the base document by which the partnership is evaluated and against which performance is measured. The charter also allows ownership of the outcomes and is a genuine symbol of recognition and empowerment for the stakeholders.

It must be remembered that the Partnering/Alliance Charter is not designed to be a legally enforceable contractual agreement. Its purpose is to focus on the working relationship and intent between the customer and supplier, not the legal relationship. The strategic partnership itself is not a legal partnership, joint venture or any other form of legal entity. It is about customers and suppliers working together for mutual benefit under a banner of trust and creative cooperation, with an intense desire to avoid adversarial confrontation. The charter is a formalisation of that desire. It is an observation that the more mature the customer/supplier relationship, the less reliance there is on legal rights and obligations.

A generic example of a typical charter is shown in Figure 6.17. Such a charter in itself won't, of course, produce the outcomes or in any way guarantee a successful partnership. It will be the people, their actions and behaviours, and the genuine intent behind the document that will deliver the real benefits over a period of time. Strategic partnering and alliance relationships are not an event, they are a process—a process based on people, skills, dedication and continuous improvement to achieve world class over a significant period of time.

Take care, however. Unless the right environment prevails, there is the possibility that the charter will become nothing more than a piece of paper that is used to instil fear and achieve short-term financial targets. This is one of the reasons why support from senior management is so important. The signing of these documents is usually followed by considerable publicity in

Partnering/Alliance Charter

Company A   &   Company B   (&C &D etc)
(+ logo)   (+ logo)

Vision
Role model alliance partners in delivering world-class results, products and services.

Mission
We will work together as a cooperative team, in a trusting environment, applying shared knowledge and skills, to achieve common goals for mutual benefit.

Critical Success Factors [or Objectives or Goals] (6–12)
(examples only)
- Cause zero harm to people, plant and environment
- Meet or exceed customer requirements and expectations
- Optimise reliability and asset utilisation
- Maintain open, honest, timely and accurate communication and information sharing
- Encourage proactive problem solving and joint resolution of issues
- Achieve an outstanding commercial outcome for all alliance partners
- Empower teams and individuals to achieve their full potential
- Promote the partnership to achieve broader business outcomes
- Establish an environment of total trust in people, systems and processes
- Demonstrate continuous and breakthrough improvement through innovation and joint benchmarking
- Have key stakeholders as advocates

Guiding Principles
- Act in a way that is best for the business
- Maintain integrity—do what you say you will
- Be fair and reasonable and act in good faith
- Do it right the first time
- Deal with and resolve all issues directly between the partners
- Commit to a 'no blame, high accountability' culture
- Promote the alliance principles in all stakeholder relationships
- Talk before you write
- Ensure no secrets, no lies and no unpleasant surprises
- Have fun and celebrate success

(Note: The signatures of all the people involved in the development of the Partnering Charter should appear on this document.)

Fig. 6.17 *Example of a partnering charter*

the form of widely distributed memos, company magazines and other internal publications. In raising the profile of the partnership, there is a large amount of promising up front. Make sure your organisation can deliver.

The process by which the charter is drafted is important and will determine the rate of success further down the line. It must be open and brutally honest. If it is to be a good charter, representative of what is to be achieved, then it will take some time to put together. You cannot enter into such a formal arrangement without understanding each other's capabilities, requirements, culture and strategies. Otherwise, each party is buying into obligations about which they have little or no understanding. From a legal perspective the use of the terms/labels 'strategic partnering' or 'strategic partnerships' are not intended to be a reference to formal legal partnerships with all the associated legal implications.

In the spirit and practice of 'no contract, no term' relationships, organisations are now complementing or replacing traditional legal, contractual agreements with a partnering/alliance agreement which incorporates a partnering/alliance charter. In complementing an existing legal contract, the partnering agreement can be a separate stand-alone document or incorporated as part of a single legal agreement. A variation on this arrangement is to have a master partnering/alliancing agreement with separate legally binding agreements for individual business cases or projects, or for a specific work scope (e.g. shutdowns). Individual project or business case agreements would then survive the master agreement in the event of termination or disengagement. The partnering/alliance principles and practices accompany any legal contractual arrangements with the traditional contract approach seen as a safety net or fallback in the event of the relationship deteriorating or collapsing.

Some of the features that distinguish partnering and alliance agreements from traditional commercial contracts include the following:

- It is a plain-English style, positive document.
- The 'fair dealing' spirit, principles and intent of the relationship, the vision and objectives for the relationship are documented up front.
- Consistent with a 'no blame' philosophy and the interdependence principle, a 'No Dispute' clause is sometimes incorporated into the agreement. This involves waiving rights to litigation between the alliance partners except in the case of 'Wilful Default'. There will be no liquidated damages of any sort. This is a true building-in of interdependence and removes the win/lose option from the relationship.
- The Executive Steering Board, which can have various titles (e.g. Alliance Leadership Team, Project Alliance Board) is the ultimate review and management body.

- The roles and responsibilities of the partnering/alliance leadership and management teams are clearly defined.
- A team approach and shared financial motivation to achieve common goals is clearly documented.
- Performance measurement processes are clearly defined, for example, KPI Balanced Scorecard/s/Performance Scorecard/s.
- Appropriate risk allocation and risk sharing mechanisms are documented and linked as appropriate to gain-sharing/pain-sharing risk/reward remuneration models.
- There is a speedy and effective issue-resolution process to ensure a win/win approach and outcomes in the event of conflict or issues arising.
- It includes a process and incentives for identifying and achieving breakthrough and continuous improvement and/or exceptional performance.

Be careful when using separate partnering and legal documents to avoid partnering for convenience. Switching between one document and the other to assert authority or for short-term gain or advantage will not be sustainable, and is not consistent with the principles and practice of partnering and alliancing. My preference is for a single partnering or alliance agreement combining both the moral agreement (i.e. principles, objectives, intent) and the legal framework, rights and obligations and other commercial considerations.

I am often asked if, when and how to involve the lawyers in partnering and alliance agreements. My answer? Get the intent, partnering and alliance principles right, agreed upon and the charters signed before involving the legal people in the formal sense. Do, however, get these people involved in the education process from the start. I have held many partnering and alliance seminars with lawyers, auditors and other legal and finance people in attendance. Many underwent a significant change in attitude once they understood the different nature of the rules of engagement that apply. For others, it was a surprisingly easy leap of faith to grasp and be supportive of the principles and practices. In some relationships there will be little to no involvement from legal people. In other relationships, where corporate policy dictates or lack of experience, size, complexity, $ value, risks and benefits are significant, or for other reasons, the relationship will benefit significantly from the input of good legal people, knowledgeable and supportive of alliance and partnering principles and practices. To that end they will add value to, rather than hinder, the process.

The relationship of choice

During the opening address of a one-day partnering workshop between a large private sector instrumentality (customer) and a critically important private sector service provider (supplier), the senior customer representative spoke the following words.

'Please, let me make it clear from the start. It is our intention with this partnering relationship not only to give *you* the opportunity to prove yourself as the supplier of choice, but that *we* as a team become the relationship of choice for the long term. This will be done because we are going to work cooperatively together to achieve demonstrable and ongoing best practice for shared benefit. As part of due process and government policy we will be taking the business out to the marketplace for review in three years. It is our aim to have this relationship, not just you the supplier, win the business openly and fairly, based on superior performance past, present, and future capability. However, if "we" the relationship cannot demonstrate peerless performance then it will be the relationship, that is both of "us", that is displaced, not just you the supplier. We will jointly share the risks as well as the benefits.'

These were truly enlightening words from a traditionally conservative environment. I realised that the step on from 'supplier of choice' is the 'relationship of choice'. Independent relationships will at best deliver 'preferred supplier' or 'supplier of choice' status. Interdependent partnerships will go one step further in forming the 'relationship of choice' between 'partners of choice'.

General workshops with customers and suppliers

Do not underestimate the value of general education (one- or two-day) partnering seminars with internal and external customers and suppliers at all levels. The knowledge, commitment and ownership gained, the ideas and step change in progress that can be generated are remarkable. This applies equally to non-partner organisations; that is, less than 8 on the relationship scale in Figure 1.4. Just knowing where they fit into the scheme of things can be invaluable. Remember: not everyone wants to be or is capable of being a genuine partner. Few organisations, however, don't want to learn and improve. There is no shame whatsoever in being part of a high performing 6 or 7 type relationship or, if appropriate, any relationship type delivering high levels of performance, that is, greater than 5 (satisfactory) on the 0 to 10 Relationship Management 'performance' scale (see Fig. 1.3).

Crisis management reviews

Still, all too often partnering and alliance relationships are born out of crisis. An upfront formal approach is often necessary if a crisis point has been reached where the business and the relationship are under threat. If it is recognised that cultural, strategic and structural changes must occur for the relationship to continue, then a summit meeting or formal review may well be required to agree on the way forward. This will probably require several meetings as well as a separate workshop with a partnership facilitator present to gain the support and commitment to move on to the next steps. Again, it is critical for senior management to be involved and committed. A workshop format similar to that shown in Figure 6.12 can be used.

It may also be that the development of the relationship to partner status requires a step change in technology or infrastructure, involving a significant investment of capital and/or resources. Support from both parties to a partnering/ alliance approach will be critical if such an important change is to be effectively achieved.

Ongoing reviews

There will be occasions where ongoing formal reviews other than workshops are appropriate and necessary. These occasions will include:

- business review and development meetings (BRADs), where progress to date and opportunities for the future are formally discussed; where specific strategic or marketplace issues or concerns are tabled;
- when there has been, or is to be, a change in management or key personnel within either the customer or supplier, so that the new people are brought up to date with the relationship and its objectives;
- agreement on future joint commitments—investment, R&D, product development;
- when capital needs to be spent or sanctioned;
- a celebration of the ongoing success of the partnership.

Informal reviews

The number and quality of informal reviews will be one of those intangible measures of the success of the partnership. An informal review involves people throughout both organisations informally and spontaneously offering suggestions, positive feedback and constructive criticism. It might be a five minute hallway discussion or a two hour technical review.

As much as anything else, it will be the anecdotal stories of professionalism, bravery, delivering service over and above, superior product quality and a thousand other amusing and interesting incidents that will nourish the relationship. The stories will be told in canteens, crib rooms, boardrooms, in the factories, in corridors, on planes, via mobile phones, on fax, electronic mail, in company magazines. We should never be surprised or underestimate how fast both good news and bad news can travel. This will be the partnering grapevine at work.

The key is sharing information

There is no substitute for openly shared information. It will be the basis for joint understanding and vision for the future. So it is crucial to set up a communication framework via which information can be exchanged internally and externally. Information will need to cross all levels, functions and departments and traverse cities, states and countries by whatever method is most appropriate—electronic mail linkups, links to the Internet, intranets and the information superhighway, fax, phone or face to face. What information should be shared? Basically, the same information that was shared internally should be shared externally with your partner. When there are no boundaries or barriers, there are no secrets. When you share common goals the partnership effectively becomes one organisation.

A fallback strategy if the potential partner says 'No thanks'

Don't be disappointed if the partner says 'Thanks, but no thanks' or something similar. They have done you a big favour, saved you considerable time and resources, and probably a lot of money. Customers and suppliers can say no to partnering/alliancing for all sorts of reasons, including:

- lack of a clear set of value propositions
- perceived or real misalignment on culture, strategy, structure, process and people that is difficult or inappropriate to correct;
- customer concern on the medium- to longer-term viability of the supplier to sustain competitive advantage due to:
  —variability in current process causing potential quality non-conformance and/or supply problems during periods of high demand
  —current technology or process approaching redundancy
  —lack of investment in the development or acquisition of new technology or process
  —financial instability (current and/or future);
- lack of confidence in and respect for senior management or other influential policy makers;
- change in supplier strategy that is incompatible with the customer's own strategy or vice versa;

- supplier has links with customer's direct competitors or other downstream competitors;
- supplier has links with other competitive substitutes for the customer's own products and services;
- potential for workplace instability that could cause an interruption to supply or reduced dependability, e.g. strikes, production slowdowns, management/worker confrontation;
- customer has a low level of trust and/or confidence in the supplier personnel servicing his or her business and vice versa.

It is a time for reflection. Retreat to a neutral corner, reassess the strategy and value propositions and implement a new action plan as appropriate. It may be only a temporary setback; if you are the supplier, keep up the current level of quality and service to reinforce the benefits and return when the time is right. Also take the opportunity to review alternative partners.

The wait-and-see approach

At the other end of the spectrum from the crisis point is the wait-and-see approach. Here, the relationship is built 'slowly but surely', based on ongoing performance and regular informal monitoring. When the time is right, take a more formal approach. Have a review meeting with some positive things to talk about, and opportunities and issues to be clarified. Then consolidate via a partnering/alliance workshop. This is often a risk-taking initiative by middle management or shop-floor champions without the full support and knowledge of senior management.

The customer partner is likely to be more receptive to partnership development if there are already tangible signs that significant and permanent change has taken place, in particular the delivery In Full On Time to A1 specification of the products or service, and the part earning of trust: that is, getting it right the first time. This sends a powerful message to both internal and external customers and suppliers. Clearly, delivery IFOTA1 will take time, depending on the environment and the rate of change within the customer and supplier organisations. Seeking a commitment before a change in performance is visible can lead to a 'prove it to me' scepticism from the customer that can often become an obstacle to progress.

The role of surveys

Surveys can prove a useful tool from both a customer and a supplier perspective. They help in understanding the supplier partner's current performance opposite the customer partner's ranked requirements, show how the supplier partner's performance (as appropriate) compares with that of the opposition and also how the relationship overall is performing. Surveys also assist customers to improve their performance as givers of timely, accurate information and to understand the degree of cooperation and teamwork in place. With that knowledge you can determine in what areas improvement is required and set about putting a corrective action plan into place. Second, surveys give you the opportunity to see how people at various levels in the customer and supplier organisations feel about the partnership. All levels of personnel, from top to bottom, should participate in surveys. The results can provide a useful starting point and ongoing measure for understanding the level of maturity and reciprocity towards partnering and even an indication of some of the people issues that may need to be addressed. Good surveys will also give an opportunity for the respondents to give their view of the pleasant and unpleasant surprises that have occurred over the period, as well as the future opportunities for continuous and breakthrough improvement.

Traditional tenders and strategic partnering/alliance relationships don't mix

The traditional 'lowest-bid' tendering process is the antithesis of both the principles and the practice of partnering and alliancing. It reduces the field of suppliers to the lowest common undifferentiated denominator. Tendering may be the crisis point or the point in time where the partnership starts, but it is certainly not the way the partnership is sustained. For organisations that are serious about developing partnering and alliance relationships, whether they are customers or suppliers, the clear objective should be to remove the tendering process from the relationship. This decision will need to be based on results achieved measured against agreed key performance indicators (KPIs), the capability of delivering on future requirements, a substantial amount of trust and a clear commitment to the partnering/alliancing process. The use of tenders in partnerships is difficult for a number of reasons.

1. Tenders display a lack of trust in the supplier and a lack of confidence in the customer.
2. They lock both parties in for a fixed term that often encourages neglect and poor performance in the early stages of the agreement with a gradual improvement in performance against objectives/KPIs as the tender period runs its course and the renewal date approaches. This can lead to

considerable variation in quality and service, with the inevitable effects on process efficiencies and productivity.

3. They create a lowest-bid or lowest price mentality even if the intent is based on total cost, total value or total quality, the effect often being poorer quality and increased prices.

4. Tenders stifle creativity and innovation due to reduced margins and the traditional confrontational, adversarial nature of communication negotiations, and general management of the relationship.

5. While on the surface tenders create a long-term commitment, the reality is a shallow, non-strategic approach that, over time, diminishes enthusiasm and increases the level of frustration for both parties.

6. The tender process itself can be very expensive for both customers and suppliers.

If you ask 'Why do organisations go out to tender?', the answer will often come back 'We have to test the marketplace'. Why do they have to test the marketplace? Because of lack of information, lack of benchmarks and because there is, on most occasions, a lack of trust. The irony is, world-class companies already have the information that their customers are seeking independently via the competitive process. They choose for one or more reasons not to share that information and not to be open and transparent. One of the mechanisms by which good alliance partners openly and legitimately avoid the tender process is by jointly testing and benchmarking the marketplace together. The Mobil Oil and Transfield Services integrated services and maintenance alliance has a cross-organisational team in place to jointly benchmark best practice around the world. Joint visits to other best practice sites occur and improvements are implemented and monitored.

Sometimes, however, tenders are an immutable fact of life: for example, in the area of public service contracts where probity considerations, government policy and accountability of public money are sensitive issues. However, this paradigm is changing with many public sector departments and functions entering into longer-term, sometimes partnering relationships where the tender process is either extensively modified or illuminated. See Sydney Water Case Study on pages 426–461 for further details.

Partnering is often commenced only after the award of the contract to the supplier/contractor. In these cases, if tendering is potentially the starting point to a partnership, both parties should take a genuinely long-term perspective on quality, service, price, innovation and relationship issues, not just the traditional price perspective. Understand before the contract is awarded the cultural, strategic and structural alignment between the organisations.

I have been involved in several partnering/alliance workshops where the process up to that date had involved a traditional hard-nosed, adversarial contractual approach from both customer and supplier. Several months after the contract had been awarded and the supplier commenced delivery of the products and services, the customer brought the various parties in the relationship together for a partnering/alliance workshop. It took half a day out of a two-day workshop to clear away the baggage and legacy of past combative practices before a constructive and cooperative approach could be taken. It then took many months of hard work to consolidate the benefits, which could have been achieved from day one if a genuine partnering/alliancing approach had been taken at the start of the process. Work on the people relationships and commit to the partnering/alliance process and all its principles up front. If the relationship is successful in partnering terms— based on observation, measurement and benchmarked performance—there should be no need to retender. In short, the incumbent supplier should have the right to retain the business on the basis of current performance against objectives and the capability to meet future requirements.

CASE STUDY

Baxter Healthcare and Mannesmann Dematic Colby (Colby)

Baxter Healthcare is the largest medical goods and services supplier to the hospital and healthcare industry in Australia. For Baxter Healthcare, the main reason for dealing with Mannesmann Dematic Colby (Colby) as their materials handling partner was the alignment that existed between the two organisations on culture, strategy and people. Baxter's high growth rates required a partner committed to the long term. Colby invested two years of management time getting to understand Baxter's business and developed a plan for Baxter without receiving any business themselves during that period. As a sign of good faith when an agreement was struck in 1993, Baxter included an 'early completion bonus' for project work rather than 'late' penalty clauses.

Performance and innovation since then has been outstanding. Distribution costs have decreased in actual terms from 1995 to 1999 despite a significant increase in activity. Additional expertise such as modelling, materials movement analysis, facilities planning, product flow and the like is also given. Individual projects are based on open costing with an agreed margin. 'The last major racking project was finished one month ahead of schedule and Baxter shared with Colby 50/50 the savings from outside storage costs no longer required,' says Ian Williams, Baxter's National Distribution Manager.

Baxter has acknowledged both the long-term commitment of Colby and their performance to date through an evergreen, open-ended relationship. Ian Williams is confident about the future of the relationship when he states, 'Through the development of trust we have eliminated the need for competitive tendering on our projects. We will continue with this partnering approach with Colby, together with the joint five-year planning process and grow the business into other states for mutual benefit.'

REFERENCES

1. Keki Bhote, *Strategic Supply Management*, American Management Association, 1989, p.16.
2. Richard Whiteley, *The Customer Driven Company—Moving from Talk to Action*, Business Books, London, 1991, p.26.
3. 'IBM wins without tendering', *Sydney Morning Herald*, 20 July 1997.

Requirements analysis (present and future)

Objective

To determine jointly the customer partner's present and future requirements and to make full use of innovation and improvement to extend previous expectations and set stretch targets.

Key points

1. Use an integrated team approach to determine current and future customer requirements; use listening and questioning skills in order to understand requirements, then confirm that a common understanding exists. Repeat the sequence whenever necessary.

2. Requirements are two-way. In the same manner understand supplier requirements on customers.

3. Use flow charts and value chain analysis to understand the processes and process flows involved.

4. Document in detail all the customer's requirements.

5. Discuss requirements with those who will ensure their delivery IFOTAI (In Full On Time to A1 specification), including everyone who is interested.

6. Carry out regular reviews of changes in requirements and new technologies.

7. Benchmark against the world's best or industry best practice. Exchange lots of information.

8. Match customer requirements to internal product/service specifications and upstream external supplier product/service specifications.

9. Understand your process capabilities with the aim of exceeding current requirements and meeting future requirements: prevention, prediction, design out; measurement; process stability; reduce variation; develop new and improved systems and procedures.

10. Determine the skills required of individuals and teams to meet these objectives.

11. Consider the future, innovation and exceeding requirements. Conduct an 'opportunity search'. Jointly discover, create, agree and then deliver those future requirements, where appropriate beyond the customer's current expectations.

> *Requirements, like measurements, are communications.*
>
> *Philip Crosby*[1]

Current and future requirements of customer and supplier partners will need to be clear, unambiguous, documented and shared with all those people who have something to do with their delivery. Once again, the importance of people and communication is paramount. Understanding and then meeting customer requirements is the starting point for all differentiation and innovation. You cannot possibly expect to gain competitive advantage by creating and developing unique value-added products and services unless, at the heart of the relationship, the basic In Full On Time to A1 (IFOTA1) specification requirements are understood, agreed upon and then met. This will involve a two-way flow of ideas, data and other information, and a clear understanding of the processes involved. Immediate customers and suppliers will not be the only ones taking part. Fundamental in this process will also be the involvement of customers' customers, other suppliers, their suppliers, distributors, consumers, government bodies and anyone who is within the supply chain or associated with it and can throw light on, or impact on, the real requirements.

We can define a process as a series of inputs to produce an output. If every process is also part of a larger process and, in turn, is itself made up of smaller processes, then the entire supply chain becomes important in understanding requirements. Flow charts can be a powerful tool in understanding processes, and thus requirements, because they define the outcomes of a process flow. Requirements are the performance or effect that the customer expects the supplier's product or service to deliver. Working back from that point to determine the various inputs required of people, design, raw materials, manufacturing conditions, materials handling, and so on needs a clear understanding of the process flows involved.

The laptop computer

In the early 1980s the Japanese had a problem. Their offices were small and so were their desks, by western standards, and their bulky, space consuming desktop computers left little room for anything else. Hence their requirement for something more compact and portable that could be put into a drawer when not in use, thus freeing up the desktop for other work.

The result was the laptop computer. Contrary to popular belief, they didn't appear because executives wanted to write reports when flying business class on intercontinental jets. However, the extension of their applications was obvious, their use and capabilities have blossomed since then and they are now at the forefront of computer technology. This is an example of how understanding and meeting customer requirements is a fundamental part of good customer/supplier relationships, and how meeting the original requirements can lead to further extended and value-adding applications.

Requirements and total quality

Philip Crosby[2] tells us that the definition of quality is 'conformance to requirements', first time and every time. This refers to all areas of business: commercial, technical, developmental, financial and managerial. From the Deming perspective, quality is about understanding processes, process stability, variation and continuity of purpose.

The supplier partner must be proactive in meeting the customer's future requirements. This will mean developing superior systems and processes, and understanding and exceeding today's requirements in order to meet the customer's future expectations. We all have an example of where a supplier has gone beyond the expected—the service at McDonald's; the tradesman who surprises us by being on time, courteous, and competent at a reasonable price; the supermarket that returned a customer's lost property to her home by courier. The result is that we continue to use the product or service. We remember the incident as a pleasing story and tell others about it at every opportunity. Of course, this scenario also works in reverse. We also remember the bad stories, tell others about them, and don't go back.

Customers remember:

1. non-conformance to requirements in a negative way;
2. exceeding of requirements in a positive way;
3. conformance to requirements with the response: 'That's what we pay you for.'

While conformance to requirements is a noble quality objective, these days it is strictly a stay-in-business strategy. In my view, no one will ever get ahead of the pack from now on by simply conforming to requirements. This applies even more to partnerships, where conformance to requirements is only a 'ticket to play'. It is the entry fee by which the organisation gains respect and credibility as being customer-led and customer-focused. Conformance to requirements gives rise to comments such as:

- 'Yes, they do everything we ask of them. They are good suppliers.'
- 'No problems, no complaints, but nothing extra special either.'
- 'They're great at being reactive—proactive is the problem.'

This is not the stuff of which partnering and alliance relationships, excellence and world class are made. What is required is performance that prompts this kind of comment:

- 'These people are incredible. They really do go the extra mile for customer service and in exceeding our requirements.'
- 'It seems as if nothing is impossible for these people. A truly leading-edge, innovative and professional organisation.'
- 'It is as if we were one organisation in the way we work together. They are here for the long term.'
- 'I was most impressed with your company's achievements over the last couple of years. It is also a reinforcement of our desire to work with you as a strategic partner.'

Process capabilities versus requirements (known and unknown)

> *The best enterprises stood out because they knew what their customers wanted and what was driving their future needs. They actively identified the key areas of benefit to customers and they acted on that knowledge. They had developed a deep understanding of their customers' value chain, and how their own supply system delivered value for money to their customers. Some of the best businesses had developed a close relationship with a leading customer that gave new insights into products and services that would be valuable to other, fast-following customers.*
> *Business Council of Australia[3]*

As you can see from Figure 6.18, strategic partnerships are about going beyond conformance to requirements. Understanding the relationship between customer requirements and supplier process capability puts into perspective the extent to which resources and effort must be focused, and the alternatives to strategic partnering should the strategy falter or not be taken up at all.

Requirements unknown/Supplier process: incapable

Forget partnerships—you are on the road to disaster, if not out of business already. This is the world of breakdown maintenance. The supplier is too busy firefighting to think about anything else. Nothing short of a revolution in management, culture and attitude, probably in conjunction with a great deal of money spent on capital, skills and the right people, will save this position. Even if this were possible, is there the time to implement? It can be done, but be prepared for the journey.

Requirements (current) known/Supplier process: incapable

This is the classic case of over-promise and under-deliver. You know what is required, you just aren't capable of delivering. If you understand why and have the vision, strategy, people, time and, probably, additional finance to improve, then anything is possible.

Requirements unknown/Supplier process: capable

You have the capability but don't understand the details. The result is a list of features that you need to turn into benefits before 'value for money' is achieved. Much time and effort can be wasted here. The real requirements must be uncovered if improvement is to be made.

Requirements (current) known/Supplier process: capable

This is about preventative relationship maintenance. Conformance to requirements is the name of the game and the stuff many a good customer/supplier relationship is made of, but it is not a partnership. However, this is an excellent starting point for partnerships if the right platform of culture, people and leadership is in place. Be prepared, the next steps to improvement will take considerable time and resources. Understand what you are letting yourself in for.

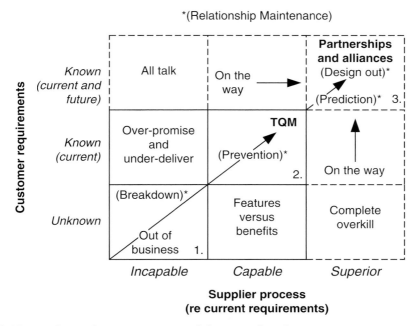

Fig. 6.18 *Understanding requirements and then exceeding them*

Requirements (current and future) known/Supplier process: incapable

This is a complete waste of time. Take a step back to reality and decide if the long hard road to recovery is desired or even possible.

Requirements unknown/Supplier process: superior

There is either a complete breakdown in communication between customer and supplier or the process itself services varied markets and customers, some more important or critical than the others. Unless there is a particular unique niche being serviced virtually free of competition, requirements need to be understood and quickly. This can also be a very expensive combination.

Requirements (current and future) known/Supplier process: capable

Understand what are the process requirements to meet future customer requirements. Hopefully, technology, capital or lack of vision and willpower will not hold you back.

Requirements (current) known/Supplier process: superior

This is well on the way. The relationship at this point should be strong enough, based on previous performance, to uncover future requirements quickly. This is where the effort should be put.

Requirements (current and future) known/Supplier process: superior

This is the stuff partnerships are made of. Predictive and design-out relationship maintenance is a way of life. Things are done in a sustainable continuous manner beyond the customer's current expectations and towards future requirements. In addition, the future is understood and being planned for with processes that are integrated, re-engineered and capable of delivering. There are very few customers and suppliers in this position today. In all but the rare exception this combination will provide genuine and sustainable competitive advantage.

How to determine requirements

> A study by the Technical Assistance Research Programs Institute in Washington, DC, found that only one-third of customer dissatisfaction was due to defects in product or service—the manufacturing failures and paper-work errors that quality programs usually try to correct. The remaining two-thirds is failure to communicate.[4]

Customer/partner requirements are directly linked to the individual partner business drivers and strategies, the value propositions for the relationship under review and a thorough understanding and analysis of the customer and supplier partner value chains. With this thorough understanding of the customer and supplier value chains, processes and process flows, ask: 'What are your requirements?' Then:

- listen (to understand)
- question (to understand)
- confirm (to ensure common understanding).

Then, if necessary, listen, question and confirm again and again until the requirements are clear and understood. It is almost as simple as that: 'What are your requirements?' This can also be determined by an integrated customer/supplier partnering team based on the shared vision and common goals/objectives for the relationship and mutual benefit. How many times have you seen a situation where obtaining requirements is like a guessing game or the pulling of teeth? The buyer is hesitant to give too much away because of a lack of trust or openness, and the seller is uncomfortable asking the question up front for fear of embarrassment or ridicule for having such a lack of knowledge. Or, more often than not, one or both parties are simply poor communicators. They don't fully understand the importance of communicating requirements, or they assume or expect that they are already known.

The other point about understanding requirements is that you have to become a good listener. This is surprisingly difficult for a great many people—we love to tell but hate being told. The requirements will be linked directly to the key objectives for the relationship as expressed in the Partnering/Alliance Charter.

Document requirements

Seek first to understand ... Then be understood   *Stephen R. Covey*[5]

Once understood, it is extremely important that these requirements are then clearly and succinctly documented for the benefit of internal personnel, external suppliers and, of course, the customer partner. The next step is to communicate and discuss in detail these requirements with those internal and external suppliers empowered with ensuring their delivery—and, for good measure, anyone else who is the slightest bit interested.

At some stage the customer requirements need to be translated into internal product or service specifications to ensure effective manufacture and delivery. This will involve agreement on tolerances, upper and lower specification limits, and so on. This link between specifications, statements of work, requirements and performance is critical.

Link requirements to agreed KPIs

Once the requirements have been determined and documented they need to be linked into key performance indicators (KPIs). The KPIs then provide the basis for measurement against performance and an effective evaluation of the pace of continuous improvement and the overall quality of the relationship. The key with KPIs in partnerships is creativity. Strategic partnering is about a paradigm shift in the way things are done. If you measure on the basis of standard KPIs it is unlikely that you will be able to measure the paradigm shift fairly, if at all. For example, how do you currently measure and track the level of fear in your organisation, the quality of leadership, sustainable, competitive advantage, the degree of empowerment, openness of communication? These are not standard measures but they certainly provide the basis for an effective partnership. My guess is that strong and effective partnerships currently operating are doing themselves a great disservice by not measuring the true impact of the relationship on their organisations. The benefits are far broader and deeper than the standard list of conventional KPIs would indicate.

Refer to Chapter 7 for a more detailed discussion on measurement and KPIs and the links with performance and return on investment/financial success.

Characteristics of a good listener

Listen with the same intensity with which you speak. Being a good listener is about attitude. It applies to both customers and suppliers and is a frame of mind that says, 'I am really interested in what is being said because it is important to me to explore and understand your needs and expectations.' Being a good listener takes practice, patience, understanding and an attention to detail. It also requires empathy for the current state of the customer's and supplier's business, and the general operating environment. Involve everyone in the listening process and invest in developing listening skills. Become a listening organisation.

Part of being a good listener involves being a good questioner, too. Asking the right questions at the right time of the right people is the hallmark of good listening. Encourage your customer with open questions, closed questions, simple, complex, confident, hesitant and naive questions—questions that cause the customer to laugh, to think and rethink, to confirm. All sorts of questions!

Requirement teams

Understanding and agreeing requirements does not have to be a one-to-one experience. The larger and more complex the organisations, the more appropriate it will be to involve others from within and outside the organisations. Forming an integrated 'requirements team' can often prove valuable in gaining not only a clear and accurate view of customer requirements but ownership and commitment as well. The requirements team may very well develop into the partnering team.

Requirements and the supply chain

Every step in the supply chain will have a specific set of requirements that needs to be meet. A simple example would be an outdoor plastic furniture set made up of four chairs and a table. The sampling of the requirements along the customer/supplier chain may go something like this.

Consumer requirements on the retailer

- Four chairs + one table.
- The chairs are to have a high back, armrests, be comfortable and strong, and able to be left permanently outdoors.
- The table is to be round, not oval, and approximately 1.5 metres in diameter.
- The preferred colours of both table and chairs as sets is avocado green, beige and white. No colour variation within a table and chair set will be accepted.
- Table and chairs will need to last a minimum of 5 years in an outdoor location.
- Stock is to be on the floor for evaluation. The consumer will not buy sight unseen.
- Home delivery is required within 24 hours of purchase.
- Credit cards will need to be an acceptable form of payment.

Retailer requirements on the wholesaler

- A minimum stock level of two sets of tables and matching chairs conforming to the consumer requirements in every detail will need to be on the shop floor at any one time.
- Any additional stock is to be held on a consignment basis.
- To avoid stockouts, the wholesaler is to guarantee restocking to at least the minimum level within 24 hours, or the same day if the request is made before 12 noon.
- Credit terms of payment 60 days from date of invoice will need to be made available.

Retailer requirements on internal staff regarding the outdoor furniture

- They are courteous and polite to customers.
- They are knowledgeable about the product capabilities and specifications.
- They maintain good relationships with the wholesaler(s).

Wholesaler requirements on the manufacturer

- Minimum stock holding of 100 sets of tables and chairs, to be paid for 30 days from date of delivery.
- Additional stock to be held on a consignment basis.
- All stock to meet the consumer requirements in every detail.
- Chairs and table are to be able to withstand a weight of 250 kg without collapsing.
- Credit terms of payment 45 days from date of invoice.

Wholesaler requirements on internal staff regarding the outdoor furniture

- They are courteous and polite to retailers.
- They ensure adequate stocks at both retailer and wholesaler.
- They maintain good relationships with the manufacturers.

Manufacturer requirements on the raw material suppliers

- The supplier/manufacturer of polypropylene plastic resin delivers the compounded resin to the agreed specification on:
  —co-polymer polypropylene
  —% ethylene content
  —melt flow index
  —density
  —impact strength
  —stiffness
  —tensile strength
  —UV stabiliser
- The masterbatch supplier delivers every time masterbatch colour compound to the agreed colour specification.
- The design of the chair and the manufacture of the moulding tool to meet specification and the relevant industry standard.
- All suppliers are to be ISO or Australian standards accredited.

Manufacturer's requirements on internal staff

- The compounded resin and masterbatch are added in the correct proportions according to an agreed standard production specification or formulation sheet.

- Injection moulding machine's conditions (temperature, pressure, etc.) are to be as per the agreed specification.
- Manufacturing schedules are to be in line with stock-holding requirements and sales and marketing forecasts.

Polypropylene raw material supplier requirements

- Quality of propylene feedstock to meet specification first time every time.
- Reactor conditions to conform to agreed manufacturing specification.
- Production campaigns to be in line with sales forecasts, stock-holding requirements and sales and marketing forecasts.

All this is just a small sample of the supply chain requirements and, clearly, we could go into more detail. The point is, even for an apparently simple product like a plastic furniture set, there is ultimately an enormous number of requirements at all points in the supply chain. For partnerships the level of complexity is far greater. There will be the need to understand not only your immediate customer/supplier requirements, but also those requirements further up and down the supply chain. They will undoubtedly have a bearing on your own immediate environment. All requirements need to be met if the ultimate consumers are to receive their goods and services In Full On Time to A1 specification. It is even critical for the raw-material supplier to understand the requirements at all the other points in the supply chain, especially the consumers.

Thinking about, or reassessing, your own process capability to meet these requirements is the next step. Also think about the skills required of individuals and teams. This is discussed in some detail later in this chapter in the section on customer/supplier skills requirements, but it is useful at this point to think generally about what is required.

Understanding requirements is crucial if conformance to requirements, and then exceeding them, is to follow.

Review requirements often

If we are to live and work in an atmosphere of continuous improvement, then it must be that requirements will change over time. How this change process is managed is important if customer and supplier partners are to maximise the benefits to be gained. Return again and again to requirements. Take every opportunity to understand how things have changed throughout all areas of the business. Depending on the nature of the business, reviews could be daily, weekly, monthly, or when required. With continuous change comes the opportunity for continuous innovation. The two are inextricably linked. Refer back to the relationship development curve on page 49. Where is the relationship on the curve, what is the next breakthrough going to look like, and where do you have to go to and who do you have to talk to in order to find out?

Understand supplier requirements

Requirements are a two-way process, applying to both customer and supplier partners. Good customers must also conform to requirements, both current and future. First, as recipients of products and services from their suppliers: forecast accuracy, timely and accurate sharing of information and technical specifications, early strategy development, early supplier involvement in concept, design product and service development, proactive win/win approach to problem solving, elimination of waste and duplication, effective and timely decision making, and access to people, systems and functions will be just some of the expectations required of world-class customer partners. Second, as suppliers to their own customers there will be a set of requirements on their own products and services.

Exceeding current requirements and delivering future requirements

Are exceeding current requirements and delivering future requirements two different things or one and the same? Answer: yes and no. Exceeding requirements is about promising and then over-delivering. If this is in the context of genuinely delivering future requirements, whether the customer is in a position to benefit or otherwise, then they are the same thing.

However, it could be a case of delivering benefits by utilising skills and expertise, products or services within the supplier organisation that are entirely unrelated to the direct product or service delivered. In this way, the supplier's credibility and reputation are enhanced and the customer receives additional value beyond the original agreed requirements. Examples might be forming a joint team to complete a skills program to upgrade computing competencies, a joint benchmarking team on workplace reform, or a joint problem-solving team. Probably, none of these initiatives will impact directly on the supplier's immediate volumes or turnover, and they are probably not part of the future requirements associated with the supplier's original product or service. However, if effectively managed and implemented, the customer will gain the benefits of an upgrade in computer skills, improved industrial relations and improved quality. Of course, depending on the circumstances, initiatives like these can also work in reverse, with the benefits also falling back on the supplier.

Solving an immediate crisis is another example. A problem has arisen with the customer, quite unrelated to the supplier's product or service, but causing the customer genuine concern, financial or otherwise. The skills of the supplier organisation—whether people, hardware or software—help to solve the problem. The supplier's credibility and stature with the customer partner is enhanced, preferred supplier status and the partnering relationship have been further secured and the customer partner is delighted to have the requirements exceeded.

Opportunity search to uncover and fulfil future requirements

Take the opportunity to search for opportunities. Whether future requirements are known or unknown to customer and/or supplier, they need to be discovered, uncovered, agreed upon, developed and successfully implemented. Regular opportunity reviews, partnering teams, brainstorming sessions, business review and development meetings (BRADs), technical reviews, use of requirements teams, site visits, benchmarking and benchmarking teams, visits to customers/users downstream in the supply chain, de Bono's[6] six thinking hats technique, and surveys are just some of the ways to determine future requirements. Not least will be the sharing of vision, strategies and general information. This whole area of searching for opportunities will be the perfect environment and breeding ground for innovation and the basis upon which competitive advantage is achieved or sustained.

Understanding whether the supplier is capable of delivering these requirements is then the next step. If not, what improvements are necessary in the areas of technology, process, people and design to conform to the agreed requirements? Within what time frame?

REFERENCES

1. Philip Crosby, *Quality without Tears*, McGraw-Hill, New York, 1984, p.65.
2. Crosby, op. cit., p.59.
3. Roderick Carnegie & Matthew Butlin, *Managing the Innovating Enterprise*, Business Council of Australia, 1993, pp.6–7.
4. John Goodman, Arlene Malech & Colin Adamson, 'Don't fix the product, fix the customer', *Quality Review*, Fall 1988, European edn, pp.6–11.
5. Stephen R. Covey, *The Seven Habits of Highly Effective People*, The Business Library, 1990, p.235 (the fifth habit).
6. Edward de Bono, *Serious Creativity*, Harper Collins, London, 1992, pp.253–4.

> ## Meeting requirements In Full On Time to A1 specification (IFOTA1)
>
> ### (a) The quick fix
>
> **Objective**
> To ensure conformance to agreed requirements IFOTA1 by putting into place, as necessary, short-term, temporary (quick-fix) solutions before more permanent quality solutions are found.
>
> **Key points**
> 1. Understand (current) requirements.
>
> 2. Measure to determine degree of conformance.
>
> 3. Institute quick-fix solutions as appropriate.
>
> 4. Look for problems and crises that can be turned into opportunities quickly and cost effectively.
>
> 5. Lay the foundations for root-cause analysis, future systems and procedural changes, and process stability.

> *The need for quality goods and services is so well understood by consumers that it is perhaps puzzling that quality is a 'problem', indeed so great a problem in marketing today that 'fixing' the problem is now seen as a source of competitive advantage.*[1]

Once the current requirements are understood and agreed with the customer partner, the supplier partner and their suppliers must determine whether they are meeting them first time and every time. This is the basic stay-in-business objective. You cannot hope to form a strategic partnership unless you can meet requirements In Full On Time to A1 specification. We are not concerned at this stage whether they are being delivered in a quality way, using SPC techniques, systems analysis, TQM principles or business process re-engineering (BPR). At this point we are more interested in the end result than the means of getting there.

In Crosby quality terms this is the 'fix department'. Understand exactly what the requirements are, then measure for conformance. Institute quick-fix corrective action as appropriate to ensure no more non-conformances. In the real world, 'quick fixes' in some form or another are inevitable. Even stable systems will produce non-conformances and special events. Ensuring stability, reducing variation and, if appropriate, generating sustainable systems changes will guarantee the greater consistency, reliability and dependability that is required. The more permanent solutions deal with preventing, predicting and designing out non-conformances. This will follow.

I remember, when working in the plastics business, we sold plastic resin in pellet form. The available packages were 25 kg plastic bags, 1 tonne semi-bulk boxes or full-bulk container loads. At that time we were selling approximately 30 000 tonnes p.a. in bags. A major problem was the delivery of damaged bags to customers for which the replacement cost alone, in terms of returning stock, raising credit notes, double handling and wastage, was $250 000 p.a. This was quite separate from the loss of goodwill, ongoing business and credibility in the marketplace. At that stage we had no real idea where and when the bags were being damaged. It could have been at the factory, when being lifted onto trucks to be delivered to the warehouse, at the warehouse before delivery to the customer, or in a number of other areas.

To avoid the time delay in waiting for a report to reduce or eliminate the problem, we made it a requirement overnight that split bags were not to be delivered to customers. That's not to say that damaged bags would not still be produced—that was a separate issue to be dealt with in a quality way over an agreed time frame. But the customers would not see them. From that point on, the damaged bags would be downgraded and sold at a reduced price as scrap.

Of course, the uproar from various people and departments was enormous. The warehouse and distribution department went crazy and said, 'Do you realise how many split bags we get? We won't have any place to put them.' What they had been doing was taping or patching them up and then sending them out to the customers. They were not concerned at all about the root cause, because for them there was no incentive to do so. The accountants and logistics people screamed that this initiative would cost a fortune to finance. The point they were missing was that customers didn't want to pay for damaged bags, and shouldn't have to. Contamination, spillage, safety and short weights were real issues and the customers were quite rightly getting fed up.

None of the concerns of the accounting and warehouse people happened, in fact. What the requirement (the quick fix) of 'no damaged bags to the customers' did was immediately to focus all efforts onto determining the root cause and finding a permanent solution. This occurred, and over the next twelve months the cost of damaged bags was reduced from $250 000 to less than $20 000 p.a.

In addition to quick-fix solutions, be on the alert for a major problem that can be turned into an opportunity. There is nothing better for reinforcing the credibility and reputation of an organisation than turning a liability into an asset in a professional and quality manner. This is a real skill that needs to be developed; genuine competitive advantage can be gained by solving a major problem.

Laying the foundations for permanent solutions

The quick fix is just that—a temporary solution until the problem recurs or until permanent, quality solutions have been found. While a clever and effective quick fix may be the start of a partnering/alliance relationship, it will in no way sustain it. The future will be about flexibility, consistency, and the reliability and dependability of products, services, systems and processes, as a base upon which the relationship can develop.

Meeting requirements In Full On Time to A1 specification (IFOTA1)

(b) Quality solutions

Objective

To develop and implement quality systems and procedures that provide the basis for permanent quality solutions, process stability, continuous improvement, innovation and the ongoing conformance to customer partner requirements IFOTA1.

Key points

1. The beginnings of the quality culture must be in place, at the very least: accreditation; TQM/SPC skills for all; workplace reform; benchmarking; effective teamwork; the development of a quality environment and quality attitude; good communication.

2. Quality solutions are as much about attitude as about systems and procedures. Do your people really believe the quality culture is worthwhile and are they genuinely committed? Is management genuinely on board?

3. Specifically opposite the customer partner, ensure that quality processes and procedures are in place to conform to IFOTA1 requirements. Understand the impact of process stability and reduction in process variability. Ensure future requirements are being handled in a similar quality manner.

4. In general, are your processes—i.e. purchasing, materials handling, design, R&D, production, marketing and sales—capable of consistently delivering internal/external customer requirements?

What has quality got to do with innovation in management methods? The connection is simple. The foundation of a quality program is a willingness to trace every quality problem back to its roots. The fact is that those roots usually reach far beyond the immediate vicinity of the problem. They reach into areas like supplier relationships, process design, information systems, physical infrastructure and the like.

Gary Hamel & C.K. Prahalad[2]

Attitude and the 'old way' of management

At some stage every manager has said, 'I don't care how it gets done. I don't care how you do it. Just make sure it happens.' The end justifies the means. Of course, that cannot happen now and certainly will not be acceptable for the future. On the surface, both managers and subordinates interpreted this approach as good leadership and delegation of responsibility, empowering people and utilising their creativity and skills in an atmosphere of freedom and cooperation. In fact, it was really an abdication of responsibility, falsely empowering those who were probably committed but not skilled enough to achieve anything near the set objective(s). The subordinates, in turn, would delegate with those immortal words, 'I don't care how it gets done, just do it', intimidating others with their new-found authority and power.

The result was almost always poor communication, increased demarcations and departmentalism, and generally a consolidation of the tribal culture. On most occasions, the outcome included a failed objective or at least a poor performance against the original demands.

In a sales and marketing environment, I know from personal experience that this leadership style was a licence to create havoc. Wheeling and dealing went on, with little discussion with other parts of the business or much thought as to how they might be affected. The result was usually a lot of unhappy, frustrated people, even more entrenched in their view that salespeople and 'terminators' were one and the same. For external customers, it was mostly a case of over-promise and under-deliver, followed by the post-mortem which gave everyone the opportunity to blame others. 'I got the order—you couldn't produce!' 'It's marketing's (or sales') fault. They obviously don't know their customer well enough.'

This attitude and approach is not sustainable in the future for any customer/supplier relationship, let alone partnering and alliance relationships. The end no longer justifies the means. The means must involve a total quality approach, utilising all the appropriate resources internal and external to the organisation. This infers delegation, ownership, teamwork, measurement, process stability, standards, prevention, prediction, designing out and good communication. All these, together with the base load of quality training, skills, competencies and attitude, must be in place.

IFOTA1 conformance in a quality way

This stage of the process involves making sure that IFOTA1 requirements, the basis for all relationships including partnerships, are being done in a quality way—from the point of view not only of systems and procedures, but also of continuous improvement and attitude. Bad attitude, poor results.

Figure 6.19 is an extension of Figure 6.18, which we looked at in relation to understanding requirements. An appreciation of where your organisation fits into the matrix of customer requirements and process capabilities must be based on sound quality principles and accurate data. The principles of total quality must be understood and their application mastered if strategic partnerships are to be a success. Your current position on the total quality learning curve will determine the next steps to be taken. Those organisations already on the total quality path will understand the amount of time, resources and commitment involved. Those that are not yet involved have a long way to go before genuine partnering and alliance relationships can be effectively implemented.

Figure 6.19 outlines the connection between an organisation's capacity to meet customer requirements, and process stability. Process stability is represented by an SPC control chart, developed over time (shown in the lower part of the diagram). Box 1 in Figure 6.19 ('breakdown') represents in SPC terms a state of complete instability. The supplier's process is incapable of meeting the customer's requirements, even if they were known. In box 2 ('prevention'), the customer requirements are known and the supplier's process is capable. In SPC terms this is process stability, aimed at reducing variation, and based on the principle of prevention.

Partnerships, however, are about a systems change. In box 3 ('prediction' and 'design out') a step change in improvement is generated from a clear understanding of current and future customer requirements, and a supplier process that is capable of delivering both. This will occur through the use of predictive tools to help manage future events, to generate world-class innovation, and to design out and eliminate wasteful and unproductive process steps.

Process stability is discussed more fully in John McConnell's book, *Safer than a Known Way*.[3]

In short, permanent quality solutions and continuous improvement are about developing systems and processes based on prevention, prediction and designing out of special causes of non-conformances and unwanted variation. It will be essential to understand your internal value chain, process flows, process stability, and the impact of process variation on your objective of conforming to both current and future customer requirements. Again, innovation will play a major role.

The basic rules are as follows:

1. Understand your value chain, the process and the process flow you want to improve.
2. Stabilise the process by removing uncontrolled variation due to special causes.

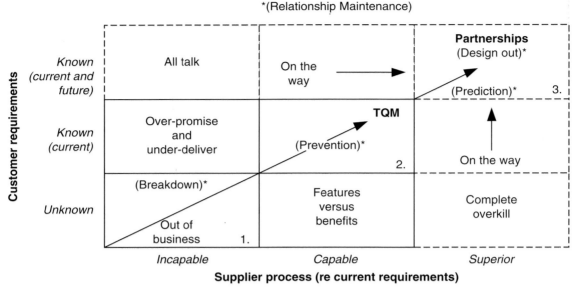

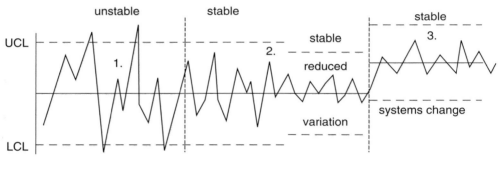

Fig. 6.19   *The relationship between customer requirements and supplier process capability*

3. Reduce variation to a level that conforms to the customer's requirements.
4. If necessary, implement a systems change to generate a step change in improvement.
5. Do it all again.

These five rules require the involvement of management and the process owners. If the system is stable, any substantial improvement must come from action on the system, not within the system. This is the responsibility of management. For a relationship to be effective it will also be essential to have an understanding of each other's independent business drivers and strategies, as well as a shared vision, common goals and value propositions.

These principles apply not only to production but to all parts of the business, from initial development and design through to production, sales and marketing, and delivery. The customer may require a 'centre cut' specification, narrowing the current upper and lower product specification limits. This may necessitate a controlled and systematic reduction in production process variability or even the implementation of a batch selection process. However, there may be other requirements opposite distribution: for example, a 24-hour delivery window or the implementation of JIT, kanban, supplier management or telemetry stock management systems to reduce variability.

Following these five principles will not ensure that mistakes won't happen and problems won't occur. They inevitably will, but they will almost always be due to special events outside the control of the normal operating system. How these issues are resolved will determine whether the impact on the relationship is positive or negative.

The other ingredients for quality solutions

Workplace reform will provide the environment within which total quality continuous improvement can occur and the basis for the productivity gains and efficiencies to be delivered. Joint benchmarking will enable a comparison of performance with the competition and the best in the world. Combined with effective leadership and skills, these practices will develop an atmosphere of trust, commitment and cooperation where the right attitude prevails. Good people working well together for common goals and shared values can produce powerful results, ensuring the delivery of both current and future requirements IFOTA1.

Business process re-engineering (BPR) can be particularly helpful in identifying, eliminating and redesigning those non-value-adding activities, and thereby improving responsiveness and increasing effectiveness. The elimination of waste, the empowerment of teams, the use of measurement, and a strong customer focus, all working to achieve step changes in improvement and creating the markets of the future, lie at the heart of good process re-engineering. It is very much a part of the continuous improvement process and consistent with the relationship maintenance concept of prevention, prediction and design out (see Fig. 2.9).

REFERENCES

1. Martin Christopher, Adrian Payne & David Ballantyne, *Relationship Marketing*, Butterworth-Heinemann, Oxford, 1991, p.6.
2. Gary Hamel & C.K. Prahalad, *Competing for the Future*, Harvard Business School Press, 1994, p.223.
3. John McConnell, *Safer than a Known Way*, Delaware Books, Sydney, 1988.

Selecting and/or reviewing partnering/alliance team members and team performance

Objective

To select, form and/or review the integrated relationship team(s) comprising cross-organisational, cross-functional, highly skilled individuals who, together with the Relationship managers, will manage the partnering and alliance relationship in the short, medium and long term.

Key points

1. The partnering/alliance teams are the core groups that are responsible and accountable for the well-being and performance of the relationship in the short, medium and long term. As leadership, management and/or operational teams they will be the nerve centre for innovation, leadership, relationship management, coordination and development.

2. Partnering/alliance team members will be chosen ideally from groups of enthusiastic volunteers by the partnering/alliance managers, senior executives, business managers and others who are close to the process and have the appropriate skills and vested interest in the success of the relationship.

3. Focus is on customer welfare, now and in the future. As appropriate, the team will develop, implement and manage short-term tasks, medium and long-term strategies, using the twelve motivators as drivers, via:
   - development of products/services/people skills/people relationships
   - adding value to the supplier package
   - cost-downs via productivity/efficiency improvements for both customers and suppliers
   - environmental initiatives
   - improving work practices
   - using effectively the resources and core competencies of each organisation to add value and synergy for all the partners
   - justifying capital expenditure as required

   The team will work in conjunction with other teams involved in these activities and with senior management to ensure continuous improvement and successful outcomes.

4. Partnering teams will be multiskilled, cross-functional and cross-organisational as well as involving other external suppliers, the customer partner and other selected third parties and groups as appropriate; for example, dealers, distributors, lawyers, accountants, engineers, designers and consultants.

5. Partnering/alliance team membership is dynamic, with personnel changes consistent with the changing needs of the customer.

6. Sponsored by senior management and guided, led and coached by the partnering/alliance manager(s), these integrated relationship team(s) will have legitimate authority and recognition and be empowered by senior management to run the relationship in every respect.

7. The partnering/alliance teams will meet formally and informally on a regular basis as required and operate under normal team dynamics.

8. Partnering/alliance team activities will link into other teams, projects, individuals and service initiatives as appropriate: for example, product/service development and design teams; process re-engineering activities; corrective action teams; strategy teams; safety, health and environment and technical service initiatives; warehouse and distribution projects; advertising and promotion activities.

A team is a small number of people with complementary skills who are committed to a common purpose, set of performance goals, and approach for which they hold themselves mutually accountable.

Harvard Business Review[1]

Suppliers, dealers (or other distribution channel members) and ultimate customers must become partners in the development process from the start. Much, if not most, innovation will come from these constituents, if you trust them (i.e. show them all information from the start) and they trust you. This is one of the most important instances of the urgent need for a shift from adversarial to cooperative relationships.

Tom Peters[2]

The benefits and successes of teams and self-managing work groups in the workplace have been well documented.[3-8] The principles governing teams and work groups are also appropriate in building and sustaining customer and supplier relationships. There is no substitute for involving as many people from as many functions as possible and appropriate, including external suppliers and customers, or for reducing the layers of management and improving the quality of communication. Tom Peters, discussing the major reason for the delay in development activities, says:

> *Rip apart a badly developed project and you will unfailingly find 75 per cent of the slippage attributable to (1) 'siloing', or sending memos and minutes up and down vertical organisational 'silos' or 'stovepipes' for decisions, and (2) ... One group essentially finishes its 'higher order' task before passing the job 'down' to the next level executor. Interaction among functions is minimal; what's done is always within the context of the hierarchy of functions—design, then engineering, at the top; manufacturing and sales at the bottom.[9]*

As the solution, Peters states: 'The answer is to commingle members of all key functions, co-opt each function's traditional feudal authority, and use teams.' This means using all internal functions—production, purchasing, sales, marketing, technical service, credit and collection, design, R&D, warehousing, distribution—as appropriate. The partner's other customers and suppliers in the extended supply chain will also need to be involved, and other parties as required who add value to the process. It has been reported in the literature that self-managed work teams are the key to productivity growth. Performance gains of 20–50 per cent have been achieved in companies that get the transition to teams right.

Both in principle and in practice, the concept of partnering teams is simple and flexible. The teams can be rigid or adaptable, as needed. The goal is to utilise the partner organisation's resources, internal and external, to maximum value; to generate and maintain commitment and enthusiasm for the customer partner, especially at the 'shop-floor' and operating level. The key individual is the Partnering/Alliance Manager—guiding, coaching, leading and coordinating. Employees must feel they are part of the success of the relationship, not forced into some time-consuming and unrewarding exercise at the behest of management.

Deep down, people do want to contribute. It's part of human nature, and it's also well documented that positive people who have confidence and a high level of self-esteem perform at higher levels. By adding skills into the equation within a team environment, you have a very powerful combination. So how can all this be made to happen? In most cases it requires a systems change initiated by management, and strong leadership. It depends entirely on the environment in which the team operates.

There needs to be a balance between structure and flexibility in the way the team operates. Too much rigidity in the composition of the partnering team or in the rules under which it operates will be counterproductive and stifle creativity and innovation, the very things you are trying to develop. Yet there must be discipline and professionalism and ultimately a structure within the business that can deliver IFOTA1 first time and every time, and more. Irrespective of all the creativity and 'blue sky' lateral thinking, there must be conformance to requirements as a base.

The challenge is, how do you manage the human imagination?

In reality, the balance will be continually moving. There will be times when structure is important: for example, in product development. There will also be times for flexibility, for brainstorming ideas for new initiatives for service developments. There will be times when the mid-point is appropriate, where the two extremes are brought together. The partnering/alliance manager will be the key player in managing the pace and directing the traffic, internally and externally. But as Tom Peters says, 'If you want to develop truly curious organisations, hire some off-the-wall weirdos.'

Do you need partnering/alliance teams?

Yes. Does it matter what we call them? No. The Alcoa/Honeywell global alliance has *lead teams*. The global lead team sets the overall direction with regional lead teams responsible for coordinating activities in each geographical area. *Steering* and *task teams* then provide functional direction in resolving issues and developing opportunities on a site or regional basis. Chrysler has *platform teams*—groups of engineers, suppliers and specialists in product planning, purchasing, finance, manufacturing and marketing—working together to guide a vehicle through the entire development process. Other partnerships and alliances have partnering or alliance leadership teams and management and integrated project teams.

As with the partnering definition in Chapter 1, the names are irrelevant; it is the principles, practices, roles and responsibilities that are important. For consistency it will be useful for our discussion to continue calling them partnering teams or alliance teams.

How do the integrated relationship teams operate?

A friend once told me, 'They don't play average teams in the superbowl.' As with professional sport, partnering and alliancing is not the world of the average or mediocre.

It is obvious that these teams cannot operate in isolation from the rest of the activities and functions within the business. Linkages with other teams, functions and departments will be critical in continuously improving the service and quality levels and ensuring innovation is alive and well. Indeed, for large customer/supplier partnerships involving multiple sites, divisions and/or subsidiaries, as well as regional or even global activities, there may be more than one partnering/alliance team linking into a central partnership steering or leadership group or partnering/alliance board. Figure 6.20 shows the typical partnering/alliance, team based governance structure.

The Partnering/Alliance Leadership Team (PLT) is normally a small group (e.g. 2–6, depending on the size and nature of the relationship) of senior executives and managers from the partner organisations who represent the final review, leadership and management body for the relationship. They are not normally involved in the day-to-day activities of the relationship and are directly accountable back to their respective organisations for the ultimate performance of the relationship. The PLT will meet regularly (normally quarterly or six monthly or as otherwise agreed). The PLT's roles/responsibilities include:

1. Approving:
   - appointment and/or removal of Partnering/Alliance Management Team members
   - changes to the Partnering/Alliance Charter and Agreement
   - the partnering plan/strategy prepared by the Management Team and reviewing performance against the plan/strategy on a regular basis (e.g. quarterly)
   - capital expenditure within authority levels
   - senior level secondments, people exchanges, succession plans and significant resource/restructuring initiatives
   - recommended variations to the remuneration model
   - the partnering relationship's annual business plans and budget
   - individual business cases or projects that may or may not require further submission to and/or approval from the respective partner organisations
   - strategies or initiatives that have been developed by the Management Team
   - any changes to the Balanced Scorecard recommended by the Management Team

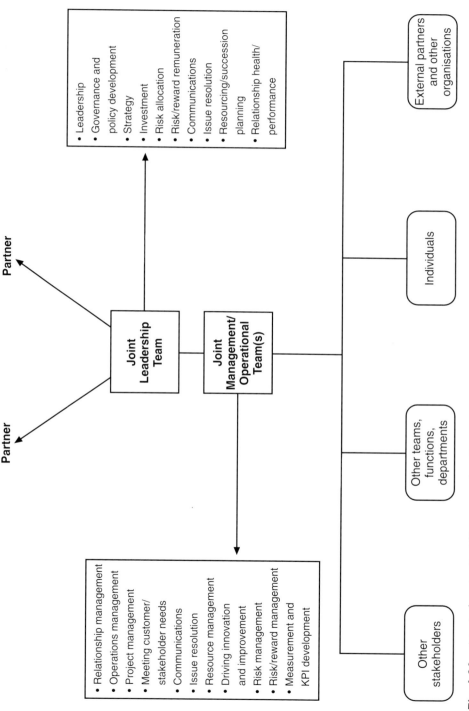

Fig. 6.20 *A typical partnering/alliance team based governance structure*

- performance based remuneration outcomes that have been recommended by the Management Team
- risk management plans, risk allocation and risk profiles of the partners as recommended by the Management Team

2. Ensuring:
   - effective governance structures and policies for the relationship are in place
   - remuneration incentives for the Management Team and other key people are established
   - the Partnering/Alliance Management Team is empowered and supported
   - the partnering/alliance principles are satisfied in all respects
   - the obligations and commitments of the relationship participants are fulfilled
   - as a team, they set the example for partnering/alliance behaviour
   - ongoing corporate and management support for the partnering and alliance approach
   - an environment that encourages honest, open, transparent and timely sharing of information is established

3. Periodically reviewing:
   - the overall 'health' of the relationship as measured by the KPI Balanced Scorecard Performance and outcomes from the partnering/alliance survey(s)
   - the achievement of specific business case or project based KPIs
   - the performance of the Partnering/Alliance Management Team

4. Being the ultimate review body for issue resolution before external mediation or 'expert' determination or other issue/dispute resolution options, as agreed

5. Providing leadership and leading the strategic and investment direction of the strategic partnering/alliance relationship

6. Communicating the views, vision, strategic objectives, value propositions and performance outcomes of the relationship to the individual partner organisations, other stakeholders and third parties

7. Being an advocate for and representing the best interests of the partnering/alliance relationship

8. Managing the inter- and intra-partner relationships

9. Where appropriate, acting as coaches, sponsors and mentors for other personnel in the relationship

10. Reporting at agreed intervals on the strategies and future plans for the relationship, and current and forecast performance against objectives

11. Facilitating meetings and contacts, internal and external to the partner organisations, that will have a positive influence on the relationship in accordance with the partnering/alliance charter vision, key objectives and principles

The Partnering/Alliance Management Team (PMT) has responsibility for the day-to-day, week-to-week operation of the relationship. It is accountable directly to the Partnering/Alliance Leadership Team for the effective delivery of the partnering/alliance charter vision and strategic objectives. It will meet more regularly than the Leadership Team—the interval could range from weekly to monthly, depending on the size, nature and current state of the relationship. Again, there may be exceptions to this on an agreed needs basis.

The management team's role includes:

- Managing and leading the relationship on a day-to-day basis at the operational level
- Meeting and where appropriate exceeding customer requirements and stakeholder expectations
- Being responsible for the cultural, strategy, structure, process/systems and people development in respect of the partnering/alliance relationship
- Ensuring there is established an environment that encourages honest, open communication and transparent, timely sharing of information
- Implementing the directions and decisions of the Leadership Team
- Establishing the partnering/alliance relationship's business plans and associated strategies
- Translating high level strategies into operational plans
- Being responsible for delivering or realising the Partnering/Alliance Charter key objectives as measured by performance against the jointly agreed KPIs and associated targets on the relationship Balanced Scorecard
- Monitoring the health of the relationship via relationship surveys and other means
- Driving and inspiring innovation, new ideas and improvement opportunities at all levels of the relationship
- Effectively managing the transition plan(s)
- Developing and/or approving business cases and project scopes for submission to the Leadership Team
- Making recommendations or submissions to the Leadership Team regarding:
  —modifications to the relationship scope and/or associated agreements
  —personnel changes, secondments, people exchange programs, succession plans
  —remuneration levels (personnel and business/relationship performance)
  —business cases and associated projects
  —business plans/strategies
  —modifications to the partnering/alliance charter and KPI Balanced Scorecard
  —unresolved issues or disputes
- Identifying and/or initiating improvement opportunities or corrective actions to enhance performance
- Ensuring personal and relationship key objectives are aligned

- Ensuring partner organisation business drivers are aligned with the partnering/alliance vision and key objectives as expressed in the Partnering/Alliance Charter
- Playing a key role in the proactive solving of problems and the joint resolution of issues via the issue resolution process
- Coaching and mentoring others in partnering/alliance principles, concepts and practices
- Managing important internal relationships and third party relationships
- Effectively allocating resources
- Effectively managing risk and risk allocation
- Managing risk/reward remuneration for the relationship and performance measurement associated with over/under-performance against agreed KPI targets
- Setting up and managing effective lines of communications and communication protocols for the relationship
- Recruiting people with the right attitudes and skills to support the relationship goals and key objectives
- Reporting to the Leadership Team at agreed and regular intervals on the:
  —performance of the relationship
  —opportunities for improvement
  —outstanding issues

The Partnering/Alliance Management Team (PMT) tends to be bigger in numbers than the leadership team and can range from four to twelve people. I have seen large teams in place in the early stages, often because of a lack of willingness to delegate responsibility to others. As the relationship develops and the trust and communication levels improve, team membership tends to become smaller. It is also normally the case that the partnering/alliance manager is the team leader of the management team and also participates in and/or is a member of the Leadership Team. On occasions there can also be a dual team leader role across the partnering/alliance managers and this often assists in building personal relationships across organisational boundaries more quickly.

The role of the partnering/alliance manager is critical to the success of the relationship. The competencies and responsibilities of these people are detailed in Chapter 9.

For both the Leadership Team and the Management Team, normal team and meeting dynamics will usually apply (e.g. set agenda headings; set and regular meeting dates with additional meetings convened by joint agreement; member roles clarified; substitutes allowed with same rights, duties, obligations; meeting location can vary; minimum quorum required; unanimous vote or joint consensus required for decision making). Team membership is also dynamic, with personnel changes consistent with the changing needs of the relationship.

In *The Team Handbook* Peter Scholtes recognises ten ingredients for successful teams.[10] They are:

1. Clarity of team goals
2. An improvement plan (objectives)
3. Clearly defined roles
4. Clear communication
5. Beneficial team behaviours
6. Well-defined decision procedures
7. Balanced participation
8. Established ground rules
9. Awareness of the group process
10. Use of the scientific/quality approach.

It is very important to apply effective rewards and recognition to the work of the partnering/alliance team. Being in the team should be seen as something special and viewed as an exciting challenge, not a chore. All types of innovative reward and recognition systems will need to be in place, based on team, not individual, performance.

The partnering team focus and remit covers the short, medium and long term

The purpose of the Partnering/Alliance Management Team (PMT) is to carry out the day-to-day, the medium-term and the long-term management of the partnering relationship. This goes against the traditional line of thinking where certain groups look after each different time frame. For example, sales looks after the day-to-day welfare of the customer and the 'tactics' that are deployed. Marketing looks after the strategy aspects in the medium to longer term, while senior management deal with the long-term, broader, strategic, investment/reinvestment aspects of the business. Given this divided responsibility, it should be no surprise that occasionally things go off the rails because of skewed priorities, miscommunication and 'siloing' within the bureaucracy and hierarchy. It is the PMT that will be responsible for linking in the activities associated with the partnership and the general business strategy to ensure there are no conflicts, inconsistencies or miscommunication. Responsibility for the short term does not mean that the partnering team gets bogged down in mundane activities or paper-bound bureaucracy. Good systems and effective IT will deliver on this. It will be the PMT that manages, leads and is accountable for the partnership process in every aspect—the motivators, the process steps and the outcomes.

For traditional organisations this new concept of ownership and empowerment will require a complete rethinking of strategy and structure, people management and people involvement.

The makeup of the partnering/alliance teams

Team membership will depend on what type of partnership you have—global, multidivisional, multi-product/service, asset-based and so on. The partnering or alliance teams are often put together at the initial partnering/alliance workshop where shared vision, common goals, joint KPIs, roles and responsibilities are agreed to. Choice of team members is made on the basis of the hard and soft skills required to meet partner needs and expectations (both customer and supplier). Consider including your partners and others as appropriate in the team-member selection process to generate 'buy-in' and commitment. Team members will be self-motivated, highly skilled, empowered individuals, committed to meeting common goals and the needs of the customer and other stakeholders in the short, medium and long term.

The integrated Partnering Management Team must be cross-organisational, cross-functional and represent most or all areas of the business that impact on the relationship. This will depend on the complexity of the partnership and the scope of specific opportunities. However, irrespective of who is in the team, they will need to have general skills in leadership and team-building, as well as a clear understanding of and appropriate proven experience in partnering/alliance principles and practice, and a solid understanding of the principles of quality management and conflict resolution. Training and skills development will have to be thought about. The skills required must match the goals and objectives set. The team could include partner representatives from:

1. Marketing or senior management, who has the big picture in view—the national/global perspective, the broader strategy—and the authority to make and/or guide the higher-level strategic decisions.
2. Sales/supply/logistics. This could be the Partnership Manager, although partnership managers do not necessarily have to live in sales or procurement. There is a strong argument they should not belong to any one department. They work for the partnership/alliance, not one particular business, function or department.

3. Technical/technical service/design, to ensure development opportunities are maximised and service levels are improved.
4. The production/operations and maintenance unit. Depending on the size, you could include up to three people who should be mostly from the shop floor with a direct input into the manufacture of the product or service.
5. Other customers and suppliers as appropriate.
6. Others on a needs basis. For example, engineering, supply, IT, warehousing, distribution, legal, finance, credit and collection, packaging.

Ideally, there will be skilled and committed volunteers from all levels and areas of the business who have heard of the formation of the partnering/alliance team(s) and are just itching to get involved. Their enthusiasm will be based on previous knowledge or experience of partnering/alliance teams, or the fact that they have heard of the partnering/alliance principles and process, like the idea and want to participate. Ultimately, this team process works because of the willingness of all parties to be actively involved and participating. This includes management. People must want to join the partnering team(s).

Newly developed teams can also be seeded with individuals from existing partnering teams to make the formation and development stage that much smoother. This will allow for cross-pollination of ideas, a faster breakdown of functional barriers and a quicker introduction to the process for the new people.

Getting people involved

This is a people process. Without people being involved, committed and working together, partnerships don't exist. Two anecdotes will illustrate the importance of people to the partnering process.

Removing the QC safety net

I was talking to the Quality Manager from a customer partner about the good track record we had built up over the last two years on IFOTA1. In fact, since a major quality complaint two years earlier which had cost over $60 000 to fix, our record was unblemished.

Much work had gone into ensuring people were aware of the customer partner's quality and service requirements. They were then skilled to meet those requirements, and systems/procedures implemented to ensure conformance. The Quality Manager told me that, as of 1 July, they would be removing quality control on our product because they had built up a level of trust and confidence in us and our ability to deliver IFOTA1. We were a quality organisation, accredited to ISO9001, so why should there be an unnecessary duplication of QC at their end? The safety net was about to be removed. It is very difficult to argue with this logic if you are genuinely a quality organisation.

It came home to me then that the Quality Manager was not in fact talking to me. I was not the one they had trust and confidence in for A1 quality. He was talking about the teams on A, B, C and D shifts at the factory, who have to ensure A1 quality 24 hours a day, seven days a week, all year round, whatever the weather. He was talking about the maintenance teams who had reduced the time of changing a stirrer on a reactor from two days to five hours, and were on call 24 hours a day to ensure product availability and plant dependability. He was also talking about warehouse and distribution and sales teams who ensured the material arrived in full and on time.

When I told the production team of the customer's intention to remove QC they were delighted. It was a matter of pride as it became apparent to them that the customer really trusted them in their ability to deliver IFOTA1. They also realised that the removal of the safety net was a two-edged sword: the consequences of getting it wrong would be disastrous, both financially and in the effect on the relationship. It also generated systems change in tightening up our own testing procedures, and this in turn made people focus more on the customer.

Involve these people, because they lie at the heart of the partnering process. Committed and empowered, they will be one of your greatest vehicles for continuous improvement. Uninformed and uncommitted, they can be your worst nightmare and no amount of slick selling will make up the difference.

Michael and the seagull

There are always special events during the partnering process that provide the catalyst for change. Some years ago, at one of ICI Australia's manufacturing plants, I gave a presentation to each of the shifts (A, B, C, D) over a three to four week period. In the control room I delivered an up-to-date account of strategies, customers, competitors and general business performance. The objective was, of course, to share information, gain some trust and commitment, and make a start in terms of involvement. I also wanted to reinforce the importance of their role and the good job they were doing in getting the quality right in terms of meeting customer requirements.

The time was 3 pm and I had arranged my presentation to 'A' shift to fit in with other meetings later in the afternoon. (The relevance of this will become clear further on.) Halfway through I sensed that things weren't going well. I thought the presentation was fine and I was in full flight. So why was one of the operators visibly pacing up and down at the back of the control room, becoming more and more frustrated and angry with every minute? I stopped the presentation and asked Michael whether there was a problem with what I was saying. It was like releasing a pressure valve. A barrage of pent-up frustration was unleashed upon me.

The gist of what Michael said went something like this:

'That's all very well. You people come up here from your head office ivory towers and you feed us all this information and tell us what a good job we are doing and to keep up the good work. Well, that's all bulls——. You don't know what sort of work we do. You have no idea of the conditions we have to work under and the sort of outdated equipment we have to use. It's a miracle the product gets made at all. If you really cared about what actually goes on and if you really cared about meeting customer requirements, you would . . .'

He then outlined a whole series of modifications and changes he thought should be made to enable a smoother-running and more effective operation. He finished off by saying:

'No disrespect, but you people are like seagulls. You fly up from your ivory towers once a month, drop a load of s——. on us and fly back. If you are really interested in the role of the plant and meeting customer requirements you should spend some real time with us, especially on the night shift [12 hours, 6 pm to 6 am], to understand what it's really like.'

I stood there aghast, totally speechless. Michael was absolutely right. Over the years, other managers and I had occasionally cruised in from our respective comfort zones to present some information (irrelevant for them), ask a couple of questions (irrelevant to them), and then returned to 'our world'. Of course, in years gone by, managers would have taken Michael's outburst as a complete breakdown in discipline and morale. Very quickly rumours would have spread throughout Head Office that things on the plant were out of control, and disciplinary action would probably have followed.

I took a different view. As I subsequently discovered, Michael had worked for the company on this plant for over twenty years. As a plant operator he had reached the highest skill level and was one of our best. There was nothing he didn't know about the operation of the plant. So why did he speak out the way he did? Not because he was a deliberate troublemaker or because he took the attitude, 'I couldn't give a damn', but because he cared enough about the plant, its operation and the importance of quality to put himself on the line and speak up and be heard.

How many times do we ask people to come into our environment in our time to talk about our business? One-way traffic. How many times do we ask people if we can go into their environment in their time to talk about their business? What Michael was saying was: 'Why should we be interested in your business when you (i.e. the rest of the organisation) are not interested in our business?' And the best time to start to understand Michael's business was on night shift, not at 3 o'clock in the afternoon in between a series of my meetings.

It didn't take me long to say that if there was an invitation to do a night shift then I would be delighted. Within a week I had done a night shift and, within a month, a day shift. It was one of the most rewarding experiences of my working career. There is no management around on night shift, no support staff, just the workers. For twelve hours, half the working day, they were totally responsible for ensuring the customers received A1 quality material. If the reactors went down, if there were problems with gearboxes, bearings, drive shafts, pumps, product quality or packaging, they had to make the decisions. During this time they were managing assets worth approximately $100 million replacement value. Being a 24 hours a day, 365 days a year operation, they had to make the product to the same specification whether on a cold Sunday morning or a burning hot Friday afternoon.

The particular night shift I attended was a busy one. There were some breakdowns and the reactors had to be brought off-line several times. I saw first-hand the skills and teamwork required, the decisions that had to be taken, the initiative that had to be used and the conditions they had to work with. I also saw that these people cared about and were committed to what they were doing. Literally overnight, it made my job easier when communicating with customers and suppliers (internally and externally) and reduced my level of frustration and anxiety. I was far more aware of the process and its capabilities. The threat of over-promising and under-delivering on customer requirements was greatly diminished and the potential to develop, innovate and add value was greatly enhanced. For example, I now had a far better understanding of the balance between customer forecasts, process capabilities, required stock levels and working capital costs.

I did a day shift some ten days later, again with 'A' shift. During the night shift, Michael had spent hours with me explaining the process. One of his biggest and most frustrating problems was the regular and sudden changes that had to be made to the production schedule. Because the changes came down from the schedulers on a piece of paper with no explanation, and in many cases required large changes in process conditions, extensive clean-down procedures and considerable additional costs were incurred.

Michael and the shift team were continually bewildered and frustrated. It appeared that the whole forecasting, scheduling system and the people running it were out of control. In most cases there was a legitimate reason for the change but, because it was not relayed back to the shift, eventually it became a 'dig a hole, fill the hole' exercise. Very frustrating and demotivating. The scheduler, who was in Head Office 800 kilometres away, had been to the plant many times but had never spent any time there talking to the guys and understanding the process.

I invited Sam the scheduler to do the day shift with me so that he too could gain the benefit from understanding the process better, but in particular to talk to Michael about scheduling. They spent hours talking about each other's job roles, objectives, difficulties and frustrations. Out of this session came a better understanding of requirements and capabilities, resulting in changes to process and scheduling that made for an easier and more effective way of managing production and stock levels.

I would be totally embarrassed telling this absolutely commonsense story if it were not for two things. First, the amount of questioning and ridicule I received when I said I was doing the night shift: to me it was an embarrassment that I had not done it before; in contrast, it was an embarrassment to others that I had thought of it at all. They asked all sorts of questions. Why would you in your role as Sales Manager want to do a night shift? What on earth can you possibly accomplish? Haven't you got better things to do? Don't you have a job? It was an extraordinary reaction. Second, the reaction from many people when I subsequently told them of this experience—surprise, enlightenment, shock, delight. You actually did a night shift! That's fantastic, it's terrific. It was a revelation to some, a revolution to others.

Once I had started doing the night and day shifts and people saw not only a change in me but a change in many of the shift workers, most of them realised the benefits and some followed my example. Others, the gatekeepers and the roadblockers, returned to their bunkers and carried on. If you haven't already experienced a night shift, or something similar—then do so. It works and it's important.

The point of this story is that the people who actually make the product are a critically important part of the process. Many of them genuinely want to participate in the continuous improvement process. Remember, when customers speak about the confidence they have in your quality and reliability, they are not talking about sales, Head Office or marketing but about production, maintenance, product development teams and others directly involved in the manufacturing process.

While this is a story about production and operations, the principle applies to all parts of the business: marketing, sales, maintenance, supply and distribution, R&D, credit and collection, finance, design. If partnerships are to be successful, every part of the business contributing to their success must be understood and recognised and allowed to play an active part in the process. Having a greater appreciation of what other functions do, how and why they do it, and the environment in which they operate is crucial. So have some of your best production people spend a couple of days with senior management, marketing or sales. Have staff involved with credit and collection spend time with production, technical service and distribution. Have your finance people spend time with production and sales. Have sales spend time with the supply team, and any other useful combination you can think of. How many 'Michaels' are there in each of these areas, frustrated and silent? How important is it to harness their ideas, enthusiasm, commitment and energy and involve them in the process? Good people want to get involved.

REFERENCES

1. Jon Katenback & Douglas Smith, 'The discipline of teams', *Harvard Business Review*, March/April 1993, p.110.
2. Tom Peters, *Thriving on Chaos*, Harper & Row, New York, 1987, p.217.
3. Mary Walton, *The Deming Management Method*, Perigee Books, New York, 1986.
4. Peter Senge, *The Fifth Discipline*, Doubleday, New York, 1990.
5. Jerry Spiegel & Cresencio Torres, *A Manager's Official Guide to Team Working*, Pfeiffer & Company, San Diego, 1994.
6. Peters, op. cit.
7. Masaaki Imai, *Kaizen*, Random House, New York, 1986.
8. Charles Margerison & Dick McCann, *Team Management*, Mercury Books, London, 1987.
9. Peters, op. cit., p.217.
10. Peter Scholtes, *The Team Handbook*, Joiner Associates, Madison, 1991, pp.6–11.

Site visits (customers and suppliers)

Objective

To bring together people from all parts of the customer/supplier partner organisations, to see where everyone works, and to understand the importance of conforming to requirements, sharing information, benchmarking, building trust and developing friendships.

Key points

1. Jointly share all types of information, both personal and business, to build trust.

2. Understand the culture of your partner organisation as well as the financial accounts, plant and machinery aspects.

3. Meet as many people as possible in order to understand their requirements fully, and to build ownership and commitment among your own people.

4. It is often simple but sincere statements from shop-floor personnel that make a strong and lasting impact on your partner organisation. Get people at all levels involved.

5. Use site visits to build the partnership from the bottom up, as well as the top down, in both customer and supplier organisations.

6. The benefits of site visits apply equally to internal as well as external customers and suppliers.

7. Customer/supplier etiquette training is essential if site visits are to be a success.

8. Agree within your organisation a set of commonsense rules and guidelines for conducting site visits.

9. Don't forget to visit other third-party benchmark organisations, including other customer/supplier partners, in order to learn, benchmark and understand the opportunities for innovation and improvement.

Site visits would seem an obvious move in any customer strategy but it is surprising how few people in your company have even seen external customers or suppliers, let alone contributed in any significant way to their success. Site visits are simple. Make them events, make them special. Senior management on both sides should not only know what is happening, they should be involved.

Share information, meet people who are dependent on you yet are the keys to your company's future. Make friends, reconfirm commitment, exchange ideas about business, the partnering process, golf handicaps, the weekend football. It's easier to let down people you have never met and know little about. It's a lot harder to disappoint a friend who has trust in you and your organisation. Self-respect and pride become involved. If you are the host, 'show off' your place. World class is something to be proud of. If you're not yet world class, be honest about it and your goal to become so.

The kind of site visits I am talking about here are not just looking at machinery, hardware or software, but more about understanding the culture of the organisation, the people, their moods, their visions and goals for the future. Aim to get a feeling for the soul and spirit of the organisation, those basic belief and value systems that keep it going. In short, gain an understanding of 'the way they do things around here'. You won't see or feel that by looking at balance sheets or profit and loss accounts, reading magazines, newspapers and faxes, or talking on the phone.

I have seen some special events occur on site visits. People get to see, hear and feel at first hand the customer's requirements and realise how important it is to understand them if they are to do their own jobs effectively. All sorts of emotions and feelings may surface—pride, disappointment, determination to improve, excitement, happiness. Site visits are very much a learning experience. On one of our first visits to a prospective customer partner, our factory team comprised four or five people from 'B' shift, some engineers and maintenance people, a total of fifteen in all. This particular company had a very impressive site, consistent with their overall professionalism and commitment to world class. A presentation on the company's background and strategies provided the initial interest. We spent two hours looking over the site, followed by lunch in the company canteen with their management and some of their operators.

Dave and Neil were two operators from 'B' shift who had given up their day off to join the visiting team, in order to meet their customer's staff and understand their requirements more fully. The transformation of the ICI team after the visit, especially Dave and Neil, was remarkable. It really was an eye-opener for them to see a world-class customer in action. Within two weeks

Dave and Neil had designed a special production checksheet specifically for their grade, so that the production results could be tracked more easily and the production process controlled more effectively.

News of the visit spread throughout the ICI plant and within the next nine months the customer's management and shop-floor workers made four visits to the ICI plant and the ICI team another three visits to the customer. Not because management on either side had said 'Thou shalt' or 'I want you to', but because requests came from the shop-floor workers themselves.

On another occasion, about 18 months later, the Managing Director and Production Director of the same customer partner visited the ICI manufacturing site at Botany in Sydney. The highlight of the visit was not looking over the 1.5 billion dollars' worth of pipes, pumps, reactors and other related hardware and software associated with a large petrochemical site. The high spot came with some simple straight-from-the-heart comments from one of the process operators over lunch, who said, 'I and the rest of the guys on the shift would take it as a personal failure if we were to deliver poor quality. You're so important to us as a customer that we put everything into place to ensure you get the right quality all the time.' He went on to explain the changes that had taken place over the last two years and the effort that went into ensuring the customer received A1 quality first time and every time. The visitors were amazed at this level of commitment from the shop floor and made the comment: 'This is quality in action. This is what quality is all about and what we are all striving for.'

So you can see that partnerships don't necessarily have to be complex things. Those comments were a simple yet powerful reminder that people lie at the heart of good, strong customer/supplier relationships, and that site visits can bring these people, MDs and process operators alike, closer together. The positive effects of those visits, which then flowed on to our systems and processes, were remarkable. Internal relationships between factory and sales also improved out of sight. No longer was there the perception of sales as high flyers driving around in company cars with mobile phones.

The strategic partnering process was really starting to have an effect, but it was also being driven from the bottom up as well as from the top down. Those site visits to one customer precipitated an avalanche of visits to other customers over the next twelve months. Again, it was a case of providing the catalyst and the opportunity, and the rest will follow. This is another example of the motivators operating within one partnership impacting positively upon other customer/supplier relationships.

Apply exactly the same principles to internal customers and suppliers and you will derive the same benefits. Get engineering and maintenance out to see the sales staff, production in to see marketing, senior management to see warehousing and distribution, sales to visit design/R&D. The results will surprise you. This is not MBWA (management by walking around) but forging constructive and lasting links with other parts of the business.

Customer/supplier etiquette training

Rewarding site visits don't just happen. They require a great deal of preparation by the organisers and a great deal of involvement from the participants. You will find many of these participants quite hesitant even to attend, let alone show interest or ask enthusiastic or relevant questions. This is not because they don't want to be there or don't care. The usual reason is that they have never done this before. In their normal jobs they don't have to communicate in such a manner. Add to this the stories they have heard from sales about monumental confrontations between customers and suppliers and you will begin to understand why they are not too enthusiastic about revealing their innermost thoughts and feelings.

In many cases, the people making site visits will have had no training in communication skills at all and cannot be expected to possess the ability to break down the barriers of traditionally adversarial customer/supplier communication without help. There may be the need to run sessions on simple etiquette: how to behave in front of customers and suppliers; what to say, what not to say; what sort of questions to ask; what questions not to ask. Of course, such skills can also be used internally to great effect in helping to break down traditional hierarchical and departmental barriers. This may all seem common sense, but you would be surprised how difficult it can be for people to act naturally outside their normal work or social environment.

Conducting a site visit

The following are some general guidelines for achieving a successful site visit.

1. Agree, from supplier and customer perspective, the objectives of the site visit(s). The primary objectives will be:
   (a) to gain a better understanding of the culture of the other organisation and its requirements at first hand;
   (b) to meet the people and understand their roles;
   (c) to set up suitable and effective lines of communication;
   (d) to discuss specific issues of concern or opportunity;
   (e) to understand the processes.

2. Agree dates, times, format, agenda, maximum/minimum numbers that can attend. Allow time for a round table discussion to share ideas.
3. Decide who is to attend and how they will get there.
4. Both host and visitor should arrange for their own people a pre-visit briefing about the other organisation that includes:
   (a) the nature of the business relationship, e.g. volumes, costs, products, services and trends;
   (b) problems and opportunities (current and future);
   (c) an overview of the requirements (from both sides).
5. Whether you are the host or the visitor, identify areas of special interest and prepare to cater for them as appropriate.
6. The group should be welcomed by a member of the senior management of the host organisation to indicate and symbolise the importance of the event and the relationship.
7. If appropriate, the host company could provide a gift or memento of the occasion, to signify a special event.
8. The visiting organisation should agree in advance on a spokesperson who will publicly thank the host for the visit at its conclusion. The host likewise should have chosen a spokesperson to respond.
9. The rules:
   (a) Be on time.
   (b) Be courteous and polite, and appropriately dressed.
   (c) Ask plenty of questions. Find out beforehand suitable questions to ask and the questions to avoid.
   (d) Listen a lot.
   (e) Don't 'big note' yourself or your own organisation.
   (f) Don't embarrass your host or visitor in the event of a performance or technology gap.
   (g) Do exchange as many ideas as possible.
   (h) Don't overstay your welcome. Stick to the timetable.
   (i) Avoid sensitive or confidential issues, or areas of conflict, until trust and friendship have developed.
10. Conduct a follow-up discussion after the visit to review the benefits and shortcomings of the visit and what was learnt from it overall. Consider the next steps that should be taken.

Don't forget visits to the customer's customer, the supplier's supplier and other benchmark organisations, along a similar format.

Site visits are special events that can lead to other special events. Great things happen from bringing people together.

Third-party site visits

Joel Barker[1] says the person most likely to change your paradigm is an outsider, someone who has little or no vested interest in your current paradigm. Utilise other customer or supplier partnerships wherever possible to impact positively on the current partnership, to challenge norms, generate new ideas and opportunities, to solve old and new problems.

Remember the partnering definition from page 2. Genuine partnerships will have a positive impact elsewhere in the organisation; they will be used as a benchmark, role model, centre of excellence for other relationships. Two-way site visits involving other partners and other world-class benchmark organisations will prove invaluable as catalysts for change and in developing and sustaining the relationship.

REFERENCE

1. Joel Barker, *Paradigm Principles*, video, ChartHouse International, 1996.

Reviewing and implementing customer/supplier skills requirements

Objective

To create a learning environment where skills and competencies are continuously developed to support and drive the ongoing innovation that sustains the partnership and the organisation's competitive advantage.

Key points

1. Determine the skills required to meet current and future customer requirements.

2. Assess the current skills profile of your organisation, and that of your partner(s).

3. Carry out gap analysis; agree on the training and skills required and the levels of competence to be achieved.

4. Implement training programs and review the level of competence achieved by those who are trained.

5. Change your organisation from a traditional training culture to a competency and learning culture. Become a 'curious' organisation.

6. As with customer requirements, constantly review via a gap analysis, agree on the skills and competencies required and implement upgrade programs as appropriate.

7. Search far and wide for talented trainers, facilitators, educators, coaches and leaders who will change the current skills base and the organisation's way of thinking and looking at the world. These people will generate the systems change in learning required to take you to the next level of the partnering process.

> *In a workplace based on commitment the individual will have a job that is flexibly defined and part of a comprehensive career structure with opportunities for advancement through skill acquisition. The organisational structure is flat with management systems that emphasise involvement and mutual influence.*
>
> *Dr Michael Deeley*
> *Managing Director, ICI Australia, 1991*[1]

Competitive advantage through skills development

Few people would argue with the old cliche that 'our people are our greatest asset'. These assets and their intellectual capital are the source of all competitive advantage, differentiation and value adding. If this is so, then training, skills development and competency must be among our top priorities. The logic is simple, but how many businesses put such logic into practice? As Tom Peters says:[2] 'Workforce training must become a corporate (and indeed national) obsession.' With strategic partnering and alliancing it must indeed become an obsession.

There is also a direct link between skills and innovation and the degree of commitment and common purpose among employees. A study by the Business Council of Australia[3] declared:

> *Talented people were a key resource for innovating companies. Deploying scarce talent in the places that had the biggest impact on innovation was essential to sustained success. The best enterprises were able to build on the experience, skills and creativity of their people.*
>
> *Their businesses were characterised by shared values. A common purpose throughout the enterprise was another key performance criterion. Successfully focusing the people on building the business and drawing out their creativity and experience required clear communication throughout the business. In the best enterprises, people at all levels had the same ideas about business objectives, priorities and how to satisfy customers. These issues are closely linked to systematic approaches to innovation and improvement in the supply system.*

There is nothing more dangerous and unproductive than a highly skilled, highly educated employee coming to work with a bad attitude. Empowered and committed people with the right skills and on the right learning curve can be a powerful and effective force. If the standards have been set and the challenge of becoming world class and developing partnerships has been accepted, skills and learning must follow. However, this is not about throwing training courses at unsuspecting subordinates and ticking the boxes on completion. It is about developing skills and competencies which are then incorporated into the overall partnering process. If you are to succeed, the traditional training culture must be replaced by a culture based on competence and learning. This will involve the effective application of knowledge, skills and attitudes up to and then exceeding the standards set by the partner organisations and the external marketplace. Continuous and breakthrough improvement will accept nothing less. This is not an overnight objective. It will take real vision and leadership to uncover, plan and implement skills development for the future.

People at all levels—shop floor, middle management, senior management—will need to be challenged on their current skills. A useful tool in understanding where you are, where you want to be, and how to get there, is a skills gap analysis. This involves identifying current and desired skills levels, deciding who needs to acquire what skills to fill the gap, and agreeing on a timetable for implementation. The skills gap analysis must be seen and developed from your own partnering perspective with the flexibility to change with changing needs.

Management involvement

There can be no procrastination here on training budgets and resource allocation. Management must not only be supportive, they must also provide the funds. Otherwise, all the talk of partnerships and alliances and world class is mere rhetoric. Management (senior and middle) must also participate in the process, both as teachers and as students. In particular, they play an important role in getting the shop floor to understand and believe in the partnering/alliance vision and its enabling strategies. How do your employees currently learn about the organisation's vision and become skilled in understanding and believing in it? How is their commitment to the vision developed?

Apart from the obvious personal issues, people fail in their jobs for two fundamental reasons. One, they are the wrong individuals for the job, that is, square pegs in round holes. They have been chosen incorrectly. The selection process has failed. This is a management problem. Unfortunately for the poor individual who was not initially aware of the incompatibility, it also becomes his or her problem. Second, the right person has been chosen for the job but insufficient skills have been developed, thereby affecting competence, confidence and self-esteem. This is also a management/leadership problem. Management have the responsibility and obligation to set the standards and provide opportunities for skills development. This includes creating an environment in which the full potential of individuals and teams can be achieved.

Joint training and skills programs

Joint training and skills programs between customer and supplier partners will be one of the critical success factors for the partnership. For example, improving communication, conflict resolution, problem solving or total quality would prove extremely useful. Even joint training in the partnering/alliance principles, process and practices would be valuable in terms of a common view, shared information and the development of trust and respect. Common understanding leads to common language which leads to common practice.

Consider also the benefits of people exchange programs and co-location of partnering/alliance personnel—secondments to the other partner with the aims of specific upskilling, sharing information and values, understanding requirements and building on the partnership. Such an arrangement is quite common within organisations, but what about between customer and supplier partners? Any part of the business could be involved in people-exchange programs with the secondment periods varying according to the objectives set. For example, apprentices, process operators, tradespeople (mechanical and electrical) and finance, marketing, sales and management personnel are all candidates for short-, medium- or long-term secondments. The effect of exchange programs on individual skills, business performance and the partnering relationship can be profound.

Continuous improvement means retraining and upskilling

There is no question that, relative to the competition, training, skills and competencies must be continuously improving. Procrastination or, worse, negligence in failing to reinvest adequately in this intellectual capital, which through innovation, growth and competition is always depreciating, will lead to commercial or technological death. Either way the end result is that the organisation is out of business and the employees (once the company's greatest asset) are out of a job.

The solution is relatively simple: train and retrain, skill and upskill, then retrain and upskill some more. Throughout this never-ending process, match the improvement in skills with an increase in ownership and empowerment of those on the shop floor and at the coalface. There is a simple yet often overlooked relationship here.

Skills + Leadership + Empowerment + Commitment + Ownership = Innovation

Sustained innovation relative to the competition will yield competitive advantage. Competitive advantage is what is needed to keep the partnership alive and well and your own organisation successful.

Ask for help everywhere

When you were at school, do you remember those teachers who had the greatest influence on you, held your attention for longer and helped you to learn faster? They enthused and inspired you to think 'outside the square' and expand your frame of reference. They helped you to be more creative and sometimes even determined a career path for you that would not otherwise have been. They made the complex look simple, the unclear appear obvious. Perhaps there was something a little different about them. Maybe even a little eccentric. Was it their passion, devotion and commitment to their discipline, their knowledge and experience, the way they spoke in simple, clear, commonsense terms?

Whatever it was, you will need these types of people as trainers, facilitators, coaches, mentors, educators, leaders. Their skills and enthusiasm will be one of the major catalysts for change and, in fact, they may themselves become part of the innovation process. Find them and use them wisely, especially at the coalface and shop-floor levels.

REFERENCES

1. Managing Director, ICI Australia, 1991. Quoted in Tony Mealor, *ICI Australia: The Botany Experience*, Industrial Relations Research Centre, University of New South Wales, 1992, p.86.
2. Tom Peters, *Thriving on Chaos*, Harper & Row, New York, 1987, p.323.
3. Roderick Carnegie & Matthew Butlin, *Managing the Innovating Enterprise*, Business Council of Australia, 1993, p.71.

Reviewing supplier relationships upstream

Objective

Irrespective of whether you are the customer or supplier partner, to improve the quality and effectiveness of the relationships with your suppliers upstream so as to enhance your ability to service your customer partner(s) and customers generally.

Key points

1. Determine/review your general supplier strategy and the quality of your supplier relationships. Decide which suppliers you want to be a vendor to, a customer to, or a partner with—and why. What relationship types as per Figure 1.3 do you want to develop with suppliers? Complete a 0 to 10 Relationship Strategy Map for your suppliers— that is, agree on the current states and desired future states for the relationships.

2. Review the number of your suppliers. Can they be reduced? Establish a list of preferred suppliers based on agreed performance criteria and single source wherever possible, to improve quality and reduce variability.

3. Search jointly for benefits based on agreed requirements. These will be driven by the twelve motivators. That is, does the benefit add value; reduce costs; improve communication; develop trust; resolve conflicts; remove hidden agendas; provide leadership; empower people; gain commitment; develop ownership; break down departmental barriers; remove fear?

4. Establish a varied assortment of teams that bring together committed and skilled people to achieve common goals.

5. Encourage two-way training, retraining, skilling, upskilling. Share and develop existing skills and competencies for mutual benefit.

6. Form partnering/alliance relationships with selected suppliers.

7. Conduct regular reviews with suppliers to share information and ideas and to innovate. Involve your customer partner(s) in these reviews whenever possible or appropriate.

8. Encourage cooperation between suppliers for mutual supply chain and customer benefit.

9. Set up agreed measures and key performance indicators (KPIs) for improvement in performance for both your own organisation and your suppliers'. Establish feedback loops for continuous improvement.

Innovating enterprises looked two ways—they focused on satisfying their customers, and they emphasised building a profitable supply system... Another form of assistance was helping to change the culture in the supplier's workplace. Working systematically on the relationship with suppliers did not bring overnight success. Success came through building up the capabilities of the business and in the suppliers, and was based on trust, information and shared interests.

Business Council of Australia[1]

Suppliers are as important as customers

There should be few surprises here. Most progressive organisations have reached the stage where they understand the importance of suppliers and their delivering of IFOTA1 to agreed requirements. Just as you want to develop vendor, supplier and partner relationships downstream with customers, so there will need to be a clear recognition and management of the relationships with your suppliers upstream.

The supplier/customer chain is only as strong as its weakest link. The quality, availability and dependability of supplier raw materials, plant and equipment, spare parts, services, hardware, software, advice and information will all have a critical bearing on your ability to meet current and future requirements from your own customers. Therefore, don't assume that your supplier relationships are any less important than your customer relationships. The quality of your relationships upstream with suppliers will need to be consistent with the quality of the relationships downstream with customers.

From the perspective of the partnership with your downstream customer, strong, stable, high performing and effective relationships with your suppliers will be essential, whether they are vendor, supplier or partner based. Effective relationships in this area will be one of the key performance indicators for successful partnerships. They will also be based on the principles of trust, skills, clear and common goals, shared information and the empowerment of both teams and individuals.

Ask the question 'How much of your organisation's revenue do you pay to suppliers?'. The answer is probably somewhere between 50 per cent and 80 per cent. This is a significant number and reinforces the fact that suppliers and high-performing supplier relationships need to be a critical part of your business and partnering/alliance strategy.

Selecting suppliers

Vendor, supplier and partner relationships flow throughout the supply chain so selecting suppliers will require a process similar to that used in the step 'Selecting a partner'. Use application importance (strategic value vs commercial value) and organisation trustworthiness (willingness vs capability) as the basis for selecting major, key and other suppliers. These relationships should be reviewed over time based on supplier performance. The objective should be to improve supplier relationships continuously, so that they move to the most appropriate relationship type and performance levels and you have the right mix of vendor, supplier and partner relationships with suppliers.

Preferred supplier lists

In conjunction with the selection process, identify how and when the number of suppliers to your organisation can be reduced. This is all in the spirit of improving quality and reducing variability. Directly connected with the reduction in the number of suppliers has been the use of preferred supplier lists. They have proved to be a useful tool in improving internal interdepartmental communication and sending clear and unambiguous messages to suppliers on performance standards and expectations.

A preferred supplier policy, for example, eliminates the traditional internal rivalry between the engineering department that puts quality, reliability and availability first, irrespective of cost, and the purchasing department that has price as the first priority. Whether this is the perception or the reality, each department genuinely believes it is doing its best for the organisation and its customers. How many times have we seen initially simple miscommunications on unclear requirements develop into outright confrontation, with each department undermining the other to achieve its individual objectives? The results are poor quality, delays, increased variability, increased costs, suppliers who feel cheated and, ultimately, unhappy customers.

The process of preferred supplier selection is just as important as the list itself and how it is used. This selection will be based on results achieved against agreed performance criteria. The criteria and standards will change according to the nature of the business and the requirements agreed upon. Be sure to communicate to your suppliers the philosophy and process behind preferred supplier selection and assist them via education and training if required. Otherwise, confusion will reign and the mutual benefit so eagerly sought will prove illusive.

A preferred supplier policy has several advantages:

- The list provides a ready reference for supplier selection.
- The policy puts a brake on supplier proliferation and 'back-room deals'. The requirement is that only those on the preferred supplier list can be used.
- The policy provides a set of clear and agreed standards and requirements for both customer and suppliers, whether the suppliers are on the list or striving to be.
- The list provides suppliers with clear and unambiguous guidelines that are fair and equal for all on how preferred suppliers are selected.
- The policy encourages early and more open supplier involvement without fear of being traded off at a later stage by suppliers offering a cheaper price.
- A 'lowest price' mentality is replaced by a philosophy of lowest overall cost and highest overall value.
- Innovation and continuous improvement are facilitated by the more trusting and open environment.
- Preferred supplier lists stimulate a longer-term, more stable approach to buying. Ultimately, they can be the stimulus for partnerships and all the associated benefits for customer and supplier.
- The lists encourage teamwork and more effective communication across functions and departments by providing an opportunity for all those interested to play a part in the selection process. Tribalism and interdepartmental rivalry are reduced or even eliminated. The customer requirements are agreed requirements. A win/win situation exists for all.
- Through early supplier involvement, target costs, target quality and specifications can be agreed on virtually at the conceptual stage of design and development. Again I want to reinforce that these preferred suppliers can span the 0 to 10 Relationship Management spectrum for all the right reasons. They must also deliver on the performance levels required for the relationship approach taken. World-class companies are building a 'virtual' shelf of preferred or pre-qualified partner organisations, consortia groups and communities for large projects. This is saving both time and money and adding increased value for lower costs.

Single sourcing versus sole sourcing

The discussion on monopolies and partnerships in Chapter 3 is also applicable here. It is necessary to draw the distinction between single supply status, which is preferred, and sole supply, which is to be avoided. In single supply arrangements, there are several available suppliers, of which one is the supplier of choice. In sole supply there is no choice—there is only one source of supply with all its inherent pitfalls. If dealing with monopolies is unavoidable and there are no substitute products or services to benchmark against, then every effort must be made to communicate the importance of delivering agreed requirements IFOTA1. Of crucial importance here will be implementing the appropriate commercial, relationship, technical or logistical initiatives and innovation.

Single supply is quite different and should not be seen as an opportunity for supplier blackmail. Instead, as has been amply demonstrated, if the customer/supplier relationship is based on two-way trust, cooperation and commitment for mutual advantage, with remuneration linked to performance where possible, then the result is competitive pricing, improved quality and reduced variability. If these qualities don't exist, then the supplier is clearly not worthy of such a position. Single supplier arrangements and partnerships are closely linked but are not the same.

First- and second-tier suppliers

As appropriate, select first-tier key suppliers or supplier partners to manage a group of second-tier, 'other' suppliers of similar or related goods and services. This approach can have several advantages.

1. Frees up customer time and resources.
2. Generates ownership and loyalty in the second-tier supplier managers and is a point of differentiation over their competitors.
3. Can reduce overall number of suppliers.
4. Reduces total costs for the customer.
5. Generates additional second-tier supplier manager income via a management fee linked to the performance of the second-tier suppliers.

Clear and consistent rules/guidelines will need to be developed and agreed upon as to how to manage the second-tier suppliers. These will be based on a common understanding of the business strategy and consistent values between the customer and second-tier supplier managers.

Search jointly for benefits based on agreed requirements

Understand across your supplier base where there are opportunities to add value and/or reduce costs. Identify the opportunities for innovation and development. Conformance to agreed requirements IFOTA1 will become the basic challenge for all suppliers and provide the basis upon which all further development work takes place. Agreeing and articulating the requirements is essential if conformance is to follow.

The benefits from strong and effective supplier relationships, irrespective of whether they have reached partnership status or not, are numerous for both customer and supplier. Those same benefits can, of course, be transposed to the next step in the supply chain for the customer, who is then in the position of a supplier. These benefits include:

Customer benefits
- Improved quality, fewer rejects, less waste
- Reduced inspection time
- Dramatically reduced customer complaints about non-conformances
- Lower prices in real terms
- Superior performance or effect at the same (or even higher) prices, i.e. greater value for money
- Improved productivity and efficiencies
- Shorter lead times
- Improved reliability and dependability of supply
- Improved cash flows and reduced working capital costs
- Lower inventory and cycle times
- Reduced product/service development time
- Improved skills from joint training
- Fewer hassles and less frustration
- More time and resources available for downstream customers
- Increased profits and ROI
- Improved communication and people relationships

Supplier benefits
- Larger volumes
- Longer-term stability of supply
- Improved production efficiencies and cycle times due to greater stability of forecasts
- Lower costs in real terms
- Fewer hassles and less frustration
- Improved skills from joint training
- Increased profits and ROI
- Fewer customer complaints and less waste
- Improved communication and people relationships
- Aggregate purchasing
- Supplier-managed inventories

Take advantage of the benefits of aggregate purchasing. The combined purchasing power of the organisation as a whole will prove far more effective than the buying power of individual businesses, divisions, departments or functions on their own. Also take advantage of this network and combined purchasing power with your customer and supplier partners. Both supplier and customer partners can benefit enormously in reducing costs and in many cases improving quality by simply combining their purchasing power with preferred suppliers.

Teams and teamwork will be essential

Skilled and committed individuals working together for common goals will provide the vehicle by which the benefits can be achieved. Provide the environment, set the challenges and measure for improvement. Team membership should not be confined to the one organisation. Wherever possible, involve members from the supplier, your own organisation and, as appropriate, the customer partner. The use of teams and their subsequent successes will provide one of the catalysts for breaking down departmental barriers and allowing greater cross-functional activity within and external to the organisation. Possible joint team activities could include:

- product/service development teams
- problem-solving/corrective-action teams
- process re-engineering teams
- joint design teams
- benchmarking teams
- special project teams
- aggregate purchasing teams
- requirements teams
- innovation/opportunity teams
- quality improvement teams

Establish the mechanism for joint training and upskilling

As the organisation's greatest asset, invest in human capital as much as in hardware. The same principle that applied to your customer partner(s) is also applicable to suppliers. Wherever possible, enter into joint training arrangements and skills exchange. Imagine the possibilities for innovation and creativity in a situation where individuals from the customer partner, your own organisation, selected suppliers and even a supplier partner are learning and upskilling together at the same place and time. There should be no limit to this involvement. The list below is not exhaustive and each market, each organisation, each customer/supplier relationship will have different priorities based on specific costs and benefits.

Areas for joint training and skills development include:

- TQM/SPC
- partnering/alliance training
- computing
- production process
- maintenance
- design
- partnering
- marketing and sales

- engineering in areas of common interest
- management and leadership skills
- team building and facilitation
- customer service
- problem solving
- conflict resolution
- technology
- strategic supply management

Do not limit these initiatives just to joint training and skills development. Look at people-exchange programs where individuals (or even groups or teams) are seconded upstream to suppliers or downstream to customers, with the specific aim of improving skills and competence and building a network of relationships. The extent of these people-exchange programs is optional. They could last for a week, a month or even a year or more, depending on their nature and the scope of the skill. For example, an apprentice-exchange program may require up to a year or longer to develop fully the skills required. Clearly, there is no reason why these initiatives could not work equally well with customers and in particular your customer partners.

Forming partnerships with selected suppliers

> *Partnerships with suppliers have helped Chrysler improve performance significantly by speeding up product development, lowering development costs, and reducing procurement costs thereby contributing to increases in Chrysler's market share and profitability.*[2]

One of the spin-offs from the partnership process is that it has the potential to uncover, discover or generate opportunities for further partnerships upstream or downstream. The issue of developing supplier partnerships is particularly relevant and important in building extended supply chain partnering networks. Certainly, the development of selected supplier partnerships will in many cases be critical to sustaining customer partnerships.

Reviews with suppliers

As with customer reviews, supplier reviews can be very varied. Generally, however, they should be held regularly and involve a review of performance against requirements and KPIs, a joint sharing of information that has relevance to the business, and a discussion about the future and opportunities for innovation. Also use these sessions to recharge the creative batteries. Take these opportunities to do something different—brainstorming, lateral thinking, involving people internal or external to the organisations who wouldn't normally be there. In particular, include shop-floor people who, in most cases, are the direct users of the product or service.

Supplier seminars

When the time is right, get your suppliers (major and minor) together with a mix of your own people, from shop floor to senior management, and a range of people from your customer partner(s). Encourage your suppliers to meet the representatives of your customer partner(s) and to exchange ideas and information, benchmark for improvement and understand at first hand the customer's business and requirements. Make sure shop-floor and front-line people are involved.

Some of my most memorable partnering experiences have occurred while delivering one- and two-day in-house partnering seminars to an organisation's internal and external customers and suppliers. The step change that can be achieved by gathering together numerous links in the supply chain is quite remarkable. This involves talking about the principles and practice of partnering and the approach the organisation is going to take opposite the key, major and other suppliers (refer to Fig. 1.2).

Make provision for key suppliers to 'live in' and 'co-locate'

As the relationship becomes increasingly seamless and the barriers, internal and external, come down and trust develops, consider providing a permanent place to stay for key suppliers. The logic is simple: make them feel at home, as you would treat internal employees and as you would wish to be treated by your own customers. A 'base' for key suppliers could range from a fully equipped office to a workstation or workbench, to open access to work areas, equipment and people. It could be on a part-time or full-time basis. The effect of co-location on teamwork, communication, decision making and general performance can be dramatic.

If your organisation is a large user of transport and you have a preferred supplier, visualise the benefits of having a representative, account manager, engineer or coordinator on site. Remember, freight, maintenance and service organisations can often be your second sales force. It could be invaluable for a major raw material supplier of a large and/or diverse range of products or services to have a fully equipped office or work area with electronic linkups back into the supplier organisation. This on-site presence will prove particularly useful where people relationships are important. In the area of engineering and maintenance services requiring the ongoing use of hardware, software, spare parts or diagnostics, a permanent work area may provide for a more responsive, flexible and effective service.

Chrysler has increased the number of resident supplier engineers who work alongside Chrysler employees from fewer than 30 in 1989 to over 300 in 1998.[3] This has resulted in greater trust and more reliable and timely communication of important information. Improved coordination, cooperation, quicker response and development times between Chrysler and suppliers and across suppliers has been impressive. Honda also talks about seamless relationships between their employees and external suppliers where it is impossible to distinguish between the two on the shop floor. Equity rules!

Develop and encourage co-supplier relationships

For the automakers Honda, Chrysler and Ford, 70–80 per cent of the cost of their vehicles lies with suppliers. The achievement of world class is unthinkable without cooperative relationships, not only with the car manufacturers and their suppliers but between the supplier organisations themselves. These co-supplier relationships often involve single-supply, dual-competition arrangements where single, preferred suppliers develop and produce like products and services but for assembly into separate models. The suppliers then benchmark and share best practice across the models, within agreed boundaries and rules of engagement. Chrysler has established an advisory board comprising its top fourteen suppliers, and its top 150 suppliers meet annually to facilitate more effective interaction between suppliers.

The importance of measurement in improving performance

I am a great believer in total quality measurement techniques and statistical process control (SPC). A thorough understanding of process stability and the role of variation in reducing—or even eliminating—rework, downtime, complexity, unnecessary bureaucracy and other forms of waste is essential for every organisation, large or small. The alternatives of reacting to the 'last point on the curve' and short-term decision making will on most occasions result in frustrating failure.

I am not going to tell you what to measure or how to measure it. Your own people, customers and suppliers are in the best position to know. However, measurement must be planned. The following questions need to be answered.

- *What* is to be measured and what training is required?
- *Who* is to do the measuring?
- *How* is the measurement to be done and how will the information be used?
- *When* is the measuring to be done (frequency/timing) and when will feedback be given?
- *Where* is the measuring to be done and where are the results to be displayed?
- *Why* is the measurement being done?

Remember, it will be the gathering and effective analysis of timely, accurate and relevant data and information that will allow for intelligent discussion of the facts, as opposed to arguments based on emotion. To this extent, control charts, Pareto charts, cause and effect diagrams, flow charts, and Gantt and PERT charts will prove extremely useful. Effective measurement will track performance against agreed requirements and future expectations and provide the basis for understanding continuous improvement. It is then the feedback loop between customer and supplier that will allow both the relationship and the benefits to be developed upon.

It is true that *you can't manage what you can't measure*. However, there are three general rules of thumb that should be followed:

1. Measure the right things in the right way. Whether it is first-pass efficiency, reject rates, cycle time, deliveries in full on time, customer complaints, or percentage success rate of new products, it must be relevant to the original objectives.
2. Don't over-measure. Measuring everything that moves, walks or talks will only confuse the measurers and devalue the information gained.
3. Do something with what has been measured, and I don't mean go away and manipulate the figures. Information for the sake of information can be more damaging and dangerous than no information at all. First, it takes time and costs money and, second, people become frustrated and lose interest in the process if they don't get the feedback.

CASE STUDY

Hazelwood Power and Alstom Power

'Alliances are first a matter of choice, from there, they are a matter of commitment,' says Alistair Tompkin, Director, Power Generation at Hazelwood Power, one of Australia's largest electricity producers. Through a deliberate corporate strategy, Hazelwood has committed to alliance arrangements for almost all its routine and defect maintenance work, major overhauls and capital investment program. So far, alliances have delivered results beyond expectations—in particular, the relationship with Alstom Power has been a major success story. The alliance has evolved over four years, from an initial invitation to develop a precipitator replacement program, to the current activities which include overhaul of generation equipment, the design, building and installation of new precipitators and major turbine and generator refurbishment. This work scope is linked, on a project-by-project basis, to some or all of five primary performance measures, which are cost, revenue loss, time, safety and quality of outcomes. Alistair Tompkin is passionate about effective measurement and mutual benefit: 'Good performance targets for each project are critical and they are carefully sculpted to create an alignment of outcomes that directly impact on the bottom line of both companies. We win or we lose together. The win/lose option is eliminated.'

Strong and supportive leadership from the top of both organisations has been critical in making the alliance approach work, and driving it from concept to successful reality. This is manifested in the integrated structure and team-based accountability. The alliance leadership team comprises one person from each company at General Manager level. Reporting to the leadership team is a cross-functional, cross-organisational team of eight managers who manage the various projects. This is made easier through the co-location of Alstom Power personnel on site.

A combination of innovation, hard work and driving leadership continues to deliver positive change and improved results. Alstom Power has been able to effectively tap into its vast organisation. Bringing its expertise and extended knowledge base, as well as a contractor perspective and negotiating skills into the relationship has been extremely valuable. For example, subcontractors costs have been reduced by 15 per cent. Hazelwood outage costs have reduced by over 10 per cent in two years and are set to reduce further.

When asked about the keys to success for good alliancing, Alistair Tompkin sees it simply as 'a clear simple alliance agreement with good performance measures, strong positive leadership, a good (team-based) structure that integrates the partners, no duplication of activities, one-system, sitting together, having a vision of a virtual company with common goals and high levels of trust. This has to happen, but it does require a leap of faith'.

The alliance approach has positively affected all aspects of the way business is done. The leadership team has had to resolve only one conflict in four years. Attitudes and behaviours of people have changed significantly for the better. David Wilson, General Manager, Alstom Power, Environmental Segment talks about the growth potential arising from the alliance: 'Based on performance we are leveraging the benefits of this relationship elsewhere. There can be nothing more powerful than having your alliance partner as an advocate when discussing new business opportunities with prospective or existing customers.' This statement is backed up by Alistair Tompkin of Hazelwood: 'We (Hazelwood and Alstom Power) are now jointly carrying out work with a third party and as a customer I have become a lead salesperson for Alstom Power. For alliances to be successful you have to love your partners' profit.' Even for Hazelwood themselves, there are opportunities to expand the alliance approach. For example, the Hazelwood coal mine has not been involved with the alliance process to date. However, they have seen the benefits and sought support from the power station to move to alliance arrangements.

Hazelwood's expectation is that they will further improve their performance through alliances and extend their application. How do you ensure success and build interdependence? 'As one team, we sit together, work together, think together, succeed together,' says Alistair Tompkin.

REFERENCES

1. Roderick Carnegie & Matthew Butlin, *Managing the Innovating Enterprise*, Business Council of Australia, 1993, p.66.
2. Jeffrey H. Dyer, 'How Chrysler created an American Keiretsu', *Harvard Business Review*, July–August 1996, p.46.
3. Jeffrey H. Dyer, op. cit., p.55.

Technology requirements (current and future)

Objective

Customer and supplier partners to understand the opportunities for changes in technology (current and future) and, if mutually agreed, to implement those technology changes that will achieve, maintain or enhance competitive advantage by reducing costs and/or increasing differentiation for the customer and/or supplier partner.

Key points

1. Carry out a gap analysis of the technology needed to achieve IFOTAI and the current technologies in use, to determine whether improvements need to be made. Do this throughout all business functions, not just product technology or the basic manufacturing operation.

2. Analyse future customer requirements and future technology needs (product and process).

3. Benchmark current and future technology requirements opposite customers, suppliers, competitors and other organisations in other markets where comparison and understanding of the technology will add value or reduce costs.

4. Understand the impact of new technologies on strategy, development costs, competitors, resources required, and people.

5. Agree with your partner(s) the strategy and detail of any technology change, the impact on costs and benefits overall and the role each party needs to play.

6. Review areas where there is the potential for technology integration, exchange or exploitation among business units, customers and/or suppliers.

7. Evaluate the role of acquisitions, joint ventures and licensing in your technology strategy opposite the customer partner.

Understand the technology gap

The quotation below in no way plays down or maligns the importance of the role of technology in either the development of customer/supplier partnerships or in the application of business strategy in general. It does, however, reinforce the point that technological change for its own sake is unimportant. It can also be time-consuming, resource-depleting and ultimately counterproductive. People and attitude lie at the heart of innovation, not vast arrays of hardware and software. Again and again, success comes back to people, in this case to their level of skill and competence in developing and applying technology and to the way they relate and communicate the subject matter.

> *The first and principal conclusion of our research is that innovation in Australia in the 1990s is about people and enterprises, not about science and technology. For the vast majority of enterprises, science and technology are vital tools that need to be applied effectively and developed selectively. But for these enterprises, innovation is more a matter of flexible, productive and focused employee relations in the workplace than it is a result of technological resources or the impact of science and science policies . . . The real world of innovation that we saw has little to do with laboratories and everything to do with attitudes.*
>
> *Business Council of Australia* [1]

There is no doubt that technology gives the lead players in the marketplace an opportunity to change the rules of the game. Microsoft and Intel are good examples. If 'applied effectively and developed selectively', technology will provide the necessary tools for the partnership to flourish and be sustained. There is a direct link between innovation, technology and competitive advantage. This stage of the process is all about understanding where technology can be used or modified more effectively to the mutual benefit of the customer and supplier partners; identifying where technology and technological change can directly affect or indirectly influence a firm's competitive advantage by lowering costs or increasing differentiation and value. Competitive advantage and innovation are two of the cornerstones of successful customer/supplier partnerships.

Technology also lies within every step of every process within every function of every business. Too often we confine our definition of technology to the area of production and manufacturing. Technology is everywhere and, in the process of evaluating opportunities, all parts of the business need to be investigated to see where technology can be beneficially improved upon or exploited. Michael Porter,[2] in *Competitive Advantage*, eloquently outlines some of the technologies in the context of the value chain. These are shown in Figure 6.21.

Technology can also range from 'low tech' to 'high tech'. Many important innovations have been born, not out of huge step changes in technology or great scientific breakthroughs, but by the application of unique and effective low-tech designs and ideas.

The first step in understanding the opportunities for technology will be to identify the technology gaps in fulfilling the customer requirements IFOTA1. Remember: the basic requirements need to be fulfilled first time and every time in a quality way if the partnership has any hope of getting off the ground. This goes back to ensuring a clear understanding of the customer partner's requirements and of the processes by which they can be fulfilled. This will determine the impact of changes in technology that may be required to deliver the solution. It must be said, however, that too often we look for solutions in technology when the root cause, and the solution, lie with management, leadership and people.

Once the technology opposite the current requirements is understood and in place, turn your attention to the technology(ies) needed to fulfil the customer partner's future requirements. These are the real keys to the innovation treasure box of sustainable, long-term success. As before, this will involve the analysis of technology in its broadest sense across all functions of the business. Hamel and Prahalad, in *Competing for the Future*, suggest there is no industry today that is not technology-intensive, be it airlines, banking, computing or communications. They also draw the connection between understanding the customer's business requirements (current and future), as discussed in an earlier step, and the technology (current and future) required to support those needs. They state:

Lacking a point of view about customers' future needs, there is a danger that a company will invest only in those technologies that correspond to current expressed customer needs. This is short-sighted. The link between technology and customers is not just currently articulated needs, but also product and service concepts that promise to satisfy unarticulated needs. The goal is to be neither narrowly technology-driven nor narrowly customer-driven. The goal is thus to be broadly benefits-driven—constantly searching for, investing in, and mastering the technology that will bring unanticipated benefits to humankind.[3]

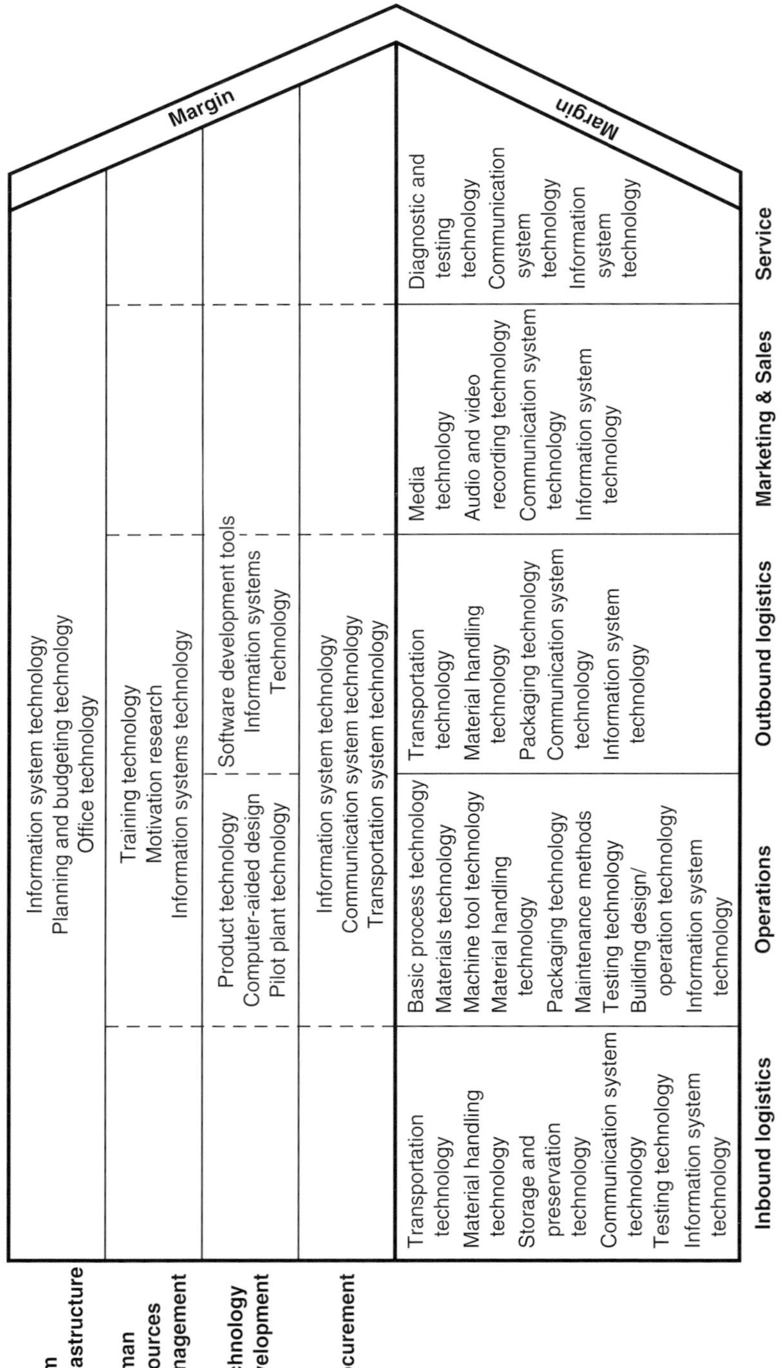

	Inbound logistics	Operations	Outbound logistics	Marketing & Sales	Service
Firm infrastructure	Information system technology Planning and budgeting technology Office technology				
Human resources management	Training technology Motivation research Information systems technology				
Technology development	Product technology Computer-aided design Pilot plant technology	Software development tools Information systems Technology			
Procurement	Information system technology Communication system technology Transportation system technology				
	Transportation technology Material handling technology Storage and preservation technology Communication system technology Testing technology Information system technology	Basic process technology Materials technology Machine tool technology Material handling technology Packaging technology Maintenance methods Testing technology Building design/ operation technology Information system technology	Transportation technology Material handling technology Packaging technology Communication system technology Information system technology	Media technology Audio and video recording technology Communication system technology Information system technology	Diagnostic and testing technology Communication system technology Information system technology

Fig. 6.21 *Representative technologies in a firm's value chain*

Benchmark technology to advantage

Ultimately, if genuine innovation is to take place, understanding the technology/benefits gap between your organisation, your competitors and the best in the world will be necessary for directing your strategy and providing a catalyst for change. For partnering and alliance relationships to be successful they must be able to demonstrate on an ongoing basis that they are delivering value over and above the alternative on an ongoing basis. This is the basis of the 'value question': 'What value is this relationship delivering for this organisation over the alternatives?'. Benchmarking will be one of the key mechanisms for doing this. Benchmarking, however, should not be limited to competitors. Your customers, suppliers and many other world-class organisations inside and outside your industry or market sector will provide the basis for comparison by which improvement can take place. There is also the opportunity for greater teamwork via joint benchmarking teams (refer to the Transfield Worley case study) between your supplier and customer partners. Related specifically to partnerships and alliances, the basic steps to benchmarking are:

1. What strategy, value propositions, relationship types and performance levels do you want to achieve? Not all relationship types and performance levels need to be benchmarked (see Fig. 1.4, the 0 to 10 Relationship Management matrix).
2. Identify and prioritise the Key Results Areas (KRAs), Key Performance Indicators (KPIs) that are critical to the long-term success of the partnership; that is, those that impact upon total cost reduction or increased value, and on the other ten motivators. These KPIs will vary enormously, but could include strategic, commercial or cost-based KPIs, as well as maintenance, flexibility, customer satisfaction, reduced cycle times, availability, reliability, dependability, bulk handling, electronic communications, production output, quality, and software/hardware design capability KPIs.
3. Establish the gap in performance between your organisation and other key 'best in class' companies, whether they are competitors (yours or your partner's) or not. Where appropriate, look outside your industry or traditional frame of reference for data or practices that can often provide breakthrough improvements.
4. Document and use that information to make improvements as required. These could include modification of the business strategies and action plans, and operational, maintenance and service practices.
5. Identify specific benchmarking partners who are outstanding opposite specific KPIs and benchmark with them for mutual benefit and continuous improvement.

6. Gather information from other sources to add to or support existing data. Use library sources, public documents, trade shows, trade journals, professional benchmarking associations, benchmarking forums, consultants, academics and other companies (customers/suppliers or otherwise). For example, in the oil refining business the Soloman Survey is widely used as a source of benchmarking data and performance ranking.

7. Continue to close the gap on the performance of critical KPIs between your organisation and the 'best in class' to ensure continuous improvement.

Benchmarking is now a widely used tool among world-class companies for achieving competitive advantage. It will also prove very useful for partnering and alliance relationships. Transfield Services and Worley have established a benchmarking forum working with key customers and partners from a wide spectrum of industries, ranging from oil and gas to steel and telecommunications.

The alternatives to benchmarking

There will be occasions where benchmarking is not as easy to do as it first appears. Unique applications, lack of 'apples for apples' comparisons, confidentiality of industry data, intellectual property restrictions, a lack of willingness to share information for competitive or personal reasons will be some of the challenges that can confront partner organisations keen to compare notes. Significant time, resources and money can also be spent 'normalising' data or collecting benchmarking data that is either irrelevant, difficult to interpret or not used effectively for improvement at an operating level. This can lead to frustration and give benchmarking a bad name for the wrong reasons.

Often internal benchmarking is a viable alternative. I worked with a multinational, multi-divisional engineering services company that recognised there were real benefits to be gained by comparing operational and performance data across business units and customers. This not only generated specific technical and operational improvements but, in sharing previously restricted information between traditional business unit 'silos' and functional 'stovepipes', improved significantly the internal relationships and the openness and transparency of communications. This then carried over to the external customer and supplier relationships.

Irrespective of whether benchmarking data is appropriate or available for partnering and alliance relationships, continuous improvement based on shared goals/objectives and target KPIs is non-negotiable. This will mean having a clear understanding of the improvement trends required to ensure that the relationship is delivering ever increasing value over and above a clear baseline starting point and projected trends. Safety frequency rate trends, rates of conversion, new products time to market, percentage of rework reduction, revenue and total cost improvement trends are just some examples.

Attend to the details and sign off with your partner

Once the new technologies are understood, there are several details that need attending to. They are all commonsense steps you probably already undertake in the normal course of business. They are:

- determine the feasibility and fit with strategy;
- understand the time frame for implementation and the overall costs of development and ongoing operation;
- quantify the effect on cost/benefits, value and differentiation opposite competitors, the customer partner and suppliers; in other words, determine the nature of the competitive advantage;
- detail the resources that will be required and evaluate the impact on people and skills.

At all stages of the partnering process up to this point there has been an ongoing dialogue with the customer and/or supplier partner at many levels, but there comes a time when two-way commitments need to be made. This is particularly important if the actual technology change (depending on its nature and scope) significantly affects one or both partners in the areas of capital expenditure, resources and timing. This commitment, or 'signing-off', can formally manifest itself in various ways such as a joint venture, MOU (Memorandum of Understanding), secrecy agreement, general agreement or formal letter. Depending on the circumstances and the amount of trust and understanding involved, a verbal recognition from senior management of the changes and their importance for and effect on the partnership may be all that is required. The use of secrecy agreements may at first sight appear incongruous, when the spirit of partnerships is based on trust, openness and complete honesty. In certain circumstances, however, where issues of confidentiality, intellectual property or exclusivity are concerned, secrecy agreements make sound commercial sense and support the value of the partnership rather than detracting from it.

At this point there needs to be mutual agreement with your partner to:

- continue with the partnership strategy and implementation of any technology change;
- agree on the impact on costs/benefits overall for the partnership;

■ agree on the role both supplier and customer partner will play in the technology change, considering such details as financing, resources, facilities, equipment, project management, stock levels if regular production is interrupted, and so on.

This signing-off process is important in formalising any major commitments from both sides and recognising the value and importance of the relationship. The partnering/alliance leadership and management/operational teams will play a key role in putting the business cases together and ensuring the approval process is timely and free of complications.

The benefits of technology integration and exchange

There are two other areas involving technology that can have a significant impact on the performance of the organisation and the partnership/alliance.

1. The finding, exploiting and creating of technological inter-relationships between the various business functions and departments within your own organisation is essential. Again, we return to people, management, leadership and the willingness to break through traditional departmental barriers and roadblocks to sharing, whether information, people, skills or, now, technology.

   Eliminating the 'not invented here' syndrome applies as much to technology as it does to any other business activity. There are extraordinary benefits to be gained from technology integration in terms of reducing costs and adding value. Add to this the benefits of introducing new technological skills, invigorating existing skills and just generally upskilling, and it is not difficult to see how technology can impact well beyond the original application and frame of reference.

2. The second area where technology can have an impact involves discovering opportunities for the exchange of technology and skills among your own organisation, your suppliers and the customer partners in areas of deficiency or immediate crisis. In every organisation, no matter how big or small, there will be areas for improvement even though they may be at different stages of recognition. This involves areas of improvement that are:

   ■ recognised, with improvement plans in place;
   ■ recognised, but ignored because of priorities, lack of funding, poor management or apathy;
   ■ existing, but not yet recognised or uncovered.

   It must be one of the major obligations of both partners to exchange or offer solutions and assistance in the upgrading of areas for improvement.

This will be one of the main sources of innovation and continuous improvement. One of the roles of the partnering/alliance leadership and management teams, or even a separate technology improvement team, could be actively to look for as yet uncovered areas for improvement or to put known areas of improvement on a faster track.

As previously discussed, there is nothing better than fast, permanent, quality solutions to an immediate crisis to reinforce the value of a partnership. This is where the application of existing as well as new technology can have a lasting and significant impact.

I remember a phone conversation with a customer partner who told me of problems they were having with loud, irregular noises coming from two large sets of gearboxes and bearings that ran their two main plastic extruders on the lamination line. If the gearboxes and bearings failed, the extruders and effectively the whole production line would stop. Being special-purpose gearboxes and bearings from Europe, there were no spares and a 6–9 month lead time for replacement. They had very few diagnostic skills on site to determine the nature and extent of the problem. As we spoke, the extruders were running at only half rates, and they were planning to shut down the line completely within a couple of days if the nature of the problem could not be uncovered. There was no doubt this was a major problem with a considerable (and possibly immediate) impact on costs, stocks and production downtime, with all the other downstream implications.

While this problem and its cause had nothing to do with the direct product that we (ICI) were selling them, I made inquiries through our own engineering and production people about our own experiences and the alternatives available. A series of phone calls discovered that our engineering group not only had world-class technology but also people with world-class skills in the condition monitoring and vibration analysis of gearboxes and bearings. They were experts in the field of gearboxes and bearings, and preventative, predictive and design-out maintenance. Understanding the nature of problems when they arose and predicting with considerable accuracy the 'time to failure' was their forte.

Within 24 hours one of the ICI engineering gearbox and bearing experts had visited the customer's site. Initial tests were done and a plan agreed with the customer for immediate corrective action and longer-term preventative and predictive maintenance. It turned out that there were major problems requiring attention. However, the time frame and the time to failure were such that the customer was able to plan for a scheduled shutdown some three months out as opposed to an unscheduled shutdown immediately. Production immediately went up to full rates, and condition monitoring to track the deterioration in gearbox and bearings was put into place by our engineers. The customer's process operators were trained in the basic skills of condition monitoring and self-diagnosis.

This was a good news story for several reasons.

1. The customer partner was delighted we were able to help out in finding both short-term and long-term solutions to an immediate crisis. The application of this technology and its associated skills was estimated to have saved the customer more than $200 000.
2. We were both surprised that ICI actually had those skills. What other skills and technology lurked undiscovered in the background that could add value to both customer and supplier relationships? There was no blame to be placed on any individual or department—it was simply that the connection between direct products and services paid for, and other non-direct but value-adding benefits, had not been made.
3. This experience precipitated a range of other similar good news stories, involving not only this particular customer partner but many other customers and suppliers. There also developed very quickly a two-way exchange of technologies and skills to the mutual benefit of all concerned.
4. ICI Engineering eventually entered into a long-term contractual arrangement with the customer for the ongoing condition monitoring of all their gearboxes and bearings. Not only was one business unit adding value for another—they were also being paid for their services on a regular basis: it was a three-way win/win situation between two internal functions and an external customer.

Every good organisation will hold these 'centres of excellence'. The challenge for all in the organisation is to recognise, communicate and promote these skills, and seek out opportunities for their application. The rewards and benefits will more than return the necessary investment of people, time and skills.

The role of acquisitions, joint ventures, joint technology agreements and technology licensing

I will go into little detail on these here as they are complete subjects in themselves and clearly have cultural, strategic and structural implications for the business as a whole. However, they can be useful in accessing, effectively securing or relinquishing technology. The key question to ask is: Do these activities gain technological and commercial competitive advantage for the buyer and seller partners? If the answer is yes, proceed with caution as this is a high-risk business. If the answer is no, save your time and money.

REFERENCES

1. Roderick Carnegie & Matthew Butlin, *Managing the Innovating Enterprise*, Business Council of Australia, 1993, p.xxxvi.
2. Michael Porter, *Competitive Advantage—Creating and Sustaining Superior Performance*, The Free Press, New York, 1985, p.167.
3. Gary Hamel & C.K. Prahalad, *Competing for the Future*, Harvard Business School Press, 1994, p.321.

Reviewing inter- and intra-partner networks

Objective

To understand the number and types of supplier/customer relationships and agree with the other partner(s) the future relationships to be developed and the mechanism of succession planning in the event of people change.

Key points

1. (a) Review the number and quality of supplier/customer inter-company relationships.
   (b) Review the quality of internal relationships within the other partner.

2. Within the customer partner, determine who are (a) the economic buyers, (b) the user buyers, (c) the technical buyers and (d) the coaches.

3. Draw up a matrix flow chart of these relationships.

4. Agree on the future relationships to be developed.

5. Share this information with your partner, agree on its contents and continuously improve the quality of inter-company relationships. Carry out a joint gap analysis and agree on an action plan to develop the 'missing' or poor relationships.

6. Agree on a succession planning mechanism to deal with changes in personnel.

7. As always, continue to share information, vision and strategy.

Reviewing customer and supplier networks may look simple enough, but this is a tough one because people are involved again. Their attitudes, personalities, conflicts, likes, dislikes, prejudices, strengths and weaknesses all need to be looked at from an open and honest perspective. How does your customer partner improve his or her internal relationships as you are developing within your own organisation? This will have its own complications and be no less difficult. Coaching, training and facilitating may be required (jointly or otherwise). Remember: for the partnership to work, the good relationships and friendships that have been developed within your own organisation need to be matched by the quality of the relationships between you and your partner, and within your partner. Otherwise, the imbalance created will affect attitudes and the quality of communication between the two organisations.

Relationship mapping

You will need to draw up the contacts and relationships as they currently stand, using the relationship mapping technique. First, define with your partner what good communication looks like in specific terms for the relationship, performance characteristics, behaviours and attitudes. Then use Figure 6.6 as a guide to draw a map of the inter-company customer/supplier relationships and the partner's internal relationships. Use a solid line to indicate good communication and a strong relationship. A broken line will indicate a poor relationship and communication skills that need improvement. It will look something like Figure 6.22. Then fill in the details of these relationships on the chart shown in Figure 6.23. This looks at the number, quality, breadth, depth and nature of the relationships, and the actions that need to be taken— by whom, when and for what benefit. Each relationship is then documented, allowing for the monitoring of progress for improvement.

Organisation charts will prove useful here in understanding individuals' roles and how the departments, and in some cases tribes, interrelate. Tom Peters is right, however, in saying that organisation charts are often destructive in vindicating the influence of one tribe or department over another, falsely delivering power and influence to those who least need it or deserve it. But if that is the reality at the time, then that is what has to be dealt with.

Who are the buyers and who are the coaches?

There is a strong connection between traditional strategic selling and strategic partnering. In their book *Strategic Selling*, Miller, Heiman and Tuleja[1] put forward a very effective approach to the more complex aspects of strategic selling. They see every 'complex' sale as unique, one in which several people must give their approval before the sale can take place. These people and their roles in the complex sale may change depending on the circumstances. Nevertheless, understanding these key players, their roles and how receptive they are to your product and/or service proposal will be critical.

While the process described by Miller et al. revolves around achieving a successful outcome to a single sales objective, many of the principles they discuss can also be applied to developing and sustaining long-term, strategic

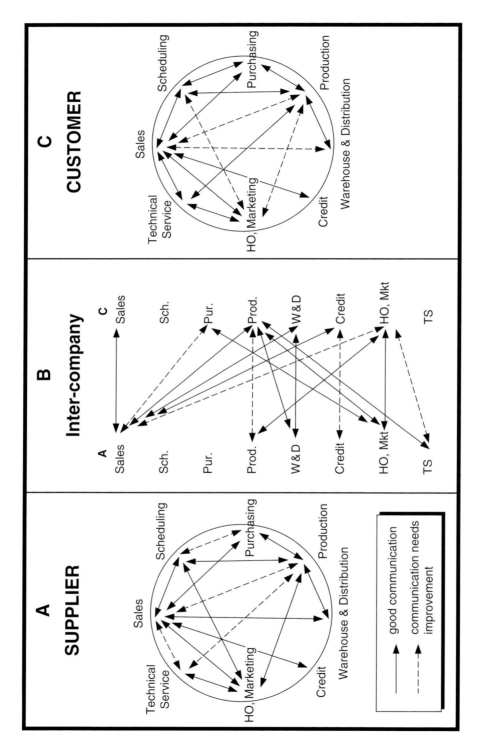

Fig. 6.22   *Relationship mapping: lines of communication*

External Customer/Supplier Relationships					
Relationship number	Contacts (C/S)	Action	Who	When	Benefit
1.					
2.					
3.					
etc.					
Internal Customer Relationships					
Relationship number	Contacts	Action	Who	When	Benefit
1.					
2.					
3.					
etc					

Fig. 6.23 *Relationship mapping: charting the details*

relationships. As they say, strategic selling is about 'seeing your customer as a partner in your success, not an adversary to be overcome'.

In particular, the authors' concept of 'buying influences' is relevant. In complex or strategic selling—no matter how many people are involved in the buying decision—there will effectively be only four buying influence roles. They are:

- The economic buyer
- The user buyer
- The technical buyer
- The coach

The same principle applies to partnerships. The relationships between buyers and coach are always there and must be recognised and developed. In particular, the role of the coach will be important in understanding the true inner workings of your customer partner.

The economic buyer

The economic buyer is the person who gives the final approval to buy your product or service and has legitimate power of veto. The economic buyer could be an individual or a board of directors, a selection committee, or another decision-making body acting as a single entity. There is only one economic buyer per sale with the focus being the bottom-line impact you make on the organisation. In partnerships, this is the return on investment or financial success in the short, medium and long term. The economic buyers in a partnership are particularly interested in how the supplier's value-adding initiatives impact upon their own competitive advantage.

The user buyer

User buyers are the people who actually use the supplier's product or service and make judgments about its performance or effect. 'How will it work for me?' is their primary concern. Their focus is much narrower than that of the economic buyer. They are interested in areas more immediate and short-term, such as reliability, availability, dependability, fit for purpose, retraining required, ease of operation, productivity, maintenance, safety, impact on morale. User buyers want to see good performance, not only for the sake of productivity and efficiencies but also because of the personal win or success involved—does your product or service make them look good as individuals?

In any organisation, there is likely to be more than one user buyer. User buyers are critically important. The way they use your product or service, 'for better or for worse', directly affects how that product or service is viewed by everyone else in the organisation, whether their perception is realistic or not.

For example, how many times have you seen an agreement reached with purchasing or senior management only to find that the production people are particularly annoyed because they were not directly involved in the process? After all, they are the people who use your product or service and can most easily influence your success or failure. Onside user buyers can be very supportive and cooperative individuals. Offside, they can be downright saboteurs. For them there is no such thing as a pleasant surprise.

The technical buyer

As Miller et al. put it: 'User buyers can be difficult but technical buyers have to be. Technical buyers make judgments about the measurable and quantifiable aspects of your product or service based on how well it meets a variety of product and/or service specifications.'[2] Their fundamental role is to screen out suppliers by limiting or reducing the field of sellers based on technicalities. They do not have the level of authority to say yes to your product or service, as does the economic buyer. But they can say no, based on technical grounds or specification non-conformance.

Technical buyers will normally make recommendations to the economic buyer for consideration. They can change your position for better or worse, literally overnight. Changes in product or service specifications for reasons that may be environmental, political, social, related to health and safety, statutory, or productivity-based can dramatically affect the supplier/customer relationship. Identify the technical buyers, and future trends and specification requirements. You will then be in a position to predict possible changes or recommend improvements to your product or service. Avoid confusing the technical buyers with the economic buyers as both the focus and the role are quite different.

The coach

Coaches are an essential element in running partnerships or, indeed, any good customer/supplier relationship. They can be found everywhere—within the supplier partner or customer partner, or external to both. A coach is an adviser, friend, confidant, an individual who can direct and guide you on specific situations or on the general development of the relationship. Your success is their success and they have your best interests at heart.

Coaches must not only be found, they must be developed. The relationship with a coach is based on trust, openness and respect and this will take time. Your coach may also be one of the other buying influences. The best possible position, of course, is when the economic buyer is also your coach. In a partnership there will be a number of coaches for both sides. In fact, the number and quality of coaches will be one of the key success factors of the partnership itself. It will be your coach who will help you to understand the relationships between customer and supplier and the internal customer relationships shown in Figure 6.22, and advise you how these relationships can be improved. Do not doubt the importance of a good coach.

Developing future relationships

The information gathered about buyers and coaches, together with a clear understanding of the customer partner's current and, in particular, future requirements, will indicate what relationships should be developed and with whom. If it is agreed that people, trust, communication, leadership and hard work lie at the heart of partnerships, then these relationships will be the key to partnering success.

Understanding current and future requirements is important because, without this knowledge, it is difficult to know where the priority areas and the primary influencers will be. It will also reveal the relationship gaps, for which solutions need to be found. It will be the quality of these future relationships that will provide the basis of a sustainable partnership. Also identify the innovators, early adaptors, followers and terrorists in the change process (see Chap. 1). The match between the buying influences and these agents of change will indicate the difficulty or ease of the task ahead.

Sign off your intentions with your partner(s)

Rarely do two organisations develop in the same way at the same speed, so be sensitive to the differing rates of change and the impact on people. It will be up to the partnering/alliance manager(s) to monitor and track the quality and progress of the relationship. Share the information gained about the relationship with your partner and specifically with the coach if you have one. Agree with the partner what relationships need to be developed for the partnership to improve.

The importance of succession planning

> *Partnering and alliance relationships must be able to survive and thrive beyond the life of key people.*

Because of its importance and impact on the very existence of the partnership, the subject of people change and succession planning will be dealt with in some detail in Chapter 8. It will suffice to say here that one of the greatest challenges in sustaining the partnership will be managing the process of people change, because partnering and alliancing are fundamentally about people and relationships. Unfortunately, it is inevitable in the western business world that people at every level of the organisation will change their positions, for all sorts of reasons, probably on average every three to five years and for senior management even less. On a partnership scale, this is a fairly short period of time if you consider that it probably takes a minimum of five years to develop a strong partnership.

In most well-run companies succession planning provides a means by which an element of prevention and even prediction can smooth the way for people change. Whatever is currently done internally in the area of succession planning should be extended to your partnering and alliancing relationships. This will involve senior management as well as the partnering/alliance managers, coaches and other key personnel active in the partnership throughout both organisations.

The other alternative, of course, is to create an environment where people don't move on as readily as they do now, especially good people—leaders, partnership managers, good communicators, innovators. Change is ultimately inevitable and in many cases provides opportunities for improvement for both the individual and the organisation. But many would argue that in the western world we change jobs too often; that three to five years is barely enough time to witness the outcome of many of the decisions that are made; that five to ten years is the more effective time frame. Certainly, few senior managers have the opportunity to live for any length of time with the results of their medium- to longer-term decisions. In many cases five to ten years would be a more suitable time frame as it would give individuals sufficient time to expand the job role, to live for a reasonable length of time with their longer-term decisions, and for the organisation to gain a genuine return on its investment.

Creating a world-class, stimulating and challenging environment where good people want to stay rather than go must be one of the major objectives of the partnership itself. This ultimately depends on management, their vision and their leadership.

REFERENCES

1. Robert Miller, Stephen Heiman & Tad Tuleja, *Strategic Selling*, Warner Books, New York, 1985, pp.70–86.
2. Miller et al., op. cit., pp.79–83.

Developing, implementing and reviewing the strategy/action plan

Objective
To develop a partnering strategy/action plan that will bring together the strategy and activities from the other eleven steps in the process and monitor their progress, as well as providing the opportunity to fill any activity/strategy gaps, innovate further and generally challenge the ongoing effectiveness of the process.

Key points
1. Consolidate the strategy and activities of the other eleven steps and review the progress of the agreed key performance indicators (KPIs).

2. Look for gaps in strategy, process, specific activities and general information.

3. Use the action plan as a basis for further innovation, key people involvement and 'buy-in'.

4. Circulate the plan and seek input widely.

5. Review and update on a regular basis.

The complexity of partnering and alliance relationships cannot be managed on the back of a postage stamp. The strategic partnering/alliancing action plan is where the stages of the process are all brought together—the melting pot of activities and actions, a cross-linking of vision, strategy and tasks, people and priorities. It is a living document that will change according to the nature and progress of the relationship. The partnering/alliancing action plan is important for a number of reasons:

- The action plan becomes a road map for the partnering process, showing where it is, where it has come from, where it is going. It puts the relationship 'big picture' into perspective, the structure, strategy and tactics, from which standpoint the overall progress and effectiveness of the relationship can be viewed in the short, medium and long term.
- It provides the link between the activities of the other eleven steps and an opportunity to test the validity and robustness of the partnering principles and process.

- A consolidating document, it should be succinct and easily read by anyone in the customer or supplier organisation. It provides the link back into the corporate strategy.
- The action plan brings together all the cross-functional, interdepartmental activities that impact upon the partnership. It can remove roadblocks and help to break down departmental barriers if used effectively. This enables early alignment and 'buy-in' from key personnel, key influencers and partnering champions.
- It will be the central control document that the partnering/alliance manager and the partnering/alliance management team will develop and use to coordinate activities and manage the progress of the partnership as a whole.
- The action plan will bring in all other activities that are not caught in the net of the other eleven steps.
- It will provide another opportunity for innovation:
  —'What haven't we thought about?'
  —'What else can be done?'
- It provides a database facility and a memory for the partnership and can also be used as a reference for other customer/supplier relationships.

The performance against the plan is a direct measure of the quality of communication and ownership in the relationship. For example, tracking the number of outstanding actions and overdue actions from the action plan as a percentage of the total actions is a direct indication of whether people are doing what they said they would do. Outstanding actions are those actions that need to be completed but are still within the allocated deadline for completion. Overdue actions are those actions that have passed the allocated deadline date. Early warnings and extensions of time may be given, but if too many extensions take place this indicates a lack of commitment to getting things done 'In Full On Time to A1 Quality' and a 'red flag' should be raised. I remember a relationship in the early stages of development where the target for overdue actions was less than 5 per cent but the actual figure was 55 per cent. This, of course, was generating angst and frustration. At an ensuing discussion it was realised that both resources and commitment were issues and corrective actions were subsequently successfully put into place.

As discussed in the introduction to the strategic partnering process (p. 143), there must be a balance between structure and flexibility. A leaning too far either way can reduce the effectiveness of the process. The action plan is no different. At first sight, it may appear a very structured and rigid step, but it will be the way the plan is managed that will determine where the balance really lies and its ultimate value to the partners.

Preparing and using the plan

There is nothing special about the action plan itself. As a guideline, the basic headings for consolidating the activities of the plan could be:

- Executive summary/fit with corporate strategy
- Partnership strategy/objectives/KPIs and targets and performance against them
- Related activities/actions/expected outcomes/milestones/action owners
- Partner alignment (i.e. culture, strategy, structure, process and people) and SWOT analysis
- Risks/benefits analysis; risk management
- Return on the partnering investment (i.e. financial success)
- Resources required
- Opportunities for growth and improvement

The plan will also track the progress of the Key Performance Indicators as agreed by the customer and supplier partners. This will involve some measure of the twelve motivators and the six outcomes (see Fig. 5.1). At this point we are well beyond conventional techniques for measuring customer/supplier performance, such as quality, delivery, service and price. How will the development of trust be determined? How do you measure the level of empowerment, and ownership? Understanding how many departmental barriers have been demolished and how the level of fear within and between the organisations has been reduced will not be easy.

Measuring ROI or financial success as an outcome is one thing, but how do you measure change in attitudes, the difference in the corporate cultures, the level of innovation, competitive advantage or customer satisfaction? In most cases it will require a genuine change 'in the way we do things around here', a complete rethink of performance measurement. Performance measurement is discussed in detail in Chapter 7.

It will be the partnering/alliance manager, as part of his or her role as the overall coordinator of the relationship, and leaders of the relationship's management/operational team(s) who will maintain the action plan. It will also be the partnering/alliance manager's role to update the plan, circulate it and call for reviews.

In practice, I have no doubt that plans such as this already exist for strategically important customers and suppliers (current or potential). In some cases, they will have all the detail and creativity of a good partnership plan but may not have the management support or the communication network links required to make them work in a partnering context.

The plan and the associated KPIs and targets will have a direct link to the Partnering/Alliance Charter and the KPI Balanced Scorecard.

Look for the gaps

There is bound to be something missing from the partnering process and this is the step that will allow you to find it. The partnering/alliance manager, partnering team members and others, including the customer and/or supplier partner, will be required to examine critically the process and its progress. This in itself will be an exercise in communication and people management. From the 'big picture' perspective, consider these questions:

- Are some activities no longer valid?
- Are there further bridging activities between steps that could be introduced?
- Are there previously unseen initiatives that now come to light via the overview?

Challenge the process for more innovation

Innovation is the lifeblood for sustaining the partnership and its competitive advantage. Wherever possible, with whatever techniques and tools are available, challenge the people involved to extend the web of innovation. Involve not only your own organisation and all its functions and your partner, but also suppliers, consultants and others who can contribute. Give them the freedom to imagine, create and discover opportunities for adding value outside the traditional 'black box'. Often bringing all the activities together from one perspective will provide the opportunity for just that. The climate for innovation is set by management and nurtured by attitudes developed over time by focused, skilled and empowered people.

Circulate the plan widely and review regularly

Such an action plan deserves wide circulation for a number of reasons:

1. All those involved in the process need to know and understand the 'big picture' and their place in it. Again, it's about sharing information!
2. It will give others who are not involved the opportunity to contribute if they wish to.
3. As a summary of the process and progress to date, the action plan can be used as a benchmark for other upcoming partnering/alliance relationships and, indeed, all other customer/supplier relationships.
4. It will provide the mechanism whereby those not involved with partnerships/alliances can understand and value the individual initiatives and their relevance and application to their own environment. That is, they can 'cherry pick' the activities, initiatives and areas of innovation that will be of greatest benefit to them.

As for reviews of the strategy/action plans, these will depend on the nature and scope of the relationships. Generally, they should be held at regular intervals and vary in both the people taking part and the location. I have held reviews in locations that ranged from the customer partner's boardroom to the reaction control room at our production plant. Basically, reviews will include:

- reviewing the progress of previously agreed strategies/actions and performance against agreed Key Performance Indicators and Targets
- agreeing, or confirming, old or new dates for completion of outstanding actions
- agreeing new activities that should appear on the actions list
- recognising achievements and continuous improvement
- identifying new areas and opportunities for improvement.

As with site visits, make these reviews special events. They should be challenging, interesting, rewarding and enjoyable.

CASE STUDY

BP Australia and Lanskey Construction

Retail sites for oil companies are literally the shop front and window to the marketplace. BP Australia has established a partnering approach and a highly successful partnering relationship with Lanskey Construction involving all aspects of service station and retail shop development. This takes in everything from site identification and evaluation through to design and construction.

Generally, BP sees partnering as a fundamental component of their business strategy. 'Where our needs and associated services are critical, a partnering type supplier relationship is paramount in obtaining the "value" opportunities that give competitive advantage,' says Trevor Bielski, Manager Marketing Procurement, BP Australia. He adds, 'Working in partnership with selected suppliers allows us to link our customer offer in a seamless way and to offer processes, technology and other leveraged advantages that we would not be able to achieve on our own.'

The initial focus has been on external relationships, but it has also been recognised that these relationships and the principles upon which they are based can be used as a vehicle to improve internal relationships—for example, leveraging a relationship across Oil Marketing business units such as retail and Air BP, then looking at exploration or Solarex streams. BP would also like to develop partnering type relationships that will allow them to more effectively bundle, automate and simplify their Low Value Spend (LVS) categories, that is those worth less than $10 000 per transaction. In the downstream businesses, LVS is around 50 per cent of the third-party spend, and comprises 90 per cent of the transactions.

While only around five per cent of current procurement involves partnering relationships, and this is mainly in the area of construction and environmental services, the goal is to increase this figure to 50 per cent or more by 2005. The BP/Lanskey partnership is proving to be one of the role models by which this objective can be achieved.

BP has effectively implemented a structured approach to partnering. Stuart Moodie, BP Relationship Manager for the Lanskey partnership, adds further, 'We have a clear process for deciding whether a partnering relationship is appropriate. Mutual alignment of goals, establishing a joint partnering charter, and linking each partner's Key Success Factors (KSFs) or business drivers to agreed Key Performance Indicators (KPIs) and appropriate Performance Measures (PMs) has proved critically important. There is then an ongoing process of open dialogue, regular measurement and review.'

Typical of many partnering relationships and alliances, the BP/Lanskey relationship has evolved from a relationship based on tenders and negotiated contracts, to a more formal partnering arrangement now in its third year. 'The continual search for value improvements has led us to this point. We had an internal 30 per cent capital productivity improvement challenge, which we involved selected suppliers in helping us achieve. We more than achieved the 30 per cent target, then it was a question of where to next, and how? Already, through the partnering approach, a further 10–15 per cent has been taken out of external construction costs,' says Trevor Bielski.

The current BP/Lanskey partnering relationship involves a Memorandum of Understanding (MOU) setting out the relationship goals and rules of engagement. The MOU sits over a commercial contract, which because of the nature of the services involved, is required by law. It is an open-ended agreement with no period or term involved—that is, the tender process has been removed from the relationship. An open-book arrangement based on cost, plus a guaranteed margin is in place with incentives, split 50/50, applying for better-than-expected performance against targets of quality, cost and schedule. Performance as measured against agreed KSFs, KPIs and PMs is reviewed on a three-monthly basis. To ensure transparency and openness, an independent third-party review of the cost outcomes takes place to ensure best-in-class benchmarks are being achieved.

Paul Lanskey, CEO of Lanskey Constructions, is delighted with both the process and the relationship developed: 'In the construction industry most companies would do themselves a big favour by partnering. The open-book, trusting approach allows us to achieve both a fair and acceptable profit margin and a continuity of work. This in turn allows us to more effectively manage our resources and to offer greater stability of employment for our people. The uncertainty that surrounds the traditional tender approach and the associated fixed price, lump sum based, tightly managed contracts has been removed. BP in return get a better quality outcome at a lower total cost.'

As is always the case with partnerships and alliances, trust is the basis upon which the relationship works. With BP and Lanskey, trust looks like having a willingness to share what was previously considered 'sacred' information. This included sharing each other's business strategies, receiving input and taking advice from each other in the development of tactical plans. Lanskey has been empowered to make decisions involving BP funds, thereby saving time and ultimately reducing risk. They are involved in everything from site evaluation through to the approval process with regulatory authorities.

The results so far have been significant. Through innovation and teamwork, $150 000 has been removed from the cost of each retail build. There is now a consolidated team across all trades and disciplines involved on each site build. There is on-time delivery of projects with no rework. Contract variations and disputes have disappeared. Risk is now managed out of the project cost base and not transferred 100 per cent to the contractors as with the traditional contracting. The cost levels achieved for a retail store build are the best within the BP Amoco group and are used as a global benchmark. Through early Lanskey involvement in the design and planning phases, building of a retail site can start with 100 per cent defined cost in a matter of days from approval of BP's Financial Memorandum (FM) or business case. This is regarded as the leading edge benchmark in the industry and is of considerable competitive advantage to BP. The completed retail sites are regarded as world-class as benchmarked internally on a global basis with all BP Amoco retail business units, and occasionally benchmarked externally with organisations like McDonald's.

As a result, the BP/Lanskey relationship has had a positive effect elsewhere within BP. For example, the partnering approach was used for their QSR (quick service restaurant) strategy development, as a value creation benchmark generally, and is being used as a template and role model for other critical supplier relationship development.

Obstacles to forward progress are still encountered internally and externally to BP Amoco. These are mainly in the form of outdated mindsets and attitudes, which result in individuals trying to destabilise the relationship. So how are the cynics, sceptics, roadblockers and the occasional terrorists dealt with? Trevor Bielski suggests, 'through showing the runs on the board, benchmarking, coaching and facilitating workshops. If they don't fit with the new culture, and don't see the benefits, they normally leave over a period of time.'

The future of the relationship looks bright. Expansion of site builds continues throughout Australia. The partnering process for which the BP/Lanskey partnership is a role model is currently being investigated in Asia, and there is considerable interest from Europe.

It is too easy to underestimate the strength of leadership, the challenging of organisational norms and the level of risk-taking that has occurred to bring this partnership to its current state. It is the same vision and courage combined with good long-term strategy, sound process and outstanding people that will take the BP/Lanskey relationship to its next level of profitable growth and competitive advantage.

CHAPTER 7

Linking measurement, performance, risk/benefit and remuneration

In understanding how to maximise the Return on the Partnering Investment (ROPI), there are as many options as there are relationships. Again the principle is simple enough. You have two or more trusting and trustworthy organisations with a shared vision and mission and common goals—based on a strategy of world class/best practice and value adding performance—which give rise to hard and soft, leading and lagging key performance indicators (KPIs), involving short-, medium- and long-term time frames. The overall outcome is a win/win result where 'their success is our success', based on an interdependent sharing of risks and benefits. Sounds all very well, but what of the details?

How does the return on the partnering investment manifest itself? How, and on what basis, do you measure the return on the partnering/alliance dollar and the resources invested, over and above vendor or supplier relationships? How do you keep the financial bean counters, nay-sayers, cynics and occasional terrorists from cutting short your 'brave new world' expedition with their corporate sorties on the relationship's credibility and overall net worth? Without question, this is proving to be one of the bigger challenges for partnering and alliance champions.

The fact that many senior executives today are in a great hurry and under a lot of pressure to deliver short-term-focused shareholder wealth does not improve the quality of long-term decision making. The opportunity or desire to grow—like a big old oak tree—long-term, successful partnerships and alliances is often absent, lost, diminished or at least inhibited. A different mindset behind new eyes will be required.

THE TWELVE PARTNERING PARADIGM SHIFTS

Developing customer/supplier partnerships and alliances is clearly about the management of a significant change process that will involve paradigm shifts in traditional thinking, attitudes, behaviours and practices. Figure 7.1 lists twelve paradigm shifts for partnering. There are more than twelve but I consider these to be the major ones. You may want to consider others in the context of your own relationships.

Paradigm Shifts for Partnering

1. No-contract, no-term relationship or equivalent (ref. p. 8, p. 217)

2. Customer/supplier partner interdependence (ref. pp. 52–54)

3. 'We are no longer interested in your margins, we are now interested in your ideas' as an operating philosophy (ref. pp. 119–122, 329–330)

4. Getting paid on performance and effect, not unit price (ref. pp. 119–123)

5. 'No tender' relationship (ref. p. 10, pp. 223–225)

6. Co-supplier relationships and joint benchmarking (ref. p. 10, p. 285)

7. Joint 'Trust Charter' agreed and operating (ref. pp. 199–202)

8. Joint partnering/alliance strategy, charter and KPIs (ref. pp. 214–218, 318–328)

9. Joint succession planning for key influencers and partnering champions (ref. pp. 306–307, 356–357)

10. 'Reverse negotiations' (i.e. partners negotiating on each other's behalf) or 'one-team negotiations' (i.e. mutually agreed decisions) based on shared information, for mutual benefit (ref. pp. 363–364)

11. Open access to previously hidden 'treasures' and opportunities (ref. p. 321)

12. 'Supplier of choice' to 'relationship of choice' (ref. pp. 218–219)

Fig. 7.1   *Partnering paradigm shifts*

Referring back to the discussion of Figures 1.2, 1.3, 1.4 in Chapter 1, moving from 7 to 8 (i.e. supplier to partner status) will not just involve an incremental or even a step-change improvement in current practices. The reality is, there will be some paradigm shift(s) required. A paradigm shift is defined as a fundamental change in the rules and the ways in which things are done, creating new boundaries, new problems and new solutions. The collaborative, open, trusting, long-term approach is clearly a new paradigm for many organisations and individuals.

For a genuine partnership in the early stages of development, three or four of the twelve paradigm shifts will need to be in place. A robust, developed and well-performing partnership will have up to six paradigm shifts operating. An outstanding world-class partnering relationship and alliance will have nine or more paradigm shifts being demonstrated. Check them off against your own customer/supplier relationships. They will also need to be reflected in the development of the relationship Key Performance Indicators (KPIs) or Measures of Performance (MOPs).

PARTNERING KPIs—MEASURING JOINT PERFORMANCE

The partnering vision, mission, critical success factors (CSFs)/key objectives and the associated Partnering/Alliance Charter and Agreement have already been discussed as part of the partnering process (see pages 214–218). The KPIs result from and are directly related to the CSFs/key objectives. To reinforce the hard and soft, leading and lagging nature of partnering KPIs, I refer you to the discussion on the overlap of marriage and partnering in Chapter 1. A successful marriage is based on the same principles as business partnering—that is, trust, long-term commitment, shared information, common goals, resolution of conflict, adding value, interdependence. While measuring the performance of a good marriage often involves 'feel good' experiences, in business we are required to be more specific.

I have analysed the outcomes and performance indicators from the Chrysler partnering/alliance experience with its suppliers in Figure 7.2. There are five key points to be made. First, these KPIs are representative of the total Chrysler/supplier relationships, not any single organisation. I have segmented the indicators/outcomes under the six partnering outcomes. As is well known, Chrysler came back from the brink of extinction in 1989 via a well-documented[1-4] partnering/alliance strategy to become the world's most profitable automaker some eight years later. Second, it is important to note that these indicators did not all come about in 1989 but evolved over a period of years. Third, they are a mixture of leading and lagging, hard and

Financial Success
Return on Investment (ROI)

- Return on Assets (ROA)
  – highest among US automakers
- Profit/vehicle
  – $250 (80s) to $2110 ('94)
- 'Target costing' used to agree supplier prices
- Increase in Chrysler market share,
  e.g. 14.7% ('94) 25 yr high vs 12.2% ('87)
- SCORE savings
  e.g. cumulative savings '89–'95, 5300 ideas
  = $1.7 billion savings
  – 1996 SCORE goals exceeded by $1billion
- Recognition that suppliers need to make a profit

Customer Satisfaction

- Suppliers increased investments in dedicated assets, i.e. plant equipment, systems, processes and people
- Average distance between Chrysler and suppliers decreased (e.g. by 26 miles for Belvidere plant)
- Almost all suppliers purchased same CAD/CAM software, i.e. CATIA
- Successful introduction of SCORE prog. (1990) 'Supplier Cost Reduction Effort Program'
- Top 150 suppliers meet yearly
- Advisory board of executives comprising top 14 suppliers

World Class

- Reduction in supplier numbers: 2500 (89) to <750 (98)
  – Extensive benchmarking between competitors (e.g. Honda & AMC)
- Focused competition between suppliers
- Visible exemplary leadership
- Choosing suppliers early in the concept/dev. phase and giving them significant or total responsibility for cost, quality, delivery
- Single supplier(s) given responsibility for entire component systems, e.g. Johnson Controls and Allied Signal
- Common email system
- Suppliers replicating SCORE program
- Replacement of sales reps by engineers

Chrysler & Supplier Partnership KPIs

Attitude

- Feedback encouraged from suppliers, two-way flow of information
- High trust through shared information, risks and rewards
- Cross-function/organisation 'platform' teams
- Customer takes supplier to lunch
- Customer got their own house in order first
- Customer listened to supplier suggestions and followed through
- Customer/supplier assistance in a crisis
- Recognition of past performance and track record
- Cooperative/trusting positive sum game

Sustainable Competitive Advantage

- Life of model relationships and beyond (for 90% suppliers)
- Detailed contracts given way to oral agreements or 1 page only supply agreements
- Removal of competitive bidding (i.e. best of 3 quotes)
- 'Single supplier dual competition' approach
- Complex supplier evaluation—price, quality, delivery, technology and opportunities for improvement
- SCORE program on-line for suppliers to track progress
- In-house resident supplier engineers 30 (1989) to >300 (1997); has improved communications and trust

Innovation

- New vehicle development cycle time, e.g. 5 yrs ('89) to less than 3 yrs ('98)
- New vehicle introduction, e.g. 4 new vehicles 1980–89, 6 new vehicles 1990–96 with no increase in eng. staff (Neon, Dodge Ramtruck, Cirrus/Stratus + new mini van models)
- Reduced vehicle weight, warranty claims and complexity
- Increasing number of innovative proposals from suppliers + $ gained/saved

Fig. 7.2 *Chrysler and supplier partnering KPIs*

soft indicators, or measures. Hard KPIs are generally those indicators based purely on objective measurement—for example, financial measures like return on assets, profit per vehicle and plant operating efficiencies. Soft KPIs are based on purely subjective assessment of performance or a combination of objective and subjective assessment. Environmental, community-based KPIs or those measurements resulting from surveys are typical examples. In the case of Chrysler, results from two-way feedback surveys, the performance of cross-organisational platform teams and the number of on-site, co-located supplier engineers would be regarded as soft measures of performance. Leading and lagging through a process of cause and effect identifies the performance outcome measures (lagging indicators) and the performance drivers (leading indicators) of those outcomes. It was not recognised for some time that the average distance between the Chrysler plants and its suppliers was diminishing. That is, relationships improved because of changing attitudes, earlier involvement in design and development, co-location of supplier engineers and many other 'lead' indicators. As a result of this, suppliers were investing in plant and equipment closer to Chrysler and further away from competitors like GM. The measure, or KPI, of average distance between Chrysler and suppliers' plants is a genuine soft and lagging KPI that in conventional relationships would be neither recognised nor measured. Yet in hindsight it is a real measure of the strength and sustainability of the customer/supplier partnership that impacts significantly on the bottom line.

Fourth, the ROI indicators tell us about the current state of the relationship while the other five categories are a measure of the quality and sustainability of the relationship. The financials alone don't give you the information you need as to the longer-term impact of partnerships and alliances and the nature of their competitive advantage. Fifth, it is often the softest indicators that are the toughest to achieve, yet can have the greatest impact. Convincing Chrysler engineers of the benefits of resident supplier engineers was not easy or initially well received. The number has grown from 30 in 1989 to over 300 in 1998. And this move has been one of the major drivers behind early supplier involvement in design and development, and in the reduction in vehicle-development cycles—the time from concept approval to volume production—from five to less than three years.

Other KPIs are symbolic. At the time Chrysler was heading down the partnering/alliance route, General Motors was doing exactly the opposite. Jose Ignacio Lopez, GM's newly installed purchasing chief, was demanding double-digit price cuts from suppliers and breaking long-standing contracts. To avoid the development of long-term, cooperative relationships Lopez was prohibiting his buyers from accepting lunch invitations from suppliers. In contrast, Thomas Stallkamp, Chrysler's head of purchasing, was instructing his buyers to take suppliers out to lunch. This is an example of differing attitudes which ultimately delivered significantly different results.

It could be argued that all these KPIs are ultimately reflected on the bottom line, but, in not measuring them, their relevance is often ignored, the broader benefits are lost and the dollars not always correctly allocated back to the partnering relationship. Partnering managers and the partnering team are doing the relationship and themselves a great disservice in not capturing this information. I have seen many situations where, if it were not that a partnership was being used as a benchmark and role model, additional business opportunities would not have been gained. Genuine partnering and alliance relationships allow access to what I call 'previously' hidden treasures. These are opportunities that would not have been realised had the relationship in question not existed. Without double counting, this contribution from the partnership needs to be recognised and captured somewhere in the KPIs. For example, Honeywell won US$9 million of instrument-upgrade business over a period of years at the SIGECO power facility at Warwick, Indiana, part-owned by Alcoa, on the strength of the global Alcoa-Honeywell alliance (refer Case Study 1).

THE 'VALUE QUESTION'

> *What value is this relationship delivering for this organisation over the alternatives?*

This true story of some years ago has almost achieved mythical/legendary status. The new CEO of the customer partner in what had been widely publicised as a very large, highly successful alliance relationship had called a meeting at short notice with the two customer/supplier Alliance Managers. It was some two years on from the signing of the agreement so the honeymoon or transition period was well and truly over. The Alliance Managers were somewhat apprehensive and wary as their mail had been telling them that the new CEO was not a partnering/alliance fan. In fact his reputation from his previous roles was one of a typical 'tough guy', hard nosed, hard dollar and bottom line driven.

They arrived at his office. True to form, he got straight down to business. 'I've heard a lot about this alliance relationship but little of the detail. So what value is it delivering for this organisation over the alternatives?' he asked, clearly in no mood for casual conversation. Caught more than a little off-guard their response, naively, was 'Really well'—they might as well have added thank you for asking and caring! The CEO countered, 'No, I'm interested in the detail. How is this relationship delivering value over the alternatives? Because I think I have some!'

It's difficult to think quickly and clearly when your heart has just skipped a beat and a state of semi-panic has set in. To cut a long story short, while they had plenty of information to give, plenty of good stories to tell and ultimately plenty of good results to share, they did not have the time to present them and the data was not in a form that was easily presentable. The CEO gave them two months (i.e. two Alliance Management Team meetings) to successfully demonstrate the 'value question'. Their response after some agonising discussions was a simple KPI Scorecard that linked directly to the key objectives and value propositions for the relationship, and graphical trends against industry best practice that demonstrated best value was being delivered and through the strategies in place would most likely be sustained.

Not only had they never been asked the question before so bluntly, they had not prepared for it either. Nevertheless, although it was brutal, it was a fair and reasonable question to ask and deserved a clear and succinct answer. The value question provokes three sub-questions:

1. What is the value being delivered?
2. What are the alternatives?
3. How do they compare?

The message is that any partnering/alliance relationship must prepare for and be able to answer the 'value question' and be able to demonstrate that the relationship is delivering sustainable value over and above the alternatives. As the Alliance Managers told me, 'We learnt a lot that day and in the subsequent months. The previous CEO had initiated the alliance and we had total support as much on faith as on substance. Over the first two years we had focused more on performance than on measurement and had been effectively left alone by external forces. We knew the results and improvements were there, we knew the alliance was delivering but the data was not fully visible and in a form sceptics or outsiders would readily accept. Naively, we thought the support would automatically continue unchallenged. We were wrong. What followed was an 18-month program of systems development to not only ensure good data and measurement but also drive improvement. As it turned out the "value question" was the right question at the right time and the new CEO is now as big a supporter of the alliance as his predecessor was.'

You are probably wondering now what alternatives the CEO had in mind. As it turned out they were nothing more than a couple of 'back door' offers from the supplier partners' competitors of a 5–10 per cent price discount for similar services and, while attractive on the surface, they were just low ball bids to buy the business with a short-term perspective. As they were never accepted, the effect on quality and service can only be imagined!

Good partners and good partnering and alliance relationships do themselves a great disservice by not measuring effectively the ongoing and sustainable value they are delivering. Whether this involves external benchmarking against competitors, other organisations or industry standards or absolute improvement against agreed baselines it is one of the more important aspects of partnering and alliance management.

DEVELOPING YOUR OWN PARTNERING/ALLIANCE OF KPI/BALANCED SCORECARD

I have found the Balanced Scorecard approach[5] to be the ideal format to effectively represent the hard and soft, leading and lagging nature of partnering and alliance performance measures. The Balanced Scorecard approach to performance measurement is appropriate at any level or in a business unit in the organisation where there is a strategy in place to support a vision and/or mission. As discussed in the previous section, it is not just the 'hard' financials that have to be measured and managed. We need to understand the performance-driving, lead indicators as well as the outcome-based, lagging indicators and the cause-and-effect links between them.

Measuring joint performance in a partnering or alliance relationship is little different from the top-down process used for measuring your business performance. The key difference is that it is a shared process between the alliance partners, producing a shared vision, mission and key goals/objectives. Each key goal/objective will have an associated set of initiatives, milestones or action plans. The success of each goal/objective will be determined by actual performance as measured against jointly agreed KPIs and associated targets.

Figure 7.3 shows a general worked example of the Balanced Scorecard template that can be used to develop your own set of partnering and alliance KPIs. It is based on the Balanced Scorecard process detailed by Robert Kaplan and David Norton in their outstanding book *The Balanced Scorecard.*[5]

The partnering and alliance Balanced Scorecard is based on the vision and/or mission and key objectives (goals or Critical Success Factors (CSFs)) obtained from the partnering or alliance charter. The vision and mission statements are reproduced for the relationship at the top of the scorecard. A summary statement of each objective is then highlighted across the top of the columns of the scorecard. The nature of the cause-and-effect link between the

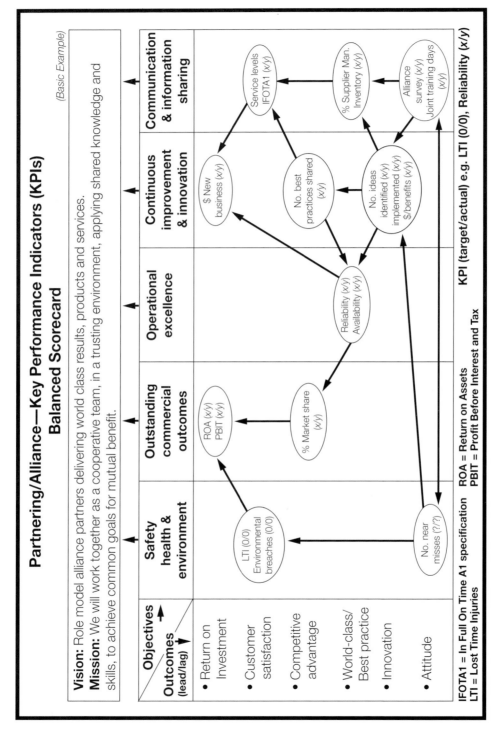

Fig. 7.3   *Partnering/Alliance Balanced Scorecard*

KPIs can be seen via the arrows connecting the KPIs. In this example, KPIs such as the number of near-miss incidents reported, alliance survey results and the number of joint training days are soft, leading performance drivers that will ultimately have a cause-and-effect impact on the hard, lagging, Return On Assets (ROA) and the lost time injury (LTI) performance indicators. Capturing innovation via measuring the number of ideas identified and implemented, and the resulting associated $ and other benefits, will be just one of the conduits by which overall success is measured.

The Balanced Scorecard of partnering/alliance KPIs is often put together, at least in draft form, at the initial partnering workshop. The right cross-representation of people is present, with the right intent and understanding, and they also happened to have developed the Partnering/Alliance Charter. Refer to the partnering step 'Reviewing process/progress with partner and sharing information' (page 203) for details on the partnering and alliance workshop format and agenda.

The steps involved in building the scorecard include:

1. Review of the Balanced Scorecard process as applying to partnering and alliance relationships and the concept of hard and soft, leading and lagging performance indicators.
2. Review existing KPIs for the relationship, if they exist.
3. Depending on the number of participants at the workshop, split up into subgroups, based on areas of workshop participant interest, involvement and/or expertise. Have each subgroup brainstorm one to four objectives to generate the first draft of KPIs, aligned opposite the six vertically listed partnering outcomes—i.e. Return On Investment, customer satisfaction, competitive advantage, best practices, innovation, attitude. Use examples like the Chrysler data and other partnering/alliance KPIs as a guide. Also brainstorm any opportunities for improvement (OFIs) opposite each of the allocated key objectives and identify any barriers to implementation.
4. Return as a full workshop group and review presentations from each of the subgroups on the KPIs generated and their vertical alignment opposite the six outcomes as well as the OFIs and barriers to implementation. Integrate this initial KPI list into the scorecard and review for overlapping or duplicated indicators. Question, challenge, modify, add to, delete from the KPIs generated. Understand the cause-and-effect link between the remaining KPIs and their connection back to each objective.
5. Return to the original split groups to finalise a short list of KPIs. Each subgroup at this stage also looks at the performance targets associated with each of the short-listed KPIs.
6. Return as a full workshop group to compile the scorecard on a central whiteboard or via a projected PC screen.

7. The full work group does a final review of the KPIs and agrees on the cause-and-effect links between the leading and lagging KPIs (see Fig. 7.3).
8. In ensuring that you have the right balance of KPIs, cross-check that there is at least one KPI and target for each objective (vertically) and at least one KPI/target representing each of the six vertical outcome headings (horizontally).
9. Agreement is then reached as to how the scorecard, in conjunction with the partnering/alliance charter, is communicated to all stakeholders not represented at the workshop, and buy-in achieved from them all. The partnering team will be responsible for finalising the scorecard if it cannot be completed at the workshop. Note, in terms of giving the subgroups enough time to complete the KPIs and targets for their given objectives, there can be as many iterations as required between steps 3 and 5.

An alternative and simplified process for smaller groups or where time is limited is to complete the Balanced Scorecard exercise as a single, large group.

The KPIs and, therefore, the balanced scorecard is a dynamic document and the performance indicators need to be continually reviewed, updated, deleted and replaced as appropriate. Once the scorecard is implemented, the actual results that are generated are then listed beside the targets where appropriate or possible (see Fig. 7.3). The KPIs should also reflect the paradigm shifts required to sustain fundamental change. If gainshare/painshare remuneration applies, you then determine which of the KPIs on the scorecard are risk/reward linked. How these KPIs are then used to determine the level of supplier partner profit applicable will be discussed in the next section. Subsequent ongoing reviews, partnering team meetings and workshops are ideal times to review the details of the Balanced Scorecard. In particular, there would normally be a monthly review of the KPI Balanced Scorecard by the Partnering/Alliance Management Team and quarterly reviews by the Leadership Team.

The idea that you should have a myriad of performance measures filling each square of the objectives/outcomes matrix of the scorecard runs counter to its intention. Getting the right mix or balance of hard, soft, leading and lagging performance measures to genuinely capture the current and future health and well-being of the customer/supplier relationship is the key to having performance indicators drive improvement, as well as measure performance. Getting a smaller number of the right indicators will be more effective than a larger number of average indicators. For example, Alcoa and Honeywell in 1999 had only four primary measures for their global alliance. They are: safety and environmental conformance relative to process control; customer satisfaction as measured by a specially designed survey; $ benefits achieved; business volume and Profit Before Interest and Tax (PBIT) against plan.

In summary:

1. The KPI Balanced Scorecard represents the performance of all the partners, not just the supplier partner(s), and the overall well-being of the relationship.
2. Not every cell/box in the Balanced Scorecard needs to have a KPI and target represented. It is the right number of the right KPIs that is important. There needs to be at least one KPI and target for each objective and at least one KPI/target representing each of the six vertical outcome headings.
3. Get the right mix of hard and soft, leading and lagging KPIs and use them for performance improvement as well as performance management.
4. Determine which KPIs will be risk/reward linked and which will be non-risk/reward linked.

From a relationship management perspective there are three different levels or categories of KPIs that need to be understood when putting the scorecard together: that is, strategic, relationship and compliance KPIs. It is the strategic and relationship KPIs we are interested in when putting together the KPI Performance Scorecard.

Strategic KPIs reflect the overall performance of the partners and will most likely involve additional activities outside the relationship scope or control. For example, the Mobil and Transfield Services Altona oil refinery strategic alliance involving maintenance, operations support and engineering services has several strategic or business KPIs, such as refinery profitability and total site LTIFR performance, upon which Transfield Services' profitability is partly based.

Relationship based KPIs reflect the measures of performance the partnering/alliance relationship is directly responsible for delivering. In the Mobil/Transfield Services alliance these would include scheduled maintenance work and project performance.

Compliance KPIs represent the lower level, day-to-day measures that would be present irrespective of the partnering/alliance relationship being in place. These might include second- or third-tier KPIs as part of safety, quality or environmental plans; performance levels or operating conditions associated with specific pieces of equipment; service level KPIs that don't warrant a place on the Balanced Scorecard but are useful in the day-to-day running of the relationship; and selective regulator or operating licence KPIs.

One of the best sets of performance indicators I have seen involved the relationship between a coal mining company and the supplier of underground mining equipment. Clearly this is a relationship of high impact but also high $ value. The primary measure of performance, which was directly linked to remuneration, was 'feet advanced in the coal seam per eight hours'. This indicator—associated with other key performance indicators of reliability, availability of critical equipment and machinery, costs per tonne of coal and safety—measured clearly and simply what the relationship was trying to achieve in delivering lowest cost coal to the marketplace.

To deliver on the agreed targets for 'feet advanced in the coal seam per eight hours' required an enormous amount of cooperation, information sharing and innovation between many players. For example, geologists, mining engineers, design engineers, management, maintenance technicians and schedulers, effectively trained and competent workers, and union members who operated the underground equipment worked in eight-hour shifts. Everyone was linked into, driven by and focused on this prime set of indicators upon which everyone was in part risk/reward remunerated. The benefits of having shared vision, common goals and jointly agreed upon and accountable performance indicators cannot be underestimated.

Traditionally the business for the supplier was about selling as much equipment as they could at the highest price and extracting as much from maintenance and service costs as possible. For the customer it was the reverse, minimum equipment purchases at the lowest or rather cheapest procurement and maintenance costs. Not surprisingly such conflicting objectives and performance drivers developed poor behaviours, bad attitudes and created many operational, communication and interpersonal problems.

SHARING RISKS AND REWARDS

Risk will be a function of probability of occurrence, the consequence of the occurrence and the context or degree of involvement in the activity. The level of risk taken will be commensurate with the level of benefit received. Identifying and accepting the risks then become two separate issues. This will be based on allocating the risk via risk management analysis to the alliance partners best able to manage the risk. Successful partnerships and alliances are based on effective risk management rather than total risk transfer. Partnering and alliance KPIs should then be linked to the shared risks taken and the shared benefits received by the partners. In that regard risk management, risk allocation and risk/reward are separate activities that can be linked in different ways, depending on the nature of the terms and conditions of the relationship. In alliance/partnering this is done within a 'no-blame', high accountability environment.

For example, a small firm involved in the critical role of boiler maintenance at a power station may sign off on a risk/reward incentive program to get the plant back online early. While the attraction of sharing equally the millions of dollars per day additional income in coming back online prior to the scheduled date in the new deregulated environment is obvious, the downside of coming back online days late could send the smaller company broke. A discussion and even negotiation will need to take place on the probability and consequence of delay and the degree of involvement in everything from the decision making to the activities schedule. Ultimately, some capping of both the risks and the benefits may be agreed to.

I also know of occasions where the larger partner, understanding the catastrophic downside of overruns or failures for the smaller partner, has agreed to accept virtually all the downside risk but left in place a major portion of the upside incentive. Then partners in an environment of good faith, high competence and clear, common objectives worked to achieve the positive result rather than watch each other's backs to avoid a negative result.

This obviously raises the critical issue of effective partner selection. Some years ago a senior executive from the Honda motor company told me that Honda will often accept much or all of the downside risk with supplier partners, preferring to focus on good partner selection, long-term relationship building, effective project management with shared objectives, and the overachieving of those objectives.

Chrysler SCORE-type program

Chrysler's SCORE, or Supplier Cost Reduction Effort,[6] has become the company's most important method for building trust, lowering costs and improving communication. It is based on the principle of being interested in the implementation of ideas, not in the reduction of unit prices. Unveiled in 1990 at a meeting of Chrysler's top 150 suppliers, SCORE involves the generation of supplier ideas to reduce total system-wide costs for Chrysler and suppliers, while improving rather than hurting suppliers' profits. Opportunities for improvement such as reducing vehicle weight, warranty claims and complexity, and suggestions for operational changes are captured, evaluated, approved and then tracked online through to completion for both Chrysler and suppliers to see.

The secret to SCORE's success lies in sharing with suppliers the savings generated from their suggestions. The supplier can either claim half the savings or give up to 100 per cent of the savings to Chrysler to boost its performance rating and potentially obtain more of Chrysler's business. Even though there are SCORE cost-reduction targets equalling 5 per cent of the suppliers' sales to Chrysler, the automaker does not penalise suppliers if they do not achieve them. Potentially, this could have a bearing on long-term business volumes from Chrysler.

Magna International, one of Chrysler's largest suppliers, provided seat systems, interior door and trim panels, engine and transmission systems and other products between 1993 and 1996. They successfully submitted 130 SCORE proposals for total cost savings of $76 million. Magna gave the $76 million to Chrysler rather than claim their half. The result was that Magna's sales to Chrysler for the period 1990–96 more than doubled from $635 million to $1.45 billion.

SCORE's success is unchallengeable. As noted in Chrysler's 1996 annual report, suppliers have exceeded SCORE goals each year: $250 million in 1993; $1 billion in 1996. Another large automaker, however, tried unsuccessfully to implement a similar SCORE program. The reason for lack of success was the unwillingness of the automaker to share the savings with suppliers.

Performance-based risk/reward models—General overview

Figure 7.4 outlines the simplest form of performance/reward payback. As the customer's total costs come down and/or the added value is increased, the supplier's profitability goes up. All too often, supplier profitability resembles curve A. That is, customer total cost and/or total value improvements are gained at the expense of supplier profitability. This situation is unlikely to deliver a successful or sustainable relationship. Performance/reward formulae can be as simple or complicated as the parties desire, depending on the complexity of the assets involved, the number of variables and uncontrollables impacting,

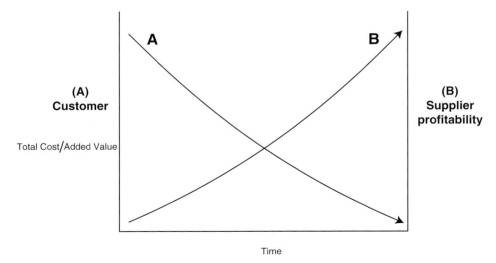

Fig. 7.4 *Relationship between performance and reward*

the number of organisations participating and any combination thereof. Avoid too much complexity—it can adversely affect understanding, communication and, on occasions, trust.

Figure 7.5 shows a typical gainshare/painshare, performance-based risk/reward model. In essence, positive or better than expected performance and negative or worse than expected performance, as measured against an agreed Business As Usual (BAU) target on the horizontal axis, is linked directly to $ reward or $ loss figures on the vertical axis. This model can apply to a wide variety of hard and soft performance measures or objectives. These range from quality, profitability cost and time, output, market price, reliability, availability and efficiency measures through to safety, environmental, industrial and community relations.

Common in project-based alliances like Sydney's Northside Storage Tunnel Project[7] and the highly successful Wandoo B Offshore Oil Platform located 75 kilometres north-west of Dampier in Western Australia,[8] this approach allows the alliance partners to effectively align the common goals to performance, measurement and remuneration. The result is an ongoing focused approach to pursuing best value and continuous improvement through innovation and an open-book, win/win, transparent approach to relationship management. The win/lose option is removed as a potential outcome. In building interdependence the partners either win together or lose together.

While the percentage gainshare/painshare split is negotiable in the spirit and practice of the relationship, a 50/50 split between the alliance partners often applies. If there is a group or consortium of customers and suppliers, the 50 per cent share can then be broken up in proportion to the involvement of each partner.

Depending on the size and nature of the relationship, a fee modifier is sometimes implemented to limit or cap either the maximum reward available or the maximum risk taken by the supplier(s). In the case of the Sydney Northside Storage Tunnel, the maximum contribution that the private sector supplier alliance partners make to the cost overrun is capped at total profit plus overheads.[9] In a complex relationship where there are a number of risk/reward-based performance measures, the fee modifier principle can also operate to ensure poor performance in one measure is not offset by strong performance in another.

In areas like safety, environment and community and industrial relations the perceived value of the better than expected performance is less tangible. Reward payments can be either made from an initial agreed pool of money specifically allocated to these areas or funded via the better than expected

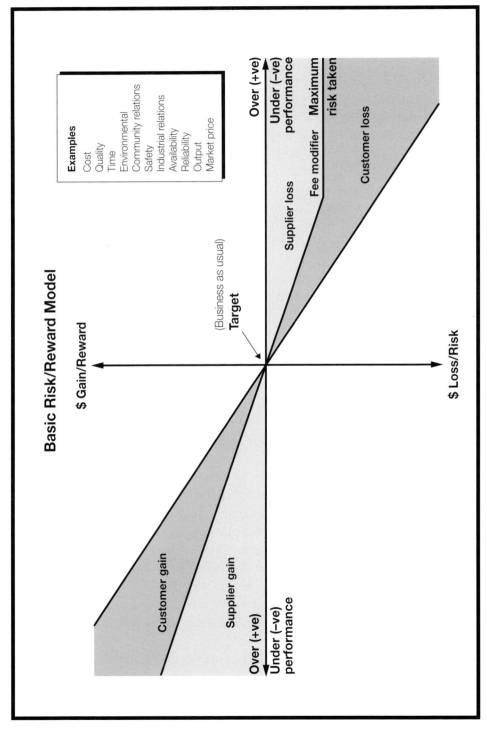

Fig. 7.5   *Gain-share/Pain-share remuneration model*

performance in the direct cost or the more financially quantifiable objectives. Determining targets and measuring performance in these less quantifiable areas will involve benchmarking best practice and developing a set of lead/driving indicators as well as lagging/outcome indicators, which are then linked to agreed $ figures. An alternative approach, especially for smaller, less complex relationships, is a subjective process involving agreeing to key performance areas and associated performance weightings. These are then reviewed and rated by the alliance or partnering team or other representative groups on a regular basis.

RISK/REWARD, PERFORMANCE BASED REMUNERATION FOR STRATEGIC PARTNERING AND ALLIANCE RELATIONSHIPS: THE DETAILS

> *You have to learn to love your partner's profit.*
> *Alistair Tompkin, Director Power Generation, Hazelwood Power*

Tompkin also says partnering and alliance relationships 'are first a matter of choice, from there, they are a matter of commitment'. Importantly, many but not all partnering and alliance relationships have risk/reward, gainshare/painshare remuneration models. Before you adopt the risk/reward remuneration model you must have the right people, with the right attitudes, doing the right things in the right way. The risk/reward model then adds the focus and the incentive to maximise mutual benefit from the shared vision and common goals. As for loving your partner's profit, this is not just about tolerating or condoning profit but a genuine commitment to and desire for the supplier partner to earn better than expected profits based on better than expected benefits delivered to the customer partner. Our success is your success. For many this idea is counter-intuitive, but the reality is that the more money the supplier partner(s) makes from the relationship, the better off the customer partner is. The risk/reward remuneration (REM) model itself is not a panacea, but when implemented well it is a very effective tool in aligning goals, attitudes, mindsets and performance outcomes.

When you think about it, all customer/supplier relationships have profit at risk. The real issue is the level of openness, fairness and transparency with which the risk and the reward details are communicated and managed, as well as the business drivers and personal intent of the individuals involved. I have seen partnering and alliance relationships and projects based on fixed price, lump sum arrangements, or other non-gainshare/painshare commercial arrangements, in part or whole, where the outcomes have been very successful because of the early engagement, open, transparent approach, mindset and attitudes of the people managing and leading the relationship. The individual business drivers were aligned up front and shared vision and common goals were agreed to. It comes down to good partners and good judgment.

That said, the gainshare/painshare, risk/reward based, performance based remuneration (REM) model is one of the main mechanisms for ensuring that the value propositions are delivered and individual partner objectives and business drivers are aligned. It is a common feature across successful partnering and alliance relationships irrespective of market sector or location. The REM model provides the key link between performance, measurement, behaviour/attitude, risk management and remuneration. This is performance based on agreed desired outcomes and on a Balanced Scorecard of risk/reward and non-risk/reward based Key Performance Indicators (KPIs). Put more crudely, a good REM model ensures that all partners have 'skin' in the downstream, customer satisfaction and value adding game.

How does the REM model work? In short, the supplier's financial remuneration and financial success, in most cases represented as profit, is linked directly to the customer's own success in the marketplace, as well as to the performance and/or effect of the products and services delivered within the partnering and alliance relationship. The supplier partner is, therefore, rewarded on the quality of the solutions and benefits generated, not on the cost or features of the purchased technology, products or services. The supplier partner earns profit on the quality of outputs and outcomes, not the cost of inputs. The percentage of agreed profit and/or revenue, gain or loss, above and below the agreed target, is based on the over-performance or under-performance against agreed KPI targets. The extent to which profit and/or revenue will be put at risk will depend on the scope of the business case or project activities and the risk profile the customer/supplier partners are prepared to accept.

The other prime rationale for the REM model is to instil and drive the right behaviours, mindsets and attitudes at all levels in the partner organisations. This creates a 'one team' culture and an environment of open communication, transparency, teaming and a proactive willingness to deliver agreed common goals for mutual benefit. The REM model, therefore, provides the fundamental link between performance, financial success and people. There is a link between the REM model and governance in terms of a shared 'we' accountability and the potential link between gainsharing/painsharing business outcomes and rewarding/recognising individual or team performance in achieving those outcomes.

The REM model also provides comfort to other stakeholder groups within or external to the partner organisations, showing that the strategic partnering/alliance relationship is demonstrably delivering best value for money. An understanding of the REM model is useful in allaying any fears or concerns that others may have in terms of uncompetitive and non-contestable pricing, secretive 'back room' deals, collusive or anti-competitive behaviours between the partners. The competitive assurance aspects associated with a good REM model (i.e. benchmarking, transparency of market information between the partners) provide a particularly useful checkpoint in this regard.

The REM model is, therefore, able to demonstrate the new paradigm approach to contestability. That is, the contest and contestability are no longer between customer and supplier partners but rather the real contest is now between the partnering/alliance relationship and the marketplace as the partners are linked via common goals, joint solutions, shared accountabilities and shared risks/benefits.

In summary, when done well and for the right reasons the performance based, risk/reward remuneration (REM) model is one of the most important aspects in ensuring and demonstrating the success and sustainability of the partnering/alliance relationship and the delivery of the associated value propositions.

The principles and the mechanics

All too often practitioners get bogged too early in the details and the process before signing off on the principles that underpin the risk/reward model. Others are obsessed with the 'cost and profit' breakdowns and definitions, building of risk/reward curves and Performance Scorecards before they understand the behaviours and attitudes that drive a successful risk/reward model. Get the right principles, behaviours and attitudes understood and agreed first, then deal with the mechanics (i.e. the process and the details).

The principles

In the context of the REM model, principles are the fundamental ground rules by which the risk/reward model will function and be managed. In particular, with REM models each relationship will be in some small or large way different. The same REM template has many variations appropriate to the circumstances and can apply to ongoing product, maintenance and service delivery relationships or projects with a defined scope and time frame. It is for the relationship partners to negotiate what is in their combined best interests. This will depend on the people, their intent and experiences as well as the size and nature of the relationship itself.

This is a non-prescriptive, generic list of REM principles that can be tailored to suit specific relationships.

- The supplier partner incentives are funded out of benefits gained by the customer.
- There is total openness and transparency by all partners, including selected sub-contractors if/as appropriate.
- The risk/reward model is based on win/win or lose/lose principles. Win/lose options are to be eliminated.
- Agreed levels of revenue and/or profit and corporate overheads are to be at risk, to gain or to lose, above or below agreed targets based on over/under-performance achieved against agreed Business As Usual (BAU) KPIs and targets. Variations to this principle can be agreed on a case-by-case basis (e.g. fixed price, lump sum, no caps, steps, 'flat spots').
- As a general rule direct costs and direct overheads are reimbursable (i.e. not at risk). This is negotiable and jointly agreed on a case-by-case basis.
- Direct costs (DC) are to be clearly defined, for example: DC = DL + SB + M + DM + DOHs + third party costs + materials where DL = direct labour, SB = salary burdens, M = mobilisation costs, DM = demobilisation costs, DOHs = direct overheads.
- Individual project or business case remuneration can run the full spectrum from lump sum to full risk reward models as agreed and as appropriate. An 'open book', risk contingency pool can apply to lump sum arrangements. The risk/reward model(s) are linked to the risk management plan and the risk profile(s)/allocation that the partners accept.
- Performance measurement would be via a KPI Balanced Scorecard and/or Performance Scorecard approach of financial, non-financial, hard and soft, lead/lag KPIs and linked directly to the shared vision and joint key objectives for the relationship.
- Performance based remuneration models will be jointly agreed so that the percentage of profit gainshare/painshare reflects the risk/reward profile accepted.
- The service provider partner will be paid 100 per cent agreed profit based on the delivery of the agreed KPI targets.
- By negotiation and mutual agreement on a case-by-case basis, profit gain and/or profit loss may be capped or unlimited or anywhere in between.
- Poor performance in one KPI should not be offset by good performance in another KPI.
- Pay target amount monthly and review and adjust risk/reward performance regularly (e.g. three monthly, six monthly, yearly) or as appropriate and agreed.

- Total cost performance and non-cost performance at or beyond the upper performance limits can be linked to contract extension.
- Actual results are determined by joint audits/review and/or third-party determination.
- Performance exceptions outside the upper and lower KPI limits will be managed via the governance process, issue resolution process and the Leadership and Management Teams as appropriate.

In return for entering a common goal, shared accountability, open book, transparent, risk/reward, gainshare/painshare environment based on the principles listed above, certain traditional practices and behaviours need to change or are fundamentally challenged. For example, liquidated damages, security guarantees, unlimited liability requirements, latent conditions, latent defects, the right to litigation, management control/compliance and others are often absent from partnering/alliancing agreements and the relationship. A good REM model is based on one team with common goals working in one direction.

Figure 7.6 is a summary of the process surrounding the REM model. The starting point is the partnering/alliance charter comprising the shared vision, joint key objectives and guiding principles for the relationship. Refer to pages 214–218 for further details. The key objectives link directly to the balanced scorecard of risk/reward and non-risk/reward based jointly accountable KPIs and targets. The risk/reward based KPIs are normally, but not always, a mix of strategic and relationship based KPIs. That is, supplier partner remuneration and, therefore, profit is linked in some way to the overall performance of the customer partner. At this point there are many who would say, 'Why put profit at risk on a KPI over which you have little or no control?'. This is the win/win, lose/lose philosophy at work. If the customer is doing it tough but the supplier's own part of the world is fine, why should the supplier gain all the benefits in isolation? The reverse logic also applies. When the customer partner is doing better than expected in their downstream operational activities or markets, the supplier partner will also gain greater than expected results. At this point a risk analysis and risk allocation discussion will have taken place to identify and agree who is best able to handle each component of risk and what actions to reduce the probability and consequence of an event have been put into place.

The analysis and allocation of risk will then be reflected in the KPI weightings, KPI targets, upper and lower performance limits, and KPI and profit performance expectations. A table is built weighting the KPIs on importance and detailing for each KPI the target performance levels and the upper

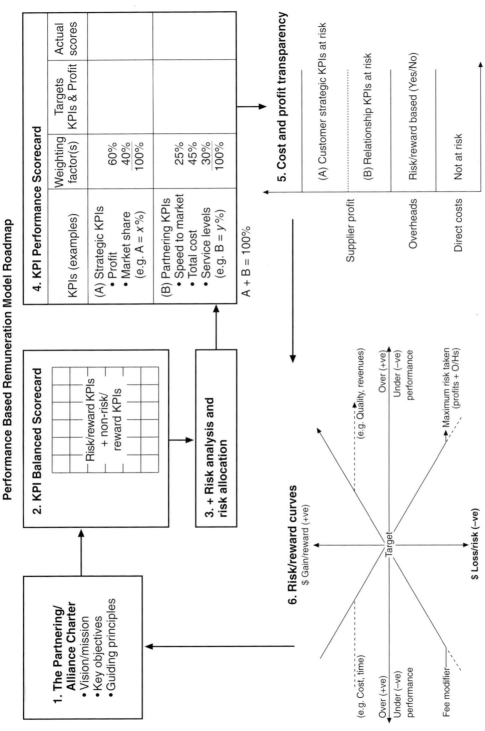

Fig. 7.6 *Process surrounding the REM model*

and lower limits of performance expectations. Also included on the table are the supplier partner's profit targets and the upper and lower profit limits associated with the respective performance levels.

The process to this point and the actual profit numbers are determined from an open book, transparent approach to cost data and profit and performance expectations. This is a discussion that will take place between the partners, based on the principles discussed earlier. As a guide, in many partnering and alliance REM models 100 per cent of the target profit is put at risk with direct costs being reimbursable, but this is entirely negotiable. Some partners believe that corporate overheads should not be put at risk as they are a necessary part of the overall business operation, often including R&D, innovation and management activities that do reflect back onto the relationship. Other partners believe that corporate overheads are outside the scope of relationship activities and, therefore, should form part of the risk component. Both arguments and any variation are valid. This is negotiable and the most appropriate option will depend on the size, intent, value propositions, scope, timing and location of the relationship.

From the data determined to this point the risk/reward curves can be developed. These curves represent the relationship between KPI performance and profit levels. The percentage of profit gain or profit loss above or below the agreed KPI targets is directly linked to the over-performance or under-performance achieved opposite the KPI targets. Standard supplier partner payments (e.g. monthly) can be based on the targets and adjusted against actual KPI performance outcomes three monthly, six monthly, yearly or as appropriate and agreed.

The REM model approach can apply to any relationship, be it ongoing or project based, any market, any part of the supply chain, and in the public or private sector. The over-riding concept is really quite simple and the variations are many.

The direct cost reimbursable, profit at risk REM model should not be seen as one of cost recovery. This is sometimes the view of the cynics, sceptics and non-believers or people that play somewhere else on the 0 to 10 RM scale (refer to Fig. 1.4). First, good partners will not do business with organisations that find cost recovery acceptable or sustainable. From a REM model perspective little or no profit means poor or unacceptable performance. Good organisations, and certainly good strategic partners, are also interested in reputation, credibility and referrals as a fundamental component of their profitable growth and sustainable competitive advantage. It is simply unacceptable for the supplier partner not to make a profit. In well-constructed partnering and alliance agreements sustained and even intermittent periods of significant poor performance can lead to relationship termination or disengagement, or to a change in relationship approach.

Having the supplier partner's success linked to strategic KPIs also generates a focus on improvement outside the relationship scope. For example, in the case of the Mobil/Transfield Services (construction, maintenance and engineering) alliance at the Altona oil refinery, there may be safety issues or poor practices that are outside the relationship scope but could affect construction, maintenance or engineering activities or overall refinery performance. Because their profit is directly linked to refinery performance KPIs, there is an incentive for Transfield Services, with full Mobil approval, to be proactive and initiate improvements wherever opportunities appear, be it inside or outside the scope of the relationship.

A worked example

I'm sorry to tell you but there is nothing prescriptive about REM models, no magic formulas, no one size fits all. There are many variations on a theme. The discussion and worked example that follows is one variation. You will need to form and fit your own circumstances and requirements to the general model.

Figure 7.6 outlines the six steps involved in putting the REM model together.

Step 1: The partnering/alliance charter

The assumption here is that partnering/alliancing is the right approach. The right partners have chosen each other and the value propositions are clear and agreed. The Partnering/Alliance Charter comprises the shared vision, common goals/objectives and guiding principles for the relationship and this has been discussed in detail in previous chapters (see pp. 214–218). Figure 7.7 is a simple, sample charter for the purpose of working through the REM model process. It is a general charter and could apply to many organisations and relationships. Importantly, it is also jointly developed and agreed to by the partners.

Step 2: KPI Balanced Scorecard

In the spirit that you cannot manage what you cannot measure, from the charter comes the KPI Balanced Scorecard, the matrix of leading and lagging, hard and soft, risk/reward based and non-risk/reward based performance indicators that measure the current performance and future improvement of the relationship. The risk/reward based KPIs are also used as the basis for remuneration, which in many

Strategic Partnering/Alliance Charter

Vision: Role model partners making a difference by delivering best practice outcomes and valued solutions through spirited teamwork.

Key objectives

1. Zero harm to people, plant and environment.
2. Deliver efficient and effective services that meet or exceed customer requirements.
3. Achieve sound commercial outcomes for all the partners.
4. Innovate for continuous and breakthrough improvement.
5. Build and maintain honest and open communication and information sharing.

Principles

- Act in a way that is best for the business, safe, legal and logical.
- Do what you say.
- Ensure no unpleasant surprises.
- Commit to trust, integrity, probity and professionalism.
- Solve problems proactively and resolve issues jointly.
- Be fair and reasonable.
- Commit to a 'no blame' culture.
- Have fun and celebrate success.

Fig. 7.7   *A strategic Partnering/Alliance Charter*

cases means profit gain/loss above or below target, being put at risk based on the over/under-performance achieved against the jointly agreed KPI targets. The KPI Balanced Scorecard was discussed in detail earlier in the chapter. Figure 7.8 is a sample KPI Balanced Scorecard developed from the Strategic Partnering/Alliance Charter in Figure 7.7. The risk/reward based KPIs are highlighted in bold.

The initial set of KPIs may also reflect the transition period or the initial building of the alliance. Subsequent KPI scorecard reviews will focus more around ongoing performance based KPIs.

Step 3: Risk analysis/risk allocation

At or about the same time as the charter and balanced scorecard are being developed, a risk analysis is normally done on the relationship scope and

Vision: Role model partners making a difference by delivering best practice outcomes and valued solutions through spirited teamwork.

Key objectives → / Outcomes (lead/lag) ↓	1. Safety, health and environment	2. Meet/exceed customer requirements	3. Sound commercial outcomes	4. Continuous improvement and innovation	5. Communication and information sharing
Financial success (ROI)			Customer profit % Budget (100%/140%) Relationship budget Costs (100%/90%)	Innovation and improvement $ as % forecast (80%/90%)	
Customer satisfaction	Total LTIFR (3/3) Relationship LTIFR (x/y) Environmental breaches (0/0)	Service levels IFOTA1 (95%/97%)			% Systems performance or access (x/y)
Competitive advantage			% Available business (>90%x/y)	Time to market (20% reduction /y)	
Best practices standards	SHE plan(s) progress (100%/x%)	Equipment availability (x/y) Project performance (90%/85%)		Number best practices shared (x/y)	Actions overdue (0%/y)
Innovation				Improvements identified (x/y) Implemented (x/y)	
Attitude	Near-miss learnings implemented (100%/x%) SHE safety audit plan —actions overdue (0/y)				Relationship survey results (95%/97%) Joint training days (x/y)

IFOTA1 = In Full On Time to A1 specification

LTIFR = Lost Time Injury Frequency Rate

KPI (target/actual), e.g. LTIFR (3/3), reliability (x/y)

Fig. 7.8 *KPI Balanced Scorecard*

activities and the allocation of responsibility for managing that risk is jointly agreed on by the partners. This then becomes an exercise of risk sharing and risk management rather than risk transfer. It involves identifying the potential risks involved for the relationship and its activities, the probability and consequence/impact of occurrence, any mitigating actions that can reduce the probability or consequence and the agreement on which party(s) is best able to manage and mitigate each area of risk. This is done within a 'no blame' but high accountability environment where the partner/alliance folk are working together as an integrated team for a common purpose. Steps 2 and 3 are closely linked and will be done most times as joint or connected exercises. They also provide the platform for building the Performance Scorecard.

Step 4: The Performance Scorecard

The Performance Scorecard associated with the worked example is shown in Figure 7.9. It is a table of the risk/reward based KPIs, the weightings associated with each of the strategic and relationship KPIs totalling 100 per cent. The KPI target, upper and lower KPI performance limits align to outstanding or unsustainable performance levels. Also on the Performance Scorecard are the target/upper/lower profit expectations that relate directly to the KPI performance levels, together with the actual performance score and profit outcome. Profit for each KPI is represented as a multiple of the total profit, in this case 8 per cent (±8%), and the weighting factor associated with each KPI. In this example corporate overheads have not been put at risk and form part of the reimbursable component. For ease of understanding and explanation and not to confuse the discussion with numbers, the KPIs in this example are mostly represented as percentages. They could just as easily be represented as numbers. The process and mechanics would be the same. A traffic light system (e.g. red, amber, green) can then be used to clearly identify where the areas of high, low and on-target performance are. In this example, overall profit achieved is 10.3 per cent, 2.3 per cent over target. Project performance is the only KPI not to achieve an above target outcome with an actual score of 85 per cent against a target of 90 per cent. The overall performance on a 0–100 scale is 64.3 per cent, which sits in the 'satisfactory' range on the total performance scale.

Over- or under-performance on the strategic KPIs can also be calculated as a multipler, a number above or below '1', which is then used on the relationship KPIs to produce a final performance and profit outcome. Other alternatives are where the actual KPI results have been standardised to a 0–50–100 scale based on the lower, target and upper KPI limits respectively. The standardised scores are then multiplied by the weightings and the results summed to a total relationship score from which the profit is calculated.

	Weighting	KPI Performance Levels			Profit Targets			Actual Score	Actual Profit
		Lower	Target	Upper	Lower	Target	Upper		
Strategic KPIs									
Customer profit % budget	10%	0%	100%	200%	0%	0.8%	1.6%	140%	1.1%
Total safety LTIFR	15%	6	3	0	0%	1.2%	2.4%	3	1.2%
Relationship KPIs									
Budget direct costs	20%	120%	100%	80%	0%	1.6%	3.2%	90%	2.4%
Service levels	20%	90%	95%	100%	0%	1.6%	3.2%	97%	2.2%
Relationship survey	10%	90%	95%	100%	0%	0.8%	1.6%	97%	1.1%
Project performance	10%	80%	90%	100%	0%	0.8%	1.6%	85%	0.4%
Innovation and improvement $	15%	60%	80%	100%	0%	1.2%	2.4%	90%	1.8%
Total supplier partner profit	100%				0%	8.0%	16.0%		10.3%

Performance score (0–100%)

	Unsustainable	Poor	Satisfactory	Excellent	Superior
	0–25%	25–49%	50–75%	75–99%	100%
Total relationship performance			64.3%		

Fig. 7.9 *Risk/reward REM model Performance Scorecard*

It is critical that the Performance Scorecard be built by a joint team, taking into account the information and understanding from the previous steps. For many newcomers to partnering and alliancing it is the openness, transparency, honesty and trust required that proves more challenging to deal with than the mechanics of the risk/reward process and calculations.

Step 5: Cost and profit transparency

Open mind and open book are the keys here. Irrespective of whether you are building the cost model from the top down (e.g. target costing) or the bottom up (e.g. activity based) or both, there has to be complete two-way transparency of information and data. The supplier partner must be open and transparent in the cost and profit expectations and their willingness and capability to deliver. Likewise the customer partner must be open and transparent with their cost, operational and business expectations and their approach to risk management.

Each organisation will have their view on the definition and makeup of direct costs, corporate overheads and profit so I will not pursue further detail here. The total target cost will normally be developed with a joint integrated team approach within a workshop environment and will involve area experts, estimators, auditors and third parties as appropriate to work up the total cost/budget targets. This exercise will be repeated periodically (e.g. annually) in line with relationship and business requirements where KPI performance targets, upper and lower limits, risk contingencies and profit expectations can be challenged and, in the spirit of improvement, reset if appropriate.

Step 6: Risk/reward curves

The final step is to produce the risk/reward curves, or in this case straight lines, gained from the information and data from the previous steps. Continuing our example, Figure 7.10 is the risk/reward curve for the KPI 'service levels' which accounts for 20 per cent weighting and a target profit component of 1.6 per cent out of a total target profit of 8 per cent. The REM curve is the visual representation of the relationship between 'service level' KPI performance and profit expectation. Actual profit figures can be calculated either from the Performance Scorecard or directly from the straight line formulas for the risk/reward curves. If you are working with the straight line formulas, the actual profit is calculated by substituting the actual KPI score for 'X' and calculating the profit 'Y'. The total relationship performance and associated profit can also be represented as a single risk/reward curve using data from the Performance Scorecard (see Fig. 7.11).

Risk/reward curves are particularly useful for explaining how the performance remuneration model works as well as being a very useful tool for monitoring and managing the overall performance of the relationship and its

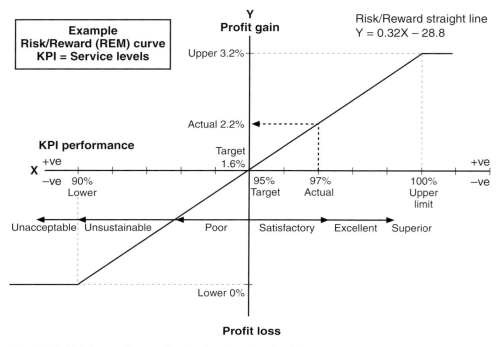

Fig. 7.10 *Risk/reward curve for the KPI 'service levels'*

individual risk/reward components. A risk/reward curve can be built for each risk/reward based KPI and/or a single curve can be made for the relationship as a whole. Figure 7.11 is the risk/reward curve for the total relationship, the data for which has been obtained by converting the actual score for each KPI to a 0–100 per cent performance score and then summing these individual performance scores, which have been multiplied by the associated weighting factors. Risk/reward curves have many variations and can include flat sections where there is a zero effect on profit with changes in performance, as well as curves that have varying slopes and steps. In non-cost areas such as service levels, safety, quality, time, reliability, availability and so on, reward payments can be funded from an initial agreed contingency or non-cost incentive pool, or out of cost savings or $ value adding benefits achieved. Examples of these risk/reward curve variations are shown in Figure 7.12.

In terms of measuring, managing and driving improvement it is critical that the starting point or base line cost and non-cost performance data for the process be known as accurately as possible. This will ensure that improvement is acknowledged and recognised. Periodic reviews (e.g. annual) of performance and profit levels, targets and actuals can then occur. As appropriate, a resetting of the 'performance' bar expectations and targets upwards can then

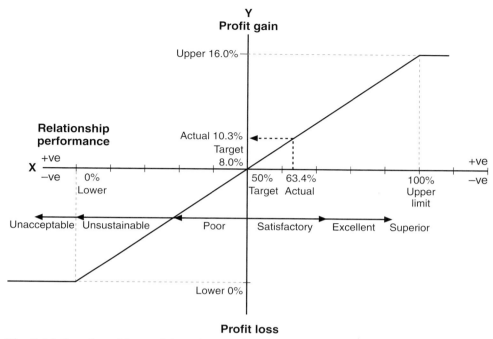

Fig. 7.11 *Sample risk/reward (REM) curve for total relationship performance*

take place, to ensure an ongoing focus on, and delivery of continuous improvement.

There does not have to be a large number of KPIs involved. Keeping things simple works just as well for REM models as it does for most other aspects of life. I worked on a large alliance project that involved a $40 million modification to an oil refinery. While the KPI Balanced Scorecard had fifteen KPIs—leading and lagging, hard and soft—to measure and manage overall project performance, there were only two KPIs linked to the risk/reward model, cost and schedule. The partners' view was that performance in all other KPIs in some way impacted upon cost and schedule. Anywhere from four to ten risk/reward based KPIs is common for strategic partnering/alliance relationships.

Dealing with exceptions

What happens when performance falls outside the upper and lower limits agreed to? These are the 'exceptions' and they can range from outstanding and unexpected positive breakthroughs to the negative impact of catastrophic failures, market collapses and natural disasters. The joint governance process and the leadership and management teams will be involved to agree the most

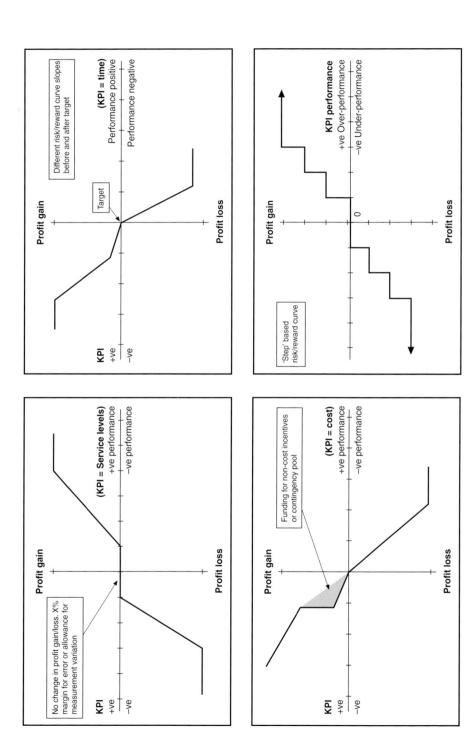

Fig. 7.12 *Risk/reward curve variations*

suitable way forward. The options can range from significant rewards over and above expectations to termination or disengagement in the most extreme of circumstances. In cases where the exceptions have a negative impact, the leadership and management teams will invoke the joint accountability principles of proactive problem solving and the joint resolution of issues, and engage the issue resolution/escalation process as appropriate to ensure the best solutions or corrective actions are found.

Consider a 'settling in' period

It can occur that the REM model is fully and formally implemented only after a 'due diligence' or 'settling in' period is completed (e.g. six or twelve months). It may be a new relationship, there may be a lack of baseline data or the partners may lack experience with or are initially uncomfortable with the risk/reward model approach and how it works. The REM model can run as an off-line parallel process for an agreed period. Target profits are paid until the REM model is proven and agreement is reached to activate the REM model as the operating model. This can also allow time for the partners to become comfortable and familiar with the mindsets, practices, behaviours and process mechanics involved. Performance adjustments can then be backdated as agreed and appropriate.

REFERENCES

1. Jordon D. Lewis, *The Connected Corporation*, Free Press, 1995.
2. Jeffrey H. Dyer, 'How Chrysler created an American Keiretsu', *Harvard Business Review*, July–August 1996, pp.42–56.
3. 'Crunch at Chrysler', *Economist*, 12 November 1994, p.121.
4. Paul Ingrassia & Joseph B. White, *Comeback: The Fall and Rise of the American Automobile Industry*, New York: Simon & Schuster, 1994.
5. Robert S. Kaplan and David P. Norton, *The Balanced Scorecard*, Harvard Business School Press, 1996.
6. Dyer, op. cit., pp.52–5.
7. A.D. Henderson and R.J. Cuttler, Northside Storage Tunnel Project paper, Tenth Australian Tunnelling conference, 1999.
8. Australian Constructors Association, 'Relationship Contracting—Optimising Project Outcomes', p.28.
9. Allan Henderson, Case study—The Northside Storage Tunnel Project, QSA/SIA/EIA conference paper, 8–9 September 1999, p.7.

THE PARTNERING AND ALLIANCE MANAGER

CHAPTER 8

Managing change and complexity in partnering and alliance relationships

HOW COMPLEX CAN PARTNERSHIPS BE?

It is rare that you find a world-class partner with a single site, a single product/service, and without that cross-divisional overlap that provides those enormous opportunities for adding value and, in turn, differentiating both supplier and customer partners. What happens when you are working with truly international companies with offices, production, sales, marketing, warehousing and distribution in Europe, Asia, North America and Latin America? How do you deal with different languages, cultures and ways of doing business?

Within Australia itself, what happens when your partner is located in all major capital cities with five to ten regional distribution centres? How do you manage the distances, site rivalry, internal customer politics, the 'Head Office versus the rest' mentality, communication, and so on?

Your partner's business is itself a multidivisional, multifunctional operation, internally crossing various product groups and several different market sectors. Add to that the fact that various groups or subsidiaries within your own company are dealing with the customer partner to varying degrees and you start to get a very complex set of relationships and networks to manage. The possible combinations of all the above are virtually limitless. The complexity of such relationships is quite daunting, even for the most experienced relationship managers and the most world class of companies.

Good communication, the right people and easy access to relevant and accurate information will be the keys to managing these networks. They will provide an outcome where the 'whole' relationship is greater than the sum of the parts.

PARTNERING/ALLIANCE MANAGERS AND PARTNERING TEAMS

The more complicated the networks, contacts, sites, divisions and products, the greater the need for strong and capable partnering/alliance managers, and not just one from the supplier side. Large, complex, diverse partnerships may require relationship managers from both customer and supplier, to work together with the leadership and management team, other teams and individuals. In addition, multi-site, multidivisional, regional or global partnerships may require multiple partnering/alliance teams. Selected individuals from these teams can coordinate the sum of the parts into the whole via an overall steering group. No layers, no hierarchy, just an effective structure to coordinate direction, activity, information and communication. Refer back to Figure 6.21, which outlines the structure discussed in the partnering team step.

It is surprising how complicated and significant in dollar turnover or contribution this network of relationships can be when all the links are connected. In most organisations this interlinking will require a complete rethink of the structure and accountabilities from top to bottom. Internal roadblocks and structural barriers must be broken down for the partnership to work. Communication must be at a fever pitch. How is your business structured? Is it asset-based, product-based, market-segment-based, customer-based? When managing partnerships, the focus will be on teams and teamwork in conjunction with, or overriding, the existing structure.

In developing a complex partnering and alliance relationship across multiple sites, divisions and products, avoid the 'shotgun' approach. Target centres of excellence where the chances of success are high and visible. Use these as points of crystallisation for subsequent areas of development. This will effectively prioritise the partnership development activities as well as optimising the use of available resources.

THE IMPACT AND MANAGEMENT OF RECIPROCAL BUSINESS IN PARTNERSHIPS

In many customer/supplier relationships the roles can be reversed by the nature and volume of reciprocal business. Generally, this is not well understood or managed, and in many cases not known or recognised at all. Partnerships—the process and the people involved—will allow for reciprocal business to be managed more effectively and the benefits to be more rewarding. Reciprocal business will add to the interdependence of the relationships, the benefits of which have already been discussed. This synergistic effect will mean the relationship is easier to operate in practice. The obvious problem, whether existing or potential, of trading off one customer/supplier relationship against another is best left to the partnership manager(s) and the partnering teams to deal with.

MANAGING PEOPLE CHANGE IN PARTNERSHIPS

> *There may be a hidden cost when senior managers rotate across jobs every two or three years. What most often prompts a change in strategy in a large company is not a new competitor, new technology, or regulatory upheaval. What most often prompts change is a new executive in the corner office . . . We know of no company that has achieved a ten- or fifteen-year strategic intent with a succession of two-year executives in key jobs.*
>
> Gary Hamel & C.K. Prahalad[1]

Change in senior management

Senior management set the vision and broad strategies. Their leadership style and direction will quickly filter through the organisation. A change in senior management could thus signal a change in vision and strategy.

It is very important that a senior management handover involves contact with the partnering/alliance organisation to ensure that the current relationships and future direction of the two companies is explained and the guiding principles, relationship approach and common goals understood and committed to. Ideally, sign-off should be reached to continue the relationship building. If the new manager(s) is of the same mindset regarding vision and strategy, there should be no problems. However, if there are any significant differences a major review will need to take place. On average, senior managers change position every three years so at some stage this predicament will have to be faced. Plan for such an event.

I remember an instance where the general manager of a very large customer ($25 million sales p.a.) left after ten years with the organisation. Very good relationships had been developed over this time and the organisation was potentially a future partner. The incoming GM had a completely different set of priorities. He was really in vendor mode (combative and tribal) and, as part of his new strategy, deliberately kept suppliers in the dark with regard to forecasting and actual off-take, and constantly played off one supplier against the other. Overnight, within the customer organisation, there came into being a new style of management—autocratic, centralist, based on fear, compliance, control and poor communication. The relationship collapsed over the next three months. This could have been avoided through a prevention rather than cure strategy.

Change in key customer/supplier personnel

Changes in key personnel can also have significant effects on a partnership. What happens if you are not yet at the stage where you have a strong, long-term, trusting relationship? You have chosen the customer, understood requirements and developed plans, and are working hard on the key relationships. Then a key contact departs or changes roles. It depends where you are along the partnership scale (1 to 10) shown in Figures 1.2 and 1.3, and on the partnership development curve, as well as on the character and personality of the new person, as to how difficult the change will be. To a certain extent it is like starting all over again.

How do you start any good business or personal relationship? Ask questions, be a good listener, define and redefine requirements and then deliver them, discover likes and dislikes, understand the personality, character, objectives, goals, ambitions and time frames. Trust and respect will need to be gained and the relationship rebuilt. Explain the partnership principles carefully until they are fully understood and commitment to them is forthcoming.

But what happens when you get someone who really does not fit the partnership mould? Make your feelings known among the existing relationships and networks and ask their advice. Use your coach for advice and feedback. You will need the help of all your key people, combined with the existing strength of the partnership, to effect a change in the thinking and attitude of the newcomer. If there is a genuine partnering/alliance relationship in place even the toughest corporate rottweiler will at least give the relationship time to prove itself.

The depth, breadth and interdependence of the relationship is vitally important if continuity and continuous improvement within it is to be maintained. This, together with a prevention, prediction or design-out approach to relationship maintenance, rather than a breakdown approach, will ensure a smoother journey.

Succession planning

How do you sustain the relationship beyond the life of key people? What is purported to be a strategic alliance or partnership is often nothing more than a good working relationship between a few good people. When one or more of those people move on, the relationship can often suffer significantly or even terminate.

With people change the key lies in the joint planning. We carry out succession planning within our own organisations so why not joint succession planning when it comes to partnering/alliance relationships? That way there are no surprises, no breaks in communication.

Systems and procedures should be in place for grooming suitable employees for promotion and contingency plans drawn up to deal with unexpected departures of key personnel. World-class partners will have jointly discussed this eventuality of people change. It becomes an expected event, planned for and well executed to ensure a smooth handover.

Think about it. You have key strategic customers and suppliers with competent and ambitious individuals doing outstanding jobs. Eventually they will want new challenges because challenge is what drives them to be successful individuals in their current roles. There is probably no better role than that of a partnering/alliance manager to groom someone for a senior management position. Use the principles and practice of succession planning in the planning and development of your partnerships as you would in the planning and development of your business.

Succession planning and the following guidelines should enable you to avoid most of the people problems that normally arise.

1. Discuss jointly from the start the importance of senior management's commitment and active participation in the partnering process and the potential impact of people changes.
2. Senior management on both sides should talk frequently about imminent people changes that may impact on the relationship.
3. An induction program on partnerships and alliances should be in place to enable new personnel to understand the history, nature and importance of the strategic partnering/alliancing to all partners and stakeholders. The partnering/alliance workshops may well fill this role.
4. Continually build up the depth and breadth of contacts, relationships and networks between the partners. Any one change then becomes less likely to have a negative impact on the partnership.

WHY DO PARTNERSHIPS FAIL?

Like marriages, partnerships and alliances fail for all sorts of reasons but, almost without exception, the problems and ultimate failure arise from people. Their basic beliefs, perceptions, decisions, actions or intentions will underlie a failed partnering/alliance relationship. The manifestation of this may be failure of plant and machinery or systems and networks, poor In Full On Time delivery performance, poor quality and financial performance, poor communication, diminished competitive advantage or reduced trust, but the root cause will rest with people.

Some of the ways partnerships can fail are:

- A change in management or CEO gives a new direction at odds with the partnership philosophy.
- A change in company vision and strategy occurs, with or without new management; for example, there is a shift from a customer focus to sweating assets and cash cows. Ultimately, this will affect the organisation's culture.
- There is poor alignment on culture, strategy, structure, process or people.
- Judging is via short-term financial results versus long-term objectives.
- Little or no interdependence is built.
- People at the operating levels, who must make it work, are not informed about, or involved in, the partnering/alliance process.
- Partners' values, motivations, expectations are unclear.
- There is a lack of mutually agreed performance measures.
- The wrong choice of markets or partners, or both, is made.
- Perception is out of line with reality. What was really in existence all along was a vendor or supplier relationship, not a partnering/alliance relationship.
- Partnering/alliance 'champions' may leave the organisation due to lack of a career path, or for better opportunities, and be replaced by someone unsympathetic to partnering/alliancing. Or they may leave and not be replaced at all. 'Champions' could range from the partnering manager to anyone with positive influence and active involvement in the relationship's success, such as innovators and early adaptors. Lose your champions, lose your will, then lose your way.
- A state of diminished competitive advantage develops, via increased costs or reduced differentiation relative to the competition, that is, the expected value from the relationship does not materialise.
- Market demise occurs; there is a lack of demand for the product or service.
- There is poor integration of business or operating units and tribalism continues to dominate.
- Senior management from both customer and supplier partners fail to lead and inspire the process or eliminate the roadblocks and gatekeepers.
- Customer complaints are handled badly; for example, a 'crisis' in product/service performance results in financial claims that are not resolved to the satisfaction of both parties.

- There is a lack of commitment or willingness to participate in step changes in technology (process or product). This may involve financial restrictions, strategy limitations or both.
- The required progress in workplace reform and TQM is not forthcoming, affecting innovation, skills development and productivity.
- The rhetoric does not match the reality. A case of over-promise and under-deliver exists. One party—or perhaps both—was not capable from the start i.e. poor partner selection.
- A permanent loss of trust occurs, leading to a dramatic reduction in information exchange.
- Achievement of monopoly status reinvigorates arrogance, complacency and inefficiency.
- There is a misconception that the 'end point' has been reached, that continuous improvement is no longer applicable and therefore the relationship is no longer useful.
- Not enough time is given or patience developed to build the relationship.
- There is disagreement over shared benefits, risk management and risk allocation.

It is the obligation of all those involved in the relationship to pick up and manage successfully all the stresses and strains that are involved. This is a skill to be learnt, developed and coached. Used wisely and effectively it may mean the difference between success and failure or, at the very least, the saving of much time, frustration, confusion and valuable resources.

Just as many marriages are saved by the intervention of a third party—family, friends, relatives, or professional facilitators such as marriage counsellors—so the same principle can apply to partnerships. Of course, there are instances where the marriage should never have happened in the first place. However, if the partnership is in the position of degenerating or dissolving and it is clear that the issues cannot or will not be resolved by the two parties themselves, then use third-party facilitation. This could be in the form of work colleagues, partnering managers from other divisions or organisations, other supplier or customer partners or experienced consultants. They will bring a new perspective to bear and hopefully open up avenues of reconciliation that would otherwise not have been possible.

How to exit a partnership—Disengagement

You exit a partnering/alliance relationship the same way you enter it—in a spirit of cooperation, openness, trust, mutual benefit and assistance, and in accordance with the original guiding principles. Not all relationships can go on forever. Market dynamics, competitive pressures in innovation and technology, takeovers, business/product/service life cycles and the like will see to that. Good partners see the changes coming and jointly plan for transition. This does not mean the relationship dissolves acrimoniously into extinction. Partners may help each other to find alternative suppliers, customers or partners. For all the right reasons, the relationship may go from 8+ on the 1 to 10 relationship scale to 8–, that is, the supplier category. This situation can also be worked through cooperatively between the partners. Often alliance partners agree up front what the 'rules of disengagement' are for the relationship. A process is agreed to, outlining the steps, issues and areas that need to be addressed in the event that the relationship is to terminate, or be wound back to a less critical or strategic relationship. This could range from people and other resource allocation, fair and reasonable access to training equipment and sites, appropriate confidential information and fair and reasonable pricing to intellectual property issues, maintenance and service issues, spare parts and hardware/software upgrades. A disengagement plan can be developed to ensure an orderly and staged exit. The 0 to 10 RM scale is dynamic, with relationships moving up and down according to their state and rate of development and the forces operating in the external marketplace.

NEGOTIATIONS IN A PARTNERSHIP

> *The new model for the 1990s [and the 21st century] (i.e. a win/win partnership) makes the old win/lose contest between customer and supplier obsolete.*
>
> *Keki Bhote*[2]

Be a good negotiator but don't negotiate

From personal experience, negotiations in an established partnership are really quite a different experience from the 'aim high, fall back, walk away' brinkmanship that usually occurs in traditional supplier/customer negotiations. The traditional confrontationist, adversarial relationship between customer and supplier just does not exist. Because there is a relationship based on shared vision, common goals, trust, openness, good communication and an absence of hidden agendas, the negotiation really isn't a negotiation at all. It becomes a discussion, or series of discussions, based on shared information, the outcome of which is a set of mutually agreed decisions that benefit both parties. A real win/win situation.

I have been involved in negotiations with a partner where we have both literally thrown our information on the table, all of it, no secrets. We then reviewed it jointly and sometimes argued about it, but at the end of those discussions a common solution always seemed to emerge that was acceptable to both parties. The reason was that both organisations were totally committed to continuing to do business together and were interested only in a mutually acceptable result. That's not to say that there wasn't an aim-high position or a fallback position, or indeed trading of concessions—there was. The difference was that it was all done in open and joint discussion. In fact, on many occasions we tabled aim-high positions, fallback positions, concessions and anything else we had in the traditional bag of tricks prior to the discussion. We then worked out the best win/win solution for both parties.

Negotiations that would traditionally have taken weeks or months of tough, hard-fought confrontation were dealt with in one or two amicable discussions. It really can be that easy. The focus is on the longer term; discussions on price terms and conditions are just small ongoing steps in the relationship that need to be managed and dealt with.

Depending on the circumstances and the nature of the relationship, this principle can be extended to 'open-book' costings and profit gain/pain share. The open sharing of costs must, of course, be two-way and used in conjunction with a high level of trust and common objectives for mutually beneficial outcomes. Open-book arrangements are not necessarily appropriate for every customer/supplier partnering/alliance relationship but they can be useful, for example, in helping to remove the traditional adversarial tendering system.

The ease with which negotiations are completed is in fact one of the measures of success of the partnership itself. And the reason for this, in one word, is trust. Absolute, total and unquestionable trust. How many relationships, personal or business, do you have that you can honestly say are based on 'absolute, total and unquestioning trust'? Out of complete trust will come shared, accurate and timely information, a common understanding of each other's objectives and the commitment and willingness to cooperate for mutual benefit.

That is why many of our current negotiations are lose/lose or win/lose confrontations. There is no trust!

I am always amazed by traditional negotiating, in particular from the seller's perspective:

1. Everyone uses the same classical negotiation skills, varying only in the degree of complexity. They are based on the principles of:
   - Gather information
   - Know your competition

- Know your customer and get his or her 'shopping list'
- Determine authority levels of both customer and supplier
- Agree aim-high, fallback, main objective and walk-away positions
- Draw up a list of concessions to trade

2. There were never any buyers on the training course to give you their version of life on the other side of the fence.

3. Totally unbeknown to us sellers, the buyers were doing virtually the same training course and learning the same principles, but from the buying perspective.

4. After all this training, buyers and sellers launched themselves upon their poor unsuspecting opponents with the objective of outwitting and outsmarting them at every turn.

In many respects we negotiate with our customers and suppliers as we would treat our competitors. We withhold information, hoping they haven't done their homework on the latest information, costs and comparative prices, so that we have an advantage; hoping they make a mistake in our favour before they make a decision, then holding them to the commitment agreed upon. This is very much a short-term perspective. What is then precipitated is a 'Don't get mad, get even' backlash that spirals the relationship back to confrontation and mistrust, and all too often to litigation. This is a world built around liquidated damages and the like.

But there is so much more to be done than worrying and haggling about price, terms and conditions—things like discovering, developing and providing world-class products and services, for starters. That's the main game. Traditional negotiations take your mind off the main game.

Who does the negotiating?

Partnering/alliance managers and the associated integrated teams have overall responsibility as they are in the best position to understand all the issues and sensitivities, and the impact of potential outcomes. What breadth and depth of resources they wish to use or consult with will depend entirely on the environment and the circumstances surrounding the discussion. For example, members of the partnering/alliance leadership and management teams will be of great value in a partnership negotiation. Their specialist skills and experience with the partner will help in sharing relevant information and in the clarification of specific issues.

Business managers and marketing clearly have a vested interest in the outcome, but they will be involved at the direction and discretion of the partnering/alliance manager(s).

How often do you negotiate?

Contrary to popular belief, as often as possible. As negotiating is now about 'one-team negotiations', making joint decisions, for mutual benefit, based on shared information, then share a lot and share often. It may be weekly, monthly or quarterly, depending on the business and circumstances.

Partnering/alliance managers need to be good negotiators

It may seem strange in view of all I have said that strong and proven negotiating skills will be an essential quality for the partnering/alliance manager. But when I talk about partnerships, shared information, no confrontation, no brinkmanship, no walkaways, I am talking about a point many steps into a long process. A lot of water must pass under the bridge before this point is reached. As can be seen from the typical partnership life cycle in Figure 1.9, the relationship can often start from a low point, a crisis. This will require an ongoing series of genuinely negotiated win/win positions, aim-highs, fall-backs and traded concessions. Gaining respect and trust is about continuous improvement; it is earned over time, not given on demand. You will need to win your 'partnering/alliance stripes', which initially will not be easy. If you are building the relationship from a low point, scepticism and cynicism will need to be extinguished by building trust over time.

If you are the supplier partner in the relationship put yourself in the customer's shoes and do some purchasing and procurement. Go to your procurement department and ask them if you can participate in their next supply negotiation. Ask them about how they negotiate. How do they develop their skills? What books do they read and learn from? What are their strategies, tactics, objectives and outcomes? How do they determine preferred suppliers?

As the relationship develops, ask if you can be involved in your supplier or customer partner's negotiations to get a broader understanding of negotiating and their business in general. Likewise, for anyone involved in purchasing goods or services, experience what it is like from the selling perspective. Get involved with sales negotiations. Carry out joint customer visits with the account, key account and partnership managers. Do everything you can to understand what life is like on the other side.

Reverse negotiations

The logic is simple, the practice more difficult. Assume as before that genuine partnering and alliance relationships are about shared vision, common goals, awesome trust (competence and character), open and honest communication sharing and all the other 'stuff'. Turning 'them' and 'us' into 'we'. That being the case, negotiating partners should be able to negotiate on each other's behalf and come up with the same or similar outcomes as if negotiations had occurred normally. I call it *reverse negotiating* or effectively 'one team' negotiations. Swap sides and put yourself in your partner's shoes. For most organisations this is a paradigm shift and unthinkable in traditional vendor/supplier relationships.

If team negotiations are involved, try swapping half of each team or half the key members over to the other side. The negotiation, of course, isn't a negotiation in the traditional sense at all. Very quickly you will find not two or more negotiating teams but one team with one mission—to get the best possible result for all. It's all about no sides, mutual benefits and agreed outcomes, based on a partnering attitude and shared information.

Try it first as a role-play, perhaps after the successful completion of a normal negotiation. This will provide the comparison benchmark. The physical act of reverse negotiating is not difficult if the right mindset is in place.

REFERENCES

1. Gary Hamel & C.K. Prahalad, *Competing for the Future*, Harvard Business School Press, 1994, p.176.
2. Keki Bhote, *Strategic Supply Management*, American Management Association, 1989, p.29.

CHAPTER 9

Strategic partnering and alliance managers

> *But you no longer evaluate an executive in terms of how many people report to him or her. That standard doesn't mean as much as the complexity of the job, the information it uses and generates, and the different kinds of relationships needed to do the work.*
>
> Peter Drucker[1]

We have looked at the qualities and characteristics of organisations and the types of structures, culture and strategic thinking that will be required to develop successful partnerships. We have also discussed the process for developing and managing the partnering and alliance relationships for the short, medium and long term. What has not yet been discussed in detail is the profile of the individuals who are going to be responsible for managing these relationships, the partnering/alliance managers.

If developing successful partnerships is critical to our future success then it is going to take special qualities and special people, first to unravel and then to manage such complexity. They are rare beasts indeed, partly because of the depth and breadth of skills and experience required and partly because business traditionally has not been in partnership mode. The whole experience is quite new and so people have not been skilled or coached in the ways of strategic partnering/alliancing.

Again, we could look at the analogy between business partnerships and marriage and perhaps draw the conclusion that society as a whole has difficulty understanding the general concept of partnerships. Marriage can be seen as a measure or an indicator of society's ability to form social partnerships. That being so, the fact that at least two in five marriages end in divorce would indicate that our track record in managing these relationships effectively is not only poor but getting worse. Why should we not assume, then, a similar trend and lack of understanding in the world of business partnerships? The way we relate to each other at a social level does not make the task of developing strong, long-term strategic relationships at a business level any easier.

Strategic partnering and alliance managers: who are they and where do they come from? What competencies and skills are required? How are these competencies and skills coached and developed? How are they recognised and rewarded? Where do they go from partnership management? What are the next steps and in what time frame? Understanding and successfully managing these issues will be no less critical than the nature of the partnership itself.

PARTNERING AND ALLIANCE MANAGER COMPETENCIES

We often talk about the types of training and academic qualifications required, years of experience gained, previous job history. This will surely vary depending on the nature of the position, the marketplace, even the country and its culture. Rather, we should be talking about the fundamental skills and competencies required. The general competencies required of a partnership manager will change very little from job to job. The types of specialist skills, particularly technical skills, and experience required will vary dramatically.

To understand the general skills, knowledge and attitudes required of a partnership and alliance manager, it is necessary to understand the competencies required of the individuals who manage the other types of buyer/seller relationships—that is, the vendor and supplier relationships. We are talking here about the sales representative, trader, account manager and key account manager (see Fig. 1.2). As I have said before, knowing where you are is just as important as knowing where you want to go. In part, managers of other buyer/seller relationships also provide the benchmarks by which the skills and performance of the partnering/alliance manager can be judged. In terms of relationship management, there is a clear 'add-on' effect of competencies required, particularly going from account manager to key account manager and then through to partnering/alliance manager. In Chapter 1, I spoke in general terms of these roles and their effectiveness in relationship management. It is critical, however, to understand how and why these competencies differ. Then it becomes possible to match those competencies opposite the individual(s) and position(s) in question.

Remember: the strategic partnering process is not only about managing partnerships. It also involves the effective relationship management of the rest of your customer and/or supplier portfolio. It is crucial to identify which customers/suppliers want to see you as a vendor and which customers/suppliers want to see you as a genuine supplier, and then manage them appropriately. Not every organisation wants to be treated as a partner. Putting an account manager into a partnering/alliance manager's role will generate frustration and ultimately failure. Likewise, putting a genuine partnering/alliance manager in an account manager's role will be an enormous waste of resources and will also ultimately end in frustration and failure.

Detailed below are the competencies required of sales representative, trader, account manager, key account manager and partnering/alliance manager. Use this list as a basis for understanding where your own organisation sits in terms of the type and quality of relationship managers employed and the types of customer relationships wanting to be developed. Also, just as importantly, use it as a basis for understanding where your competitors lie on the relationship management scale.

There will, of course, be many other people and job titles involved in managing relationships, directly or indirectly. In fact, anyone in any job has to manage relationships—purchasing managers, asset managers, business unit managers, project managers, general managers, customer service officers, business development managers, operations managers and the list goes on. While their job descriptions will vary, when managing relationships they will take on many of the characteristics of the five roles described here. In fact these roles are just an attempt to capture some of the broad qualities, competencies, attitudes and behaviours associated with any job position and with managing relationships on the 0 to 10 Relationship Management scale.

I appreciate I am at risk here, in what follows, of totally alienating all those with 'Sales Representative' stamped on their business cards. However, it is important to understand that it is the sales representative competencies, as I define them, and not the individuals that I have reservations about. I am not interested in titles on business cards but in the quality of the individuals who hold them and the management and culture that support them. Actions, behaviours and attitudes speak louder than position or title. As always, no individual is likely to fit exactly into any particular set of competencies. It will be a balance based on skills and experience.

The Account Manager and Key Account Manager competencies are based on the ICI Australia career progression matrix which, as a project team member, I was involved in putting together. They are presented here with permission.

◆ Sales representative competencies (deficiencies or weaknesses)

Business effectiveness

- Lives within a world of tribalism and interdepartmental rivalry, making selfish, short-term deals and decisions at the expense of strategy and the support team.
- Has little understanding of, or time for, other departments, particularly production, marketing and management.
- Focuses primarily on price and getting the order.
- Understands the competitors but is poor at documenting this information and relating its significance back to the marketing or business plans.

Management effectiveness

- A 'Lone Ranger' operator, not a team player; has difficulty with the detail of sales and marketing plans, and with the need for them.
- Would regard coaching other staff and exchanging information as a threat, not a benefit.
- Interested in fulfilling quotas and budgets at any cost.

Personal effectiveness

- Despite an outgoing, friendly personality, in reality is a poor communicator and influencer (oral and written).
- Has a 'back to the wall' attitude under pressure, and solutions tend to be *ad hoc*.
- Has basic negotiation skills that normally result in win/lose outcomes.
- Displays initiative, drive and persistence but this is often mismanaged and misdirected.

Customer relations and communication

- The relationships developed are usually superficial and based on poor support from the business units and limited trust or respect from the customers.
- Tends to ignore, or fails to uncover, customer requirements and therefore tends to sell features not benefits.
- A poor networker internally and externally whose main contact with the customer is through purchasing.
- Problems (about stock availability, quality, service) often arise, with poor or protracted outcomes.

New business

- A 'hunter' of new business to fill quotas or budgets.
- The driving force is often money in the form of bonus or commission.
- New business has a high focus due to the difficulty in sustaining repeat business.

Presentation and selling

- A good talker but little substance in what is said.
- Negotiates more on gut feeling and emotion than on facts and a well-prepared strategy or plan.
- Due to a poor understanding of process capabilities, the result is usually a case of over-promise and under-deliver on quality and service. The fallback discussion revolves around reductions in price, conflict and complaints resolution.
- Competent at the quick fix, but permanent solutions are rare.

Safety, health and environment (SHE)

- Has little or no understanding of this subject and little interest in it. SHE issues create problems, not opportunities.

Debt collection and credit risk assessment

- Does not see this role within his job remit, which is fundamentally to get the order.
- Has little or no interest in or understanding of a balance sheet or profit and loss account and their impact on business viability.
- The credit and collection function is seen as another tribe whose role is more of a hindrance than a help. Will often trade additional volumes or services for extended trading terms.
- Has a poor understanding of the cost of extended trading terms and the impact of slow payers and bad debts on the bottom line.

Professional expertise

- Has poorly developed professional selling skills.
- Has a general knowledge across a range of industries but lacks the vision and capability to integrate strategy and tactics to achieve win/win outcomes.
- Is a task-oriented individual and sells on personality, not substance or skill. Interested in the short term and has real difficulty in sustaining medium- to long-term continuous improvement relationships.
- Customers can be small or major accounts depending on the size and professionalism of the organisation.

◆ (Good) trader competencies

Business effectiveness

- Understands company/customer/competitor structures and values and has an appreciation of the relevant product/services and their applications.
- Will tend to be reactive rather than proactive on product/service developments, technical service and complaints resolution.

- Places emphasis on speed of sale and delivery of products and services at a margin.
- Sees repeat business is as important as new business.
- Understands trade practices and other legal requirements.

Management effectiveness

- Works essentially unsupervised and is responsible for profitability and contribution as well as volume and $ turnover.
- Is essentially interested in the outcome, not the process; hence strategies and plans—while focused—tend to be short, succinct background documents.
- Is a strong and effective networker of resources within and outside the company.

Personal effectiveness

- Has effective interpersonal, negotiating, influencing and networking skills at most levels of own organisation and customers'.
- Can communicate both technical and business issues.
- Works best under pressure and tight deadlines, finding quick solutions to customer problems.
- Has the ability to think quickly, demonstrating initiative, drive and persistence. Focus is short to medium term.

Customer relationships and communication

- Builds strong relationships with key individuals in customer organisation but lacks a true multilevel selling base.
- Is responsive and flexible to customer requests with a clear focus on conformance to requirements, but lacks the developmental and technical support base to sustain strong, broad-based, long-term relationships.

New business

- Constantly seeks to identify new opportunities from all sources and assess their value to the company.
- Takes an 'ear to the ground', 'heard it on the grapevine' approach.
- Is innovative, creative and persistent in tracking down leads and making cold calls.

Presentation and selling

- Is a skilled and effective negotiator at all levels with a focus on the task at hand rather than on the long-term big picture.

- Achieving beyond-budget results is the primary driver of performance and is often linked into bonus or commission schemes.
- Makes use of basic multilevel selling and, in some cases, advanced multi-level selling.

Safety, health and environment (SHE)

- Understands the relevant requirements and standards and keeps up to date with changes in requirements relevant to own work area.
- Understands the interaction between use of products and the environment and the impact of products on the customer's environment.

Debt collection and credit risk management

- Is conscious of the ramifications of poor debt management on the bottom line.
- Will carry out a risk assessment before commencing new business, and monitors existing business for changes in financial stability.
- Extended trading terms often given automatically or used as a concession to be traded during negotiations.

Professional expertise

- Has genuine professional selling skills and broad business skills.
- Achieves primarily short- to medium-term, budget-based targets and goals through determination and a sound understanding of the marketplace, customers and competitors.
- Is adaptable to change, often gathering the credibility and respect of both customers and competitors. Customers are small, direct and major accounts.
- The appropriate organisational structure, culture or systems support are unlikely to be in place to sustain key account management or partnerships.

◆ Account manager competencies

Business effectiveness

- Understands the products and services of own business unit in detail, and company-wide products and services in general.
- Understands the relationship between the application and performance of these products and services, known customer requirements and the capability of the organisation to meet those requirements. This includes being aware of sales plans/actions/strategies of other business units in respect of their customers.
- Understands own company structures, departmental and functional inter-relationships, target customers/markets and competitors.

- Appreciates the position of own business unit within the relevant business or industry sectors, the general operating environment and overall economy.
- Contributes to strategy development through the collection of customer/ competitor and other general market information and trends, together with the input of ideas and recommendations.
- Has a good understanding of the consequences of own actions on business performance and their implications for other parts of the company.

Management effectiveness
- Prepares sales and action plans to meet objectives on key performance indicators as agreed with management and based on the business/marketing plans and agreed customer requirements.
- Understands company procedures and systems and their utilisation.
- Coordinates and networks the activities of other individuals and teams, utilising resources within the company, suppliers, customers and elsewhere, to ensure the fulfilment of both business objectives and customer requirements.
- May act as coach or mentor to less experienced staff or others in a non-sales environment via the transfer of knowledge and skills as appropriate.

Personal effectiveness
- Has a clear understanding of, and commitment to, the company vision and values, which is embodied in both actions and words.
- Employs effective interpersonal, negotiating, influencing and networking skills at all levels, internal and external to the organisation, gaining support and commitment from other company functions/departments and customers.
- Prevents conflict wherever possible and resolves conflict where necessary.
- Possesses the requisite verbal and written communication skills to make presentations within own areas of expertise at all levels of an organisation, be they technical or business issues.
- Is an effective team player, and can also act as coach or team leader as appropriate, ensuring objectives are clear and effectively communicated.
- Possession of the personal skills listed above allows the account manager to work under pressure, effectively prioritising issues and searching out and implementing solutions to customer problems.

Customer relationships and communication
- Establishes and develops relationships with major customers by understanding their short-, medium- and longer-term priorities, together with determining and then fulfilling their agreed requirements.

- Establishes effective internal communication of agreed customer requirements and associated action plans, working closely and effectively with all appropriate functions and departments to ensure successful implementation.
- Manages and is responsible for the customer/supplier relationship and the corresponding results opposite the key performance indicators in the short to medium term.
- Takes every opportunity to develop and strengthen the customer relationship by bringing together key personnel from appropriate levels within the customer/supplier organisations for the cross-fertilisation of ideas and mutual benefit.

New business

- Identifies new business opportunities, assessing their value to the organisation and the customer in terms of strategic fit, cost/benefits, potential risks and financial exposures.
- Recognises the opportunity for new or modified products and services and champions their development and introduction.

Presentation and selling

- Uses a diverse range of selling skills to persuade the customer at all appropriate levels (breadth and depth) of the product/service benefits offered.
- Negotiates and influences successfully to meet the needs and expectations of own organisation and of the customer.
- Applies multilevel selling techniques for major and key accounts.
- Utilises a sound understanding of the organisation's business/marketing plan, the competitor's pricing and general business strategy, and general market trends, in achieving agreed business objectives.

Safety, health and environment (SHE)

- Recognises that the understanding and communication of relevant SHE issues and procedures is an essential part of doing business.
- Has a general appreciation of regulatory requirements and company standards with specific and detailed knowledge of hazards and safety procedures opposite areas of own expertise.
- Ensures conformance to agreed SHE requirements, utilising informed judgment and effective evaluation techniques and drawing on all relevant resources internal and external to the organisation.
- Implements a 'prevention rather than cure' approach wherever possible.

Debt collection and financial risk assessment

- Accepts the accountability and responsibility for debt management and financial exposure opposite nominated customers.
- Continually determines and assesses the financial viability and stability of nominated customers and potential new accounts, enlisting assistance of credit, financial and other management expertise as appropriate.
- Works effectively in conjunction with management, credit and collection and other financial teams to minimise and monitor overdue payments, bad debts, excessive financial exposure, credit limits, stock levels.
- Manages the sensitive balance of minimising risk while maintaining the relationship.

Professional expertise

- Is recognised both internally and by the customers as a selling professional who utilises professional selling skills to achieve consistently the business goals and objectives while meeting customer requirements.
- Demonstrates a proven commitment to quality and the continuous improvement approach, with a high level of skill, initiative and enthusiasm.
- Operates within company and statutory standards and guidelines across a wide range of markets, customers, corporate functions, products, services, processes and personalities.
- Customers are predominantly small and major accounts.

◆ Key account manager competencies

Business effectiveness

- Has extensive knowledge of target industries and market sectors with a comprehensive understanding of key customers, their value chain, vision, objectives (short/medium/long term) and other issues of significance.
- Has a clear understanding of the business objectives.
- Manages intercompany relationships by working across departments, functions and other business units as they affect the nominated key customers, utilising well-developed negotiation, conflict resolution and team-based skills.
- Is seen as a coach, adviser and facilitator on competitor and customer strategy development.
- Is involved up and down the supply chain with suppliers and customers' customers, on behalf of own organisation and the customer, in joint benefits, special projects (technical and commercial), financial issues, product/service back specification.
- Has a specialist understanding of legal, legislative and commercial issues as they affect the target industries, markets and customers.

Management effectiveness

- Acts as a mentor and coach and provides training to less experienced account managers and other nominated members of own organisation, suppliers and customers.
- Contributes to the management of own work unit, be it self-directed or otherwise; for example, natural leader role, budgeting, people issues, resource allocation, skills development and conflict resolution.
- Prepares sales and customer plans/profiles for key customers as well as comprehensive analyses of target industries and market sectors.
- Can lead and/or be a part of special projects directly related to the target industries, market, customers, or otherwise. These could include product/service development, quality improvement, corrective action and investment projects.

Personal effectiveness

- Utilises a wide range of interpersonal, technical, administrative and networking skills to ensure that sales and customer strategy/action plans are effectively implemented for key and major accounts.
- Puts together and presents critical presentations at senior management levels (internal and external).
- Draws on the expertise of a wide range of resources, well-developed networks and personal relationships, internal and external to the organisation, to resolve major issues or develop major opportunities.
- In handling problems and opportunities, thinks outside current or conventional boundaries and develops creative and innovative solutions.

Customer relationships and communication

- Develops effective working relationships at senior site, division and national levels with key strategic accounts.
- Assists in the development and implementation of sales strategies across industries and products.
- Understands and can manage long-term selling cycles, seasonal trends, product/service life cycles and other controllable influences associated with a global working environment.
- Can work as part of a team or independently, exercising personal judgment in making decisions and managing the customer relationship.

New business

- Plays a major role in, or leads, significant market/product/service development projects.
- Can identify and follow through on opportunities at a strategic level.

- Utilises extensive business and interpersonal skills, together with a detailed knowledge of the marketing and sales strategy, competitor activity, customer strengths and weaknesses and general market conditions, to negotiate for major new business.

Presentation and selling

- Utilises multilevel selling to its fullest extent.
- Has fully developed professional selling skills and can influence and persuade senior management within key strategic accounts as well as own organisation.
- Carries out complex and major negotiations independently or as part of a team.

Safety, health and environment (SHE)

- Ensures compliance with statutory and company requirements and standards through effective communication and the mobilisation of appropriate resources.
- Identifies areas for improvement and recommends changes where necessary.
- Assists customers to understand the implications of relevant regulations and standards for their business.
- Anticipates movements in community standards and the impact they will have on the running of the business.

Debt collection and financial risk assessment

- Utilises preventative and predictive tools to anticipate where potential bad debt and financial exposure problems could lie.
- Proactively works with customers, developing, agreeing and implementing strategies and action plans, and networking the appropriate resources internal and external to work through financial difficulties.
- Initiates and assists in the development of win/win solutions to improve own organisation and customer's financial position and performance.

Professional expertise

- Has skills in account management and key account management that are recognised throughout all levels of the organisation.
- Has extensive knowledge of, and experience in, a wide range of industries, markets, products and commercial practices, and a broad understanding of individual character types and job roles.
- Has a high level of credibility at senior levels of customers' and own business units, based on proven performance and the development of specialist skills.
- Customers are predominantly key accounts.

◆ Partnering/alliance manager competencies

Business effectiveness

- Has a comprehensive understanding of the supply chain, including all external influences, and a sound understanding of competitors and their strategies.
- Has a full understanding of the internal relationships in the organisation's business units and functions, within customers and suppliers, and of the interrelationships between them, nationally and globally as appropriate.
- Has a high level of technical understanding of markets and is regarded as an expert within the partnership marketplace.
- Is consulted at all levels (breadth and depth) of the organisation and the customer/supplier partner on specific partnering/alliance issues and partnering/alliance relationships in general.

Management effectiveness

- Leads, manages and coaches the partnering/alliance teams and overall is responsible and accountable for the well-being of the relationship(s) in the short, medium and long term.
- Makes a significant contribution to the development of the marketing and business plans in respect of the partnership, and to the linkages and influences in other areas of strategy and general business activities.
- Makes a significant contribution to the organisation's broader strategy and vision.
- Has a role that also includes developing and implementing remedial plans, individually or within teams, in the event that the partnering/alliance relationships are at risk or other key strategic accounts need to be retrieved.
- As appropriate, takes a management and leadership role over people and teams that don't report directly.

Personal effectiveness

- Leads the process and significantly influences senior management within the organisation, customer and/or supplier partner in gaining their agreement to the partnering/alliance strategy and action plans.
- Communicates effectively at all levels and is widely consulted and respected on partnerships/alliances (principles and practice); also consulted in areas of general knowledge and experience by the business units/functions, customers and suppliers.
- Is regarded as a master troubleshooter and coordinator in areas of problem and conflict resolution on major and critical issues.

- Has the ability to mobilise and utilise a wide range of internal and external resources for the resolution of problems or the development of opportunities.
- Is a team player and a supporter of the team approach and its associated benefits; however, can also act independently as required.
- Is capable of managing, and effectively working within, complex and diverse team structures and is well versed in team dynamics.

Customer relations and communication
- Manages critical customer relationships of strategic long-term importance to the organisation, specifically strategic partnerships and alliances; is fully accountable and responsible for the development and management of those relationships.
- With the skills of a high-level troubleshooter, is able to turn a crisis (internal or external) into an opportunity, to build or rebuild the relationship to the mutual benefit of both parties.
- Is able to extend this influence and skill to other relationships, acting in a third-party consulting capacity.

New business
- Identifies long-term strategic opportunities at a national/international level.
- Contributes to new business strategies at a corporate level within or external to the partnership.

Presentation and selling
- Operates within a complex environment from a structural, geographical, product, customer/supplier profile, relationships perspective.
- Uses fully developed professional selling and broad business skills to persuade, influence, coach and facilitate at all levels from senior management to the shop floor.
- Exercises appropriate judgment, independently or as part of a team, on a wide range of business issues.
- Possesses a clear understanding of the short/medium/long-term objectives and strategies of the partnership and how to achieve them.

Safety, health and environment (SHE)
- Advises on the strategic, business, customer and community implications of movements in standards and requirements of the relevant business units.
- Works closely with senior customer management in the development of SHE strategies.

Debt collection and financial risk assessment

- Works with customer/supplier partners to develop financial strategies to protect and add value to the financial interests of customer, company and supplier.

Professional expertise

- Has a broad understanding of target industries and markets and their international environment and relates strategic issues for the partnership/alliance to that understanding.
- Is sensitive to company and customer/supplier cultures, organisation issues and market pressures, and is able to integrate them at a strategic level.
- Possesses high-level negotiation and leadership skills, and industry/market specialist skills that are recognised at a national/international level.
- Has a high level of trust, respect and credibility within the partnering/alliance relationship and throughout the supply chain.
- Understands what is required to develop and sustain partnerships and has the capability, skills and commitment to make them work.

MANAGING THE ASSETS

> For more and more companies today, the ratio of market value to asset value is 2:1, 4:1, even 10:1. The difference between asset value and book value is not goodwill, it is core competence—people-embodied skills.[2]

To put the importance of the partnering/alliance manager's role in perspective, think about the role of the typical business manager or general manager. Their fundamental role is the effective management and deployment of assets, be they in the broadest sense hardware, software or service-based. This may involve millions, tens of millions or even hundreds of millions of dollars. They are empowered quite legitimately by the organisation to manage these assets to achieve certain outcomes.

I put it to you that the partnering/alliance manager's role of managing critical and strategic long-term relationships is no less important. Figure 9.1 links the traditional view of return on assets and the partnering/alliance view. In this case, it is the relationship that is the asset. For example, take your prospective partner(s) and in general terms note down the effect of the relationship on your business in terms of current and, more importantly, future returns. This is ultimately the real test of asset management. From this perspective the traditional

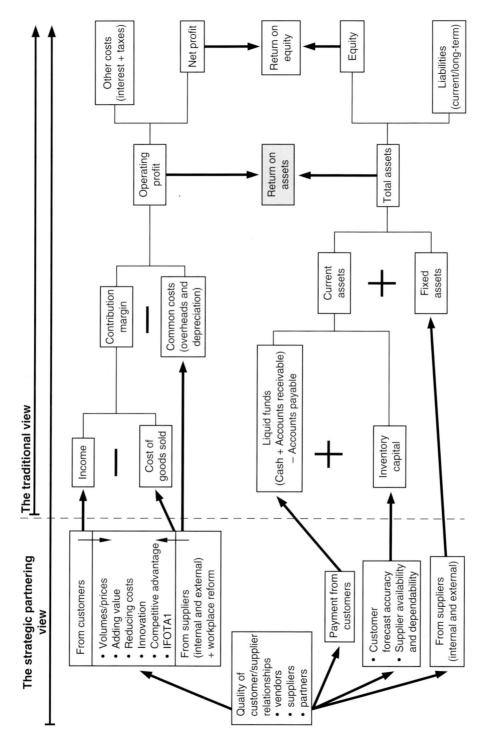

Fig. 9.1 *Managing the return on assets: traditional versus strategic partnering (IFOTA1 = In Full On Time to A1 specification)*

view of asset management is secondary to the management of the real drivers of the business, which are people, and the quality and understanding of your customer/supplier relationships. These are the prime assets to be managed. They will determine whether the traditional asset-based indicators can be met.

What I have said here in no way diminishes the importance of good manufacturing and manufacturing strategy. In fact, quite the opposite. The link between manufacturing strategy and relationship management is critical. Think about a world turned upside down where you have individuals close to, or at, the coalface responsible for relationship asset management and no business managers or general managers in the traditional sense. These new relationship/partnership managers will be linked into the various functions to ensure the traditional returns on investment are met, with the key performance indicators being based on the quality and management of relationships. This will put a completely new focus on partnership outcomes and the link to return on assets and investment.

WHERE DO PARTNERING/ALLIANCE MANAGERS COME FROM?

Partnering/alliance managers will come from all kinds of weird, wonderful and unexpected places. Internal, organically grown and developed partnering managers will have a strong knowledge of the company culture, products, services and supply-chain complexities. However, their development will take time, particularly in a culture that needs to change and where inbreeding of poor attitudes and low performance levels is to be avoided. If the organisation's culture, strategies and structure need changing, an experienced outsider may be just the solution required. The mid-ground is to seed external experienced partnering managers into the organisation with part of their role being the coaching and development of partnership managers internally.

A further option is a task-force approach. This involves an external project team of professional partnering coaches and managers deployed into the organisation with the mission of setting up the environment, systems and processes whereby the partnering relationships and managers are identified and developed. The task force would also assist with the partnering strategy development, cultural change and implementation of the required team-based structure.

Internal or external to your organisation, partnering/alliance managers will include:

- Young, capable, intelligent and ambitious individuals on the way up. Depending on their skills and expertise, they will probably want to move on after a reasonable period to a senior management role.

- Older and experienced senior managers with the right qualities and attitudes, wanting something different.
- Commercially experienced individuals from other areas of the business—again with the right qualities and attitudes—who are challenged and excited by such an opportunity and see it as a long-term career role.
- Tom Peters' 'weirdos' who are eager to push beyond the traditional limits, think 'outside the square' and take risks.

A generic position description is shown in Figure 9.2. Use this in conjunction with the partnering/alliance manager competencies (pages 377–9) as a starting point in your own organisation to select and develop your partnering champions of the future. In the right environment these innovators, paradigm shifters and pioneers will be invaluable.

HOW ARE PARTNERING/ALLIANCE MANAGERS COACHED AND DEVELOPED?

Unless you already have change agents in your organisation who are capable of, and committed to, nurturing future partnering/alliance managers, you will need to look externally. It may be that you already have experienced partnering/alliance managers on board—possibly under a different name—who can be a coach as well as a player, but this is unlikely.

First, be clear about who you are looking for—the trainer or the trainee. Does either exist internally or externally? We now have a better understanding of the competencies required of the partnering/alliance manager. What about the competencies of the trainer?

If there is no one suitable within the organisation, there is no other alternative but to bring in a partnering/alliance coach to start the process of upskilling and/or recruiting. Then, with the support of senior management, create the environment in which these individuals can develop and flourish. This will not be a one-step process and will cause you, quite rightly, to revisit the core vision, strategies and internal structures to determine whether the principle and application of strategic partnering is sustainable or appropriate. Look back at Figure 1.4 to determine what level and quality of customer/supplier relationships exist. Identify the gap and the solutions to bridge it. The quality of your current customer/supplier relationships and the individuals managing them will dictate what needs to be done, by whom and when.

(Draft)
Partnering/Alliance Manager
Position Description

Job purpose

To lead and manage the overall well-being and continuous improvement of the Strategic Partnership, in the short, medium and long term.

Responsibilities

- Manages the complexity and the networks of the partnership.
- Partnering Team Leader.
- Management and leadership role over people and teams that don't report directly.
- In conjunction with the partnering leadership and management teams is responsible for the development, implementation and delivery of short-, medium- and long-term strategies.
- Owns the Partnering Charter and the associated KPI Balanced Scorecard and Performance Scorecard and is responsible for delivering.
- Reports periodic progress to senior management.
- Member of the senior management steering group.
- Master troubleshooter and problem solver.
- Is innovative and creative in developing technical and non-technical opportunities.
- Maintains and develops internal and external relationships of importance to the partnership.
- Works with coaches, counterparts, other teams and individuals for continuous improvement.
- Persuader, influencer, coach, facilitator at all levels from senior management to shop floor.
- Develops and delivers against partnership key performance indicators (KPIs).
- Understands and improves partner organisational alignment opposite culture, strategy, structure, process and people.
- Leads the development of new ideas, incentive programs, training and development programs.

continues

Fig. 9.2 *Partnering/alliance manager: position description*

- Builds trust, respect and credibility within the relationship's key shareholders.
- Links the immediate partnering relationship to the 'bigger picture' and the achievement of longer-term organisational and partnering/alliancing goals.
- Balances company and partnership loyalties.
- 'Champion of the cause' in taking strategic partnering/alliancing from rough concept to practical application.
- Takes calculated and educated risks to achieve continuous and breakthrough improvements.

Skills:

- Communications
- Interpersonal
- Leadership and management
- Coaching
- Problem solving
- Total quality
- Specific technical skills as required

- Strategic influencing
- Strategic thinking
- Innovation/creativity skills
- Team building
- Conflict resolution
- Financial
- Project management

Fig. 9.2 *Partnering/alliance manager: position description (continued)*

WHERE TO FROM HERE?

There is no doubting the significance of successful partnerships and alliances for individuals, teams, organisations and supply chains. Strategic partnering/alliancing will generate superior value for customer and supplier organisations, as well as value for employees and other community and environmental stakeholders. We have entered a new era of globalisation and economic recovery where the strength and quality of relationships between customers and suppliers will be the key to sustained growth and prosperity. Strategic partnering and alliance relationships will provide the paradigm shift required to sustain this competitive advantage. In monitoring and challenging your progress, always remember three things:

- **Keep the faith**—in the principles and the fundamental underlying values upon which the relationship is based.
- **Stay focused**—on the purpose, the value propositions, the shared vision and common goals/objectives for the relationship and their achievement.

■ **Enjoy the journey**—and have some fun in learning and developing as individuals, teams and organisations.

REFERENCES

1. Peter Drucker, in an article by T. George Harris, 'The post-capitalist executive: an interview with Peter Drucker', *Harvard Business Review*, May–June 1993, pp.114–24.
2. Gary Hamel & C.K. Prahalad, *Competing for the Future*, Harvard Business School Press, 1994, p.255.

CASE STUDIES IN STRATEGIC PARTNERING AND ALLIANCING

CASE STUDY 1

ALCOA and HONEYWELL

A global alliance from humble beginnings

How is it that a global strategic alliance between the world's leading producer of aluminium and alumina and the world's leading automation controls company can be born from humble beginnings in Perth, Western Australia? This is the case with Alcoa and Honeywell with worldwide sales in 2002 of US$20.3 billion and US$22.3 billion respectively. As with many partnering and alliance relationships the answer lies in the three critical elements of passion, experience and risk taking in the hands of key influencers and champions who are prepared to take a vision and turn it into reality, and who have a passionate belief that partnering and alliance relationships are critical to their organisations' future.

Alcoa mines bauxite and processes this base raw material through to alumina, then aluminium and on to a variety of finished products. Honeywell enables the Alcoa refining plants to run safely, effectively and efficiently via their control systems. Honeywell's products, systems and services are involved in critical areas of plant performance and control and have a high impact on the profitability and competitiveness of Alcoa's business. It involves development and installation of hardware, software, safety management systems, field devices, other support services and training. Engineering and advanced control applications also have a strong influence in improving plant yields and efficiencies.

The relationship began in 1977 with Honeywell selling the first process control (systems) equipment and instrumentation to the Alcoa alumina refining plant at Pinjarra, Western Australia. The years between 1977 and 1991 were typical of many customer/supplier relationships: adversarial, non-exclusive, showing little trust, with limited multilevel contacts developed and little understanding of each other's needs and objectives. Unit prices and volumes based on a short-term financial focus led to a large but under-utilised installed base of equipment. This far from ideal situation resulted in adverse effects on efficiency, productivity and flexibility of plant operations and on the relationship itself.

This environment of simple ongoing purchase and maintenance prevailed for many years. As is typical of so many alliances the relationship reached a crisis point in 1991. Both organisations realised that something fundamental had to change for the relationship to improve and for genuine competitive advantage for both parties to be sustained. The fact that both Honeywell and Alcoa had developed a quality internal training culture created an opportunity for joint activity. At this point the two companies started a formal relationship development process leading to the formation of a cross-organisational Australian 'Lead Team' in 1992. Its role was to identify and address key issues impacting the relationship and to challenge the norms, comfort zones and prevailing paradigms within and between their organisations. More than 160 issues were brainstormed and used via teams as the basis for improvement. It was also the Lead Team's role to progress the local alliance to a global relationship in the common interests of both parties. Kim Mitchell, the then General Manager—Engineering & Construction, Alcoa World Alumina, initiated the alliance and Lead Team concept. Then the commitment, active support and participation of a team of key players were needed to drive the process from rough concept to practical application.

Part of the lead team's analysis included each organisation's perception of the other's approach to the relationship. The conclusions were enlightening. A summary is given in Table 1.

In many cases the perceptions of the two organisations were directly related in a circular cause and effect (chicken and egg) manner.

The period 1992–95 was then a proofing period whereby problems were solved and trust and credibility gained by delivering agreed products and services and other requirements **In Full On Time to A1 S**pecification. This was a typical phase 1 of the partnership development curve (see Fig. 1.9) and the basis for further innovation and new initiatives. In 1995, a Heads of Agreement was signed defining the mechanism and deliverables to extend the relationship to a Global Alliance.

The formalisation of the alliance process occurred with the signing of a Global Alliance Agreement for process control products and services on 4 April 1997 at the Head Quarters of Honeywell's Industrial Automation & Control division in Phoenix, Arizona. As an indication of the degree of commitment to the alliance, the agreement was signed by Bob Slagle, then President of Alcoa World Alumina, and Michael Bonsignore, then Chairman and CEO of Honeywell Inc. The agreement makes Honeywell the supplier of choice for process

Alcoa perceptions of Honeywell	Honeywell perceptions of Alcoa
■ Honeywell driven by hardware sales	■ Purchase hardware only—no application services required
■ Product support poor	■ Same problems from multiple sources within Alcoa
■ Little knowledge of alumina process applications	■ Difficult to communicate with the right people
■ Good products	■ Alcoa expected project services to be provided beyond financial allowance of orders
■ Support services lack value for money	■ Honeywell not involved in project definition, installation, etc.
■ Market the product without knowing the need	■ Unaware of sensitive issues (e.g. IR)
■ Alcoa spends time teaching Honeywell engineers	■ No escalation (issue resolution) path within Alcoa

Table 1

control equipment and instrumentation and sets the strategic direction for the future of the relationship. Founded on quality principles and joint teaming it is not just a price agreement but a document defining the nature of the relationship and the behaviours required. For ease of use, accessibility and openness the agreement has been put on the Alcoa and Honeywell intranets.

This is a really important step for Alcoa. We are a global business, a commodity business, so the ability to produce at the lowest possible cost is terribly important. Therefore, the idea of spreading the best things you do as fast as you can everywhere in your system, is the road to success in our business. This alliance takes us to a new level, and for me, is a measure of the future success of the business that we have been able to put this together.

Bob Slagle, President of Alcoa World Alumina

Some of the implications for the future with this agreement include:

- increased production
- reduced (total) costs
- reduced capital outlay
- reduced site inventories

The theme of the alliance is taking the best of what is done around the world and applying it to the relationship globally. The driving force behind working more closely with Honeywell was the need for a total value approach on a global scale as opposed to unit price on a regional or site basis. Clive Nielsen, Procurement Manager Alcoa World Alumina Australia, the commercial lead for the Alcoa/Honeywell relationship, outlines the need for change: 'Alcoa had made a very significant investment and commitment in Honeywell's process control equipment and it was recognised by both partners that this equipment could be used to much greater effect, providing added value through "smarter" control applications. The benefits and experience gained from the Australian experience could then be leveraged to operations elsewhere in the world.'

What emerged from this period (1992–97) was an increasing interdependence, which continues to grow. Honeywell saw Alcoa as a critically important customer and Alcoa saw process automation of critical strategic importance to its future success.

Both in the spirit and the practice of 'no contract no term' relationships there was no formal agreement in place between 1991 and 1997 despite very significant commitment in time and effort by many people from both companies. Even the Global Agreement entered into in 1997 is open-ended with annual reviews. In that context it operates in the true spirit of no contract, no term.

Typical of world-class alliance and partnering relationships a formal team structure is a core component of the Alcoa/Honeywell alliance. A Global Lead Team (Board) sets the overall strategic direction. Regional Strategy and Planning or Lead Teams provide input to the business plan and coordinate activities in each geographical area while specific project and support teams provide the functional delivery of products and services on a site or regional basis. Task teams are also formed to undertake specific actions or address a defined problem. They are usually disbanded upon completion of the task. A formal but simple escalation process has been agreed and is used very effectively in the timely resolution of issues and problems, big or small. It is based on the principle of empowerment and resolving issues at the lowest possible level. If not resolved within agreed timeframes, the issue is escalated to the next level. The type, number and degree of escalation are part of the measures of the success of the alliance.

To ensure the required commitment and support from senior management all teams are sponsored by executives of both companies or by the next level of team. They have independent charters with associated deliverables and Key Performance Indicators (KPIs) that are integrated back up to the Global Lead Team (Board) Mission. As an example, the Global Lead Team Mission adopted when the Heads of Agreement was signed in 1995 is detailed in Figure C1.1.

Alliance Managers from both organisations were appointed to manage the ever-increasing complexity of the relationship. These individuals, in conjunction with the Global and Regional Teams, were responsible for the development and well being of the alliance in the short, medium and long term. In this case these three individuals—Bob Turner (Senior Engineering Consultant Electrical—Alcoa), Clive Nielsen (Alcoa) and John Taylor (Honeywell)—led the process from the start. Residing in Perth, Western Australia, their role became global. As you could imagine, effective communication was a key issue covering time zones as well as distance. Apart from extensive travel and face to face communication, effective use of IT was and still is critical at all

---

Alcoa—Honeywell Alliance
GLOBAL LEAD TEAM MISSION

Achieve breakthrough performance against Alcoa and Honeywell IAC business objectives by strategically applying process control and information technologies.

BY

- Common global commercial processes and procedures
- Continuous improvement in the provision and application of process control and information products and services in accordance with common Alcoa World Alumina and Chemicals standards
- Ongoing reduction of operating costs and improvement of the profitability and quality performance of both businesses
- An infrastructure and environment that encourages open and effective exchange of information
- Aggressive support of technical interchange and effective supply chains for goods and services in the Americas

Fig. C1.1 *Alcoa/Honeywell Global Lead Team Mission*

levels. Email, video conferencing, conference call facilities, the Internet, Intranets and mobile phones are all utilised.

As an indication of a paradigm shift that occurred, most issues are resolved on the basis of what is best for the 'joint business', not the individual organisations. For example, a two-way open book arrangement exists whereby pricing and terms are determined by taking the view that the alliance is a 'joint business' providing the process control products and service needs to Alcoa's alumina refining industry. As an indication of the openness and trust that exists, all prices are shown on both Alcoa and Honeywell Intranets.

> *This sharing of information is done in a way that adds value to the joint business or it isn't done at all.*
>
> *Clive Nielsen*

Senior management commitment is seen as essential and extends to CEO/President levels. There is also regular contact between global management and regional executives. However, no greater statement of support and commitment could be given than that made by the Chairman and CEO of Honeywell Inc., Michael Bonsignore, at the signing of the Global Agreement in Phoenix on 4 April 1997 when he said:

> *This is a big deal for me personally, and a wonderful day for our two companies. It has been a vision for Honeywell to establish alliances with major clients like yourselves. The reason I feel so good about it, is how well-aligned we are philosophically and operationally, and how compatible the cultures of the two organisations are. I am very proud of the people in this room. What management owes you is our commitment to build this relationship from the bottom up, to have clear and unambiguous channels of communication and responsiveness.*

As an indication of the breadth and depth of communications and the networks established there is frequent cross-training, site visits and interaction at all technical, commercial and operational levels. This is the routine way of conducting the business. In terms of direct skills development and specific support for the partnering process a formal deployment/training program was implemented, covering the alliance agreement principles, relationship concepts and operational mechanisms. Other initiatives in communicating the nature and importance of the alliance have been a joint newsletter, internal video news presentations and joint internal and external seminar/workshop presentations.

Understanding the team process and facilitation skills has been a particular focus for both partners, all within a quality framework. In fact the relationship is founded on quality principles and is dependent on total quality management (TQM) being an integral part of both corporate cultures, to the extent that each partner has been significantly involved in structural change processes of the other. For example, there is extensive cross-membership within problem solving teams and workshops. Alcoa has provided significant input into the Honeywell teams that are currently reviewing new product developments, including how Honeywell licenses its software.

Teamwork has allowed for the high level of trust to be developed, enabling open and honest communication on any issue no matter how sensitive. This level of trust and openness raised many eyebrows in the more conservative and traditional ranks of both organisations. The traditional sales/purchasing single point of contact approach was removed. Sales and procurement staff, although still important, play a supportive role. There was a joint Alcoa/Honeywell selection panel for interviews for new Honeywell staff involved with the alliance. There was a broad multilevel teaming structure approach where engineers were at the main interface. For example, eight Honeywell engineers worked full time on the Alcoa Pinjarra site servicing the process control project engineering needs of three refineries in Western Australia.

As with all world-class alliances, innovation is the key and the lifeblood of the relationship. Continuous improvement is written into all team charters and, while there is as yet no formalised benchmarking process, the benchmarking done so far and other anecdotal evidence suggests that this alliance is at the forefront of equivalent relationships. For example, there is joint involvement in each other's planning and forecasting processes, and this continues to lead to the development of new products and the realisation of a number of value adding opportunities.

In the case of Alcoa and Honeywell, innovation first involves the new and creative business structure and mode of operating that has developed between the two organisations and, second, provides leading edge technology and solutions. For the most part, the products and services delivered are world class, and where they are not, the alliance is committed to make them so. As the alliance expands so does the ever-increasing variety of products and services delivered.

There is a difference here from traditional relationships. It is the alliance that is spoken about, the relationship, the joint business plan, the joint approach, 'us' as opposed to 'us and them'. A seamless relationship is being developed based on a shared vision and common goals. It is not just a case of doing what has always been done but now doing it a whole lot better. A mind-set shift has occurred. Fundamental changes have taken place—changes that were once thought impossible but that have now changed the way business is done and is thought about between the two organisations.

The following metrics were developed to measure the business and operational performance of the alliance in Australia:

- Safety—zero TRIR and environmental exceedences for Honeywell/Alcoa relative to process systems implementation, operation and support
- Customer satisfaction—multiple surveys for specific activities at each location
- Value of the alliance to Alcoa World Alumina & Chemicals business (AWAC) total incremental audited annual benefits from installed applications
- Value of the alliance to Honeywell—business volume and PBIT (Profit Before Interest and Tax) against forecast

These key performance indicators were the responsibility of the lead teams to manage. It must also be understood they were continuously refined to reflect the true nature and performance of the relationship.

A joint business plan has already been developed and is revised on a rolling six-month time scale. The primary measures are small in number— only four in fact: TRIR and environmental exceedences; customer satisfaction rating; total incremental annual audited benefits; business volume and PBIT against plan. The tendency to have too many indicators was resisted to facilitate timely measurement of the results. This will generate a greater focus on increased returns for each alliance partner. For example, in the key measure of safety and environmental exceedences, zero exceedences and incidents was achieved in 1999, that is, a score of 5 out of 5. To measure customer satisfaction, thirty-two surveys were conducted in 1999. They were specific to a particular activity or project as opposed to general 'across the board' surveys. An overall satisfaction score for on site services of 92 per cent (versus a target of 85 per cent) of 4 and 5 scores on a 5 point scale was achieved.

The benefits over and above the existing performance levels have been considerable:

1. reduction in the (total) cost of doing business, e.g. bar-coded automated parts management on a global scale, electronic trading;
2. significant plant operating improvements, e.g. the development of a common suite of process applications for alumina refining;

3. major production benefits;
4. improved project implementation performance;
5. jointly funded developments;
6. increased profile for the mining and minerals business of both organisations.

The future of the alliance was summed up in 1999 by John Taylor, Honeywell's Global Alliance Manager.

> *The longer-term view of this alliance is a seamless relationship with Honeywell as a 'co-producer' in Alcoa's alumina business. The ultimate in teamwork, 'one team, one goal'. The common goals are for Honeywell's process control leadership to provide a sustainable competitive advantage for Alcoa and to expand the scope of the alliance into other business units of Alcoa and Honeywell. This will critically depend on the ability to deploy current and future achievements globally.*

The alliance structure was reviewed and in 1999 a 'white paper' was jointly developed to re-engineer the relationship, to position it as a joint business, a virtual joint venture, with greater direct management by the ultimate users of the joint business, the plant operations. This was seen as a logical development of the alliance, with Alcoa and Honeywell as 'co-producers' in Alcoa's alumina business. The emphasis is on the business drivers of both companies, with Alcoa and Honeywell sharing a portion of the benefits as well as some of the pain in the lean times. In addition, the risk of technology change is transferred to Honeywell, who, as owners of the technology road map, are seen as the logical choice to manage that risk.

The new business model, called QUASAR (QUality Automation Solutions in Alumina Refining), is based on a long-term (10 year) service arrangement (co-sourcing not out-sourcing), which includes the provision of infrastructure, resources and technical refresh. A portion of the payment is linked to achievement of key results—a balanced scorecard. The equipment and services are provided on a fee-for-use basis that provides positive cash flow by removing the need for large amounts of capital to be invested up front, and the usually lengthy time for investment payback (especially with infrastructure). Historically, benefits from process control tend to tail off after a period of time for many reasons, including plant changes and redeployment of personnel. Under the new model, fees are also linked to the sustaining and improvement of benefits from process control over time. While, at US$300 million, QUASAR represents the largest ever single contract for Honeywell's process automation business, it is also a huge commitment for Alcoa, as well as Honeywell. It requires significant re-assignment of resources involving literally hundreds of people, including stakeholders in the businesses, boards of directors and additional staffing. It is spread across six countries, embraces four languages, many cultural differences and the full spectrum of technical and commercial disciplines. The program was—and still is—subject to rigorous analysis and justification, which has facilitated its progression through critical corporate approval processes. Initial successes of the program in Spain and Jamaica are supporting the initial vision of the benefits of working as true co-producers: 'one team one goal'.

The development of a relationship such as this is never without its obstacles. The key is to be honest and mature enough to admit their existence and get on with the solutions. The following obstacles have been recognised and are being tackled.

- internal barriers and politics; territory protection; baggage—people's past issues either with the alliance partner or with other organisations, making it hard for them to accept the changing relationship;
- fear of being open and, therefore, being taken advantage of;
- inflexible positions by traditional custodians of the corporate rules.
- lack of formal structures and financial mechanisms to handle a global 'business' alliance;
- changes in culture and management direction as a result of mergers and acquisitions;
- global changes—political and business—resulting in extreme, short-term business perspectives;
- centralisation of authority, micro-management, control and less regional autonomy;
- high rate of turnover of executives (lack of long-term sponsorship);
- issues relating to reaction of joint venture partners to QUASAR.

The first two obstacles have been addressed through the teaming process and the extensive use of quality tools to resolve issues. For example, a serious customer dissatisfaction issue resulting from misalignment of regional boundaries (territories) was resolved in 1999. The solution was jointly agreed by implementing a structure for business from the region involved, to be managed through a dedicated Honeywell team based in Houston. The result provided a single point of accountability for performance measurement of the alliance and a more efficient means of managing the complex supply chain issues prevalent in that region. Inflexible positions were, and are, being resolved by executive intervention.

Challenges introduced by mergers and acquisitions have been mitigated, to a significant extent, by stability of sponsorship—particularly within Alcoa—and a stable 'core team' who have worked to maintain focus and defend the alliance culture in the face of significant cultural opposition. Also, the possible effects of impending mergers and acquisitions have been looked at through a series of risk analyses to ensure a positive view and future for the alliance is maintained.

Global business changes have increased the need to analyse the benefits and demonstrate the value of the alliance, and cost management programs and initiatives have been stepped up as at least one of the enablers to achieve this. Shifts to centralise business structure and authority have reinforced the importance of executive sponsorship. Sponsors at this level have fostered an understanding of the benefits of long-term relationships and are able to exert considerable influence at the 'centres of corporate control'.

Both Alcoa and Honeywell have established joint ventures in certain locations or certain operational areas and, while the complexity of dealing with both companies' many locations, somewhat differing focus areas and diverse views on the Alcoa/Honeywell relationship is difficult enough, the added task of bringing these joint venture partners to the required level of understanding and acceptance has been an enormous challenge.

Further solutions to achieve the most effective global business structures and financial mechanisms are still being developed. None of the obstacles above is unique to Alcoa and Honeywell, however, and many organisations would do well to learn from their experience. Of critical importance is the resilience of this (and any relationship) to survive these obstacles. That the Alcoa–Honeywell relationship has overcome so much difficulty is testament to the commitment of the alliance teams, to their passion, willingness to take risks and determination to keep pushing what is right: alliance interest, not self-interest.

While not a focus to date, the development of multi-way alliances with other suppliers and customers is being investigated to maximise the potential from an extended supply chain involvement, delivering greater synergy and added value.

Without question this alliance will continue to have a strong influence and positive impact on both organisations outside of the immediate relationship itself. It is viewed as a benchmark for relationship development by both organisations. However, no one is suggesting the road ahead is easy. Understanding the 'what and how' of the innovation and attitude-change required to take the relationship to the next level is proving both challenging and rewarding.

The fascinating fact that both Alcoa and Honeywell are over 100 years old should not be lost on the inquiring mind. Arie de Gues in the July 1997 *Harvard Business Review* talks at length about 'living companies' whose lives span more than 100 years, far beyond the 20–30 year term of the average corporation. Gues states:

> *. . . living companies are very good at 'management for change'. Living, learning companies stand a better chance of surviving and evolving in a world they do not control. The high levels of tolerance inside the living organisation create the space for more innovation and learning.*

In the case of Alcoa and Honeywell, I think there is a direct correlation between the lifespan and success of living corporations and the quality and sustainability of the customer/supplier relationships they seek to establish. Both organisations are undergoing continual change with major mergers and acquisitions adding to the diversity of business units, as well as building on existing principal core focus areas. This provides a dynamic backdrop that will test the mettle of this alliance.

Genuine alliance relationships take years, not months, to develop. The Alcoa/Honeywell alliance is testimony to the courage and persistence of key individuals and the high level performance of teams. It is also about leadership at the executive level taking a visionary, long-term approach in supporting and actively participating in a relationship they see as a fundamental measure of their organisation's future success. This is a global relationship producing world-class results and getting better.

TRANSFIELD SERVICES and WORLEY

A tale of two companies

What was originally an analysis of two separate companies, Transfield Services and Worley, turned into an inspiring tale of two special organisations doing, jointly and separately, some extraordinary things in the area of strategic partnering and alliancing. This is part of their story.

The objective of this case study is twofold. First, to explore some of those independent and interdependent relationships, the best practices as well as the lessons learnt and, second, to understand how these and other relationships interconnect as part of the broader, developing Transfield Services and Worley 'community' approach to relationship management that directly supports their long-term visions and corporate strategies.

Both companies are at the leading edge of alliance implementation and have been doing business together in varying forms and on various projects for over 20 years. As with many free spirited and visionary companies their early relationship development was more an evolutionary process than a structured strategy. While there has been a planned and strategic approach to relationship development in recent years, the entrepreneurial and collaborative spirit continues to guide their progress.

Prior to becoming a publicly listed company in May 2001, Transfield Services operations were part of the privately owned Transfield Group of companies. Transfield Services business activities have seen a dramatic expansion in revenues, profitability and client base since their inception in 1993. Transfield Services is now one of the leading providers of operations and maintenance services to private and public sector organisations in Australia, New Zealand and South-East Asia. With revenues expanding to $846 million in 2002, profitable and sustainable growth has been, and continues to be, based on a highly successful, strategic and long-term approach to relationship management, underpinned by a clear and focused partnering and alliance philosophy. With over 5500 direct and 6000 subcontractor employees and $3 billion of work in hand across 11 industry sectors, Transfield Services has secured operations and maintenance contracts through to 2030.[1] Transfield Services has become a significant service provider and is now listed on the ASX 200.

Worley is an Australian based, global design and project services company. Formed as a private company in the early 1970s and having gone public in November 2002, Worley has become a leading provider of professional services to the energy, resource and complex process industries, such as oil and gas, refining, petrochemicals and chemicals, minerals and metals, power and water, and industrial and infrastructure developments. Employing over 4000 people, Worley's aggregated revenue has grown from $214 million in 2000 to a forecast $495 million in 2003, of which 28 per cent is planned to come from alliance based, long-term relationships.[2]

While the numbers and the growth rates are impressive they tell only part of the story. The real success story lies in the people, the processes and the strategies behind them. Both companies work in market sectors traditionally noted for their adversarial, hard-nosed and often combative and tribal approach to contractors, suppliers and customers alike. Where relationships are often typified by detailed, one-sided, fixed price, lump sum, win/lose, prescriptive contracts based on paper-thin margins, there is little or no risk sharing and even less trust. These contracts are most times won via a lowest bid tender or traditional competitive bid process. Often the contractor's price reflects potential loopholes in the contract and the possibility of exploiting variations at a later point in time. Given these non-aligned and often conflicting goals and objectives, it is no surprise that failure to meet quality, cost and schedule requirements, as specified in the contract, often results in a punitive backlash or litigation between supplier and customer, contractor and client.

Transfield Services and Worley have turned their backs on this traditional approach and embraced, wherever appropriate or possible, strategic partnerships and alliances. On occasions this has meant walking away from potential business, since any self-interest based, short-term gain would have been at the expense of long-term mutual benefit. On other occasions this has meant both companies deliberately and strategically joining forces, leveraging core competencies and collaborating. An interdependent web is evolving, an interactive 'community' of cooperative relationships and people that is robust, long lasting, flexible, responsive and very difficult to compete with. Strategy, process and people lie at the heart of the Transfield Services and Worley story, which involves both separate and integrated approaches. They are potential collaborators and competitors as well as independents pursuing separate projects and ongoing business relationships. It is the successful management of this 'fuzziness' and complexity that distinguishes these two companies from others in the market place.

The commitment to alliancing comes right from the top of the organisation. 'Alliance-based revenue derived from long-term relationships with leaders of the resource and energy sectors is the foundation of the Worley business,' says John Schubert, Chairman of Worley. John Grill, Worley CEO and co-founder of the company, agrees: 'Alliances are a key part of our approach to business and our successful strategy. Because we structure our alliances on an open book, cost only basis, and then share the risks and rewards with our clients, Worley is totally committed to making sure the alliance works. Our joint ventures are founded on mutual respect and recognition of each partner's skills. We joint venture with partners whose skills complement ours to ensure a project's success.' This view is echoed by Peter Watson, Managing Director of Transfield Services: 'Our ability to deliver win–win, integrated service solutions through strategic alliances with our clients has been key to our business success.'

Transfield Services have over 70 relationships across Australia, New Zealand and South-East Asia, with alliancing and partnering the most common approach taken. The key features being:

- agreement terms and conditions designed to create a partnership with the alignment of each party's objectives;
- total transparency of financial and commercial arrangements with revenue based on cost reimbursement and profit at risk;
- Key Performance Indicators (KPIs) jointly developed with the client to ensure Transfield Services' activities are aligned with the client's desired outcomes.

Worley, since the early 1990s, has championed an alliance based approach that has allowed their clients to focus on core competencies, delivered more efficient project delivery and aligned alliance partners' interests by sharing in risks and rewards.

While there are many Transfield Services and Worley relationships that could be explored, three will be discussed in some detail to show the nature of their separate and integrated strategies. They are:

1. Transfield Services/Mobil Oil Alliance
2. Transfield Worley Woodside Integrated Services Alliance
3. The BHP Steel/Transfield Services Alliance

As a general observation, the Transfield Service and Worley relationships are a mix of project based, life of asset, evergreen and term based relationships spread across many different market sectors. There is also a mix of public and private sector involvement. As well as the three relationships mentioned above other relationships will be drawn on as general examples.

THE TRANSFIELD SERVICES/MOBIL OIL ALLIANCE

The Transfield Services/Mobil relationship at the Altona oil refinery on the outskirts of Melbourne commenced in 1991 with Transfield Services winning, via tender, a standard maintenance contract. The relationship evolved to a point where in 1995 a formal alliance arrangement was entered into. 1991 to 1995 was a proofing period for both organisations. Cultural change was occurring within Mobil with a move from a control and compliance environment with high levels of supervision and skills demarcation to an environment of teams, multiskilling, empowerment and clear accountabilities at all levels. In the early days contractors were seen as both a cost to the business and a threat to employment security. All decisions were made by Mobil, contractors were not allowed to use the Mobil canteen, they had separate work areas and were not allowed into the Mobil workshops. Not an easy position to move forward from!

Moving from a point of low trust and poor communication to the current level of high trust, openness and transparency has taken almost 10 years. A change of Mobil management also took place in 1995 and an alliance agreement was struck with the focus on improving safety, reducing total costs and increasing asset utilisation. This was based on the Transfield Services performance to that point and the future willingness and capability of Transfield Services to deliver the necessary improvements in safety and plant reliability to secure Mobil's future in a highly competitive and cost focused market place. Since that time senior management from both organisations have driven the alliance process forward with the participation and commitment from the operating levels. Today the alliance relationship covers total structural, mechanical, civil, instrumentation and electrical maintenance and minor project works for the Altona Refinery. It is an evergreen relationship with remuneration based on a management fee plus reimbursable costs, with all profit based on performance and linked directly to Mobil's own scorecard of performance indicators.

Below are just some of the practices and initiatives currently in place that make this relationship different and special.

- Cleverly, Transfield Services has developed a supporting cluster or alliance network with other high impact suppliers to Mobil, involving critical product/service applications. They are:
  —Worley, since 1999 a full alliance partner in the delivery of engineering services, drawings and process and instrumentation diagrams

—Saunders for tank management and design
—Contract Resources for industrial cleaning of tanks, steam lines and the like
—Tomballe for insulation and asbestos removal

- The goals and objectives for each of these organisations have been aligned with Transfield Services and their performance linked with Transfield Services' performance in the overall delivery of the Mobil alliance goals and objectives.

- Transfield Services are represented on every committee on the site, including the Union Consultative Committee and the Occupational Health and Safety Committee. In that regard the union relationship is rightly seen as critical and inextricably linked to the well being of the alliance. In the words of Mike Van Der Linden, former Maintenance Resources Manager for Mobil, 'The Enterprise Bargaining Agreement is in fact seen as an alliance in itself'. The operators are seeking a yearly review with union member remuneration linked to the alliance KPIs. If the business fails, they fail. This is a remarkable cultural shift.

- There is now a far greater social interaction between Mobil and Transfield Services people, with a greater degree of friendship developed. The old attitude and approach of 'them and us' has turned into 'we'. 'It's simply a far more enjoyable place to work. People are learning, performing and enjoying themselves', says Transfield Services' Colin Chadwick.

- Safety, Health and Environment (SHE) training programs have been developed by Transfield Services staff for the Mobil operators with joint SHE 'toolbox meetings' being held every month.

- Joint Mobil/Transfield Services training is held for site related activities.

- A number of Transfield Services and Worley employees are in permanent roles that are traditionally exclusive to client control.

- There is now in place a formal alliance agreement, which is 'evergreen', based on ongoing and outstanding performance opposite agreed Key Performance Indicators (KPIs). These KPIs then form the basis of the risk/reward model whereby Transfield Services profits are put at risk to gain or to lose, above or below agreed targets based on the actual performance achieved. The KPIs are a weighted mix of Mobil Business KPIs and specific alliance KPIs. The Mobil Business KPIs include Total Reportable Injuries and Reportable Incidents, Soloman Mechanical Availability and Altona refinery's total business expense and profitability. The specific alliance KPIs include the Soloman Maintenance Index, Continuous Improvement initiatives, Productivity Improvements, % Maintenance work scheduled and project delivery performance. Transfield Services' performance is formally reviewed every six months and should there be a failure to deliver to requirements over three consecutive reviews (i.e. over an 18 month period) the agreement and the relationship can be terminated. With the focus on win/win, mutually beneficial outcomes it is, however, the intention of all parties involved not to let this happen but rather for the alliance to go from strength to strength.

■ To ensure that the relationship remains world class, a joint Mobil/Transfield Services benchmarking team was formed to understand best practices and assist with their implementation as appropriate to the Altona refinery. The team went on a number of benchmarking tours to the United States and other alliance sites. They are also linked directly into the Transfield Worley Services Best Practice forum, which will be discussed later in the case study.

■ A customer satisfaction survey is completed every six months with a 360-degree feedback process in place.

■ There is a team based structure in operation to manage the relationship. The Alliance Leadership Team (ALT) is made up of two senior managers from both partners. Meeting on a quarterly basis the ALT has the responsibility of looking at future growth and expansion opportunities. The Site Operations Team (SOT) is again a cross-organisational, multiskilled team responsible for the ongoing well being of the relationship at the operating level. The SOT meets monthly and reports directly to the ALT.

■ The alliance is now used as a training ground for developing alliance champions and practitioners for other relationships and has become a virtual on-site university for relationship management and operational practices.

■ Since the alliance agreement was struck in 1995, the Alliance has achieved a dramatic reduction in the numbers of suppliers to the refinery under their management, from 160 to 30. This has reduced total systems costs and significantly streamlined communications.

■ Applying a 'best for client approach', Transfield Services utilises and deploys competitors' services where they, as a diversified, multi-divisional organisation, cannot deliver the best overall value for money for a particular job.

■ Both organisations now take advantage of aggregate purchasing of a wide range of products and services and this has produced significant benefits and savings for both organisations.

■ As a manifestation of trust, Transfield Services personnel place Mobil work orders on Transfield Services and their subcontractors, and then arrange both the Transfield Services invoice and subsequent payment on behalf of Mobil. To ensure appropriate checks and balances to this open book approach there is an independent review every six months.

- There is a process in place called 'A Better Way' which captures innovative ideas from all levels. The best ideas are implemented and the benefits measured. For example, $300 000 was saved by taking up the idea from a Transfield Services employee to lease scaffolding and manage it internally rather than use an external scaffold supplier.
- As an example of sharing synergies all apprentices come through Transfield Services, rather than the two organisations as occurred in the past. Both organisations agree they will receive better training and greater job security.
- To ensure seamless and effective communication, Mobil and Transfield Services use the same Lotus Notes software, with Mobil providing all the PCs in the Transfield Services office.

These work practices and initiatives have not happened overnight but over a period of nearly 10 years. In the words of Joseph Sadatmehr, COO Transfield Services, 'You have to work at it every day, just like a marriage. It is also invaluable when all parties are on board with the principles and the practices.' Joseph is passionate about the four Transfield Services values and how they relate not only to the Mobil Alliance but all Transfield Services relationships. 'Firstly it's about satisfying my customers, internal and external to the organisation. This is about integrity and doing what you said you would do. Secondly, people are our greatest asset. It is their understanding of the customers' requirements together with their commitment and skill that adds value for the customer. Thirdly, as management we must provide a safe environment in which our greatest assets, that is our people, can work and learn effectively. Nothing but zero defects is acceptable and this means getting it right the first time. If we get the first three values right, then profits will follow.'

The acquisition of Mobil by Exxon in 2000 created a reflection point for the alliance. Exxon did not have an alliance of this kind operating anywhere in the world and as an organisation they were generally unfamiliar with the alliancing approach. This required a resetting of the relationship and developing a common understanding of the alliance goals, mindsets, guiding principles and practices that applied. Exxon brought a new set of eyes and systems/procedural requirements, which initially tested the open, transparent and trust based relationship that had developed over the previous eight years. As Dave Robinson, the Transfield Services Alliance Manager, says, 'In hindsight it was good for the alliance as it forced both Transfield Services and Mobil to review formally what had been achieved, implement new rigour and structure to the alliance and understand what were the next improvement opportunities.'

The results have been remarkable. Since 1996 Mechanical Availability has risen from 93 per cent to over 99 per cent while maintenance costs have been reduced by over 50 per cent. There is a high level of integration via cross-organisational teams with shared accountability. Openness, honesty and applying the 'best person for the job' philosophy have produced an outstanding world-class safety record and very low employee turnover. The Serious Injury Frequency Rate (SIFR), serious injuries per million hours worked, has gone from 25.9 in 1994 to zero in 2002, a world-class achievement. There has been only one day lost due to industrial disputation in six years, the best record in the region. Many hundreds of thousands of dollars have been saved via The Better Way program. The refinery won successive Maintenance Excellence Awards for their achievements.

In 1995 the Soloman Survey, the acknowledged benchmark for the Asia Pacific region, rated the Altona refinery performance at eighth position out of the nine Australian refineries. 'A virtual basket case', as one Mobil Manager commented. By the end of 1998 the Altona refinery was rated at number one in Australia and second out of fifty-six refineries in the Asia Pacific region. That record has since been maintained, a remarkable achievement.

There have been many innovations that have produced significant benefits, in particular ones relating to procedures. Welding and other work now takes place on 'live' units, via effective by-pass, safety and operating procedures. In the past the units would be shut down with the resultant loss of production.

Both Transfield Services and Mobil agree the success to date would not have been achieved in a standard contractual arrangement. There is one particular story told to me that typifies the level of trust built between the alliance partners and the commitment jointly made to the long term. Mobil was going through a tough time with external market prices and profitability was poor. Transfield Services had just earned themselves a good profit for outstanding maintenance performance, a large portion of which they gave back to Mobil on the basis that true alliance partners gainshare and painshare together. Transfield Services took the approach that this was the wrong time and sent the wrong message to 'bank the bonus'. There is no question that this level of support and commitment will be reciprocated in the long term.

The alliance 'performance bar' is being continuously raised and the challenge for the alliance partners in the future is what will be the next set of breakthroughs, unreasonable goals from which the new paradigm will appear. The Altona relationship is sharing best practices with other key and connected petrochemical facilities in the region, which in turn is generating benefits back to Mobil and the alliance partners. It is no surprise that the Mobil/Transfield Services Alliance has become the benchmark for learning and transformation and a role model for others to follow.

TRANSFIELD WORLEY SERVICES (JV)/WOODSIDE ALLIANCE (TWW ALLIANCE)

Located on the North West Shelf of Western Australia over 1670 kilometres from Perth, at a cost of $12 billion, the North West Shelf Gas Venture is the largest and one of the most important natural resource developments undertaken in Australia. Based on the huge North Rankin and Goodwyn gas fields and the Cossack, Wanaea and Hermes oil fields the venture supplies gas to domestic and industrial markets in Western Australia, LNG for export to Japan, and LPG condensate and crude oil to global markets. The project is a consortium of six companies: Woodside Energy, BHP, BP, Chevron, MIMI and Shell, with Woodside the project operator.

In late 1994, Woodside, as the operator of the North West Shelf Venture, proposed to the five joint venture participants that it should move to a single integrated services arrangement on a partnering model. This was quite different from the more traditional, competitive bid process that had been operating since production began in the mid 1980s. In July 1995, the 50/50 Transfield Worley (TW) Joint Venture, now called Transfield Worley Services, was awarded a contract by Woodside Energy for integrated services at its onshore gas treatment plant in Karratha and its three offshore facilities, North Rankin A, Goodwyn A and Cossack Pioneer. The performance based contract and relationship, with an annual turnover for Transfield Worley Services of approximately $75 million, is for the life of the assets, estimated at around 25 years. The scope of alliance activities includes project management and project execution, engineering services, procurement, construction, commissioning, maintenance and shutdowns.

This original contract started life as cost plus profit and corporate overhead as a percentage of turnover. In the spirit and practice of sharing both risk and reward the alliance has reached the point where Transfield Worley Services' profit gain or loss, above or below agreed targets, is now directly linked to Alliance Scorecards for each of the onshore and offshore operations. These Key Performance Indicator (KPI) Scorecards are then rolled up into a single alliance Performance Scorecard. In the words of Paul Harrison, the Transfield Worley Services Alliance Manager, 'the alliance KPIs are aimed at providing consistent measurement, enabling trending and benchmarking as well as achieving the strategic goals of the alliance through aligning business drivers of the alliance partners'.

Transfield Worley Services see the alliance broken into **four key areas** of people, relationships, systems and results.[3] The alliance has recognised that in the services and solutions business, sustainable competitive advantage comes from the capacity of its **people** to lead, challenge and create. This is manifested in the performance of the alliance exceeding customer expectations. Regarding people development in the field of project management competency, four alliance personnel have achieved the highest level of accreditation, that of Master Project Director. A recent assessment by the Australian Institute of Project Management (AIPM) indicated that a high level of project management skill is present within the alliance. The alliance has also shown a significant commitment to the development of its graduate engineers and is the only Australasian organisation recognised and accredited by the Institute of Chemical Engineers of Australia (IchemE). Paul Harrison comments, 'With the appropriate people empowered to make the correct decisions at the right time, the alliance can address the key business driver of reducing direct and indirect business costs. Cost effective projects can be delivered, workflow processes and deliverables rationalised, re-work minimised and all non-added value activities eliminated.'

The alliance also understands that **relationships** are vital. Significant co-location and people exchange has taken place to ensure a better understanding of joint roles and objectives of the alliance and has clearly improved the relationship between Transfield Worley Services and Woodside. In 2001 the number of Woodside personnel actually working within the alliance went from three to ten. 'People integration has been two way, with people both moving into (Woodside) Technical Services from the alliance, and moving to the alliance from Technical Services', says Clive Saxton, Offshore Technical Service Manager. A reorganisation of the alliance interface has also delivered improvements in relationships. This involved the centralising of business support services and a team focus through the establishment of Front End, Engineering Projects, Implementation and Simple Technical Changes teams. Due to the significant use of piping, flanges and fittings and their critical application, the alliance entered into a Strategic Partnering Agreement with One Steel in January 2001. In entering this collaborative, long-term arrangement the alliance has reduced material, transaction and inspection costs, reduced inventory holding costs, improved supply and shortened lead times and improved quality.

'The alliance relies on its **systems** to convert the talent of its people into value for the customer. Systems are key to sustaining the culture of continuous improvement' (John Black, Quality Team Leader). As an indication of the focus that has been placed on systems improvement and the delivery of quality services, Transfield Worley achieved the ISO 9001:2000 standard for Quality Management System Requirements. The 'Enterprise Management System' that underpins the entire alliance operation was a joint alliance/Worley

Corporate initiative. It is an open and transparent management information system that allows for effective planning and accurate tracking of progress (quality, cost, schedule, safety and environmental) of individual projects, top level performance drivers and business objectives. This achievement was recognised as leading edge in the deployment of Management Systems by reaching a finalist position in the West Australian Engineering Business Excellence Awards in September 2001. Transfield Worley Services also shared success with Woodside and a Worley Subsidiary, I&E Systems, in receiving an Institution of Engineers Australia engineering excellence award for the North Rankin Fire and Gas Upgrade project.

The **results** to date have been extraordinary, as indicated by 'best practice' achievements on the 2002 Performance Scorecard. The 2002 TWW alliance Performance Scorecard is shown below. The overall alliance performance fell just short of outstanding for the 12 month period to December 2002 and represents a clear indication of the high value being delivered for Woodside.

Some of the specific highlights have been in the project delivery area. The TWW Alliance over the last six years has expended over 1500 man-years on projects, the majority of which have been less than $100 000. The skills, capabilities and experience gained on the smaller projects benefits the work done on the larger projects, such as the recently completed Echo Yodel project. The Transfield Worley Services scope of the $205 million project was $35 million and included design, procurement, fabrication and installation of brownfield modifications on the Goodwyn A offshore platform. It represented some real challenges:

- implementation of one of the most significant upgrades ever on a live Woodside offshore platform
- implementation of new technology
- aggressive work schedule
- managing the project in an integrated team environment

The project was completed three months ahead of the 24 month schedule, on budget and reinforced the flexibility, innovation, quality and integrity standards of the alliance. The success of the alliance is acknowledged by Jakob Sedic, the TW Echo Yodel Project Manager: 'Using the alliance provided significant advantages as team members were familiar with the design of Goodwyn A and the intricacies of modifying a live platform; both essential ingredients in successful brownfields projects'. It is the alliance approach and its continuity of service that has enabled Transfield Worley Services to deliver the best value for money for Woodside.

KPI description	Score	Performance score			
		0% Poor	50% Satisfactory	75% Good	100% Outstanding
KPI 1 Duty of Care					
1.1 HSE:* TRCF	8.21	>13.8	<13.8	<11.7	<10.3
1.2 HSE: Improvement Plan Progress	100%	<90%	>90%	>95%	>98%
1.3 HSE: Safety Leadership	96%	<80%	>80%	>85%	>90%
1.4 Integrity: Audit Close Out Rate	0%	>10%	<10%	<7.5%	<5%
1.5 Integrity: Closeout Rate of Projects	−10%	>20%	<20%	<10%	<5%
KPI 2 Delivery					
2.1 Quarterly Targets (Qtr 1, 2002 Score)	92%	<80%	>80%	>85%	>90%
2.2 Schedule Performance	−1%	>20%	<20%	<10%	<5%
2.3 Incentivisation	2.06	<1.00	>1.00	>1.60	>2.00
KPI 3 Cost Management					
3.1 Fees	100%	>105%	<105%	<100%	<95%
3.2 Annual Savings Register/ Suggestion Scheme	$0.83M	<$0.25M	>$0.25M	>$0.5M	>$0.75M
3.3 Cost Performance	−8%	>10%	<10%	<0%	<−10%
KPI 4 Alliance Health					
4.1 Customer Feedback	4.06	<3.5	>3.5	>4.0	>4.5
4.2 Annual Alliance Improvement Plan	99%	<85%	>85%	>90%	>95%
4.3 Unplanned Personnel Turnover	5%	>15%	<15%	<10%	<5%
OVERALL ALLIANCE SCORE	93.13%	<50%	<75%	<100%	=100%

*Health, Safety and Environment

Fig. C2.1 *TWW Alliance Performance Scorecard: 2002*

Innovation and establishing best practice is also a hallmark of the alliance. The alliance Performance Scorecard is used both to measure and drive performance improvement and to reward personnel. Business support and supply chain management technology have been developed within the alliance. A project risk identification and treatment database is in place and an Internet site for offshore material handling equipment has been developed. An estimating norms database with over 20 000 items has been developed regarding project estimating for brownfield upstream and downstream oil and gas facilities. These are just some of the innovation and best practice initiatives.

The alliance has not always been smooth sailing, however. Apart from the cultural changes required of Woodside in becoming an alliance partner, maintaining a committed, empowered, responsive and customer focused culture in a remote location under these circumstances has not been easy for Transfield Worley Services. As often happens in large relationships like this, Woodside's unexpected increase in work scope and project activities at the beginning of the alliance initially caused significant growing pains for Transfield Worley Services and the workforce went from 120, through the expected peak of 200 to over 800 people in less than two years. Partly because of this initial rapid growth, systems and procedures development suffered and this led to a lack of control over individual projects.

There was a reflection point in late 1997, two and a half years into the relationship, when both Transfield Worley Services and Woodside sat down to seriously review progress to date. While both qualitative and quantitative evidence suggested that improvements had been made over and above the existing arrangement, an absence of good base line data and inadequate management systems made it difficult to quantify the extent of the improvement. The alliance partners set up a two year process of management information systems (MIS) development and a proofing of project performance. Several benchmarking trips were also made over the next two years to Aberdeen in Scotland, a major hub for the North Sea oil and gas operations, and other sites around Australia.

This MIS has proved so effective and successful that Transfield Worley Services is currently rolling similar systems out to other Transfield and Worley business units. This will ultimately provide a single information system across the companies that will allow for a broader sharing of support and operating costs and thereby produce direct cost savings. 'Real difficulties occurred in the early days because of a lack of good base line data to track performance against. It is critical for any project and relationship such as this to have a clear starting point. What we have now is at the leading edge of information systems and the right people with the right attitudes are in place' (Iain Ross, Worley Alliance Director and former TWW Alliance Manager).

There was a period after the contract was awarded in 1995 when Transfield Worley Services and Woodside fell back into the traditional 'client/contractor' relationship and 'please the client mode', where commitments were made that were not achievable. Learning to challenge your partner and say 'No' when this is the correct response and then finding alternative solutions is an important quality of good alliance partners. 'Being able to respectfully yet effectively challenge each other and what we do, to find better ways and better solutions is critical for our joint future,' states Mark Warren, former Transfield Worley Services Team Leader for Business Services.

To understand why this alliance is going to be sustainably successful for the life of the asset, it is worthwhile visiting two of the underlying Transfield Worley/Woodside alliance principles. The first is **trust**: the relationship between Woodside and Transfield Worley Services is conducted with openness, cooperation engendering the development of mutual trust and confidence. The second is **institutionalisation**: the philosophy and values of the alliance relationship must become enduring and part of Woodside's and Transfield Worley Services' fabric, making them robust to changes of management and personnel. These two principles, in particular, manifest themselves in the strategy, the practices, the attitudes and behaviours deployed in this relationship.

The future for the TWW Alliance is summed up by Iain Ross, Alliance Director: 'The business objectives of Transfield Worley Services are aligned with Woodside's through our contract, our KPIs and through the methods by which we motivate and reward our people. In essence, our organisation is driven to assist Woodside in delivering against its business targets. Our focus over the following years will be to help drive down operational expenditure and maximise the value of capital expenditure while maintaining and/or improving "health safety and environment" (HSE), technical integrity and the availability of the North West Shelf facilities.'

Frank Thistlethwaite, WEL Engineering Services Manager, also reinforces commitment to both the alliance and the future:[3]

The Transfield Worley Woodside Alliance contract is all about working together to achieve common goals and objectives. The alliance principles appear straightforward but in reality are challenges. The TWW Alliance contracting style is leading edge, requiring all parties to adopt new ways of working based on shared values, mutual trust and achieving bottom line improvements to Woodside's business. This takes time and commitment from all parties.

Transfield Worley Services has all the technical processes, systems and people to deliver against Woodside's requirements. Focus is now shifting from engineering and project management to improving the broader value to the business. Supporting this evolution of the contract is an established, conscious improvement culture. I am confident that the alliance is now in a position to further 'raise the bar' and become a benchmark within our industry.

This relationship has all the hallmarks of a breakthrough alliance. The right teams and people are in place, working with outstanding information systems, and completely focused on uncovering value adding opportunities and cost improvements for long-term mutual benefit. Add to this an eight-year investment in time, people and learning and you have a 'standout' alliance relationship.

BHP STEEL ALLIANCE

The BHP Steel/Transfield Services relationship is typical of two mature and professional organisations following a classic development path for high performing strategic alliances. The Port Kembla Steelworks is the largest integrated steelworks in Australia, with over $2 billion per annum in turnover, producing in excess of 5 million tonnes per year of steel products in slab, hot rolled coil, plate and packaging products for the domestic and export markets. In early 2001 BHP Steel conducted a review of their maintenance activities in order to identify ways to achieve an overall improvement in the maintenance performance, including a quantum improvement in maintenance downtime, plant and equipment reliability, and cost improvement. It was agreed that the existing 'in house' approach to maintenance would not deliver long-term sustainability for the Port Kembla Steelworks, particularly given the critical nature and timing of their de-merger from BHP Billiton in July 2002 and the heightened importance of delivering on equity market expectations. The bottom line was that BHP Steel was under real pressure to deliver excellence in every aspect of their business.

After much internal deliberation it was agreed that a collaborative, open book, transparent, performance based, long-term, strategic alliance approach, with an external partner as a change agent, would best deliver on what were clear and compelling value propositions. The value propositions being:

- Increase opportunity for BHP Steel to focus on its core competencies.
- Achieve significant improvements in plant reliability and plant availability.
- Deliver a quantum reduction in maintenance costs.
- Gain access to best practices and supporting processes, systems and technologies.
- Improve career development opportunities for staff who were to be transferred to the new alliance partner.
- Use the strategic alliance as a transformation vehicle for internal cultural and operational change.

Following an intensive evaluation process Transfield Services were selected as the preferred partner and commenced work in December 2001, for what was to become Australia's largest strategic alliance relationship, with in excess of $100 million per annum turnover. This required over 400 people to be recruited into Transfield Services to support the alliance, 300 of whom had previously been BHP Steel employees. The cultural change required has been significant.

The five year alliance term with an annual five year roll-over option, is based solely on the performance achieved against a jointly agreed Performance Scorecard of risk/reward based Key Performance Indicators. Transfield Services remuneration or profit is put at risk to gain or to lose, above or below expectations based on performance against five weighted criteria: safety (15%), commercial performance (35%), reliability (25%), conversion costs (20%) and customer service (5%). This makes the alliance effectively an evergreen arrangement based on delivering demonstrable value to the customer and mutual benefit for the alliance partners and gives assurance to both Transfield Services and alliance employees that the relationship is sustaining itself for the long term. Typical of the governance processes associated with many alliances, an Alliance Management Team is responsible for the day-to-day activities of the alliance and reports to the Alliance Leadership Team, which meets quarterly.

As would be expected, Transfield Services successfully used the Mobil and Transfield Worley/Woodside alliances as benchmarks and role models for what could be achieved with BHP Steel. This involved site visits and discussions at all levels to generate an understanding of Transfield Services' willingness and capability for alliancing. The scope of the alliance is considerable and continues to expand based on the strong performance and demonstrable improvement from the baseline. The scope of service provided by the alliance to the Port Kembla Steelworks includes:

- mechanical, fabrication and electrical planned maintenance services
- detailed planning and execution of routine, planned and unplanned breakdown work
- detailed planning and management of major shutdowns
- management of major subcontractor works
- site-wide resource management and coordination of:
    —industrial cleaning services
    —mobile crane and equipment services
    —scaffold services
- facilities maintenance services to buildings, industrial buildings, industrial services (e.g. air conditioning, roofing and sheeting)
- health, safety and environment, human resources/industrial relations, finance and administration services to support the operation

The first twelve months of alliance operation, the transition period, have seen some extraordinary changes and exceptional results, a number of reality checks as to the work yet to be done, plus the opportunities still to be realised. Safety as measured by the combined LTIFR (Lost Time Injury Frequency Rate per 1 million hours worked) has improved 75 per cent from just under 4 to 0.95 after twelve months operation, production records were set in five of the eight plants in which the alliance operates and total costs for which the alliance is responsible were reduced by more than 20 per cent or $30 million per annum in the first twelve months. Improvement ideas generated by the workforce produced documented savings of over $1.5 million. All this was completed within an environment of intense change for both the alliance and BHP Steel generally.

So what did the alliance do that was different?

It could be argued that what has been achieved is a paradigm shift. What did the alliance team do to make such a difference? On safety there was a refocus on training and an improved compliance with existing safety systems, the implementation of a subcontractor safety management program and a greater compliance with incident reporting, investigation and rehabilitation procedures. On maintenance service delivery there were a number of new initiatives implemented.

- Small decentralised plant based teams were put in place and supported by a Transfield Services central resource team, second tier alliance partner organisations and selected subcontractors working as composite teams, sharing best practices, resources and expertise. This was quite different from the independent, plant based and siloed approach of the past.
- Plant based detailed planning of work orders, linked to site-wide resource scheduling and coordination improved resource utilisation. The average number of maintenance personnel per day involved with on-site contract and internal services has been reduced from 800 to 450, which has produced a significant cost saving for BHP Steel.
- Development of joint Alliance Business Plans and a supporting Key Performance Indicator (KPI) Performance Scorecard that is linked to gain/pain share, profit at risk remuneration and aligned opposite BHP Steel business drivers. This approach is driving a performance 'can do' focus.
- There has been joint management of issues, budgets and resources.
- There has been a rationalisation of subcontract service providers with an alignment to alliance type performance based terms and conditions.
- A shutdown and project team was created to focus on planning and execution of major shutdowns and projects.

- Transfield Services Quality Assurance and Customer Service Systems were implemented.
- An existing 'adversarial' and 'silo' based culture was changed to a 'can do with less' culture, in particular with the former BHP Steel personnel who transferred to Transfield Services.
- All work is now captured on work orders, enabling greater control and transparency.
- Introduction of 'Activity Based Budgeting' and cost estimating and control techniques enabled a more accurate delivery against target estimates.

A specific example of the success of the alliance was a major shutdown on the Hot Strip Mill. 'The $6M Hot Strip Mill shutdown that occurred in Feb 2003 is a clear example of the changes that have occurred and the commitment being shown at all levels of the alliance partners,' says Kiehl Quinn, Transfield Services Alliance Manager. He adds, 'The project came in one day earlier than schedule, on budget with no lost time injuries or medical treatment injuries. It was the most successful shutdown in BHP Steel's history.' One of the BHP Steel shutdown managers commented at an alliance review workshop that was being held at the time of the shutdown: 'I have just come from the morning shutdown meeting and the BHP Steel people tell me the shutdown is going much better than expected. They also told me "they feel safe", more so than any other shutdown. This is one of the key differences the alliance is having.'

There can be no higher accolade for the alliance and the shutdown project team than that from Lance Hockeridge, Vice President of BHP Steel, who said, 'I would like to pass on my thanks and congratulations to everyone involved in what has been a very successful campaign. The safety effort was first class, given no Lost Time Injuries or Medical Treatment Injuries, and was achieved with a degree of passion, planning and innovation that I do not think we have previously seen. Operationally, a very wide range of tasks was accomplished in a very timely and efficient manner. I was very impressed with the level of cooperation and integration with Transfield Services.'

The key learnings

As with every high performing alliance, when the limits are being pushed, it is not always smooth sailing and there are always lead and lag indicators, events, behaviours and practices that provide reflection points and opportunities for improvement. The first 12 to 18 months of the BHP Steel and Transfield Services Alliance are no different. Some of the more significant learnings have been:

- Get the benchmark, baseline data accurate and in place early. The existing BHP Steel systems made it difficult to understand the extent of the improvements that had been made.
- Ensure that the redirecting or consumption of $ savings into other activities is carefully managed, otherwise the cost benefits can be lost, redirected or misunderstood.
- Align budgets, reporting mechanisms and KPIs early in the process to avoid misperceptions.
- Ensure early and continuous education of all stakeholders at all levels in the principles and practice of alliancing/partnering to avoid the temptation to revert to 'old' practices and behaviours.
- Ensure early development of relevant and integrated business systems, for the control and reporting of budgets is critical.
- Recognise that a high level of communication and information sharing at all levels is required to ensure stronger and more open, transparent relationships. It took time for the alignment of alliance partner cultures and for some BHP Steel folk not to see the alliance as a threat but a benefit.

Overall the alliance partners now understand that this relationship is a journey that will take time and that people, skilled and committed, at all levels are the greatest asset. The challenge is to engage the broader work groups, in particular at the operating levels, to share a common understanding of the alliance principles and practice and how that manifests itself in their workplace, together with a mindset that is based on joint/shared accountabilities. Identifying, developing and empowering 'shop floor' alliance advocates/champions will be one of the greatest opportunities for the alliance.

The future

A joint business plan has been developed to manage the safety, relationship, operational, value adding and people aspects of the alliance. This will enable the alliance partners to deliver on their promises and continue with continuous and breakthrough improvement.

The alliance and associated improvements could not have come at a better time. There is currently a strong demand and higher market prices for BHP Steel products, and this is reflected in a strong financial and share price performance for BHP Steel. The first year of alliance operation has delivered results far better than would otherwise have been possible and delivered demonstrable value for BHP Steel over the alternatives. On the basis of the performance to date BHP Steel has approved the annual contract roll-over option thereby maintaining the five year alliance agreement term with an evergreen intent and mindset. In doing so the alliance partners have reached the first significant milestone in realising their vision of being 'successful alliance partners in delivering world-class equipment performance at optimal cost'.

AND THE LIST GOES ON!

Each of the three relationships discussed provides a valuable insight into how and why these relationships work and the superior benefits that can be gained. There are also many other individual relationships, alliances, joint ventures and partnerships that could be discussed in similar detail to demonstrate the level of implementation, learning and the degree of success of Worley and Transfield Services organisations, jointly and separately. For example, Transfield Services and Worley, through the Transfield Worley Services JV, share a strategic plan to develop integrated services contracts and alliances in the resource and energy sector that results in a major step change in operational performance and cost reduction. Five successful, long-term Transfield Worley Services integrated services alliances with Shell Todd Oil Services (NZ), New Zealand Refining Company, Mobil Adelaide, Mobil Altona and Woodside are evidence of this strategy in action. These integrated service arrangements have an extensive scope covering activities like design, and project services, maintenance and upgrades as well as reliability and integrity management. Transfield Services independent partnering and alliance relationships with Australian Rail Track Corporation (ARTC), the Transfield Telstra Facilities Management Alliance, NSW Police Service, ACT Housing, Mackay Sugar and Worley's independent relationships with BP Kwinana, Huntsman, Qenos, Worsley Alumina and WMC provide a growing list of collaborative and strategic relationships moving forward from different starting points and travelling at different rates of development.

The relationships discussed also give an understanding of the broader strategy that drives both the individual and the joint goals and objectives of Worley and Transfield Services. The bigger picture is how they interconnect both as complementors through their integrated service and alliance relationships and as a growing community of best practice, jointly learning and sharing for mutual benefit.

> *We must be understanding of and flexible to clients' needs. One of our strengths is we have learnt to adapt different relationship models to suit their expectations and relationship management knowledge and maturity.*
> *Joseph Sadatmehr, COO Transfield Services*

BENCHMARKING

Any experienced alliance manager will tell you that the most challenging aspects of running an alliance are demonstrating that the relationship is delivering sustainable value over the alternatives and benchmarking the alliance performance against best practice. Is accurate, relevant data readily available? Is it an 'apples for apples' comparison? How can this information be used for continuous and breakthrough improvement? These are questions that good alliance and partnering managers continuously concern themselves with.

Transfield Worley Services has established a Business Excellence Network, a 'virtual business community' of best practice and improvement. The network was initiated in March 2001 with a Best Practice Forum, and the original vision was to create a forum working with existing partners to benchmark and share best practice between contracts. As well as the annual Best Practice Forum, an interactive website has been developed with the growing alliance and integrated service contract network, to communicate and share best practice. Seven primary initiatives have been identified and developed, and the associated best practices are being implemented across the network alliance partners. These benchmarking/best practice initiatives include safety, technical integrity, small capital projects, shutdown risk management, productivity estimating norms, tank cleaning strategies and technology, and resource management. A steering group comprising alliance partners also meets quarterly to track and drive progress and formally recognise outstanding achievements.

This best practice model is in itself at the leading edge of relationship management best practice. Through the Business Excellence Network Transfield Worley Services provide the synergy, administration and network access but the network members themselves take ownership and drive the initiatives forward. These initiatives will then be self-funding for the network through benefits gained and the intellectual property developed will be shared between the members, thereby delivering superior value for all involved.

In the words of Peter Meurs, CEO of Transfield Worley Services, 'We must keep developing, learning, sharing and institutionalising best practice. When a company has the opportunity to work with blue chip clients to capture and implement best practices over its own learnings, business performance improvement is significantly improved.' Peter Meurs adds further, 'The future lies in sharing best practices and the integration of services throughout the broad Worley and Transfield Services business network. Leveraging core competencies and skills, and working together across this collaborative community will generate not only profitable growth and sustainable competitive advantage but provide a positive legacy of broader business, social and environmental benefits.'

SUMMARY

The power of reference and referral in the successful implementation of the alliance, integrated service and collaborative relationship management strategy is generating profitable growth and competitive advantage for Transfield Services and Worley, jointly and separately. Their progress and achievements have been extraordinary by any measure. Through humble beginnings with the Mobil (Altona) experience Transfield Services now provide integrated service solutions to six of the nine oil refineries across Australia and New Zealand, with new opportunities continuing to materialise. Their revenue from services has doubled to over $800 million in five years to 2002, with their Earnings Before Interest and Tax (EBIT) increasing by a factor of three for the same period. Building on the Woodside experience, Worley's alliance and integrated services contracts are forecast to contribute approximately 28 per cent of aggregated revenue in 2003.

Their existing and successful partnerships and alliances have given Transfield Services and Worley entry into whole new industries and market sectors. For example, Worley is now making inroads into the New Zealand dairy industry, utilising its design and project management skills. In March 2003, Transfield Services formed a long-term, strategic alliance with Mackay Sugar, the first of its kind for the Australian Sugar Industry. Estimated to earn revenues of $200 million over the first five year term, Transfield Services will maintain Mackay Sugar's four sugar mills, more than 800 kilometres of rail track, over 80 locomotives and all cane bins as well as operate the rail activities. From this base, the opportunities to make further inroads into the sugar industry are enormous.

Typical of learning organisations, Transfield Services and Worley have invested significantly in people as their number one asset. Their partnering and alliance success is not based on the investment of money. Rather, their success is based on the investment in time, people and attitude. A truly integrated partnering and alliance strategy could take 5–10 years to consolidate. It will be based around people, strong interpersonal relationships and clear values, and will almost always require a change in people's behaviour and mindset. One of the real strengths of both companies is their ability to attract and develop high performing partnering and alliance managers—key influencers, leaders and passionate champions who are ultimately responsible for the success of their relationships. Both Joseph Sadatmehr and Peter Meurs agree: 'Effective succession planning of these key people is the key to success for alliances and partnerships. There is a succession plan in place for every one of our alliance managers.' Peter Meurs adds further: 'We are constantly looking for and developing these key people. On occasions we will employ them where there is no immediate position on the basis that this is about the long term.'

Turning confrontation into cooperation and competition into collaboration, although common sense, is anything but easy. It is not about technology in the first instance either. Technology is the enabler. It is about attitudes and cultural change. The irony is that when you get the people and attitudes right over time these relationships are then able to take extreme advantage of technology and make the most effective and profitable use of funds. That is their competitive advantage. Peter Meurs talks about the step change that has occurred in systems development and implementation: 'Eight years ago it took two years to develop the systems to effectively manage these alliances. Today they are established and working in three months.'

To ensure there is alignment between strategy development and implementation, interactive workshop programs have been developed. 'Everyone in the organisation will be involved in the programs. It is one of the key vehicles by which we are generating the cultural change and developing the attitudes needed to sustain our long-term partnering and alliance strategy. The opportunity is also provided to share knowledge and learning across the organisation,' says Michael Craner, Training and Development Manager, Transfield Services. 'We have the leadership with the knowledge and vision to succeed but it critically requires the operating levels of the organisations to be informed, involved and committed. We can't do it without each other.'

With over 70 per cent of their business currently in joint ventures and alliances, and revenue growth rates over 30 per cent per annum over the last five years, Worley's early 1990s' goal of becoming Australia's peerless engineering services business through these vehicles has been realised. One of the initiatives was the successful development of an alliance hub at Spotswood in Melbourne, Victoria, in 1998. Alliance based, cross-organisational, cross-functional, multiskilled teams have been developed around a single location in Spotswood. These high performance teams service three alliance partners in the surrounding area: the Transfield/Mobil alliance at the Altona refinery, and the alliances with Qenos and Huntsman at their large, nearby petrochemical complexes. Cost efficiencies have been another benefit of the Spotswood alliance hub. As Russell Staley, Worley Director and initiator of the original concept, says, 'The provision of low cost overheads well below those of a conventional CBD engineering practice, spread across a number of relationships, and a location close to the facilities being serviced, illustrates the underlying strategy of cooperation.' He adds, 'We have a vision with Transfield Services for the future of integrated services in Australia, that is, to have a low-cost multi-centre alliance office in every major industrial centre.' An alliance hub has now been developed in Townsville, Queensland, to provide engineering services to three geographically remote WMC Fertilizer sites at Phosphate Hill (ammonium phosphate fertilisers), Mt Isa (sulphuric acid) and Townsville Port (storage and shipping facilities).[4] Other alliance hubs are also in place at Kwinana in Western Australia and in New Zealand.

Their own joint venture has not in any way precluded Worley and Transfield Services from developing other independent joint ventures, networks and consortia relationships. For example, Worley also has 10 other joint ventures, some of which are with organisations that would be competitors to either company in other parts of the market place, including a joint venture with ABB to deliver a full range of engineering services with Esso in Australia. TIGA is a joint venture between Worley and Fluor Daniel, performing the detailed engineering design and procurement for Phillips on the massive Bayu-Udan project in the Timor Sea.

On the flip side, Source Personnel, a Transfield Worley Services joint venture, has been established for the provision of labour hire. Also, encouraged by the Transfield Worley Woodside success, the two companies have jointly secured a $100 million alliance agreement with BOC gases to engineer, procure and construct air separation plants and other process plants for BOC in Australia. Transfield Worley Services have a 50/50 joint venture to grow their businesses in New Zealand.

This is but a part of the complex Transfield Services and Worley relationship matrix, a balancing act that requires continuous communication, strong management and great vision. I have seen and worked with many companies over the past 20 years in the area of partnerships and alliances and few have been able to deliver an integrated corporate alliance strategy with the success that Worley and Transfield Services have achieved.

If you think this is just a bunch of former tough guys running a mutual admiration society and no longer able to handle the hard-nosed, hard money world of traditional contracting, you would be sadly mistaken. In talking to the Transfield Services and Worley folk in researching this case study two observations became clear. First, the alliance partners were tough on themselves. Their search for excellence, for continuous and breakthrough improvement is uncompromising, unconditional and non-negotiable. Second, the partners are tough on each other—360 degree feedback, openness and transparency, combined with an insatiable desire for improvement, creates an environment where each organisation openly, fairly and respectfully challenges the other. I was reminded of a quote from Robert Porter Lynch:[5] 'Creativity is given birth by people in a perpetual state of enlightened dissatisfaction'. The people

I spoke to at all levels were hungry for improvement and continually searching for the next steps. They were dissatisfied with their current state on the basis that the future state was both more compelling and more rewarding.

John Grill, Worley CEO, talks about the importance of alliances and partnerships for the future success of the business in the following terms: 'One of the greatest disasters for this company would be to have a relationship fail. On the flip side, one of the real measures of alliance success is when the client goes overseas and they take us with them. Alliances for us are about making a commitment to the long term, making a fair profit, not an obscene profit, and growing something each year to be proud of which is better than the previous year.' For both Transfield Services and Worley, partnerships and alliances are a fundamental part of their business strategies, and have led to significant growth in revenues and profits and a sustainable and pre-eminent competitive position in the market place.

In their excellent book *Built to Last* published in 1994, Jim Collins and Jerry Porras wrote about what makes truly exceptional companies different from other companies. In a subsequent newspaper article Collins reinforced the need for those *Built to Last* principles in light of the new global, e-based economy and the impermanence and mediocrity it often creates.[6] He says, 'If the new economy is to regain its soul, we need to ask ourselves some tough questions: Are we committed to doing our work with unadulterated excellence, no matter how arduous the task or how long the road? Is our work likely to make a contribution that we can be proud of? Does our work provide us with a sense of purpose and meaning that goes beyond just making money?' Partnering and alliance principles and practices lie at the heart of this work ethic.

Transfield Services and Worley are not only building their companies to last but their business relationships as well. Many organisations would do well to emulate them.

REFERENCES

1. Transfield Services Limited Annual Report 2002.
2. Worley Prospectus 2002.
3. Transfield Worley Woodside Alliance Annual Report 2001.
4. Worley Annual Report 2001.
5. Robert Porter Lynch, *Business Alliance Guide*, John Wiley, 1993, p.279.
6. Jim Collins, *Sydney Morning Herald*, 4 March 2000, p.101.

THE SYDNEY WATER JOURNEY

A strategic 'triple bottom line' approach to relationship management

Few organisations have the same level of complexity, critical operational and project delivery requirements, or number of stakeholders to satisfy short, medium and long term as Sydney Water, Australia's largest water services supplier and a statutory state owned corporation. Sydney Water provides drinking water, wastewater and some stormwater services to people in Sydney, the Blue Mountains and Illawarra regions to the west and south of the city. The organisation has over 4 million customers, generates in excess of $1.5 billion in revenues, manages $14 billion in assets, employs 3600 people and services 1.5 million properties. There are also many hundreds of important private sector suppliers and a large number of key stakeholders and regulators.

Sydney Water continuously walks a tightrope satisfying customers and the general community who have rightly high expectations, the regulatory authorities that monitor and scrutinise its performance and the private sector which relies on its ongoing business, while at the same time it has to protect the environment and run a successful business. All these stakeholders expect the highest level of integrity, performance, standards and understanding. Many would argue that, with this level of complexity and performance expectation, there would be an over-riding temptation to maintain a conservative, 'steady as she goes', 'early adaptor' or, at best, a 'lead follower' approach to change and change management.

So why and how, over the last five to eight years, has Sydney Water taken such an innovative, varied and increasingly successful approach to relationship management, internal and external to the organisation, involving leadership, courage and a pioneering spirit? This strategy involves internal partnering across the major departments/functions of Sydney Water; entering into Build Own Operate Transfer (BOOT) arrangements with global competitors for a critical part of its business (water filtration); leading the world's first genuine public/private sector construction alliance; engaging the private sector in over $1 billion of capital works projects under partnering and alliance principles and practice; entering into a performance based, long-term relationship with a strategic energy partner to plan and manage Sydney Water's future energy strategy and requirements; implementing a structured and strategic long-term approach to stakeholder relationship management; and taking a 'triple bottom line' (business, social and environmental) approach to business, engaging the community in its business activities and having a major focus on environmental sustainability. Evolving is a broad stakeholder community that supports a longer term approach to running a successful business that delivers a wide range of social benefits alongside financial returns, while fundamentally caring for the environment. As a broad and developing strategy, this triple bottom line approach, combined with a 'legacy' mindset to share learnings and best practices, puts Sydney Water at the leading edge of relationship management.

While the major volume of relationship management innovation and activity has been in its Asset Solutions business, involving medium to large capital works projects, there is also a high level of relationship development activity and innovation across the organisation, with a great deal of cross-fertilisation of ideas and shared learnings taking place. It is these relationship management activities and the associated learnings, together with the future strategic directions for relationship management, that are the focus of this case study. Historically there is no one single time and place, event or initiative, or single champion of change initiating the journey. It has been this part-evolution and part-revolution that has produced a sustainable platform from which transformation has now occurred.

WHERE TO BEGIN: A HISTORICAL PERSPECTIVE

Prior to the mid 1980s Sydney Water's capital works and operations activities were done completely in house and, in the case of capital works, by a dedicated day labour force. The organisation was over 17 000 strong at this point with few effective private sector relationships. Around this time many people viewed Sydney Water as a typical, large, bureaucratic monopoly supported by a comfortable, sometimes arrogant and complacent, techno-centric culture managed predominantly by engineers with more focus on technology, assets and cost management than community and environment.

The Sydney Water workforce had the capacity to design, construct, operate and then maintain the assets, be they dams, reservoirs, treatment plants, pumping stations, pipelines, associated plant or equipment. For example, Warragamba Dam, Sydney's main source of drinking water, was designed, constructed and operated entirely by Sydney Water employees without any assistance from the private sector. As the organisation began downsizing in the mid to late 1980s, through pressures of privatisation, global competition, greater cost efficiency and value for money focus, there developed a greater necessity for reliance on the private sector. At this point the associated contractual arrangements and, therefore, the supporting relationships were typically hard-nosed, hard dollar, fixed price/lump sum or schedule of rates based and prescriptive. Most, if not all, of the risk was transferred to the contractor, and this often led to adversarial, combative and tribal behaviours and practices based around tight specifications and a high degree of control and compliance. Prior to 1990 Sydney Water still did most of the Design and Construct work and used specialist private sector contractors for mechanical/equipment assistance.

Initial resistance to change and a sceptical approach to contractors as simply 'private sector profiteers' often led to negotiations being hard fought, bitter contests. This only reinforced the insular view from Sydney Water staff that many (not all) contractors were untrustworthy, extracting additional profits at Sydney Water's expense through unnecessary contractual loopholes and variations. On the other side, many private sector contractors saw Sydney Water as combative, predominantly price focused, with little appreciation of their well being or need for profitability.

The journey from contract management to relationship management and, ultimately, triple bottom line, 'community' based relationship management probably begins around this time.

DRIVERS FOR CHANGE

As with most organisations Sydney Water over the last 10 years has gone through a number of restructures, changes in senior executives and the odd crisis here and there. The change in the early to mid 1990s to broaden the organisation's relationship approach came about for a number of reasons that in part explain why it needs to be at the leading edge of relationship management best practice, with a triple bottom line focus.

- Water, the product itself, inherently generates a triple bottom line focus, engaging everyone in the community to some degree. Managing the finite supply of water, a fundamental building block of any society, provides challenges and opportunities for improvement and innovation. Issues such as safe drinking water, population growth, water conservation, retention of water for rivers, climate change, wastewater, alternative supplies, new technologies for sewage treatment, water collection and waste water treatment are fundamental issues for society as a whole.

- Sydney Water no longer holds a genuine monopoly position. The impact of global competitors bidding for business, the power of the community and environmental groups, the interest of regulators and the influence of politics have effectively removed the monopoly structure, mindsets and practices.

- There was recognition that Sydney Water could not deliver its growing and critically important capital works program without the collaborative, long-term support of a healthy, competitive, profitable and successful private sector, together with the cooperation and support of the community.

- There was also recognition that a sustainable strategy with regard to the environment was critical.

- Risk could not be completely transferred to the contractor/private sector. Credibility, reputation and the associated responsibility could not be abdicated.

- A triple bottom line approach to business generally and a growing recognition of a triple bottom line approach to relationship management was critical to Sydney Water's long-term success.

- Bundling of projects would enable a more strategic, innovative and cost effective approach to project and relationship management and enable a more effective delivery of triple bottom line outcomes.

- The need for further Sydney Water cultural change in breaking down internal 'silos' and generating greater customer, community and environmental awareness and focus was clear.

These business drivers were encapsulated in a major milestone and centrepiece in the triple bottom line relationship management journey, *WaterPlan 21*, Sydney Water's long-term strategic plan for sustainable water, wastewater and stormwater management. Released in 1997 and since revised, *WaterPlan 21* provides clear priorities and goals to 2021, goals that are delivered through five year corporate, environment, drinking water quality and asset plans. The overall plan provides the basis for understanding how Sydney Water needs to relate to its broad group of both internal and external stakeholders. Sydney Water stakeholders are many and varied and range from the Board of Directors and executive team, regulators such as the Environment Protection Authority (EPA), NSW Health and Department of Urban and Transport Planning, councils, community and environmental groups, customers, private sector suppliers and employees. One stakeholder group is no less important than the other but all require different approaches and a clear understanding of the performance levels required of each relationship, based on a joint understanding of each stakeholder's needs and expectations.

BUILD OWN OPERATE TRANSFER PROJECTS (BOOTs)

The first real foray by Sydney Water with the private sector in a fundamentally new way came with the BOOT filtration plants. Entering into four successive BOOT arrangements with the private sector in the early to mid 1990s for the filtration of over 95 per cent of Sydney's water supply, with 'transfer' back to Sydney Water as a long-term option, was seen at the time as ground breaking for the water industry worldwide. There had been some projects in Europe (France and the United Kingdom) but not to this degree of ownership or operation. The end result was the Prospect, Macarthur, Illawarra and Woronora water filtration plants, all operating by 1996 and filtering over 95 per cent of Sydney's water supply at a total cost of $500 million and with over 3500 megalitres per day of filtration capacity. French company Lyonnaise des Eaux was involved at Prospect, English company North West Water at Macarthur and the French company Vivendi at Illawarra and Woronora. All are world-class private sector water services companies.

The decision to undertake the BOOT projects was made at the executive level, Bob Wilson being the Managing Director at the time. These projects were seen within Sydney Water as a dramatic departure from previous practices of designing, constructing and operating such assets in house or with a limited involvement from the private sector. At the time there were a number of internal and external value propositions or business drivers for going down the BOOT path with the private sector.

- Sydney Water had an extensive and expensive capital works program, Clean Waterways, up and running and this, together with changing water guidelines, required the building of water filtration plants to deliver clean water. Up until then only chlorination had been used. The private sector was then a most attractive option for sourcing capital.
- The New South Wales government was putting a high emphasis on working with the private sector under PFI (Private Funding Initiatives) type arrangements.
- Certain tax incentives and allowances made PFIs more financially attractive.
- The executive team wanted to set up a competitive environment to benchmark and improve Sydney Water's internal efficiencies and costs. Colin

Nicholson, Sydney Water Manager Water Filtration, says, 'This was the single biggest benefit of the BOOTs. Sydney Water was heavily unionised, often with a "jobs for life" mentality. The BOOT projects really focused the mind and put the impetus on effective cultural change. This led to the outsourcing of mechanical and electrical maintenance and BOOT employees being on green field contracts. The BOOTs challenged the norms of the organisation.'

■ The BOOTs were an ideal opportunity to learn about and access current and future overseas technologies and, in return, provided an entry point into Asia for many of the international private sector water companies and service providers. Although Sydney Water had several small plants it had relatively little experience in water filtration.

In hindsight the evaluation and selection process for the BOOT partners was not too dissimilar from that used for subsequent alliances—for example, the Northside Storage Tunnel Alliance—and energy partner relationships that occurred some years later. The construction target costs and operation costs were not firmed up until the final short list of three private sector consortia was evaluated. This included total life cycle costing, with rise and fall allowances on labour, chemicals and energy.

Raj Goyal, Sydney Water Manager Strategy & Management, who, along with Colin Nicholson, led the BOOT negotiations and has been involved in their management since, says of the process: 'There was a long evaluation period, heavily scrutinised, which passed every check on probity and price. Based on the initial baseline financial and operations data that Sydney Water had done with the initial concepts and designs, plus some pilot plant work, it was hard to see how Sydney Water could lose by going to the private sector seeking further improvements. The BOOT quotes were 15 per cent cheaper than Sydney Water could have done it itself and with the same or better quality.'

The specifications for the plants were unlike any other specifications that Sydney Water had done previously. They were more focused on outcomes than traditional prescriptive input driven specifications. The BOOT candidates' selection and evaluation were made by an inter-disciplinary team involving project staff, finance, treasury and legal.

Partnering was implemented with two of the BOOTs during the construction phase, with a collaborative approach taken for ongoing operation. Risk sharing lay at the heart of the commercial principles with the private sector consortia accepting risk for Design and Construction and Sydney Water taking the risk for the Environmental Impact Study. There was obvious tension between Sydney Water and the private sector consortia as they were competitors in a broader market place. As Colin Nicholson says, 'It wasn't easy. Initially there was a strong reluctance to be open, share information and collaborate, but ultimately having a collaborative relationship made a huge difference. The four Design and Construct BOOT projects came in on time and on budget and Operations has seen good results to date.'

Raj Goyal says the learnings have been significant. 'From the first BOOT we needed to lessen the legal involvement in the process as the costs were too high. We found the best way was to agree on the principle then bring in the lawyers. This was a function of both experience and trust. Secondly, have less complicated commercial terms and conditions. This would allow for easier succession planning and broader understanding of the commercial arrangements and how they work. Thirdly, look at a more equitable spread of risk driven by financial benefits.'

The giardia and cryptosporidium outbreaks in the water supply in 1998 and the associated miscommunication over the impact on the community precipitated a crisis of confidence in Sydney Water. The incident brought home to all BOOT participants, including Sydney Water, that everyone's long-term interests would be best served by delivering the world's best service to customers and working together more as partners than potential competitors. Colin Nicholson says, 'The water crisis itself and the resultant tighter water quality expectations were a catalyst for change for the BOOT relationships. It was lose/lose for all if not handled well. Rather than assert blame, everyone looked for a joint solution. This was the making of the long-term, collaborative relationship.' He says further, 'The BOOTs were in part precursors to the current-day Design and Construct, Design Construct and Operate variants and the partnering and alliance activities.'

Ron Quill, now acting Managing Director for Sydney Water and at that time the responsible General Manager for the BOOTs, envisioned the opportunity and initiated the structure to facilitate a more effective engagement with the private sector. Regarding the BOOTs, there is now a free flow of information, a high level of trust, clear Key Performance Indicators (KPIs), regular performance and relationship reviews and a commitment by all to resolve all issues by sitting around the table together. This has led to significant improvements. Customer satisfaction is up and Sydney Water, which still runs six water filtration plants on its own, is increasing its knowledge of water treatment and filtration. This is done through joint information sharing, shared R&D with leading international water service companies and a fellowship scheme that involves people exchange programs (e.g. to France and the United Kingdom) and joint skills development. The BOOTs are now used as reference sites for the private sector operators to expand their business in the region.

Raj Goyal agrees: 'Sydney Water has learned an enormous amount from the BOOT operators. It has been a win/win for everyone. The BOOTs have also been refinanced and the benefits shared between Sydney Water and the BOOT partners. For example, Sydney Water has the ability, together with the BOOT partner, to hedge interest rates for agreed periods and this has saved many millions of dollars over the seven year period since startup. Relationships are good with all the BOOT consortia and both financial and operational performance improvements have occurred as the relationship has improved.'

INTERNAL PARTNERING

Throughout 1998 a series of internal partnering workshops took place to initiate the process of embedding partnering principles and practice throughout the two main business units and wholly owned subsidiaries of Sydney Water at that time (TransWater and Utilities). TransWater was the wholesaler, supplying bulk water and wastewater treatment services to Utilities, which looked after the (water) distribution and retail aspects of the business. Initiated and led by TransWater, a range of self-assessment interviews was conducted in late 1996 as part of its continuous improvement program. The results of a facilitated self-assessment of its business against the Australian Quality Awards Criteria and a Customer Focus workshop highlighted the need for TransWater to improve its (internal) customer focus. Accordingly, TransWater included 'delivery' and 'improvement' strategies in its business plan to ensure it met customer requirements, sustained customer satisfaction and moved towards best practice. This evolved into an internal partnering education program that would enhance the productive business relationship between TransWater and Utilities. The prime business drivers being to understand the principles and practices of partnering, the practical application for Sydney Water and to ensure the two growing businesses:

- operate as one team, in one direction with open communication;
- work together via agreed requirements for effective operation;
- give good value for money against agreed Key Performance Indicators (KPIs).

The initial internal partnering workshop took place with the Sydney Water Executive team and senior managers in February 1998, at which time a partnering charter was developed and signed. This was an important document as it showed the absolute commitment of the senior management team to the internal partnering process and the role they were prepared to play. That same charter was then used as the basis for generating a common understanding, via a common language, to develop a common partnering practice at the operating levels across the TransWater and Utilities businesses. This involved building joint performance KPI Scorecards for each region for which a joint team of Transwater and Utilities staff were mutually accountable. The Sydney Water executive team was responsible for the development of the partnering charter, its shared vision and common goals. The regional teams were responsible for its delivery.

The culture, strategy, structure, process and people aspects were exactly the same as if the relationship were between Sydney Water and external partner organisations. Also put in place were senior executive sponsors to the teams as well as a typical alliance/partnering issue resolution/escalation process where disputes and issues were handled via proactive problem solving and joint resolution of issues at the lowest possible levels. This was supported by an action plan with accountable milestones to effectively implement the improvement opportunities.

Apart from having a genuine practical application for improving internal relationships, shifting mindsets, attitudes and changing many practices, this process also proved an excellent learning vehicle for subsequent external partnering/alliance relationships. With over 500 people attending the workshops this was the largest initiative of its kind to occur anywhere in Australia.

WHAT'S IN A CONTRACT?

The Australian Standard AS2124–1986 'General Conditions of Contract', modified to conform to Sydney Water's requirements, has been the contractual backbone of Sydney Water relationships with the private sector for almost two decades, especially in the area of Design, Construct and Operate projects. Implemented in the first instance to protect the interests of Sydney Water, it has served and continues to serve the organisation well in many areas. But many in Sydney Water have recognised over the years that, depending on the relationship approach to be taken, greater contractual and behavioural flexibility is required. Along with alliance and partnering agreements, variations of AS2124 have developed to incorporate more collaborative behaviour with fewer win/lose, punitive implications. This has proved an effective compromise. Fundamentally based around a schedule of rates or lump sum value, traditional aspects of the AS2124 contract framework include securities or retention of monies and performance undertakings; latent conditions; insurance of the works; role of inspectors, superintendents, superintendents' representatives, contractor representatives; liquidated damages; delay costs; defects liability; variations and others. While perhaps appropriate for the 1980s and early 1990s, as the requirement for higher levels of trust, collaboration and sharing of risk materialised, other contractual variations or alternatives needed to be found.

For example, the three large ocean outfalls at North Head, Malabar and Bondi completed between 1985 and 1991 at a total cost of $313 million were completed by a traditional approach, being a mix of schedule of rates to relieve some contractor risk and lump sum contracts with few incentives. There was a high degree of Sydney Water supervision from site engineers and shift engineers and others. While construction was outsourced, the project design and project management were done by Sydney Water.

The other contractual alternative that Sydney Water has used selectively and effectively since its first publication in 1996 is the C21 construction contract, again modified for Sydney Water requirements and originally developed by the Department of Public Works and Services. There is a strong emphasis in C21 on cooperative contracting, early warning, clear roles, responsibilities for measured outcomes and a best practice focus, while still maintaining a traditional schedule of rates/lump sum focus.

It was the Northside Storage Tunnel Alliance that fundamentally challenged the paradigm(s) upon which these contracts were based.

NORTHSIDE STORAGE TUNNEL ALLIANCE (NSST)

Although the Sydney Water relationship management journey has a broad front there is no doubt the NSST Alliance project is one of the cornerstones of Sydney Water's experiences. As a key component of the *WaterPlan 21* strategy, the NSST project commenced physical construction work in mid 1998 and on completion in September 2000 cut 80 to 90 per cent of the wet weather sewage overflow previously discharged into Sydney Harbour. As one of Australia's most recognised and valuable tourist attractions, Sydney Harbour water quality is a key public concern and sewage overflow during wet weather was a major source of harbour pollution. The project itself comprised over 20 kilometres of tunnels, 3.8 to 6.6 metres in diameter and located 40–100 metres below sea-level, running under Sydney Harbour, and connected waterways serving a significant number of Sydney's northern suburbs. In excess of 1.8 million tonnes of clean sandstone were excavated and then transported by barge for use primarily as landfill in western Sydney. The tunnel itself has a capacity in excess of 500 million litres. The stored overflow in the tunnel would then be pumped to the existing sewage treatment plant and discharge system at North Head on Sydney's eastern seaboard.

To meet the project objectives on time, cost, environmental performance, community relations, workplace safety, industrial relations and quality, Sydney Water adopted an innovative alliance approach for the delivery of the project. In fact this was the world's first alliance based public sector capital works project and the first application of alliancing to a tunnel project.

Although not widely appreciated, the initial catalyst for the project was a proposal put to the New South Wales government from an international water services organisation to build a similar tunnel. It was this competitive environment that then set the tight timeframe for project completion prior to the commencement of the Sydney 2000 Olympic Games in mid-September 2000.

A number of alternative options for significantly reducing overflows had been investigated by Sydney Water since 1991 but these were discarded as being impractical, too expensive or having unacceptable timeframes.

In May 1997, the decision was taken by Sydney Water to construct the Northside Storage Tunnel as a pre-Olympics priority, in just three years and four months. Between May 1997 and the state government's approval of the project in late December 1997, Sydney Water evaluated and selected the alliance partners and concluded the necessary environmental impact statements in record time. In January 1998 an alliance agreement was signed between Sydney Water and the other principal partners: Montgomery Watson (systems engineers and now called MWH), Connell Wagner (design engineers) and construction partner, Transfield.

'The typical Sydney Water approach was not possible', says Allan Henderson, Sydney Water Program Director and NSST Alliance Manager. 'A project of this size and unclear risk profile completed via a conventional design-bid-build procurement process would have taken at least six years and a conventional contract would have potentially exposed us to significant cost increases and time delays.'

Greg Klamus, Sydney Water Project Director for NSST, was given the challenge by Paul Broad (Managing Director) to manage the Design and Construct and complete the project by the incredibly tight deadline, quietly, cleanly, safely and at a cost that was regarded as exceptional value for money. He agrees with Allan Henderson's view: 'The challenges were technical, commercial and relationship based. Given the size, scope and urgency of the project the alliance approach was the most sensible and practical way to complete the work.' Klamus also talks of the changes that were required, 'However, for it to be successful some fundamental Sydney Water paradigms had to be challenged.' Such as:

'Why do we, Sydney Water, need to specify the detail, be prescriptive and focus on the inputs rather than outcomes?

'Why set up a traditional "them and us" environment that will most likely lead to adversarial behaviours and poor or delayed project outcomes?

'Why can't "we" all work as one team to achieve common goals with joint accountability and shared risk?'

After robust internal discussions and reviewing the success of alliances in the offshore drilling private sector it was recommended to the Sydney Water board that an alliance approach be taken.

'For Sydney Water this was a leap of faith based more on intuition than fact', says Klamus. 'We had to divest ourselves of traditional contracting practices based on fixed price, lump sum arrangements with tough, punitive and often one-sided contractual terms and conditions.' Another distraction that made the project that much more challenging was the many changes in Sydney Water senior executives. The first two and a half years of the project saw three Chairmen, four Managing Directors and seven General Managers. This created a rollercoaster ride for communications, internal stakeholder management and ongoing commitment and support for the project, especially during difficult times. It was Ron Quill who, as General Manager of Trans-Water, was ultimately handed the executive responsibility for successfully leading and completing the project.

What makes the NSST Alliance project special is the extent to which the alliance partners embraced the one-team approach and the breathtaking extent to which they shared risk, avoided disputes and embarked upon a totally transparent and open process to achieve an incredibly ambitious and challenging set of common goals.

There are three aspects in the practical application of the NSST alliance project that are significant.

1. The selection and evaluation process of the partners

A call for proposals based on an alliance approach was issued to industry in September 1997. The evaluation and selection criteria comprised the assessment of technical experience and capability to undertake the project, capacity to manage environmental and community issues and the affinity for alliance partnering. This involved desk top evaluations of the initial written proposals through to an intensive interview phase with the short-listed candidates and, finally, two-day alliance development workshops with the final two proponents. This process and the fact that the preferred alliance partners were chosen before the final target cost was agreed were marked differences from the majority of previous Sydney Water practices.

The alliance agreement was negotiated around an open book, direct cost reimbursable, risk/reward model. The private sector partners' profit and overheads were put at risk to gain or to lose, above or below the agreed profit target, based on the over- or under-performance achieved against agreed Business As Usual (BAU) targets. These BAU targets were linked into cost and non-cost performance indicators, namely time, safety, community affairs and environment.

At this stage the risk profile associated with the project was very unclear. Relatively little was known of the precise ground conditions that would be encountered. The project budget estimate used for government approval in December 1997 was $300–400 million but this was based on a very unclear and potentially variable risk profile. Little had been done by way of site investigation and design development. Because of the time constraints, there had been no project-specific geological investigation and there was no detailed specification or defined scope of works. This caused the budget figure to be revised on a number of occasions to allow for increased scope of work. For example, added connections at Scotts Creek and Shelly Beach, cost escalation on foreign exchange rates, owner's (Sydney Water) internal costs and changes to accounting and financing charges saw the final budget legitimately expand to $451 million.

2. The approach to project delivery

Regarding **teams and project governance**, all alliance personnel, including Sydney Water staff, were co-located in a single, open plan environment to maximise open communication, information sharing, proactive problem solving and joint resolution of issues. The entire integrated alliance team then became focused on the five cost and non-cost project objectives, led by eight clear and simple guiding alliance principles of which 'Act in a way that is best for the project' and 'Commit to a "no blame" culture' were seen as the most fundamental.

Northside Storage Tunnel Alliance Principles

- Act in a way that is best for the project.
- Build a champion team that is integrated across all disciplines and organisations.
- Commit to a 'no blame' culture.
- Use breakthroughs to achieve exceptional results in all project objectives.
- Commit corporately and individually to openness, integrity, trust, cooperation, mutual support and respect, flexibility, honesty and loyalty to the project.
- Outstanding results provide outstanding rewards.
- Deal with and resolve all issues within the alliance.
- Spread the alliance culture to all stakeholders.

The Project Leadership Team, Integrated Project Team and Alliance Implementation Team provided the basis for sound governance and leadership, management and maintenance of the alliance process, and project management and delivery, respectively.

To ensure all issues were resolved within the alliance a '**no blame**' clause in the alliance agreement stated that all partners waived their right to litigation with each other, other than for wilful default. This drove everyone, their mindsets and behaviours, towards win/win outcomes and is quite different from the more traditional 'best for self and to hell with the other guy' approach that is often followed by blame, finger pointing, lawyers and, finally, litigation.

The gain/pain share, **risk/reward model** provided the link between performance outcomes, measurement, remuneration and driving the right behaviours for mutual benefit rather than self-interest. A fee modifier mechanism also applied to ensure that poor performance in one objective was not traded off against good performance in another. 'If the team fails two out of five objectives it automatically loses any incentive it gained for the other three, which reinforces the incentive to focus on the entire job', says John Callaghan, design manager for Connell Wagner at the time.[1]

Allan Henderson talks about the unique aspects of the non-cost objective performance measurement:[2] 'Measurement of performance in the environment, community and safety objectives required the determination of performance benchmarks in these areas, and the development of appropriate performance measurement methodologies. The established benchmarks define levels corresponding to "poor", "business as usual" and "outstanding" in the various performance parameters developed for each of the objectives. The benchmarks and measurement methodologies apply not only to performance outcomes, but also to the management process in the respective areas.

'Assessment of the performance against the benchmarks was carried out by independent panels throughout the project. Such benchmarking and measurement of performance in these non cost objectives is believed to be unique in world-wide contractual practice and certainly has not been attempted previously in the Australian construction industry.'

Testimony to the uncertain risk profile was the extremely poor tunnelling conditions and high water inflows encountered as the tunnel crossed under Sydney Harbour. This cost the alliance three months on the excavation timeline and significant additional materials and cost. Innovation, creativity and lateral thinking within an operating environment of high safety focus and high urgency were critical. There were 45 documented **breakthroughs and**

innovations during construction, delivering savings totalling 2 per cent on the total cost as well as significantly impacting on the other non-cost objectives. For example:

- Tunnel configuration optimisation saved in the order of $2 million and reduced both environmental and safety risks as a consequence of a reduction in construction activities. Approximately five weeks were also saved on the schedule.
- Refinement of concept design, optimisation of location, layout and process of the tunnel odour control scrubber at North Head saved over $1.5 million on the BAU target estimate.
- Tunnel design innovation included raising the tunnel in one area to position it in a more suitable rock formation and extending the tunnel in another area to improve environmental outcomes.
- An improved understanding of the rock condition enabled the alliance team to reduce the extent of concrete lining required.

Under a traditional approach, which does not always focus on win/win, such design changes and innovations may well have taken considerable time and greater cost, and involved adversarial, contractual discussions on variations, latent conditions, liquidated damages and the like. Through the alliance approach, all the partners at all levels were focused on win/win, through a performance based, no blame/high accountability and unified culture solving problems proactively, in the shortest time, at the least additional cost, while still being conscious of environmental and community needs.

3. Performance outcomes against project objectives

Cost: 'Completion of the project at a cost which is regarded, by industry standards, as providing best value for money'

Despite significant problems with unexpected ground conditions and challenges on the community and environmental fronts, the final project cost came in at $465 million, only 3 per cent or $14 million more than the final April 1999 budget estimate of $451 million.[3] However, lessons were learnt and in hindsight the 5 per cent contingency agreed and allowed for at the early stage of project development was too optimistic for a project of this scope and urgency. It was through the alliancing approach and philosophy that the partners focused on solving the technical problems together in the shortest time possible and at the least additional cost. NSST Project Management costs totalled 1.6 per cent of the project cost, which compared favourably with project management costs of 9.8 per cent for the $313 million Deep Ocean Outfalls Project completed some years earlier.

Time: 'Completion of the project by the Sydney 2000 Olympics'

The tunnel was accepted by Sydney Water on 13 September 2000, two days before the opening ceremony of the Sydney Olympic Games. This was a direct result of high and improved levels of productivity. As a benchmark comparison, the Deep Ocean Outfalls Project, delivered by a traditional design and construct contract, involved 14 kilometres of tunnelling and took seven years from approval to final commissioning. This is compared to the Northside Storage Tunnel with 22 kilometres of tunnelling completed in four years. The construction period of three years for the NSST was half that of the Ocean Outfalls.

Safety: 'The project to be characterised by world class safety, industrial relations and quality standards'

Unfortunately, a fatal accident in the first 600 metres of tunnelling reinforced in an absolute way the constant and total focus required on safety and the commitment to zero harm. The results subsequently achieved for overall project safety performance based on both process benchmarks and performance outcomes were significantly better than the industry average. For example, the measure of 'average weeks lost' per 'lost time' injury of 4.6 weeks compared favourably to 11.6 weeks for the Australian Construction Industry and also highlights the success of the alliance's Injury Management Program.

Community: 'Project community/social practices and procedures to be rated as world class with genuine sensitivity and responsiveness to community members and groups'

Meeting community expectations, managing the balance between communication and consultation with the community, and maintaining their trust proved to be the greatest challenge for the alliance. The concept behind the project to address the major sewage overflows into Sydney Harbour by a tunnel discharging to North Head Sewage Treatment Plant was highly controversial and subject to considerable public debate prior to the project being approved. This created strong and very vocal resistance to the project before the EIS was completed and the contract awarded. The project itself raised community concerns around the potential health risks from gases released at vent shafts, the visual impact, noise and vibration associated with construction sites and shaft structures and the impact on property values. This was compounded by an EIS, completed before project start up, that led to some unmet community expectations. It proved difficult to regain the community's trust once it had been lost. Lessons learnt during this time reinforced the need for early and enduring community relationship building based on open, shared information. Trust lost is difficult to regain. In the words of Allan Henderson of Sydney Water:[3] 'We were not ready for the level of community hostility and seriously underestimated the resources needed to manage this aspect of the project.' Overall this was the lowest scoring non-cost objective rated by an independent panel at just over 75 per cent.

As well as the many lessons learnt, however, there were also many significant success stories, which demonstrate the level of commitment and innovation Sydney Water and the other alliance partners put to community affairs. Over 330 community meetings, Customer Liaison Committees, public forums and technical, round table conferences were held throughout the life of the project. A key learning was that communities can improve project design outcomes, particularly for those elements that directly impact on local populations. One example was the waterfront option at Tunks Park. There was a clear community preference to relocate a large acoustic shed intended to surround the construction site at one end of a well-used park. The shed, a key component of the initial Design and Construct planning, was essential to meeting construction noise standards stipulated in the Minister's Conditions of Approval. The win/win facilitated solution was the construction of huge underground caverns to store spoil and a temporary coloured shed to blend into the environment and reduce the visual impact. This meant a significantly reduced work site area, no permanent buildings located in the park, ongoing access to the boat ramp and jetty for the community and an improved waterfront reserve. The key community learnings and a number of associated case studies have been well documented and are now freely available as a reference.

Environment: 'Project environmental practices and procedures to be world class and the project to be delivered with genuine sensitivity and responsiveness shown to the environment'

Despite working within a complex area with associated high potential risk and a very prescriptive initial Environmental Impact Study, the alliance performed particularly well, scoring 17.3 from a possible 20 from an independent assessment panel. Stringent environmental protection regimes were in place, governing control of noise, air and water pollution during the handling of excavated rock and construction materials. Located on one of the most picturesque parts of Sydney Harbour, the Little Manly Point wharf and barge loading facilities are close to a nature reserve, which is home to the long-nosed bandicoot. The surrounding waters also provide sanctuary for a colony of fairy penguins and contain sea grasses and other aquatic plants. No blasting was allowed and all tunnels in the area were bored. Temporary rather than permanent piles were used in the aquatic reserve and they were screwed rather than hammered to reduce noise levels. Even the amount of time a shadow could be cast on the sea grasses by the barges was limited and barge movements were stopped one hour before dusk to protect the birds.

NSST summary

'This alliance gave the design teams unprecedented opportunity to work closely with the constructors during the design and development phase and to resolve issues during construction. The alliance allows all parties, including the owner, to focus on solving issues and finding improvements without the traditional demarcations and concerns. And all this done in a way that keeps control with the owner' (Charles Rottier,[3] Director Major Projects Asia for MWH and member of the Project Alliance Leadership Team (PALT)).

There was no alternative to alliancing. In the words of David Iverach, Transfield CEO Group Services and Energy at the time, when talking about the challenges faced: 'Under a traditional lump sum, 100 per cent risk transfer, client/contractor approach the Tunks Park variation would most likely have shut down the project. The issues raised at Little Manly Point would have delayed the project by about a year. In both cases enormous and ongoing community unrest and significant litigation would have been the likely outcomes. It is the alliance approach that has made the project achievable.'

A team from the University of Technology, Sydney tracked the progress of the entire project from a 'future perfect' perspective—imagining the future and then seeking to realise it, subject to constant revision, on a rolling here and now basis.[4] Stewart Clegg, a team member, says of the NSST Alliance: 'The project represented a major and significant achievement, in which a new and innovative approach, which we saw as in large part being based on thinking in the future perfect, provided breakthrough results. The project grew from just 28 pages, with no design, no price and no clauses, other than an injunction to think in the future perfect and create a much cleaner Sydney Harbour. Which is what they did.'

The NSST Alliance project has become a national and international benchmark by which others learn about, manage and measure the success of their project and strategic alliances. There are still, however, polarised views on its success, driven by a lack of understanding of what occurred, a misperception of the increased and variable scope regarding the final total cost, or political motives or other agendas. Overall the Northside Storage Tunnel

Alliance is a demonstrable success with many things learnt that have been successfully taken away to other projects and ongoing relationships. The real legacy of the NSST Alliance project and approach is the knowledge, confidence and courage it has given others to travel the same path. It is a true pioneering event within the Sydney Water journey.

PARTNERING AND BUNDLING

The next phase of the journey involves an extensive array of partnering projects, involving a greater degree of bundling of traditional smaller projects into longer term strategic arms of the overall *WaterPlan 21* strategy. Two will be discussed in some detail in this case study: the Cronulla STP Upgrade and the West Hornsby and Hornsby Heights Sewage Treatment Plant Upgrade. However, there are many others that have been run along similar lines. Some were very successful, some less so, mainly because of the risk profile, partner selection and contract management practices.

Generally these projects involve a more standard contractual approach, for example, AS2124 or C21 contracts or variants thereof as a base within a partnering framework. That is, there is a partnering charter of shared key objectives, a Balanced KPI Scorecard for performance measurement, joint accountability, and leadership and management teams. The level of openness and transparency is determined by the terms and conditions of the contract and the willingness of the partners to share financial and other associated information that would normally be shared under a full performance, risk/reward based partnering/alliance arrangement.

Cronulla STP upgrade

A Design, Construct and Operate (DCO) project for the upgrading of the existing Cronulla Sewage Treatment Plant (STP) from primary to tertiary treatment was awarded in January 1999 under fixed price, lump sum commercial contract to Bovis Lend Lease, together with their subcontractors CH2M HILL, SKM and Australian Water Services (AWS). With a budget of $85 million, the Cronulla STP upgrade was the largest sewage treatment plant project for 10 years.

The purpose of the project was to improve the beach water quality within Bate Bay. As an overlay to the commercial contract a partnering approach was taken to ensure a collaborative process and mutually beneficial outcomes were achieved. This involved partnering workshops at the beginning of the project and review workshops at regular intervals. A partnering charter of shared vision, common goals and guiding principles for the project was developed and this linked into a Balanced Scorecard of Key Performance Indicators for which joint leadership and management teams held themselves mutually accountable. The KPIs covered the six critical performance criteria of cost, quality, schedule, safety, community and environment.

The project itself had some special features and non-traditional, relationship based elements:

1. The upgrade made the Cronulla STP the largest of its kind in the world to discharge such high quality effluent to the ocean.
2. It had the largest UV disinfection system in Australia.
3. It was the first DCO for Sydney Water with an extended two year operating period linked to a bonus/damages incentive scheme, if operating costs were lower/higher than those tendered.
4. No additional engineering investigation was undertaken after the EIS. The contract was based on performance rather than overly prescriptive method based specifications and managed via a quality assurance system rather than quality control through detailed inspection.

The partnering based project has been a demonstrable and outstanding success. The plant was designed and constructed on time, within 28 months, and commissioned in April 2001. The project is on track for Sydney Water to take over operation of the plant in 2003. From a quality perspective the *St George and Sutherland Leader*, the local newspaper, reported 'Beachwatch results for July (2001) showed all local beaches passed tests for the two main pollution indicators. The completed upgrade of Cronulla STP is showing very positive results for the beaches'.

The final capital cost of $77.9 million is 9 per cent under the budget of $85 million approved in 1997 with the annual operating cost of $2.6 million per annum expected to run to budget. The safety LTIFR (Lost Time Injuries Frequency Rate per million hours worked) achieved was 16, half the industry average of 32. The project had a high environmental and community focus. At the opening of the Cronulla plant, the Premier of New South Wales released a green and golden bell frog colony into the wetland created as part of the project. The community was also continually informed. There were nine advertisements in the local press advising of progress, four newsletters, five tours of the construction site by environmental groups and one open day to the public.

Two Sydney Water operators were seconded to the AWS operating team to gain experience in how AWS manage treatment plants and to provide continuity of operation when the plant is taken over by Sydney Water. Other lessons have been learnt and been passed on to other projects.

Ian Payne, Sydney Water Program Director and acting General Manager for Asset Solutions, who was the Cronulla Project Director, says, 'The partnering approach did make a significant difference to the success of the project and was particularly helpful in developing a good relationship between all project participants. For example, the partners flew people in from around the world to solve problems. Partnering built cooperation and trust and an approach of "what is best for the project", albeit this was constrained sometimes by a lump sum contract.'

West Hornsby and Hornsby Heights Sewage Treatment upgrades

A partnering approach was also used in the upgrade of the West Hornsby and Hornsby Heights Sewage Treatment Plants (STPs) in Sydney's northern suburbs.

Initially Sydney Water used its in-house design expertise to verify that the required effluent performance could be achieved on the confines of the two existing STP sites. In November 2000 CH2M HILL was engaged to develop the concept designs and manage their implementation. In January 2001 the Transfield Montgomery Watson Harza JV (TMW) team was awarded the detailed Design and Construct contract. Although traditional contractual, competitive bid, tender base methodologies were used in selecting the DCO contractor, partnering principles and practice were actively and extensively used throughout the project by all the project participants. A formal partnering agreement, supported by a partnering charter of shared key objectives, was chosen as a suitable enabling process to focus all parties on a single set of outcomes. Working as a single integrated project team (IPT), Sydney Water and partners CH2M HILL and TMW delivered fully on the project objectives without compromising the operation of the two complex sewage treatment plants.

The upgrade was completed with minimal impact on the local community and environment, on time at the end of April 2002, under the budget of $26 million and with a safety record of 1 LTI in 170 000 hours worked, which is well below industry average. Initial effluent quality results, which will be further quantified by longer term monitoring, indicate that both STPs will achieve the stringent Environment Protection Authority licence requirements.

There was a shared approach to risk, with risk allocated to the partners best able to manage them. Generally Sydney Water and CH2M HILL assumed the process risk and TMW the construction risks, with Sydney Water working closely across all parties involved in the project. Simultaneous construction on both plants, which were located close to residential areas, saw an intensive communications strategy in place throughout the project. The feedback from the local residents regarding communications management has been very positive. Co-location of all resources on site, IPT monthly partnering meetings to review progress and an emphasis on openness, cooperation and good communication also typified the working approach to the project.

For their efforts, the project partners won an Institute of Project Management Achievement Award[5] in 2002.

Start partnering early and with the right people

From their many experiences Sydney Water people say that, in hindsight, in most cases the preference is to enter into partnering based relationships, that is the approach, attitude, mindset and practice, as early as possible in the selection/evaluation process. In the case of projects this needs to happen early in the Design and Construct phases. Early involvement in planning and design, integrated project teams, people exchange and secondment, open book (to varying degrees), open and honest communication and information sharing, no blame/high accountability culture, proactive problem solving and joint resolution of issues within the relationship, joint leadership and management/project teams are common features of these partnering and alliance variants.

Irrespective of whether there is incentive or risk/reward based remuneration or, as still often occurs, a more traditional schedule of rates and fixed price or lump sum arrangements, understanding the guiding principles, having agreed common objectives, joint management of risk, and the right people, mindsets and behaviours in place will be the key to success.

Ray Abe, Sydney Water Project Director, talks of his experiences: 'With the work being done at North Head Sewage Treatment Plant, Sydney Water is working with its consultants as though in an alliance, despite having entered into a standard contract arrangement. It is not necessary to have such working arrangements strictly formalised, although from my experience there clearly are benefits in doing so. It is a case of having the right people, with the right mindset and attitudes, to focus on achieving mutually beneficial outcomes.'

A CHANGE IN DIRECTION

Another key milestone on the journey was the endorsement by the Sydney Water Board of Directors of the Asset Solutions Division 'Strategic Directions' paper in December 2000. Its author, Craig Baragry, Sydney Water Manager Project Delivery Services, says the paper formalised the way forward for the Asset Solutions business and will have a significant impact on the way Sydney Water does its business in the future. The 'Strategic Directions' paper is based around five strategies:

- Managing the capital projects via programs (large bundles) of work
- Developing a relationship contracting framework with the private sector
- Integrating planning with delivery
- Forming centres of expertise
- Prequalifying organisations for repetitive and routine work

Baragry further adds, 'As outcomes from these strategies, we will create new collaborative engagement mechanisms with the private sector, delivering improved value and efficiencies. The strategies will promote innovative solutions and ongoing improvements by bundling projects together to form more attractive packages for the private sector. There will also be a working environment and relationships created whereby management of risks is transparent. For this to happen, partnering and alliance relationships are a necessity for Sydney Water. In the near future we will have three full alliances in operation, namely SewerFix SPS (already started), Priority Sewerage Program and Bondi RIAMP.'

Before the strategic directions were developed, feedback from suppliers was that Sydney Water was over-prescriptive, adversarial in its contract management, allocated parcels of work too small to promote innovation and efficiencies, and had tendering procedures that were too bureaucratic and documentation that was excessive.

There is a need for alternative approaches. The design and construct strategy based on a traditional competitive bid, tender based selection process and a lump sum, fixed priced contract with or without a collaborative approach may be difficult for industry to sustain in the longer term. In this market place (capital works) the cost of tendering is high, on average 1 to 1.5 per cent of the contract value, and the margins relatively low at 4 to 6 per cent of sales, especially for the constructors. On that basis, tenderers need to win at least one in four bids, in an intensely competitive market place, to break even or better. On top of that it is estimated that it costs Sydney Water approximately 1.5 per cent of the project budget to prepare and assess tenders.

With a full alliance based approach initiated via different selection and evaluation processes, the target cost is finalised jointly and transparently with the preferred partner candidate rather than a list of candidates with only one being ultimately successful. The positive cost implications for both Sydney Water and the private sector are significant. Where a more conventional approach is warranted—for example, where the scope of work is better defined, the risks more certain and the time to deliver less constrained—it may be appropriate to have only two tenderers fully develop proposals.

Baragry talks of the progress so far: 'After almost two years of practical application of the new engagement mechanisms, evidence suggests that the revised strategies are having an impact upon the construction and consultancy industry. The supply chain is shortening, with larger parcels of work being offered in the market place and various strategic partnering arrangements are forming to enable suppliers to gear up their capability to meet our new standards of doing business.'

THE PRESENT STATE: CURRENT ALLIANCES

In 2001–2002, Sydney Water invested $556 million in the capital program to ensure that asset performance was not only maintained but improved. Successful delivery of this massive capital works program reflects the implementation of procurement reforms such as bundling of major projects and relationship-based contracts. Capital expenditure for the year exceeded budget by $46 million or around 9 per cent owing largely to the accelerated delivery of key projects.
Alex Walker, former Managing Director, Sydney Water[6]

Five of the eight major projects to be delivered over the next 20 years under *WaterPlan 21* will be done via relationship contracting approaches. Three projects—SPS, PSP and Bondi RIAMP—in varying stages of development will all be completed as full alliance based relationship contracts, similar in framework to the Northside Storage Tunnel Alliance. Highlights of the relationship approaches taken for these three projects are discussed below.

SewerFix (SPS)

The $200 million Sewage Pumping Stations (SPS) upgrade is a key component of the SewerFix program of work within *WaterPlan 21*. Under SPS, Sydney Water entered into a relationship based contract with the private sector consortia made up of Bovis Lend Lease, Tenix, CH2M HILL, Sinclair Knight Mertz and The Phillips Group. Work commenced early in 2002. Similar to the Northside Storage Tunnel approach, Sydney Water has formed an integrated program team to define, design, construct and commission works to improve the operational performance of approximately 300 sewage pumping stations. This involves leading and managing integrated project teams; a no blame/high accountability culture taking a best for project approach through shared vision, common objectives and guiding principles; and a Performance Scorecard of cost and non-cost KPIs, a core group of which are linked to a risk/reward, gainshare/painshare model.

One year into a four year program, the results to date have been nothing short of extraordinary, a paradigm shift in approach and performance.

- Sixty sewage pumping stations were completed in six months and a further 74 are on track to be completed in the following six months. As a benchmark, prior to the SPS program and using discrete, traditional, lump sum contracts, Sydney Water was constructing around 14–16 sewage pumping stations per annum.
- Construction time has reduced from 9–10 months per pumping station to 4–6 months.
- Planning activities per pumping station have significantly improved (e.g. 12 months to 4 months for concept design and 4–9 months to 2 months for detailed plans).
- The average time to commission a pumping station has reduced from four weeks to four days. Further, information and improvements from the commissioning processes are being incorporated into the Asset Maintenance Database. This allows contingency plans to be improved and thereby reduce the risk of sewage overflows in the longer term.
- The SPS program delivered the first tranche of work (60 pumping stations) with an $8.8 million (16 per cent) saving against the target cost.
- An independent expert assessed the non-cost performance for the first tranche as 'outstanding':
  —Zero Lost Time Injuries safety record in 244 000 hours worked.
  —A satisfaction rating of 8.4 (out of 10) from residents directly affected by the work.
  —No reportable 'dry weather overflows', a critical Key Performance Indicator from the Environment Protection agency.
  —No environmental breaches or infringements.

In speaking to a number of different people from the various disciplines and activities, at all levels, involving planning, design, project management and construction, all agreed that the performance achieved would not have been possible under a traditional approach. Typical was a statement from Dave Watts, Sydney Water Planning Manager: 'We could not have achieved what we have other than through an alliance. It's not adversarial, everyone works as a total team, getting on with the job and looking for the best solutions jointly. The most pleasing thing is the good comments we are getting from the community about what is being delivered.'

A key question is what does the alliance look like at the construction site level? Paul Scottman, Bovis Lend Lease Construction Supervisor, says, 'There is no way this work could have been done via a traditional contractor approach. On the ground the alliance makes life and the job easier. The way people treat each other is different, working together, not putting up barriers. There is honesty and trust in communications. We are also getting letters of commendation from the community.' Don Daniels, Area Supervisor for Bovis Lend Lease, adds, 'I have learnt a lot from the alliance approach. The team gels well and it is a great place to work. We all see the alliance as a new company to work for and we get to work with different environment, communications people as well as the community. It's also safer.'

Continuous improvement is demonstrated by the way the alliance resets the KPI targets at agreed milestones. Richard Van Putten, Sydney Water Sewer-Fix Program Director, explains: 'As part of our objectives we set the original Target Cost Estimate and it was then benchmarked so that each future estimate was based on the savings from the first. This meant that the first tranche savings could not be repeated without further improvements being made. This approach also applied in the non-cost areas with the extraordinary results achieved in Community and Safety now being business as usual. We then set new benchmarks for outstanding performance in the current tranche of work.'

Chris Browne, SPS Program Manager from Bovis Lend Lease, adds another perspective: 'Why is this alliance so special? The joint team was given close to an impossible task and then given a free hand within the broad rules of engagement to find out the best ways to get the job done. It's a very exciting and enjoyable place to work, when you don't shackle people down.'

It is also different for the designers, says Steve Lindforth, Director of Sinclair Knight Mertz. 'In traditional D&C project designers are often seen as "subbies in a suit", you are boxed in, at arms length from the client where communications are minimised. SewerFix is completely different. We are working with the operators. There is fast and direct communication and we are getting real feedback. Sydney Water is also more flexible in mindset and attitude with the alliance approach, as we are all part of the alliance and therefore part of their [Sydney Water's] business. The flexible and adaptable alliance approach provides a sensible and equitable basis for design.'

In discussion with alliance personnel it is the people aspects that come through most strongly. 'It's only when you get back to a traditional contract that you really appreciate the benefits of an alliance. The point of difference is the multi-disciplinary approach. Also the assessment of risk is not just based on technical solutions but also looked at from a community and environmental perspective. There is a much deeper level of analysis. It is also one of those work experiences that will live on well after the project is finished.

We will never forget what we achieved as a team', says Christine Marsden, Senior Communications Consultant with The Phillips Group.

Richard Van Putten has also seen a step change in the level of engagement and commitment that goes beyond the immediate scope of the alliance. 'The biggest change has been in the culture of Sydney Water with all divisions represented in the team at various locations from designers to site supervisors. Being trusted, open partners in the process has led to better understanding of each other's needs. After one year of the four year program we are already seeing a change in the attitudes as Sydney Water employees take the knowledge they have gained back to their work teams. The maintainers have now set up their own workshops to dissect their processes and tie them into the new pumping station operation. The story does not stop there as these groups are also looking at other civil, mechanical and electrical work practices to improve other areas of their operations and have engaged the alliance team to support them through that change. This has also been the catalyst for the alliance maintenance contracts which will be the next step in Sydney Water's evolution.'

Craig Baragry, Sydney Water Manager for Project Delivery Services, also agrees: 'Overall, when compared to the work carried out on the sewage pumping stations pre-alliance, the alliance team has achieved productivity gains of the order of five times that achieved previously using traditional procurement and project management methodologies.' Pre-alliance, the SPS work scope would probably have been put to the market as more than 50 separate projects, separately bid, evaluated and managed. The cost savings alone are huge. The pace of project delivery is so far above expectations that earlier than expected access to available capital and changing Sydney Water priorities is creating budget constraints.

There is a different approach in place regarding the $40 million pipe program associated with SewerFix, where a five year panel of approved, pre-qualified contractors has been in place for two years. They are currently using AS2124 as the base document for the work but are looking at a relationship contract or alliance framework in the future. This part of the industry is very much at the leading edge of new technology required to improve the pipe structure without extensive excavation work in built up areas of Sydney.

Bondi RIAMP

The Bondi Reliability Improvement and Modernisation Program (RIAMP) addresses the need to renew and modernise the Bondi Sewage Treatment Plant (STP). Commissioned in the 1950s, Bondi STP is Sydney Water's third largest STP, with a customer base of over 500 000 people. The RIAMP is scheduled for implementation from October 2003 to 2007.

Sydney Water, deviating from its past practice of going to the market for full Design Construct and Operate (DCO) partner(s), has retained the conceptual design team of CH2M HILL and Sinclair Knight Mertz as nominated alliance partners. This is to maintain developmental continuity and retain the institutional knowledge gained to date. They are currently seeking additional alliance partners for the detailed design, construction and commissioning of the RIAMP works as defined in the conceptual design phase. An alliance framework similar to that for the Northside Storage Tunnel project is then planned.

Priority Sewerage Program (PSP)

The remainder—seven bundled projects—of the first stage of PSP, which looks at improving sewerage services in specified suburbs, towns and villages around Sydney, is also planned to be delivered via an alliance contract approach. To date, Sydney Water has used discrete contracts for each of the five stage 1 schemes, resulting in different subcontractors for each scheme. This has created difficulties with length of tender evaluations, time delays, planning, continuity of work, safety, community and environmental issues.

Ian Payne, Sydney Water PSP Program Director, outlines the contrast between the traditional lump sum approach and the performance based risk/reward approach: 'The nature of many traditional lump-sum contracts is that they provide contractors with strong financial incentives to identify and retain any productivity gains or other cost savings and to increase project costs through claims for variations in scope. In contrast, open book accounting and the risk/reward regime of the full alliance contract provides strong financial incentives for the contractor to identify, capture and share cost savings with Sydney Water and to reduce overall program costs. Improving on the cost benchmarks from previous experience on the program will be a key performance indicator and a fundamental determinant of the contractor's remuneration. The proposed PSP relationship based delivery strategy significantly reduces the risks that have eventuated in the program to date, particularly those relating to cost increases and community relations and safety performance.'

Remuneration under the alliance contract will begin with an independently verified target cost for each scheme. Target costs will be agreed after granting of planning approvals and prior to each scheme being included under the scope of the relationship contract. Independently audited direct costs will be reimbursed to the alliance. However, access to the negotiated overhead and profit margins and any share in savings against the target cost will be dependent on overall performance against the cost and non-cost objectives for each scheme. The risk/reward model will calculate access to overheads, profit and any savings.

Ian Payne adds further: 'Innovation is a major focus under the alliance contracting approach. An alliance contract provides the incentives for thinking of better ways of delivering the program and it removes specification-focused contract barriers to implementing those ideas. The risk/reward model provides financial incentives for the contractors to deliver outstanding performance against our community, environment and safety objectives. It provides similar incentives to identify, capture and share cost savings with Sydney Water. Having provided the incentives for developing new ideas, the performance-focused rather than specification-focused contract then provides the flexibility to allow new approaches to be adopted quickly.'

With an established environment conducive to innovation, the alliance contracting approach then focuses attention on continually improving performance throughout the program. Reviewing targets against the community, environment and safety objectives at the beginning of each new scheme ensures that performance in those areas is continually improved over the life of the program. Similarly, as actual savings are achieved on each scheme, the new cost benchmarks will be applied when developing target costs for the subsequent schemes.

Traditional base, collaborative approach: some examples

Not all the major capital works projects are full alliances. Many variations of the alliance, partnering theme are developing. One such project in the early stage of evaluation and development is modifying the traditional AS 2124–1986 contract to suit an environment requiring a collaborative, innovative relationship within a more conventional risk profile and work scope. Latent conditions and liquidated damages are being removed, the time extension, dispute resolution and defects liability are being amended to reflect a more open and collaborative arrangement and a number of partnering and innovation clauses are being added, together with an incentive based remuneration model.

This is a clever and innovative variation on a traditional AS2124 contract base, in particular, the open book, incentive based remuneration model, which involves an agreed schedule of rates; fixed management fee; contingency pool; risk/reward profit pool based on performance in the non-cost areas of time and safety, environmental impact, and impacts on community and stakeholders. This is yet another demonstration of lateral thinking and learning from past experiences.

Two of the other major projects of *WaterPlan 21*, the $197 million Illawarra Waste Water Strategy and the $100 million stage 1 of the Georges River Program also have a more traditional lump sum design and construct base but incorporate many partnering and alliance principles and practices. Charters of shared vision, common goals, hard and soft leading and lagging KPIs, integrated project teams responsible for project delivery and continuous and breakthrough improvement, joint leadership and management teams are an integral part of the relationships. This, together with a no blame/high accountability approach and open and honest communication, is making a significant difference to project delivery.

'Progress to date has shown the partnering approach is delivering faster and better results with fewer and more effectively handled disputes/issues than would otherwise have been under a purely traditional approach', says Colin Heath, Program Director for the Georges River Program. 'Communications are honest and open. Where in the past there would have been many meetings, there is now only one. Trust and having people challenging traditional behaviours and attitudes is the key to the future.'

John Butow, Sydney Water Program Director Illawarra Waste Water Strategy, has similar thoughts: 'Partnering has taught us that we have to swim or sink together. There is no point in contractors losing money. Irrespective of the contract the reality is you can never transfer 100 per cent of the risk. Today's competitive environment compels us to work as an integrated supply chain.'

COMMUNICATIONS AND STAKEHOLDER RELATIONSHIPS

Sydney Water's goal for external relations is:

> *To enjoy the trust and credibility of the communities we serve by having relationships with stakeholders that are open, honest and based on a platform of goodwill, so as to deliver better business outcomes.*

One of the key platforms of the *WaterPlan 21* strategy has been the role of communication and the development of effective relationships with key stakeholders. Sydney Water has around 25 relationship managers responsible for relationships with regulators and other major stakeholders, a typical major and key account approach in the business context.

Susan North, Stakeholder Adviser for Sydney Water, comments: 'This involves undertaking stakeholder research to help the corporation identify what is important to stakeholders in their dealings with Sydney Water and develop measures for stakeholder satisfaction. From this, stakeholder relationship plans with associated key performance indicators are developed; information is gathered and entered into an associated stakeholder database. There are exchange activities, convening of joint forums and development of joint programs and initiatives. These are critical relationships to the success of Sydney Water delivering on its vision and goals and the stakeholders are responding very positively.'

Open-ended Memorandums of Understanding (MOUs) with NSW Health, Department of Land and Water Conservation and the Environment Protection Authority (EPA) have recently been updated and signed by the respective CEOs. These are simplified and streamlined documents that reflect the current relationship with these three important agencies and that provide a framework for establishing formal structures for communication at strategic and operating levels, allowing issues to be resolved in a cooperative manner. Although they are not required by legislation, Sydney Water has entered into similar MOUs with the Sydney Catchment Authority (SCA) and the National Parks and Wildlife Service to formalise the importance of these relationships.

Susan Love, Sydney Water Strategic Communications Adviser, adds: 'Getting the balance between consultation and communication is not easy when you are dealing with local communities. From the giardia and cryptosporidium drinking water crisis of 1998 and recent projects including the Northside Storage Tunnel Alliance we have learnt some simple yet powerful lessons in how we relate to the community and regulators. For example:

- Communication must be flexible. Keep language simple.
- Brief regulators early and regularly.
- Include communication requirements in tender specifications. Train partners, contractors and sub-contractors in communication practices.
- The project team, contractors and the community must understand restoration.
- Scientific data and expert opinion fails to impress communities concerned about health issues.
- Sharing information openly with the community is a powerful tool.
- Set up a coordinated project team and establish roles and responsibilities up-front.'

'We want to take stakeholder relationships to the next level and be seen as the centre of best practice for environment and community affairs,' says Susan Love.

David Hardie, Sydney Water's Communications and Stakeholder Manager, gives another perspective: 'The key is establishing relationships early in the project development. We use multi-disciplinary teams and with the internal partnering approach, "communications and environment" has the right to sit at the table. In the old days it was a matter "if they don't agree with you, you didn't tell them properly". There were a lot of technically driven solutions with a time and dollar focus. It is completely different now. There is a genuine triple bottom line approach to relationship management with all stakeholders.'

A GOOD REPUTATION IS IMPORTANT

Sydney Water's triple bottom line approach has been independently recognised. The Reputation Measurement's 'Good Reputation Index' published in the *Sydney Morning Herald* and the *Age* in October 2002 examined, through the perceptions of 22 expert and community stakeholder groups, the ability of the top 100 corporations (based on financial indicators) operating in Australia to manage those activities that directly contribute to their reputations as socially responsible organisations. The six performance categories judged were management and market focus, financial performance, ethics and corporate governance, environmental performance, social impact and employee management. Sydney Water ranked 11th in the overall rankings, 1st in ethics and corporate governance, 3rd in environmental performance, 11th in employee management and social impact, 13th in management and market focus and 84th in financial performance.

This is an outstanding result and a direct measure of the success and vindication of the triple bottom line relationship management practices that have developed at Sydney Water and continue to improve.

SYDNEY WATER, STRATEGIC ENERGY PARTNER

Continuing to break new ground, and again consistent with *WaterPlan 21*, Sydney Water, late in 2002, entered into a long-term, strategic, energy partnering relationship with Burns Row Worley and Energetics to develop and implement an effective energy management program, including purchase and sale of electricity, energy conservation and efficiency, energy monitoring and reporting. Additionally, the energy partner would manage Sydney Water's portfolio of viable renewable energy generation projects. 'Sydney Water is one of the largest energy users in NSW. With its commitment to the environment via *WaterPlan 21*, the reduction in the use of non-renewable energy sources and reducing greenhouse gas emissions is a clear imperative for the organisation', says John Petre, Sydney Water's Energy Manager. Initiated by Alex Walker, Sydney Water's Managing Director at the time, it is a full and genuine performance based partnering relationship, comprising shared vision and common goals for mutual benefit, led by a joint team with success measured via a Balanced Scorecard of performance indicators and linked to a risk/reward remuneration model. This long-term, strategic relationship was the first of its kind for Sydney Water and a first for the industry.

THE FUTURE AND THE LEGACY EFFECT

Sydney Water is developing relationship management as a core competency. Its triple bottom line approach to relationship management has differentiated it in the market place and added demonstrable value for its customers, the community it serves, the environment and other stakeholders. It is using its relationships, and in particular its partnering and alliance relationships, as vehicles for transformation and cultural change within the organisation. In doing so it has brought along a willing and capable private sector that is also gaining new knowledge and skills, thus extending those participants' own value and competitive advantage in the market place. Few organisations have taken such an extensive, engaging and strategic approach to relationship management. The success of the strategy is demonstrated in the results to date and Sydney Water's approach to the future.

Ron Quill, Sydney Water's acting Managing Director (following the retirement of Alex Walker in late 2002) and previously General Manager Asset Solutions and a prime instigator of much of the transformation, talks of the triple bottom line importance of effective relationships in terms of the 'legacy effect'. 'Sydney Water has an enormous opportunity to give back to society much of what it has learned and gained in the way of knowledge and experiences. To leave a continuous legacy that will give broader benefits or add value for the wider community and environment is very important and links directly to our values. This "legacy effect" goes well beyond just the making of money or the delivery of projects, basic products and services.'

The legacy effect flows internally through effective succession planning, shared learning, new solutions and an open, empowering and engaging culture. Craig Baragry, Sydney Water Manager Project Delivery Services, also talks of the legacy effect on the private sector service providers: 'We need to influence, educate and impart the same alliancing and partnering, relationship management principles and practices with our prime partners as well as the suballiance partners and the many other subcontractors. This is about developing and maintaining a healthy community of like-minded, interconnected organisations with common goals and a shared destiny. We must have healthy competition in the market place delivering sustainable best practice and superior performance. Therefore helping, assisting and educating those organisations that are unsuccessful in winning Sydney Water business is important, so they can continue to compete effectively and fairly in the future. This sustains the continuous improvement approach and is a fundamental part of the triple bottom line approach to relationship management. Perception or reality, we can't have a "closed shop" of partners, preferred suppliers and service providers. Part of the legacy is building and maintaining a successful, competitive and healthy business community.'

I don't want to give the reader the impression that Sydney Water is the perfect organisation. It makes mistakes. Its strength is its ability to learn from those mistakes, and quickly. It has been a rollercoaster journey with many successes and many lessons learnt that have been transferred to other relationships, projects and ongoing business operations. Sydney Water Board must also be given credit for their role in this journey. Along with the champions and pioneers they have displayed distinct courage, intuition and a long-term perspective to take up these new initiatives and, in some cases, new paradigms under a difficult operating environment.

Little or none of this change would have occurred without the presence of champions, key influencers and pioneers who have been the key catalysts for change. They are stubborn and passionate, with an unwavering belief in the power and value of relationship management and, in particular, alliances and partnering. To name a few:

- Ron Quill, for showing executive leadership, commitment and vision in relation to current and future relationship strategies
- Greg Klamus and Allan Henderson, for their pioneering roles with the Northside Storage Tunnel Alliance (NSST)
- Alex Walker (Strategy Energy Partner), Paul Broad (NSST) and Bob Wilson (BOOTs), all previous Managing Directors who have made key decisions at critical times to initiate change

Rory Brennan from Sydney Water Asset Solutions sees the future as involving consolidation of current programs with a clear strategy for moving forward. This will encompass:

- more partnering, alliancing and relationship contracting on a selected basis;
- greater bundling of projects and programs of work;
- pushing the new collaborative, high performance, partnering and alliance relationship approaches further into the Sydney Water value chain (e.g. planning, operations and maintenance);
- taking a 'whole of life' approach to performance based contracts;
- developing further Integrated Services Contracts, which aggregate a range of activities (e.g. fire services, waste services);
- developing further panels of pre-qualified suppliers;
- significantly reducing procurement costs and cost of tendering;
- continuing to use the triple bottom line approach to drive and measure the behaviours and performance of the project teams.

There is no doubting the success of Sydney Water's partnering and alliance relationships with the private sector and they will continue to find greater application on a selective basis. While 30 per cent of the current $450 million per annum capital works program is engaged in alliance and partnering relationships, this percentage will grow on a selective basis. Sydney Water understands well that these relationships are not appropriate or required in all circumstances and that there are many alternative approaches, depending on the value propositions, size, scope and risk profile involved. These alternatives also provide valuable benchmarks for the strategic partnering and alliance relationships.

An independent survey of 34 Sydney Water suppliers was conducted in late 2002 to assess industry's views on Sydney Water's new approach to delivering capital works. The survey findings confirmed industry's support for alliancing, that it was innovative and the process created value for both Sydney Water and the industry partners. The following comment is from one of the industry respondents: 'Sydney Water's shift to alliance based projects has enabled us to deliver tangible, better value to Sydney Water, by exploring better alternatives and using the best people from all organisations. This has been the case particularly with projects where complex design, delivery or operational impacts were involved.'

Ian Payne, Sydney Water Program Director, states: 'Full partnering and alliance relationships force you to sit down and understand what's important. There has been a paradigm shift over the last five years at Sydney Water. We are learning to tailor and adapt relationship models to suit the environment, for example the Cronulla STP upgrade.'

Paul Freeman, Sydney Water General Manager Asset Management, also agrees: 'There is now a growing confidence in partnering and alliancing within Sydney Water. This new performance based collaborative approach has selective but high value application in maintenance, planning and design, energy, engineering services and operations. Alliances and partnering relationships offer aligned objectives and a shared vision especially where Sydney Water lacks expertise and does not desire to develop in-house capability.'

An extended enterprise or relationship 'community' is in the making. Sydney Water is an organisation responding from the boardroom to the shop floor to a world that is demanding better business, social and environmental performance, in quicker time and at a lower total cost. This is a tough call, requiring a triple bottom line approach, a paradigm shift in the way business is done.

Protecting public health, protecting the environment and being a successful business is a delicate balance requiring a collaborative, high accountability, high performance approach to relationship management. Sydney Water is a demonstrable example of a learning organisation in delivery mode. Their continuing journey at the leading edge of best practice provides a valuable insight for those organisations wanting to travel a similar path.

REFERENCES

1. Mary Buckner Power, *ENR*, 7 June 1999, p.2.
2. A.D. Henderson and R.J. Cuttler, 'Northside Storage Tunnel Project', Tenth Australian Tunnelling Conference, March 1999.
3. Shani Wallis, 'Final Account on Sydney's Alliance', *Tunnels & Tunnelling International*, November 2002, pp.28–31.
4. Stewart Clegg, Tyrone Pitsis and Thekla Rura-Polley, 'Constructing the Olympic Dream: Managing Innovation through the Future Perfect', School of Management – University of Technology, [2001], pp.4, 28, 31.
5. Project Management Achievement Awards paper, 2002, p.23.
6. Sydney Water Corporation, Annual Report 2002, p.9.

Tony Lendrum
Strategic Partnering Pty Ltd
www.partneringcommunity.com
partner@ozemail.com.au

Index